THE NEHRUS

Motilal Nehru, Swarup Rani and Jawaharlal Nehru about 1895

THE NEHRUS

MOTILAL AND JAWAHARLAL

By B. R. NANDA

ILLUSTRATED

The John Day Company   New York

TO MY FATHER

FIRST AMERICAN EDITION, 1963

©1962 by George Allen & Unwin Ltd. All rights reserved.
This book, or parts thereof, must not be reproduced in
any form without permission. Published by The John
Day Company, 62 West 45th Street, New York 36, N. Y.

Library of Congress Catalogue
Card Number: 62-21017

MANUFACTURED IN THE UNITED STATES OF AMERICA

PREFACE

MANY people today remember Motilal Nehru as the father of Jawaharlal Nehru, just as in the nineteen twenties there were not a few in whose eyes Jawaharlal's chief title to distinction was that he was the son of his distinguished father. Both verdicts are equally superficial. The fact is that Motilal's place in Indian politics in the last ten years of his life was second only to that of Gandhi. And Jawaharlal, even in the life-time of his father, had climbed several rungs of the ladder which was to bring him to the top as the leader of the national movement and the logical heir of the Mahatma.

It is exactly one hundred years since Motilal's birth, and thirty since his death, but no biography of him has yet been written. If this has made my task more laborious, it has also made it more interesting, as the story of his life had to be pieced together from original sources, including his own papers. However, I had not gone very far in my research when I realized that it was impossible to understand or interpret his life without dealing in detail with the ideas and activities of his son, that a biography of Motilal could not but become the biography of his son as well.

Father and son played very different parts in the national struggle; but so intertwined were their lives that they influenced each other, not least when they differed. Love of one's children is a natural and common enough emotion, but in the case of Motilal it had a rare quality, which Gandhi, a deeply religious man, described as 'divine'. It was this extraordinary emotion, deeply rooted in his being and strangely incongruous in a hard-headed lawyer, which gave a new twist to the story of the Nehrus. That story was not always of a triumphal progress with garlands and banner-headlines; more often it was a chronicle of sweat and toil, loneliness and suspense, personal anguish and political frustration, against which their only defences were their proud patriotism and indomitable faith. Such of course is the stuff of which politics— the politics of nationalist revolt—are made.

The story of the Nehrus ran parallel with and merged into the story of the Indian freedom movement. A survey of that movement has already been attempted by me in my biography of Gandhi. But the Mahatma was not directly concerned with the early period of the Indian National Congress before 1915; nor was it necessary, (or feasible for reasons of space) to deal with the twenties in such detail as is essential to bring out the role of the Nehrus. The present work, therefore, supplements rather than overlaps the theme of my earlier book.

This book is primarily based on a study of original and un-published sources, the Nehru family papers, confidential official records, the Gandhi and Sapru papers. In addition, books, journals, reports and newspapers have been consulted to reconstruct the period; the select bibliography at the end, however, includes only such printed works as have been cited in the text or in the foot-notes. As a rule, footnotes refer to printed sources. Only occasion-ally have references been made to unpublished sources, since mention of all of these would have distracted the reader with too many footnotes.

Having drawn upon such diverse sources and dealt with events which, in the light of the changed relationship between India and Britain, now seem more remote than mere chronology might suggest, I have tried to see men and events in historical perspective, to understand and interpret, rather than to uphold or condemn.

New Delhi   B. R. NANDA

ACKNOWLEDGMENTS

I AM deeply grateful to Shri Jawaharlal Nehru for kindly permitting me to consult and use extracts from his private papers, for finding time, in the midst of his other pressing engagements, to meet me on a number of occasions, and for answering my many questions.

I am indebted to Shrimati Vijayalakshmi Pandit, Shrimati Indira Gandhi, Shri Brij Lal Nehru, Shrimati Rameshwari Nehru, Shri B. K. Nehru, Dr S. S. Nehru and Shrimati Raj Dulari Nehru for giving me much useful data, which helped to fill gaps in my knowledge.

Dr B. C. Roy was kind enough to prepare for me a note dealing with Pandit Motilal Nehru's health, his last illness and certain incidents. Dr K. N. Katju supplied me with useful information on the legal career of Pandit Motilal Nehru. Shri Mohan Lal Saksena, Shri S. D. Upadhyaya, Dewan Chaman Lall and Shri Brij Mohan Vyas gave me their interesting reminiscences. Munshi Kanhiya Lal gave much assistance in tracing old papers in Anand Bhawan. Shri Jhabarmal Sharma furnished some data on the early association of the Nehru family with Khetri.

I am grateful to Shri G. Ramachandran, General Secretary Gandi Samarak Nidhi, for permission to consult the correspondence of Mahatma Gandhi. The Ministry of Home Affairs granted me permission to consult and use extracts from confidential official records. Shri S. Roy, Shri V. C. Joshi and staff of the National Archives of India have been very helpful to me.

Shri A. N. Sapru and his brothers were kind enough to permit me to use extracts from the unpublished papers of the late Sir Tej Bahadur Sapru.

The Navajivan Trust Ahmedabad have been good enough to permit me to quote from the writings of Mahatma Gandhi.

I am grateful to Shri Kesavan, the Librarian, and Shri Mulay, the Deputy Librarian, of the National Library, Calcutta; to Shri Girja Kumar, Librarian of the Indian Council of World Affairs, and to Shri Dharam Vir, Librarian of the Gandhi Memorial Museum Library, for their courteous assistance at all times.

Shri V. C. Joshi has helped me in correcting proofs and my son Naren has assisted me in the preparation of the index.

I need hardly add that I alone bear responsibility for the views expressed in this book and for all its shortcomings.

And finally, I owe a profound debt of gratitude to my wife for her constant sympathy and support during the many months when this work was under preparation.

B.R.N.

CONTENTS

1. Formative Years   17
2. The Profession of Law   26
3. West Wind   34
4. Indian National Congress   45
5. Motilal the Moderate   54
6. The Only Son   62
7. Harrow   70
8. The Young Nationalist   81
9. Fateful Choice   94
10. Politics Calling   106
11. Halcyon Days   115
12. Home Rule   130
13. Reforms on the Anvil   142
14. Emergence of Gandhi   152
15. Amritsar   162
16. The Plunge   173
17. High Tide   187
18. Low Tide   199
19. Letters from Prison   209
20. Trapped in Nabha   217
21. Leader of the Opposition   224
22. Tussle with Gandhi   234
23. Evolution of Jawaharlal   245
24. Rift in the Lute   260

25. *End of the Tether*   270

26. *Rising Tempo*   282

27. *The Clash*   293

28. *On the Brink*   307

29. *Freedom's Battle*   325

   Epilogue   340

   BIBLIOGRAPHY   344

   INDEX   348

ILLUSTRATIONS

Motilal, Swarup Rani and Jawaharlal
     about 1895   *frontispiece*

Motilal about 1900   *facing page*   36
Motilal in his car about 1904   36

Motilal as Leader of the Bar   37

Father and son before and after the
     plunge into politics   166
Motilal, Leader of the Opposition in the
     Central Legislative Assembly in 1928   167

Anand Bhawan   198

Motilal launching *The Jalduta*   199

CHAPTER ONE

FORMATIVE YEARS

1, Church Road, Allahabad. A large palatial house; with its elegant furnishings, spacious lawns, fruit gardens, sparkling fountains, swimming-pools, tennis-courts, horses, carriages, cars and retinue of servants, it reminded visitors of the country mansions of the British aristocracy. It was not far from the University and the High Court and on a moonlit night one could trace from its roof the silver line of the sacred Ganges and the silhouette of the Naini Central Gaol across the Jumna. The Honourable Pandit Motilal Nehru, the proud owner of the house, was the cynosure of all eyes as he drove to the High Court every morning in a magnificent carriage drawn by a fine pair of horses and with liveried servants in attendance. Robust and rubicund, with chiselled features, a determined chin and rather formidable moustaches, well dressed (his suits were made in Savile Row), he commanded inside and outside the High Court an admiration not unmixed with awe. His ready wit delighted the Honourable Judges as much as it discomfited rival counsel. Genial, fond of good food, good wine and good conversation, a staunch friend and a straightforward opponent, he was known among his many friends, British and Indian, for his generous hospitality. He had everything a man could wish for: a fabulous income, the respect of his peers, a lovely though fragile wife, a clear-eyed son, two charming daughters. He was the idol of the Bar, the favourite of the Bench, the darling of destiny. Nothing could have been more apt than the name he chose for his house: *Anand Bhawan* (Abode of Happiness).

This image of Motilal at the zenith of his professional career was to undergo important changes in the last ten years of his life. But in the minds of his contemporaries it remained unaltered to the last and thirty years after his death it still lingers in popular imagination. It is usual to refer to him as a 'born aristocrat', with a 'princely' style of life and a 'right royal manner' of lavish hospitality. Motilal did not, however, inherit a kingdom, nor even an estate. He was not born with a silver spoon in his mouth; he had no 'gold-bearing genes'.

2

Motilal's family originally belonged to the valley of Kashmir, which is famous for its lofty mountains, dancing brooks, flower-filled meadows and beautiful women. Early in the eighteenth century it was also noted for its scholars; one of them, Pandit Raj Kaul, caught the eye of the Mughal king Farukhsiyar when he visited Kashmir about the year 1716, and was persuaded to migrate to Delhi, the imperial capital, where he was granted a house situated on the canal which then ran through the city. Living on the bank of the canal (nahar), Raj Kaul's descendants came to be known in the Kashmiri community as 'Nehrus', or rather 'Kaul-Nehrus'. Raj Kaul also received a few villages as jagir from the Mughal Emperor. But unfortunately his patron did not live long. Challenged by ambitious satraps and refractory nobles from within and powerful enemies from without, the Mughal Empire was in the last throes of a rapid dissolution. Farukhsiyar's brief reign had its disgraceful denouement in 1719, when he was dragged out of the harem of his own palace, deposed, imprisoned and finally done to death at the instance of his own ministers, the ambitious Syed brothers. Raj Kaul's royal patron thus disappeared from the scene. With the decline of the imperial authority during the following years his jagir dwindled until it amounted to no more than zamindari rights in certain lands. The last beneficiaries of these rights were Raj Kaul's grandsons, Mausa Ram Kaul and Saheb Ram Kaul. Mausa Ram's son, Lakshmi Narayan, became the first Vakil of the East India Company at the Mughal court of Delhi. Lakshmi Narayan's son Ganga Dhar – the father of Motilal Nehru and the grandfather of Jawaharlal Nehru – was a police officer in Delhi when the Mutiny broke out in 1857.

3

By 1857, the 'Nehrus', the descendants of Raj Kaul, had been settled in Delhi for nearly a century and a half. During this period the political landscape had been completely transformed.

Bahadur Shah, who was to be the last of the imperial line of the
Mughals, had been divested of all real power, though he still
maintained a shadow court in the Red Fort at Delhi with as
much dignity as his straitened finances, contumacious sons and
the whims of the British Resident permitted. The Mughal court
performed cultural, rather than political functions; Bahadur
Shah himself was a poet; his protégé was Zauk, the rival of the
famous Ghalib. The aristocratic classes of Delhi took their cue
from the King and patronized painting, poetry and local handi-
crafts. Remarkably free from religious prejudice, Bahadur Shah
observed the Hindu festivals of *Diwali* and *Holi* with the same
enthusiasm as the Muslim *Id*. On certain auspicious days, such
as New Year's Day and the lunar and solar eclipses, he followed
the Hindu custom of having himself weighed against grain,
which was then distributed among the poor. During the rainy
season, Mehrauli, a suburb of Delhi, was the scene of the
'Punkahs' festival, when Hindus and Muslims fraternized in
visits to the temple of a Hindu deity and the tomb of a Muslim
saint.

The only surviving portrait of Ganga Dhar Nehru shows him
bearded, dressed like a Mughal grandee, with a curved sword in
his hand. There was nothing surprising in a Kashmiri Brahmin
being turned out like a Muslim nobleman, if we remember that
the conventions, the ceremonial and even the language –
Persian—of the Mughal Court had, since the days of Akbar, set
the fashion for the entire Indian sub-continent. By the middle of
the nineteenth century western influences had made themselves
felt in the port-towns of Bombay, Calcutta and Madras, but had
not yet percolated to the heart of the sub-continent. Nevertheless, by 1857 even Delhi had enterprising individuals such as
Ramachandra, the mathematician, and Mukandlal, the physician,
who had received western education. Ganga Dhar's own sons,
though only in their teens, had learnt to speak English – an
accomplishment which was soon to stand them in good stead.

4

This conservative, cultured and contented society, centred on
the Mughal court, broke up on 11th May 1857, when the
mutinous troops from Meerut broke into Delhi, killed or drove
out its European residents and thrust the standard of rebellion

into the unwilling and feeble hands of King Bahadur Shah. From the outset it was a hopeless venture. No love was lost between Prince Mirza Mughal, who became the commander-in-chief of the rebel army, and Prince Jawan Bakht, the son of Bahadur Shah's youngest and favourite queen, between the royal princes and the king's advisers, or between the rebel leaders and the court. Bahadur Shah was hard put to it to save the townsfolk from the soldiers who had already tasted the fruits of indiscipline. Hakim Ahsanullah Khan, the King's adviser, who was suspected, with good reason, of communicating with the British,[1] was arrested by the army leaders, and released only after Bahadur Shah had threatened to abdicate and even to commit suicide. Lack of leadership in the mutinous regiments and in the royal entourage sealed the fate of Delhi, notwithstanding the great heroism of the rebels in the battle of the Ridge during that terrible summer of 1857.

A ghastly fate awaited Delhi when British troops shelled their way into the town in September. In the words of a British historian, 'for the citizens of Delhi, the aftermath of the Mutiny was a case of the scorpions of Rehoboam following the whips of Solomon'.[2] No man's life was safe in the city: all able-bodied men were taken for rebels and shot on sight. Three Mughal princes were shot dead in cold blood by Captain Hodson; twenty-one more were hanged shortly afterwards. 'It is a great pity,' wrote John Lawrence about the King, who had been taken prisoner, that 'the old rascal was not shot directly he was seen'; and as late as December 12, 1857, he was enquiring: 'Is private plundering still allowed? Do officers go about shooting natives?'[3] After the city had been ransacked and looted with a thoroughness which put Nadir Shah's record into the shade, the 'prize agents' of the victorious army were busy digging up the floors and walls of deserted houses in search of buried treasures. Almost the entire Indian population of Delhi, estimated at a hundred and fifty thousand, streamed out of the gates.[4] Thousands camped under the sky in the neighbourhood of the Qutab and Nizamuddin, braving cold and starvation, but hoping

[1] Sen, S. N., *Eighteen Fifty-seven*, p. 94.
[2] Spear, Percival, *Twilight of the Mughuls*, p. 218.
[3] *Ibid*, p. 219.
[4] *Ibid*, p. 218.

one day to return to their homes; others bade a final goodbye to Delhi and set out in search of safety and shelter.

5

Among the fugitives who took the road to Agra were Ganga Dhar Nehru and his wife Jeorani, their two sons Bansi Dhar and Nand Lal, and their two daughters Patrani and Maharani. One of the girls, with her fair complexion and fine Kashmiri features, was mistaken by British soldiers for an English girl. Kidnapping was a serious offence and life – Indian life – was cheap. Fortunately Ganga Dhar's sons, who spoke English, cleared up the misunderstanding and thus saved the whole family from massacre.

The upheaval of 1857 uprooted Ganga Dhar from Delhi, where his ancestors had been settled for nearly 150 years. He was lucky to escape with his family, but he lost his job and almost everything he possessed. It is not known whether he tried to restore his fortunes in Agra, but he had not long to live. Early in 1861, he died at the age of thirty-four. Three months after his death, on May 6, 1861, his wife gave birth to a son. He was named Motilal.

The death of her husband had been a terrible blow to Jeorani. It was one of those catastrophes under the weight of which many an Indian family of ancient lineage has been known to sink into permanent oblivion. Luckily both Bansi Dhar and Nand Lal were plucky boys and were able to stand on their own feet. Bansi Dhar secured a job as a 'judgment-writer' in the *Sadar Diwani Adalat* at Agra and rose to the position of a subordinate judge.

Since Bansi Dhar was in government service and liable to frequent transfers, Motilal was brought up by Nand Lal. Between these two there grew up a strong bond of affection, a happy blend of the filial and the fraternal of which the Hindu joint family, despite its many faults, furnishes perhaps the finest examples.

Through the good offices of Principal Anderson of Agra College, Nand Lal secured a job in the small state of Khetri in Rajasthan, where he became a teacher, then private secretary to Raja Fateh Singh, and finally the *Diwan* (chief minister). Nand Lal proved an efficient administrator. 'The enlightened policy and reforms of the young chief of Khetri, Fateh Singh,' ran the Report on the Political Administration of Rajputana for 1865-7, 'have already been brought to the notice of and secured the approbation of his Excellency the Viceroy and Governor-General in Council'. In his speech at the Agra Durbar in November, 1867, Sir John Lawrence cited the Raja of Khetri as an example for other princes to follow.[5] Nand Lal served in Khetri till the end of 1870. On November 30th of that year, Raja Fateh Singh died at Delhi; he had no son but had expressed a wish to adopt Ajit Singh, a nine-year-old boy, as his heir. The ruler of Khetri had a somewhat anomalous position: he was the feudatory of the Jaipur Durbar, but in certain matters dealt directly with the Paramount Power acting through the Agent to the Governor-General for the States of Rajputana. It was doubtful whether, in terms of the treaty rights, the Raja of Khetri was entitled to adopt an heir, and whether Jaipur Durbar would acquiesce in succession by adoption. Nand Lal and others who attended Raja Fateh Singh during his last illness decided to conceal the news of his death and took the dead body in a closed carriage to Khetri, where, after announcing a sudden illness, they pronounced him dead. The boy Ajit Singh was hastily summoned to Khetri. Meanwhile Captain Bradford, the Political Agent at Jaipur, had hurried to Khetri. Ajit Singh had not yet been installed on the *gaddi* (throne), but Captain Bradford, presented with almost a *fait accompli*, confirmed the adoption.[6]

Nand Lal had carried out the last command of his late master, but he lost his job. He quitted Khetri, qualified as a lawyer and began to practise law in Agra. When the High Court was transferred to Allahabad, he moved with it. The misadventure which had pulled him out of the backwaters of Rajputana to a provincial capital in British India gave great new opportunities, not only to himself, but to the entire Nehru family.

6

Meanwhile Motilal was growing up into a vivacious boy. At Khetri, where his brother was the *Diwan*, he was taught by Qazi Sadruddin, the tutor of Raja Fateh Singh. Till the age of twelve he read only Arabic and Persian. In the latter language

[5] Sharma, Jhabarmal, *Khetri Ka Ithas* (History of Khetri), p. 82.
[6] Captain Bradford to Colonel Brooks, Agent to Governor-General, December 7, 1871. (N.A.I.).

his proficiency was striking enough to command the respect of
men much older than himself. He joined the high-school at
Cawnpore where Bansi Dhar was posted. Characteristic letters
from Motilal to the headmaster, have fortunately survived:

'To   H. Powell Esq.
                    Head Master of Ch. Ch. School,
                              Cawnpore.
Respected Sir,
    I respectfully beg to inform your honour that I am quite
prepare for the examination of both classes i.e. 4th and 5th.
    Perhaps you know that when I informed to the Principal for
my promotion in the 4th class, he refused and said, "the other
boys have also right as you have". Therefore now, I wish to be
promoted in the 4th class by my own power.
    Hoping that you will grant my petition.
                                        I remain,
                                          Sir,
                                    Your obedient student,
                                      Moti Lall.'

The confidence and courage of Motilal, who was hardly twelve,
break through the barriers of the arbitrary spelling and grammar
of an alien tongue, which he had only just started learning and
in which he was before long to become remarkably fluent.
    Motilal was far from being a bookworm. Athletic, fond of
outdoor sports, particularly wrestling, brimming over with an
insatiable curiosity and zest for life, he took to the playground
and places of amusement with enthusiasm, and between whiles
attended his classes. His career at the Muir College at Allahabad
was not noted for academic distinction: his quick wits and high
spirits landed him in many an escapade, from which he was
extricated by Principal Harrison and his British colleagues, who
conceived a strong liking for this intelligent, lively and restless
Kashmiri youth. Englishmen teaching in Indian colleges may
have been no more friendly to nationalist aspirations than the rest
of their compatriots in India, but it would be wrong to think of
them as cogs in the Imperial machine like magistrates and police
officials. Between the English professors and their Indian pupils
there were often bonds of sympathy, understanding and even
friendship. On Motilal a deep and lasting impression was left

by the affectionate solicitude of Principal Harrison, one of whose letters he carefully preserved. The contact with his English professors was a strong formative influence, implanting an intelligent, rational, sceptical attitude to life and a strong admiration for English culture and English institutions. University education did not load Motilal with book-learning; but it helped to open for him a window on the world – the wide western world.

Motilal sat for his degree but, thinking he had done his first paper badly, stayed away from the rest of the examination. As it turned out, he had answered his first paper fairly well. His university life thus ended inconclusively and ingloriously. For an Indian youth who had inherited neither money nor property, to play with his educational career was to play with his future and to face the frustration of a low-paid job for the rest of his life. Fortunately, Motilal pulled himself together in time. He decided to follow the legal profession in which his elder brother Nand Lal had already achieved a moderate success. He worked hard and topped the list of successful candidates in the *Vakils'* examination. In 1883 he set up as a lawyer at Cawnpore under the aegis of Pandit Prithinath, a senior lawyer and a friend of the family.

7

Nand Lal, Motilal's elder brother, had been married at the age of twelve at Delhi in 1857, the year of the Mutiny; the ceremony was too important to be put off even in the midst of that great upheaval. Child marriage was then the rule among Kashmiri Brahmins and Motilal was also married and had a son while still in his teens. But the marriage ended tragically: mother and child both died. Soon afterwards Motilal married again. Swarup Rani, his second wife, belonged to a fresher stock from Kashmir; her family, the Thussus, unlike the Nehrus, had migrated to the plains comparatively recently. She was *petite*, with a 'Dresden china perfection' of complexion and features, hazel eyes, chestnut-brown hair and exquisitely shaped hands and feet. The youngest of four children, she had been spoiled by her parents; it was not easy for her to fit into her husband's household, peopled by a host of relatives and dominated by a formidable mother-in-law whose fierce temper was a byword in the town.

The beautiful Swarup Rani and handsome Motilal made a

charming pair. They had a few years of happiness before Swarup Rani's ill-health cast its long shadow over their domestic life. Their first child, a son, did not live. On November 14, 1889, their second child was born. He was named Jawaharlal. The birth of a son and heir is the high-watermark of happiness in a Hindu family. In Motilal's case it was an occasion for special rejoicing, because of the tragedy of his first marriage. It was, and is, customary among Kashmiri Brahmins to have the horoscope of every new-born baby cast by the priest-astrologer, who is attached to each family in the same way as a doctor or solicitor is in the West. However, Motilal had the horoscope of his infant son prepared by the court astrologer of Khetri State, whose ruler had not forgotten the services rendered to him by Motilal's brother.

Meanwhile, Motilal had made a good start with his legal practice. The district courts of Cawnpore did not offer full scope for his ambition. In 1886, after he had completed his three years' apprenticeship, he decided to move to Allahabad, the seat of the High Court, where Nand Lal had a lucrative practice. Nand Lal was so delighted when he heard young Motilal argue his first case that he embraced him in the court-room.

Once again destiny dealt Motilal a cruel blow. In April, 1887, Nand Lal died at the age of forty-two, leaving behind him his wife Nandrani, two daughters and five sons, Biharilal, Mohanlal, Shamlal, Kishenlal and Brijlal. At the age of twenty-five, Motilal found himself head of a large family, its sole bread-winner. He had come to Allahabad for greater opportunities; he found only heavier burdens. But he was not the man to be overwhelmed by adversity. The loss of his beloved brother gave a keener edge to his ambition. The exuberant energy which had been dissipated in childish pranks and youthful follies had now a single aim – success in his profession.

[7] Sharma, J. M., *Adarsh Naresh*, p. 344.

CHAPTER TWO

THE PROFESSION OF LAW

ALLAHABAD may seem a sleepy little town today, but in the last decade of the nineteenth century, to a young lawyer anxious to make a place for himself in the world, it must have seemed a land of opportunity. It was the capital of the North Western Provinces, as the United Provinces were then called. It was the seat of the university and the High Court, and the centre of the English language press which moulded the opinion of Europeans and educated Indians in northern India.

The legal profession, thanks to the purely literary qualifications required for it, was becoming overcrowded even in the eighteen-eighties. 'Briefless barrister' was a comic phrase to some, but a tragic reality to those whom it was intended to ridicule. The struggle for survival at the Bar was keen: room at the top there always was, but the top was not easily reached, nor did it accommodate more than a few. Dr John Matthai, the well-known economist and educationist, is said to have received a bunch of bananas as the fee for his first brief in the Madras High Court. Initial disappointment and a sense of failure were the lot even of those who later achieved outstanding success. For many a weary year, the new entrant to the legal profession found time hang heavy on his hands. The aimless browsing on newspapers and magazines in the Bar Library, the gossip from the courts, the anecdotes relayed at secondhand from the more fortunate seniors, scarcely filled the young lawyer's frustrating day. He had to be content with such petty briefs as came his way, until he resigned himself to failure, or found himself, by an unexpected turn of fortune's wheel, at the top of the profession. Such was the lot of C. R. Das, a Bengali lawyer, nine years younger than Motilal, whom the trial of Aurobindo Ghose brought into the limelight after fifteen years' struggle against poverty and oblivion. Such too was the lot of a Gujarati youth, M. K. Gandhi, eight years younger than Motilal, who was called to the bar in England, read books on physiognomy and sought advice from experienced lawyers on the 'art' of practising law; and when at last, after unconscionable waiting, a brief came his way, he broke down in a Bombay court while cross-examining the first witness, refunded the client's fee and retired to the small town of Rajkot to make a modest living by drafting petitions until the displeasure of a British officer drove him to seek his fortune in South Africa. The diffident, tongue-tied, self-conscious Gandhi, scanning the morality as well as the legality of his briefs, was poles apart from Motilal, who was the epitome of self-confidence, quick to seize on a point of fact or law and to stretch it to the utmost in his client's favour.

Motilal received only five rupees for his first brief, but he was fortunate in not having a long uphill struggle: his success was as rapid as it was spectacular. In his early thirties, he was making nearly Rs. 2,000 a month, a considerable sum for an up-country lawyer at that time; in his early forties his income had reached five figures. He was one of the four brilliant *vakils* whom Chief Justice Sir John Edge admitted to the roll of advocates of the Allahabad High Court in 1896, the others being Pandit (later Sir) Sunderlal, Munshi Ram Prasad and Mr Jogendranath Choudhuri. In August, 1909, he received permission to appear and plead at the bar of the Judicial Committee of the Privy Council in Great Britain.

Success came easily to Motilal because he possessed a natural shrewdness, sound common sense and the gift of persuasive advocacy. K. N. Katju, one of his younger contemporaries, thus explains the secret of his eminence at the Bar: 'Pandit Motilal was handsome. He dressed fastidiously. He was by no means eloquent, but keen in debate and incisive in argument. He radiated cheerfulness and good humour ... While Pandit Motilal was in the court and on his legs, the atmosphere seemed surcharged with sunshine.' He also had the saving grace of humour. Once in the course of his address to the jury he said he did not want to confuse it. 'Never mind the jury,' cut in the judge, 'the jury can look after itself.' 'My Lord,' Motilal replied, 'that may be so, but I want it to look after my client.'

But all his gifts would not have brought him to the top without another quality of which he had given little promise in his youth – industry. There is no short cut to success in the legal profession. Each day brings new battles of wits, new briefs with new intricacies of law, fresh masses of evidence to be sifted marshalled and digested. This means working hard late at night or first thing in the morning, as the days are taken up with interviews with clients and appearances in court.

2

Motilal was a civil lawyer. Most of his important cases were about disputed succession to property belonging to big zamindars and talukdars. The stakes were high and so were the fees. The rival claimants engaged the foremost lawyers in the land. The intricacies of the Hindu law of inheritance were further complicated by the thick folds of insinuation and intrigue in which such disputes were often shrouded. The income from an estate was large enough to make it worth while for the party in possession to prolong the course of litigation, and for the rival party to fight for it to the bitter end. One of these cases which concerned the Lakhna estate, came to Motilal in 1894 and remained with him for more than thirty years – long after he had given up active practice. A brief history of this case, which was one of the most important and remunerative Motilal handled, is not only interesting in itself but a good example of the problems with which he had to wrestle in the course of his legal practice.

A *jagir* (estate) was granted to Raja Jaswant Singh, a landlord of Etawah district, for his services to the British Government during the Mutiny. Raja Jaswant Singh married three times. He had a son, Balwant Singh, by his first wife and a daughter, Beti Mahalakshmibai, by his third wife, Rani Kishori. Unfortunately, Balwant Singh fell into evil ways, was convicted of murder and sentenced to thirteen years' imprisonment. Raja Jaswant Singh thereupon disinherited his son and executed 'a solemn deed of gift' of his property in favour of Rani Kishori, with the stipulation that if a son were born to Balwant Singh, the property would revert to him when he came of age.

In 1879 on the death of her husband, Rani Kishori came into possession of the *jagir*, which she managed with uncommon ability and efficiency. But four years later her stepson, on release from jail, claimed the property on the plea that he had been wrongfully deprived of it. Since the *jagir* had been acquired and not inherited by his father, the courts held that the disinheritance of Balwant Singh was valid under Hindu law. Events now took a dramatic turn. Balwant Singh, who was approaching his fiftieth birthday and had a wife living, married a young woman named Dunnaju. In 1894 it was announced that Dunnaju had given birth to a son who was named Narsingh Rao. To Rani Kishori this seemed part of a plot to do her out of her *jagir*. She consulted Motilal, then a rising lawyer in Allahabad. Motilal's opinion, which was later confirmed by Sir Charles Paul, an eminent Calcutta lawyer, was that Raja Jaswant Singh's gift of property in favour of a grandson unborn on the date of the execution of the deed, was bad in law.

In 1916 things came to a head when Narsingh Rao, having attained his majority, filed a suit as Balwant Singh's son and heir for the restitution of the property in the terms of his grand-father's will. He engaged Tej Bahadur Sapru, a leading lawyer of Allahabad, as his counsel. Rani Kishori engaged Motilal. Motilal was inclined to contest the suit on the legal issue, but his client insisted that legitimacy of Narsingh Rao should be disputed. On this point Narsingh Rao produced an impressive array of wit-nesses – relatives, midwives and neighbours. The evidence of Dunnaju, who was in *purdah*, was taken at her residence by the British judge. At the end of the cross-examination – which Dunnaju had stood remarkably well – Motilal casually asked her if she would submit to a medical examination. 'Not once,' she retorted, 'but twenty times, and not by one lady-doctor but by a hundred lady-doctors, provided Rani Kishori does not open the gold-bags in her treasury.' Motilal consulted a few eminent gynaecologists to ascertain if such an examination, twenty-two years after the event, could establish the fact of maternity. The advice he received was by no means unanimous, but he decided to apply for Dunnaju to be medically examined. Her counsel stoutly contested the application, describing it as *mala fide* and protesting that all the gynaecologists in the country had been consulted on behalf of the other party, that it was no longer possible to obtain impartial advice, that the examination ('the physical cross-examination',) was harmful, uncalled for, useless; that it was an intolerable humiliation for a high-born Brahmin widow. All these arguments served only to rouse the judge's sus-picions. Narsingh Rao's suit was dismissed in 1918 and the High Court rejected his appeal. Motilal's client had won the first round, but the litigation was to last for another ten years, with new developments, which will be related later.

It was this case which elicited from Chief Justice Sir Grimwood

Mears the memorable compliment that 'no lawyer in the world
could have done that case better than Pandit Motilal had done
it'. Sir Grimwood formed the highest judgment of Motilal's
talents. 'When I came to Allahabad,' he recalled, 'and was beginning to learn the names and positions of the various members
of the Bar, I was struck with the respect and pride with which
all his colleagues at the Bar spoke of Pandit Motilal Nehru.
When I had the pleasure of meeting him, I understood the
reasons for the affection with which he was regarded . . . He
had a profusion of gifts; knowledge came easily to him, and as
an advocate he had the art of presenting his case in its most
attractive form. Every fact fell into its proper place in the
narration of the story and was emphasized in just the right
degree. He had an exquisite public speaking voice and a charm
of manner which made it a pleasure to listen to him . . . With
his wide range of reading and the pleasure that he had taken in
travel he was a very delightful companion, and wherever he sat
at a table that was the head of the table and there was the
centre of interest.'[1]

3

What distinguished Motilal was not that he earned enormous
sums of money: there were other lawyers in Allahabad – Sir
Sunderlal for example – who did not earn less, and there were
quite a few in Bombay and Calcutta who earned more. But only
of Motilal could it perhaps be said that expenditure rose *pari
passu* with income. He spent generously on the education of his
children and of his nephews, who had become his responsibility
after the death of his beloved brother Nand Lal in 1887. He
moved from the densely populated city of Allahabad to a bungalow – 9, Elgin Road, in the spacious and exclusive 'civil lines'
where European and Eurasian families lived in solitary splen-
dour. It was a courageous decision. It signified a desire on his
part to live in healthier surroundings with greater quiet and
privacy than were possible in the heart of the town. It was also
a sign of the transformation which was taking place in his life:
the rise in the standard of living was accompanied by increasing
westernization. Only a few hundred yards separated the 'civil
lines' from the city, but mentally and socially the two were poles

[1] *Leader*, February 8, 1931.

apart: one could almost say, as E. M. Forster said of Chandra-pore, that all they had in common was 'the overarching sky'.

In 1900 Motilal purchased a house – 1, Church Road – from Kanwar Parmanand of Moradabad. It was situated near Bhard-waj Ashram at a spot hallowed by association with episodes in the *Ramayana*. Motilal was struck less by the sanctity of the location than by the size and the possibilities of the estate, which included a large garden and a swimming pool. The price – Rs. 19,000 – may seem ridiculously low, but the deal was made sixty years ago, and the house was in a dilapidated condition and required extensive renovation and reconstruction. Motilal opened his purse-strings to make his new home – which he named 'Anand Bhawan' (Abode of Happiness) – as comfortable as possible.

Today, Anand Bhawan (renamed 'Swaraj Bhawan') with its huge bare rooms, long verandahs, empty terraces and legend-haunted silence, is a different place from fifty years ago when it was filled with Motilal's own family, his nephews, their wives and children and numerous guests and above all with his own resonant voice. Having a lively curiosity and zest for living, he made a point of ordering the latest gadgets and improvements. Anand Bhawan was the first house in Allahabad to have a swimming pool; it was also the first to have electricity and water laid on. Motilal's library included quite a few 'manuals of applied science', which were in vogue in America and Europe at the turn of the century. One of these was *Practical Bell-fitting* and another *A Practical Treatise upon the Fitting of Hot-Water Apparatus*. Apparently before ordering installations for his house, Motilal took care to find out how they worked. The craze for the 'latest and the best' was an essential part of his make-up in those days. During his visits to Europe in 1899, 1900, 1905 and 1909 he spent much time and money in buying furnishings and fittings for Anand Bhawan. When the cycle was an expensive novelty, he ordered successive models through Raja Ram Motilal Guzdar and Company, a local firm of which he was part-owner. In 1904 he imported a car, the first in Allahabad and probably in the United Provinces. Next year, during his visit to Europe, he bought a new car. In 1909 when he was again in Europe he bought two cars, a Fiat and a Lancia. He already had a number of carriages and a fair-sized stable of fine Arabian horses. There is a good photograph of Motilal in breeches with his two daughters, eleven-year-old Sarup and three-year-old Krishna, on horseback beside him. His children learned to ride almost as soon as they learned to walk. He himself was a good rider and an excellent shot and whenever possible indulged his taste for *shikar*. His favourite sport was wrestling: when he was too told to practise it himself he enjoyed watching a bout between his servants in a part of the garden where the ground had been specially prepared for an *akhara*: he would encourage the contestants during the match and entertain them to milk afterwards.

4

Motilal's optimism and self-confidence had hastened his success at the Bar; his success further enhanced his self-confidence. Looking back, he could not help feeling that he had triumphed against heavy odds. A star-crossed destiny had seemed to shadow his early years: it had robbed him of his father before he was born, and then taken away his elder brother in the prime of life. Within a decade, however, the days of uncertainty and insecurity were behind him. He did not suffer from false humility; he enjoyed his success enormously and visibly and took full credit for it. He valued money, prestige and the good things of life and was glad to be able to command them.

Though he worked hard, he knew the art of relaxation. At about seven in the evening, winter and summer alike, he would entertain his friends in the house or garden, and good food, good wine, good conversation were the order of the day. Here the battles of the courtroom were fought over again – quite without malice, for it was all part of a game, the great game of making money. The moving spirit of these gatherings was always the host himself: his wit and exuberance were unfailing. By nine o'clock the party would be over and Motilal, still in high spirits, would join his family for a gay and leisurely dinner, sometimes eaten at table in the western fashion, sometimes squatting Indian style on the marble floor in the Indian dining-room, but always to the accompaniment of a happy flow of repartee and little intimate family jokes.

Those were the days, too, of the tennis and the big garden-parties, when the great, smooth lawns of Anand Bhawan were gay with the many coloured saris of the guests and the brightness of winter flowers; when the teacups tinkled, the guests laughed and chattered, the band played; and above the cheerful sounds of the élite of Allahabad enjoying themselves could be heard the rich laughter of the host enjoying himself most of all.

CHAPTER THREE

WEST WIND

TILL the age of twelve Motilal had been able to read only Persian and Arabic, but he employed European governesses and resident tutors for his children. His nephew Brij Lal Nehru tells how in the nineties he decreed that everyone in the house must talk in English. The result was dead silence, as most of the women and children in that large household could not speak it. The incident reveals a new trend towards westernization in Motilal's life. He had already scandalized his orthodox colleagues by taking his midday meal in the premises of the High Court. Very strict and irrational rules governed the eating habits of Brahmins; many of them cooked their own food and ate in sanctimonious seclusion which not even their children were allowed to disturb. For Motilal, whose natural independence had been fortified by bracing contact with the British professors of Muir Central College, it was not easy to acquiesce in a social tyranny which presumed to govern the minutest detail of his daily routine.

The Hindu society of the early nineteenth century was like a fossil from which true life had departed. It was scarcely aware of its great heritage; it was caste-ridden, and priest-dominated; it tolerated social inequality : it sanctified untouchability and child-marriage; it shut out girls from the rudiments of education and even from God's sun and air by the pernicious custom of *purdah*. Little initiative was left to the individual, not only in such matters as love, marriage and the choice of a profession, but even in the trivial details of everyday life. The heavy hand of an entrenched priesthood lay everywhere; no marriage could be celebrated, no birth announced, no funeral arranged without the paid assistance of the ubiquitous priest. It was forbidden to share food or drink with those outside the caste, to eat certain kinds of meat or vegetables, to have a haircut except on auspicious days, or to stir out of the village until the astrologer had conferred with the stars. This society had its good points : its profound respect for tradition and authority, its keen sense of social obligations, its placid contentment and stability. But it left little elbow-room for the growth of the individual; the strait-jacket of the society was too tightly wrapped round him. The neutrality of the British *Raj* in social and religious matters had stereotyped existing abuses and strengthened the stranglehold of the priests. The one line in the Rig Veda which was held to enjoin *sati* (burning of the widow on the funeral pyre of her husband) was, according to Max Muller, the great orientalist, 'perhaps the most flagrant instance of what can be done by an unscrupulous priesthood'.

It is not surprising that on such a society the first impact of the West should have been shattering. Macaulay's name is linked with the introduction of a system of education designed to produce 'Indians in blood and colour but European in opinion, in morals and intellect'. Nevertheless, long before Macaulay set foot on Indian soil, western education was being demanded by a vocal section of Indian opinion. As far back as 1823, Raja Ram Mohan Roy had protested in a letter to Governor-General Lord Amherst against the 'establishing of a Sanskrit school under Hindu Pandits to impart such knowledge as is already current in India. This seminary can only be expected to load the minds of youths with grammatical niceties and metaphysical distinctions of little or no practical use to the possessors or to society'. 'The Sanskrit system of education,' he warned, 'would be the best calculated to keep this country in darkness.' Six years before Ram Mohun Roy write this letter, the Hindu College had been founded in Calcutta. Its students were so intoxicated with the heady wine of the West that they saw nothing to admire or accept in their own culture. Some of them went the length of eating forbidden food and throwing the remnants into the houses of their orthodox neighbours. and most of them would have heartily endorsed Macaulay's verdict that a 'single shelf of a good European library', was worth 'the whole native libraries of India and Arabia'. The poetry of Keats and Shelley and the prose of Burke and Macaulay were discussed at dinner by educated Bengalis in the middle of the century; the enthusiasm for Shakespeare's plays could not have been less in Calcutta than in London. Quite a few of these Anglophiles adopted not only the habits and manners but also the religion of the ruling race. The efforts of Christian missionaries, the pioneers in new education, were seconded by proselytizing colonels and magistrates whose evangelical ardour became a contributory cause of the Mutiny.

'The fear of Christianity,' the historian of Indian social reform has written, 'has been the beginning of much social wisdom in India.'[1] Threatened from within as well as without, the Hindu society sought to reform itself. The *Brahmo Samaj* in Bengal and the *Prarthana Samaj* in Bombay denounced social evils which had become indefensible under the searchlight of the West. A whole generation of Hindu reformers battled against restrictions on inter-dining, female education and the remarriage of widows, and against the curse of untouchability; men like M. G. Ranade and Telang devoted their lives to the task of hastening the transition of Hindu society from the medieval to the modern by substituting rational and secular for traditional and sectarian standards of conduct and morality.

At the beginning of Queen Victoria's reign Hinduism was on the defensive, almost defenceless; when she died it had already taken the offensive. Swami Dayanand had offered in the *Arya Samaj* a purified, almost puritanic version of Hinduism, free from elements like image worship which had been particularly vulnerable to attack from Christian missionaries. For the rest, the *Arya Samaj* was pertinaciously polemical, militant, proselytizing. About the same time Bengal produced a gentler prophet of Hindu revival in Shri Ramakrishna, who interpreted the traditional concepts of *Vedanta* and *Bhakti* simply, clearly and vividly so as to reconcile the western-educated intelligentsia to the faith of their forefathers. The process of reconciliation was stimulated by the devoted researches of western orientalists and by the ardent, albeit undiscriminating enthusiasm of European admirers of Hinduism like Mrs Annie Besant. The discovery that its cultural heritage was second to none raised the *amour propre* of a people smarting under political subjection.

2

The recoil from a blind and wholesale imitation of the West had thus begun, but the process was slow. Early in the nineteenth century Michael Madhusudan Dutt, the Bengali writer, claimed that he dreamed in English; the boast could have been repeated with equal justification by the young Aurobindo Ghose when he returned to India in 1893 after fourteen years' stay in

[1] Natarajan, S., *Social Reform in India*, p. 8.

Motilal about 1900

Motilal in his car

Motilal as Leader of the Allahabad Bar

England. Every ambitious young man in India aspired to visit England to qualify for the Indian Civil Service or, as a second best, to become a barrister and return to India transformed into an English gentleman.

Motilal had not been called to the Bar in England; he was a home-bred *vakil*, but as his legal practice rose, his dress and manner of life began to conform more and more to the western style. One landmark in this westernizing process, as we have already seen, was his occupation in the early nineties of a bungalow in the 'civil lines' of Allahabad; another was a visit to Europe in 1899.

The visit to Europe was to prove a turning-point in Motilal's life. Of the taboos prevalent among Kashmiri Brahmins, per-haps none was stronger than that on foreign travel: to go abroad was tantamount to a violation of the Hindu religion and punishable with excommunication from the caste—a form of social boycott which could be very trying indeed. Pandit Bishan Narayan Dhar, a prominent lawyer of Allahabad, defied the ban, but on his return to India offered to perform a *prayshchit* (purification) ceremony – a face-saving expedient which at once condoned the transgression on the part of the individual and asserted the supremacy of the caste. A bitter controversy followed. The Kashmiri community split into two factions; those who were prepared to take Bishan Narayan back into the fold came to be known as adherents of the *Bishan Sabha*, while those who would not waive the social boycott on any conditions be-longed to the *Dharam Sabha*. Motilal's sympathies were de-cidedly with the *Bishan Sabha*. Before long Motilal and his family found themselves in the centre of the fray. Bansi Dhar, Motilal's eldest brother, who was about to retire from govern-ment service, took it into his head to visit England and witness Queen Victoria's Diamond Jubilee in 1897. All his life Bansi Dhar had meticulously followed the painfully elaborate ritual prescribed for orthodox Kashmiri Brahmins; not even his children were allowed to intrude upon him when he sat down to his meals in his own home. Any hopes he may have entertained of maintaining his orthodoxy intact in the course of his travels were dashed to the ground soon after he sailed. He fell seriously ill and had no alternative but to accept food and medical aid available on board the ship. The novel experience, despite the initial shock, broke the shackles of a lifetime; when Bansi Dhar

returned to India a few months later, after his round-the-world
trip, which included an interview with President McKinley of
the United States, he had been transformed into an English, or
perhaps an American gentleman.

3

Two years later, in 1899, Motilal himself paid a visit to
Europe. The visit was partly for pleasure and partly to canvass
support for Raja Ajit Singh of Khetri in his dispute with the
Jaipur Durbar. Motilal sailed from Bombay in August and returned home in November.

While in London he saw Sir Mancherjee Bhownaggree, the
Indian member of the House of Commons. When Motilal showed
him a memorandum on the claims of the Khetri State, he was
so impressed that he thought it had been drawn up by Sir
Edward Clark, the Advocate-General of England. 'I must confess my weakness,' Motilal wrote, 'when I say that I did feel
flattered for a time.' The affairs of Khetri did not wholly absorb
Motilal; he enjoyed every moment of his stay in England and re-
counted some of his experiences in a letter to the Private Secretary to the Raja of Khetri.

Motilal to Jagmohanlal, dated London October 22, 1899: 'I
have not been able to catch all the people for whom I had (letters
of) introduction from His Highness . . . but I have seen a good
number of them. Sir G. Seymour Fitzgerald has been of great
assistance to me in getting orders for me to see the House of
Lords on the opening day ceremony and other places of interest.
Sir W. Lee Warner is a dry-as-dust old Anglo-Indian who did
not know what to talk about except the Indian National Congress which came in for a large share of abuse. Dr Lennox
Brown is a grasping old surgeon very eager to pounce upon anyone who is unfortunate enough to have a throat affection.'[2]

Dr. Brown attributed Motilal's cough to his nose, and cauter-
ized his nostrils on the spot. Motilal came home with a lacerated
nose and minus twenty guineas. 'I must say,' Motilal wrote, 'that
on all accounts Dr Brown is one of the cleverest throat surgeons
in England . . . The late Sir Morel Mackenzie who attended the

² Unpublished (N.P.).

late German Emperor for his throat disease was accompanied by
our friend Dr Brown. His name is therefore closely associated
with Mackenzie's. When talking of them both people say *Moral*
Mackenzie and *Immoral* Brown. The reason is that the largest
class of throat patients comes from among the beautiful actresses
of England, who flock to him and receive the first and foremost
attention without paying a single guinea. He is the Hakim
Mahmood Khan of London. I wish I had been an actress, not to
save the twenty guineas, but to save the great pain I suffered,
which he would never have given me if I was capable of inspiring a tender feeling in him.'

As the time came for Motilal to leave for India he confessed
'it is for the first time in my life that I feel that it is not an unmixed pleasure to return home from a country like England . . .
I have made some friends among the nobility and gentry of
England, but have not been able to do much in that direction as
it is a very bad time of the year to see anybody. London is out of
season and all the big people are out. Besides, the [Boer] War is
the all-absorbing topic of the day and no one cares to listen to
anything else'.

On return to Allahabad, Motilal refused to perform 'the purification ceremony'. Threatened by social boycott, he was not
apologetic, but disdainful, defiant, aggressive. In a letter dated
December 22, 1899, addressed to his friend Pandit Prithinath
of Cawnpore, he explained his stand:

'My mind is fully made up. I will not (come what may) indulge in the tomfoolery of *Proschit* [purification ceremony]. No,
not even if I die for it. I have been provoked and have been
dragged from my seclusion into public notice. But my enemies
will find me a hard nut to crack. I know what your *biradari*
(caste) is and if necessary, in self-defence, I will ruthlessly and
mercilessly lay bare the tattered fabric of its existence and tear it
into the minutest possible shreds. I am only waiting for some
foeman worthy of my steel to take the field and will then be
ready to break a lance with him . . . So long as H and others of
his ilk howl and bark I will pass them by with the most studied
indifference and contemptuous silence . . .'

Motilal was excommunicated, but did not give in. Nor did
he lose any opportunity for a dig at his self-righteous oppon-

ents. 'You may not dine with me without polluting yourself,' he told an orthodox uncle who came to see him, 'but I
suppose we could share whisky and soda?' Motilal became the
leader of a third group, the most emancipated in his community;
it was at first called *Moti Sabha*, but the name was changed at
Motilal's instance to *Satya* (Truth) *Sabha*. His defiance helped to
put out the dying embers of orthodoxy; large numbers of
Kashmiri young men were henceforth able to travel abroad for
education or for pleasure, without incurring the odium or
opposition of their community.

This trip to Europe, which was followed by another in the
following year, accelerated Motilal's westernization. Thorough-
going changes ensued, from knives and forks at the dining table
to European governesses for the children. To the new influence
may be attributed the adoption of 'Nehru' as a surname. As we
have already seen, Motilal's ancestors were Kauls, and acquired
the name of Nehrus because their house was situated on the
bank of a *nahar* (canal). The double-barrelled name Kaul-Nehru
was adopted for some time; it was shortened to 'Nehru', but the
description was confined to a small circle of friends and relatives.
Motilal's eldest brother was known as 'Bansi Dhar Pandit'
during his trip abroad in 1896-7, and Nand Lal's books in the
Anand Bhawan library bear the signature: 'Pandit Nand Lal'.
Motilal was the first in the family to adopt Nehru as a surname:
'M. Nehru Esq.' had obviously a more modern ring than 'Motilal
Pandit'.

Growing westernization brought Motilal closer to the British
community in Allahabad. Many Englishmen admired this handsome Kashmiri Brahmin, the rising star of Allahabad Bar, who
dressed, lived and even looked like an Englishman. They envied
the elegant luxury in which he lived; they admired his
bonhomie; they respected his independence even though it sometimes seemed to verge on defiance. Senior officers of the I.C.S.
liked his company and enjoyed his hospitality; one of them, Sir
Harcourt Butler, who rose to be a Lieutenant-Governor, claimed
in 1920 'a friendship of thirty years' standing'. The relations between Government House and Anand Bhawan were cordial;
dinners and teas were exchanged. Motilal had not turned forty
when Sir John Edge, Chief Judge of the Allahabad High Court,
offered to propose his name for membership of the exclusively
European 'Allahabad Club', and to get the proposal seconded by

the Brigadier-General commanding the Allahabad sub-area. Motilal politely declined the offer as he sensed the width of the racial gulf and did not want to risk being 'blackballed' by the newest subaltern from England. Nevertheless, it was a fine gesture from the Chief Justice and indicated the high esteem and even affection in which Motilal was held by those at the apex of the official hierarchy.

Many years later, when Motilal gave up his profession and the luxuries of a lifetime to cast in his lot with Gandhi, he became a symbol of patriotic sacrifice. Nothing strikes the imagination of the Indian masses more forcibly than renunciation: a Buddha or a Gandhi storms his way into their hearts. It is therefore not surprising that legends should have grown round Motilal's opulent past: for example, he was said to have sent his linen for laundering to Paris. These legends, by heightening the contrast in his life before and after the plunge into the struggle for freedom, served to feed an inverted snobbery and to fulfil a psychological need of the millions who had dared to challenge the might of the British Empire. There was thus an understandable tendency to play up Motilal's phase of anglicism. But in fact it had definite limits. In the first place, though he flouted the tyranny of caste, he did not discard that characteristically Indian institution, the joint family. Unlike many a westernized Indian, he did not look down upon his relatives or wash his hands of his social obligations. The debt he owed to his brother Nand Lal he repaid many times over. He brought up his nephews as his own children; to them he always remained the beloved *Bhaiji* (respected brother) on whom they could always lean for advice and support. Secondly, Motilal's wife was too unsophisticated and deep-rooted in traditional beliefs to be converted into a full-fledged *mem-sahib*. Swarup Rani might tolerate knives and forks, and European governesses in her house, but her attachment to the Hindu scriptures, the *pujas* (worship) and orthodox ritual was unshakeable. She continued to make pilgrimages to Hardwar and Benares, though her husband often laughingly suggested that she was already living in *Prayag*,[3] the holy of holies, and could more usefully visit Japan or America.

Swarup Rani's health suffered a setback after the birth of Jawaharlal in 1889. A second child, a daughter, was born on August 18, 1900. She was named Sarup Kumari; her pet-name

[3] The ancient name of Allahabad.

Nanni ('the little one') was shortened to 'Nan' by a European governess. There was great rejoicing in 1905 when a son was born on November 14th – by a curious coincidence, the birthday of Jawaharlal. But the rejoicing was short-lived; the infant died when he was hardly a month old. Two years later, in 1907, a daughter was born on November 2nd. She was named Krishna; her nickname Betty was the choice of her European governess, but it sounded like 'Beti' (Hindustani for 'daughter'), and was readily accepted by the family. 'I hardly remember a time,' Krishna recorded many years later, 'when mother was hale and hearty, able to eat, drink and lead a normal life like the rest of us. I did not know what it was to have a mother's constant care, for she had to be taken care of herself all the time.'[4] From time to time Swarup Rani became seriously ill and was a semi-invalid for long periods. Her sister Rajvati, who had been widowed at an early age, came over to Allahabad and thenceforth spent the best part of each year nursing Swarup Rani and keeping house for her.

Rajvati's life was punctuated by a strict routine of worship, fasting and other austerities; her influence, coupled with that of the pious Nandrani, the widow of Nand Lal, constituted a strong religious pocket in Anand Bhawan which Motilal made no effort to dislodge. There was indeed a good-humoured co-existence in Anand Bhawan between the deep religiosity of the women and the light-hearted agnosticism of the men. Rajvati was too ortho-dox to touch food cooked in the western style for Motilal. She had her own separate kitchen, where she told the children fascinating tales from the epics as she cooked and served them hot *puris*. On auspicious days, such as *Diwali*, Motilal was present at the *Lakshmi puja*. And he looked forward to the colour, festivity and expense of ceremonies such as that on his son's birthday, when the boy was weighed against bags of grain which were later distributed to the poor.

This easy-going tolerance and lack of humbug exposed Motilal to no little misunderstanding and even misrepresentation. Political opponents found religion a good stick to beat him with : he was denounced as 'denationalized', anti-Hindu and pro-Muslim. Only recently a critic referred to Motilal's son as 'English by education, Muslim by culture and Hindu by an

4 Hutheesing, Krishna, With No Regrets, p. 124.

accident of birth'.[5] It is not easy to say whether this verdict is coloured more by ignorance or malice. True, Motilal's wide circle of friends included Muslims, his hospitality made no distinction of race or creed, he employed Muslim *munshis* (clerks) and servants; he was well-versed in Persian literature and fond of Urdu poetry. All this did not, however, add up to 'Muslim culture'. During the two hundred years the Nehrus had been settled at Delhi and Agra, they had imbibed that peculiar Indo-Muslim synthesis in dress and etiquette, art and literature, social customs and even superstitions, which was the product of three centuries of Mughal rule and was most pronounced in northern India. We have already seen how, on the eve of the Mutiny, Hindus and Muslims lived in harmony in Delhi. The Mughal King and the Muslim noblemen of Delhi did not see any outrage to Islam in participating in the colourful festival of the *Holi*. Nor did a Brahmin aristocrat lose caste because he was equally proficient in Sanskrit and Persian. The sharp lines of communal cleavage date from a later period, when the grinding of religious axes began to yield political advantages.

Specializing as he did in the law of Hindu inheritance, Motilal possessed a much wider and deeper knowledge of the religion of his birth than many of his critics would have allowed. Nevertheless, it is a fact that his was not a religious temperament. He was not one of those inquisitive, introspective, self-questioning spirits who, obsessed by a sense of sin, draw up a nightly balance-sheet of good and evid deeds, or experience an irresistible urge to penetrate the mystery of life. He was too absorbed by the daily struggle here and now to bother about the hereafter. He was a product of that late-Victorian 'free thinking' rationalism, which was learning to dispense with divine explanations of the working of the universe and to pin its faith on the human intellect and on science to lead mankind along endless vistas of progress. This rationalism prevented Motilal from being swept off his feet by the tides of Hindu revivalism, which rose high at the turn of the century. The doctrines of the Arya Samajists were too dogmatic, of the Vedantists too metaphysical and of the Theosophists too ethereal for his logical, practical – and unimaginative – mind.

If we must label Motilal, it would be safer to describe him as an agnostic than as an atheist. His initial rebellion was not

[5] N. B. Khare, in an article in A *Study of Nehru* (Editor, Zakaria), p. 215.

against the tenets of Hinduism but against the superstitions with which it was encrusted. Vivekananda, the great apostle of re-awakened Hinduism and a contemporary of Motilal, had bewailed: 'Our religion is in the kitchen. Our God is the cooking-pot, and our religion is: "don't touch me I am holy" '. 'I would rather see every one of you,' he had exhorted a Hindu audience, 'rank atheists than superstitious fools, for the atheist is alive and you can make something of him.'

By taking to western ways, Motilal did not seek merely to imitate the ruling race; he made a bid for freedom from the hidebound society into which he had been born. It was as if, to prevent asphyxiation, he had opened his western window for a breath of fresh air. In this, as in most other things, Motilal was more rebel than conformist. His innate spirit of rebellion was one day to lead him along political paths which neither he nor his British friends could have imagined as they drank each other's healths.

CHAPTER FOUR

INDIAN NATIONAL CONGRESS

ON December 28, 1885, when Motilal was twenty-four and a budding lawyer in Cawnpore, seventy-two Indian gentlemen from various parts of India met in Bombay. For this first meeting of the Indian National Congress, ground had been paved by a number of pioneers in the fields of education, journalism and social reform. It was, however, left to an Englishman to provide an outlet for the incipient nationalism which was still groping for expression. Allan Octavian Hume, the son of the Radical M.P. Joseph Hume, rose to the high position of secretary of a department. In 1882 he retired, after serving the Government of India for thirty-three years in the Covenanted Service. The remaining thirty years of his life were spent in the service of the people of India.

Hume was convinced that though the British had brought peace to India, they had not solved her economic problems, that the officials were perilously out of touch with the people, that the surging tide of intellectual, social and economic discontent needed to be controlled and channelled if it was 'not to ravage and destroy but to fertilize and regenerate'. Hume's first impulse had been to confine the All India meeting in December, 1885, to the discussion of social questions and to invite Lord Reay, the Governor of Bombay, to preside over its deliberations. The Viceroy, Lord Dufferin, however, advised Hume to enlarge the scope of the meeting to include political questions, so that it might perform the functions which His Majesty's Opposition did in England, and not to fetter freedom of discussion under an official president.[1] After a hurried visit to England during which he consulted John Bright, Lords Dalhousie and Ripon and other eminent authorities on India, Hume returned just in time for the first meeting of the Indian National Congress, the venue of which had to be changed at the eleventh hour to Bombay because of the outbreak of cholera in Poona.

[1] Wedderburn, Sir William, *Allan Octavian Hume*, p. 60.

As they assembled in the Goculdas Tejpal Sanscrit College in their morning coats, well-pressed trousers, top hats and silk turbans, the seventy-two delegates to the first session of the Indian National Congress could scarcely have realized the historic role they were playing. Florence Nightingale, who read a paper on the Indian revenue system at a meeting of the East India Association, and whose reformist zeal came to embrace the poverty of the Indian peasant as well as the health of the British soldier, wrote shortly before the inaugural session of the Congress:

'This National Liberal Union,[2] if it keeps straight, seems altogether the matter of greatest interest that has happened in India, if it makes progress for a hundred years. We are watching the birth of a new nationality in the oldest civilization in the world. How critical will be its first meeting at Poona! I bid it God-speed with all my heart...'[3]

The feminine intuition of Florence Nightingale was to prove keener than the political insight of Lord Dufferin.

Far-sighted Britons had foreseen that the British rule in India could not last for ever. Macaulay had pointed out that it was dangerous to impart western knowledge without awakening ambitions, and to awaken ambitions without providing an outlet for them; he had envisaged the day 'when the public mind of India may expand till it has outgrown our system'. Such a prophecy would have been dismissed as the fantasy of a Whig historian by members of the Covenanted Service, who commanded all the points of vantage in the structure of the *Raj*, whether in the districts, in the provinces, or in the councils of the Viceroy and the Secretary of State. Theirs was a close corporation of professional administrators, who behaved as, and perhaps sincerely believed themselves, in the words of Blunt, 'the practical owners of India; irremovable, irresponsible and amenable to no authority but that of their fellow members'. A small coterie of senior officers in the central secretariat formed a freemasonry which dispensed the plums of the service, decorated each other and wound up their careers in Simla, or more often in London, where from their seats in the Secretary of State's

[2] One of the names suggested for the Indian National Congress.
[3] Ratcliffe, S. K., *Sir William Wedderburn*, p. 123.

Council they could continue to promote their own policies and protégés in India. Theirs was a steel frame, solid, immobile, difficult to bend, impossible to break.

2

It was hardly to be expected that the emergence of an all All-India political organization could be welcome to the 'guardians' of the British Raj. Their point of view had been expressed often and bluntly enough. In 1853 Lord Ellenborough had observed that British policy should avowedly be 'to continue to govern the Indian people with the deliberate intention of holding them in perpetual subjection'. In March, 1877, Sir John Strachey, the Finance Member of the Government of India, frankly repudiated the doctrine that it was the duty of his government to think of Indian interests alone.[4] During the Ilbert Bill agitation, Sir Fitzjames Stephen, a former member of the Viceroy's Executive Council, wrote a letter to The Times in which he described the Government of India as 'essentially an absolute Government founded not on consent but on conquest'.[5] Even the gentle, scholarly and judicial Henry Beveridge, the father of Lord Beveridge, who confessed that 'India had burnt itself' into him, could write in 1877 that, however wrongfully the British may have got hold of India, for them to 'abandon her now would be to act like a man-stealer who should kidnap a child, and then in a fit of repentance abandon him in a tiger jungle'.[6]

What with keeping down crime, administering justice and sitting up late at night writing interminable reports for their superiors, the British officers in the districts had their hands more than full. Fretting at the climate, the loneliness and the exile, they looked forward to the long leaves and re-joining their families in England. And meanwhile they bore their cross with fortitude, supported by the conviction that the system they administered was 'the most beneficent, the most perfect and the most unalterable that can be devised'. They felt at home with the unsophisticated peasant to whom they were ma-bap, mother and father rolled into one. They could understand and even like

[4] Proceedings of the Legislative Council of the Governor-General, vol. xvi, p. 163.
[5] Gopal, S., The Viceroyalty of Lord Ripon, p. 153.
[6] Beveridge, Lord, India Called Them, p. 384.

the sly sychophant expectantly hanging around their verandahs for the favour of a job or a title. But they were repelled by the English-speaking Indian, who had the impudence not to make an obsequious bow, take off his shoes or lower his umbrella when approaching the members of the ruling race. Patronage, and even kindness towards the subject race, came more naturally to the British official than equality. The sense of racial superiority was even more deeply ingrained in the non-official Briton who, lacking official status, had only his colour to fall back upon. During the early years when the Indian National Congress was going through its birth-pangs, it was a favourite grouse of the Anglo-Indian press that the English-speaking Indians had the audacity to refer to Europeans in India as foreigners.[7]

'The merciful dispensation of Providence, which has placed India under the great British Dominion,' – such expressions were often heard at the early sessions of the Congress. It was, however, not so much sycophancy as the fighting spirit of some of the Congress spokesmen which impressed the authorities in India. At the second Congress held in December, 1886, Raja Rampal Singh, a delegate from North Western Provinces, declared that the Arms Act, which denied Indians the right to carry arms, outweighed all the benefits of British rule: 'We cannot be grateful to it for . . . converting a race of soldiers and heroes into a timid flock of quill-driving sheep.' More significant than the professions of loyalty were the demands voiced by the Congress: the expansion and reform of the legislative councils, the right to question the executive and to criticize the budget, a larger share in the superior branches of the administration. These were radical, indeed revolutionary demands. 'Representative institutions, according to a British Governor, 'were a sickly plant in their own soil'; their extension to India must have seemed out of the question. 'Democracy' was not an entirely respectable word, nor did it have a wholly pleasant connotation even in England in the closing decades of the nineteenth century. Of Lord Salisbury, the Conservative statesman, the British historian A. J. P. Taylor has written: 'He spoke all his life as though democracy was a sort of germ people catch much as people now talk of Communism that will get into the Western

[7] Cotton, Sir Henry, New India, Or India In Transition, p. 75.
[8] Banerjea, S. N., A Nation in the Making, p. 130.

world unless we keep the Greek window closed.'[9]

Gokhale, one of the ablest and sanest leaders of the Congress in its early phase, once remarked that no Indian could have started the Indian National Congress, and if its founder had not been an Englishman and a distinguished ex-official, the authorities would have found some pretext for snuffing it out at birth. Lord Dufferin quickly retraced his steps; the benevolent neutrality of his Government towards the Congress turned to a thinly-disguised antagonism. Hume also discovered his miscalculation; the response from his former colleagues of the Civil Service was disappointing; while they were sensitive to criticism, they were impervious to pleas for reform. It was futile, Hume felt, to address petitions and protests to the authorities in Simla. He decided to appeal to public opinion in India and England over the head of the unchanging and unchangeable bureaucracy. In a speech at Allahabad on April 30, 1888, he declared:

'Our educated men singly, our Press far and wide, our representatives at the National Congress – one and all – have endeavoured to instruct the Government, but the Government like all autocratic governments has refused to be instructed, and it will be for us to instruct the nations, the great English nation in its island home, and the other far greater nation of this vast continent, so that every Indian that breathes upon the sacred soil of our Motherland may become our comrade and coadjutor, our supporter, and if needs be, our soldier, in the great war, that we, like Cobden and his noble band, will wage for justice, for our liberties and rights.'[10]

3

The fact that Hume's speech was delivered at Allahabad had a special significance. Allahabad was the capital of the North Western Provinces and the headquarters of their Lieutenant-Governor, Sir Auckland Colvin. Colvin was a liberal administrator, a supporter of legislative reform in homoeopathic doses, but he had been alarmed by the bold lead Hume had recently given to the Congress. In October, 1888, Colvin wrote to Hume warning him against unleashing forces which he would not be able to control, and criticized the Congress on lines which were

[9] Taylor, A. J. P., *From Napoleon to Stalin*, p. 120.
[10] Wedderburn, Sir William, *Allan Octavian Hume*, pp. 62-2.

to become familiar during the next fifty years. He challenged the representative character of the Congress, stressed the divergent needs and aspirations of the Muslims and pointed to the hazards of premature and aggressive propaganda among an illiterate population. Hume picked up the gauntlet and refuted Colvin's arguments. He denied that the Congress was spreading hatred against the Government; on the contrary, by recognizing and ventilating grievances it was telling the people of India 'that the British Government is superior to all other governments in the world, for its fundamental principle is to shape its policy according to the wishes of the people'. Nor did he accept that the Congress agitation was premature; he was not sure that it was not already too late. As for Colvin's solicitude for the Muslims, Hume described it 'a shameful libel on the Muslims that they were inferior to the Hindus and would have no chance if a fair field is conceded to all'. 'The hostile stimulus,' Hume drily added, 'came from outside.'

Sir Auckland Colvin's known antipathy to the Congress and Hume's visit to Allahabad had brought the conflict to Motilal's door-step. The Congress session for 1888 was scheduled to meet at Allahabad during Christmas week; it became an occasion for a trial of strength between the British officials and their henchmen on the one hand, and the local Indian intelligentsia on the other. Among the latter were a number of lawyers, veterans like Pandits Ajudhianath and Bishamber Nath, and juniors like Madan Mohan Malaviya. The president of the session was George Yule, an English merchant of Calcutta and a friend of India. An attempt by a group of loyalists led by Raja Shiva Prasad to break up the session proved abortive. The Raja's buffoonery caused a little stir and much amusement and his 'Patriotic Association', set up as a rival body to the Congress, proved still-born.

Motilal had moved to Allahabad only two years before; after the death of his brother he had too many domestic and professional burdens to be able to afford the distractions of politics. But there was much excitement in the town, and the twenty-seven-year-old Motilal was too proud to keep out of the fray. The list of the 1,400 delegates of the Allahabad Congress (1888) includes 'Pandit Motilal, Hindu, Brahmin, Vakil High Court, N.W.P.' The following year at the Bombay Congress in 1889, Motilal was not only a delegate, but was also elected to the 'Subjects Committee' in the distinguished company of Surendra Nath Banerjea, Gokhale and Madan Mohan Malaviya. Two years later when the Congress met at Nagpur, Motilal was again elected a member of the 'Subjects Committee'. In 1892 when the Congress again met at Allahabad under the presidency of W. C. Bonnerji, Motilal was the secretary of the Reception Committee. A spacious octagonal hall, specially built in the grounds on Lowther Castle to accommodate 3,500 delegates and visitors, 'surpassed in elegance and finish, the best halls in which the Congress had hitherto held its sessions'.[11] Part of the credit for this grandiose structure could safely be given to the future builder of Anand Bhawan.

4

During the next decade Motilal's name does not figure in the list of Congress delegates. These were the years when he was forging his way to the top of the Bar, and hardly had the time or the inclination to stray into the by-ways of politics. Nor was the political atmosphere electric enough to evoke a response in him. The Congress had survived the initial displeasure of the authorities; it held its annual sessions with unfailing regularity; it solemnly heard familiar feats of oratory from well-known leaders, and year after year passed resolutions in similar if not identical terms. But the novelty was wearing off. The attitude of the 'Simla clique' – as Hume called it – had changed from neutrality to antagonism, and finally to a supercilious indifference. Hume had despaired of making an impression on the bureaucracy and pinned his hopes on the education of public opinion and Parliament in Britain. The apathy of the British public was, however, notorious; only a bloody mutiny or a bejewelled Maharaja could arouse its momentary interest in the distant Oriental Empire which seemed more remote even than Ireland. Nor was it an easy task to whip up the interest of the House of Commons in Indian affairs. If Providence had thrown the burden of governing India on the House of Commons (as the admirers of the Empire, British and Indian, loved to put it), the House of Commons had thrown the burden back on Providence.[12] Hume and his friends, Sir William Wedderburn, Sir Henry Cotton, C. J. O.

---

[11] Report of the Annual Session of the Indian National Congress 1892.
[12] Besant, Annie, India Bond Or Free, p. 25.

Donnell, George Yule, Dadabhai Naoroji and Gokhale made heroic efforts to educate the British public, press and Parliament through the British Committee of the Indian National Congress, the Indian Parliamentary Committee and the journal *India*, but they seemed to make little headway. They had to contend not only with abysmal ignorance of Indian problems, but also with the tide of imperialism which was running high at the turn of the century. R. C. Dutt, the president of the Lucknow Congress (1899) bewailed the 'reactionary times' through which India was passing. 'We have achieved nothing of late," he lamented, 'we have lost a good deal of what we possessed before . . . I have struggled hard to save the wrecks of established rights . . . I have been beaten, defeated, swept away by the overwhelming tide . . ."[13] In Britain, these were the years of a resurgent imperialism, of Joseph Chamberlain, Rhodes, Jameson – and Curzon.

Lord Curzon's regime marked the high watermark of British imperialism in India. Ironically enough, it also marked the beginning of the end. 'Remember,' Curzon once exhorted Englishmen in India, 'that the Almighty has placed your hand on the greatest of his ploughs . . .' For his great mission in India, as he conceived it, he had extraordinary qualifications. After a distinguished record at Eton and Oxford, he had entered Parliament at the age of twenty-seven, travelled widely in Central Asia and the Far East, in the United States and India; he had served as Under Secretary of State for Foreign Affairs, and secured the ambition of his life, the Viceroyalty of India, before he had turned forty. To his undoubted talents, vast knowledge, and prodigious industry he added a fervid imagination, but it was that peculiar brand of 'Oriental' imagination which revelled in magnificent pageants and phrases, but could not enter the minds and hearts of a subject race. His 'reforms' of the university and the corporation in Calcutta had already awakened misgivings in the western-educated classes, but the partition of Bengal (July, 1905) was his crowning blunder. Whatever the administrative merits of a scheme which sought to re-draw the frontiers of an unwieldly province populated by seventy millions and covering the present states of West Bengal and East Pakistan, Orissa and Bihar, the indecent haste and secrecy with which it was pushed through roused the suspicion and wrath of the educated classes.

[13] Gupta, J. N., *Life and Work of R. C. Dutt*, p. 319.

The Bengali intelligentsia viewed the project as a calculated attack on their political consciousness and solidarity. They felt, in the words of Surendra Nath Banerjea, 'the uncrowned king of Bengal', that they had been 'insulted, humiliated and tricked'. The atmosphere in Bengal, and indeed in the whole of India, became dangerously explosive. Hundreds of meetings were held; memorials rained upon the Viceroy and the Secretary of State; the nationalist press thundered. On October 16, 1905, the streets of Calcutta resounded with the cries of 'Bande Mataram', as thousands of men, women and children converged on the sacred ghats for a bath, and later vowed to resist the dismemberment of their province and the threat to the integrity of their race.

All was in vain. Curzon belittled the agitation as 'manu-factured', and the authorities followed the time-honoured methods of countering the agitation. In April, 1906, a conference of the Bengal Provincial Congress at Barisal was dispersed, its prominent leaders were beaten up and imprisoned; one of their offences was the shouting of 'Bande Mataram'. The pent-up anger and frustration of the people sought new outlets. They lacked the power to shut out British manufactures; but could they not through the discipline of patriotism raise invisible tariff walls? The boycott of British goods and the encouragement of *Swadeshi* (Indian manufactures) became the two pillars of the campaign against the Partition of Bengal. Such was the temper of the people in Bengal when the campaign was at its height that few people dared to purchase foreign cloth except under cover of darkness; guests retired from dinners where foreign sugar or salt was served; a six-year-old girl cried in her delirium that she would not take foreign medicine;[14] and no porters could be found at Faridpore station to carry the luggage of His Honour the Lieutenant-Governor of East Bengal, when he arrived on a tour of inspection.[15]

The partition of Bengal raised the political temperature in India. It drove some hot-headed youths along the perilous paths of political violence and created a new gulf between the educated classes and the British Government. It also widened the cleavage within the Indian National Congress: the tug of war between Moderates and Extremists was to dominate Indian politics for a decade, and to draw Motilal Nehru into the fray.

[14] Banerjea, S. N., A *Nation in the Making*, p. 197.
[15] Ibid, p. 291.

CHAPTER FIVE

MOTILAL THE MODERATE

THE Moderate leadership included well-known figures, whose association with the Congress dated from its birth: party managers like Pherozeshah Mehta, prolific publicists like Dinshaw Wacha and spell-binding orators like Surendranath Banerjea. But the ablest exponent of political moderation was Gopal Krishna Gokhale, the disciple of Ranade, the mentor of Gandhi and the idol of Motilal Nehru. Gokhale was once asked if constitutional agitation had ever helped a subject country to liberate itself. 'It may be,' he replied, 'that the history of the world does not furnish an instance when a subject race has risen by agitation. If so, we shall supply the example for the first time. The history of the world has not yet come to an end.'

No one was better qualified than Gokhale to lead a constitutional agitation. He was intensely patriotic; he had given his all to his country. While still in his thirties he was honoured as an 'elder statesman'; knowledgeable and accurate, cautious and empirical, candid and courteous, indefatigable and incorruptible, fluent and formidable in debate, his performance as a parliamentarian struck Sir Henry Cotton, M.P., the president of the Bombay Congress (December, 1904) as comparable with the best in the House of Commons.[1] From his seat in the Imperial Legislative Council at Calcutta and Simla, Gokhale directed a powerful searchlight on the grievances of the Indian people. Why had the pledge of racial equality, implicit in the Charter Act of 1833 and the Royal Proclamation of 1858, not been fulfilled? Why were Indians shut out from their legitimate share not only in the 'great' imperial services' but in the officer cadres of the 'Minor Departments' such as the Opium, Salt, Customs and Police? How was it that after a hundred years of British rule four Indian villages out of five were without a school-house, and

[1] Cotton, Henry, Indian and Home Memories, p. 289. This incidentally was the first Congress session, which Jawaharlal, who was fifteen at the time, attended with his father.

seven children out of eight grew up in ignorance and darkness? Gokhale made earnest appeals to the Government of India to recognize the changes which were coming over the country. 'The whole of the East,' he declared in his budget speech of 1906, 'is throbbing with a new impulse, vibrating with a new passion ... we could not remain outside this influence even if we would, we would not remain if we could.' He invoked a 'nobler imperialism', instead of that 'narrower imperialism', which treated subject peoples 'as mere footstools' for the dominant race. He called for a change of heart in the bureaucracy. Though foreign in personnel, would not the Government of India conduct itself as if it were national in spirit?

2

Gokhale was voicing the sentiments, the hopes and the illusions of the first generation of Congressmen. 'We hope to enjoy the same freedom,' Dadabhai Naoroji had said on his election as a member of the British Parliament, 'the same strong institutions which you in this country enjoy. We claim them as our birthright as British subjects.' Sankaran Nair told the assembled delegates of the Indian National Congress in 1897 that it was 'impossible to argue a man into slavery in the English language', and declared:[2] 'From our earliest school-days, the great English writers have been our classics, Englishmen have been our professors in colleges. English history is taught in our schools ... Week after week, English newspapers, journals and magazines pour into India for Indian readers. We, in fact, now live the life of the English. It is impossible under this training not to be penetrated with English ideas, not to acquire English conceptions of duty, of rights, of brotherhood. To deny us the freedom of the press, to deny us representative institutions, England will have to ignore those very principles for which the noblest names in her history toiled and bled.' These veterans of the Congress were not dispirited by lack of response from the Government. They had read their British history, and knew what struggles had been waged in and outside Parliament for the Corn Laws, the anti-slavery laws, the factory laws, parliamentary reform, and indeed for every piece of important legis-

[2] Natesan (Editor), *Congress Presidential Addresses*, vol. I, pp. 363-5.

lation. They knew that it could not be otherwise with con-stitutional reforms for India.

This optimism seemed wholly unrealistic to a section of Con-gressmen, who were learning to question the premises and the programme of the Old Guard. This radical section, of which the inspirer and hero was Bal Gangadhar Tilak, and which came to be known as 'Extremist', regarded as futile all attempts to pene-trate the darkness of the bureaucratic mind with luminous speeches; twenty years of petitioning had failed to bring the country visibly nearer self-government. The Extremists wondered whether self-government within the Empire was at all a prac-ticable ideal; it could mean, in the words of Bipin Chandra Pal, one of the prophets of the new school, 'either no real self-govern-ment for us or no real overlordship for England'. They wondered whether political evolution from precedent to precedent was feasible for a country like India; a subject nation did not prepare itself by gradual progress for liberty; it opened by means of liberty the way to rapid progress. It was hardly possible by a snail-slow process to convert a foreign government into its opposite; there was no alternative to a speedy substitution of Indian and democratic for British and bureaucratic rule. Indians needed not more appointments in the services, but the right to make them. Such was the logic of Tilak, who would not rest nor let the Government rest, of Lajpat Rai whose fiery eloquence electrified the Punjab; of Bipin Chandra Pal whose burning eloquence set the listeners 'aflame with the fever of a wild con-suming desire', and of Aurobindo Ghose whose ardent patriotism, mystical fervour and subtle logic fused into an explosive mixture. 'Nationalism,' wrote Aurobindo, 'comes from God. Nationalism cannot die, because it is God who is working in Bengal'.

The partition of Bengal was a godsend to the Extremists, be-cause it seemed to demonstrate the incorrigibility of the British bureaucracy in India and the futility of Moderate tactics. It drove scores of young men and women to anarchical societies, into which they were initiated with the *Gita* in one hand and the sword in the other. 'Perverted religion and perverted patriotism' – this was how an official committee later described the dark and daring deeds of these young men and women, who believed they were repaying in blood the debt they owed to the land and religion of their birth. The Extremist leaders knew full well that political violence was unavailing and indeed suicidal against a better-armed adversary. They, however, advocated vigorous measures to demonstrate the depth of the national feeling on the partition. Boycott of British goods and promotion of *Swadeshi* – Indian manufactures – became two important planks in their campaign against the Government.

3

A head-on collision between the Moderates and the Extremists seemed imminent at the Benares session in December, 1905 – the first meeting of the National Congress after the announcement of the partition of Bengal. The excitement was keen enough to draw Motilal, after many years, as a delegate to this session over which Gokhale – his beau ideal in politics – presided. Gokhale's presidential address, despite its restrained and measured tone, was a trenchant criticism of Curzon's policies and a passionate plea for a new deal for India. An open clash between the Extremists and Moderates was saved by the mediation of Lajpat Rai, the gentleness of Gokhale, the forbearance of Tilak and the absence of the formidable Pherozeshah Mehta.

Early in 1906, a rare opportunity seemed to offer itself for the opening of a new chapter in Indo-British relations. The turn of the electoral wheel brought the Liberal Party into power in England. The new Secretary of State was John Morley, the student of Burke, the disciple of Mill, the friend and biographer of Gladstone. The heart of nationalist India, as Gokhale put it, hoped and yet trembled as it had never hoped and trembled before.[3] If only Morley would rescind the partition of Bengal, carry through a substantial measure of constitutional reform and with the help of the new Viceroy inaugurate a sympathetic policy, the bitter legacy of Curzon would be obliterated. Unfortunately, Morley did not, perhaps could not, act quickly. He had to wrestle with his own council in London, packed as it was with the quintessence of Anglo-Indian reaction; he had to reckon with the entrenched bureaucracy at Simla and the vocal European commercial interests in Calcutta; he had to repel the attacks of Curzon, Lansdowne and the Conservative Opposition in Parliament, which accused him of weakening in the face of agitation and violence; he had to handle the Radical members in his own party who urged him to go fast and far in meeting

[3] Natesan, *Congress Presidential Address*, vol. I, p. 823.

Indian aspirations. 'It was no easy thing, Morley recorded, later, to make watches keep time in two longitudes at once.'⁴ In 1906 Gokhale visited England and had a number of interviews with Morley. 'My principal work here,' he wrote home, 'now has resolved into a tug of war with the officials of the India Office, as to who should capture Mr. Morley's mind. I am only one and they are many . . .' He sent word to Tilak not to impugn Morley's sincerity and to have a little more patience 'for the sake of our common country.'⁵

To Tilak the results of this secret and indefatigable diplomacy were not obvious; the partition of Bengal remained and the attitude of the authorities towards political agitation was hardening. Once again as the time for its annual session approached, the shadow of a split seemed to lengthen over the Indian National Congress. The Extremists suggested the names of Lajpat Rai and Tilak for the presidency. The Old Guard took fright and summoned Dadabhai Naoroji to the rescue. The 'Grand Old Man', now in his eighty-first year, travelled all the way from England to preside over the Calcutta session in December, 1906. His presence prevented an open rupture and facilitated a compromise on the controversial issues of *Swadeshi* and boycott. Dadabhai's presidential address delighted the Extremists by making a clarion call for *Swaraj* (self-government). The Moderates were uneasy: they had invited him to put out the fire; this he had done, as an Anglo-Indian journal gleefully put it, with kerosene. After Dadabhai's departure, the old suspicions and hatreds between the two factions welled up again. The Moderate leaders, and especially Pherozeshah Mehta, who controlled the party machine, came to the conclusion that the time had come to stem the Extremist tide if the Congress organization in India and Morley's work in England were not to be swept away. Within a few weeks of the Calcutta Congress, the Moderate offensive opened. A number of conferences were convened to educate public opinion. Pherozeshah Mehta himself presided over a conference in Bombay. Another conference was held at Raipur in Central Provinces.

4

It was against this background that the first Provincial Con-

⁴ Morley, *Recollections*, vol. II, p. 156.
⁵ T. V. Parvate, *Gokhale*, pp. 210-13.

ference of the United Provinces opened in Allahabad on March 29th with Motilal Nehru in the chair. He gave as its *raison d'être* the obvious need for supplementing the efforts of the Indian National Congress with 'small Congresses' in every province, to reiterate the national demands and to ventilate local grievances. The argument was plausible so far as it went, but there is no doubt that the real object of the Allahabad meeting was to define and defend the creed of the Moderates and to denounce the programme and tactics of the Extremists. The political barometer in Motilal's home province had recently risen. There had been a lecture tour by Gokhale, who had ably expounded the creed of political moderation; and just before the conference, Lajpat Rai had visited Allahabad and lectured on 'The New Spirit', which was another name for Extremism. He had urged a boycott not only of British goods but also of British courts, exclaiming: 'We feel like sinking in the earth when we are asked what our numbers are, and what the numbers of our rulers are . . . The history of the world points to the fact that no nation has secured freedom by another's charity or benevolence. This is written in letters of gold, nay letters of blood . . .'

That Motilal should have found himself in the Moderate camp may seem surprising in the light of later history; in 1907 it seemed natural and inevitable. Moderate politics were the only politics he had known since he attended the early sessions of the Congress. Constitutional methods of agitation fitted in with his legal training and background; able and persistent advocacy was as sure to succeed at the bar of British public opinion as at the bar of the Allahabad High Court. Motilal had boundless admiration for Gokhale. The aura of religious revivalism that overhung Extremist politics in Bengal and Maharashtra repelled him. He came to respect Tilak, but had little patience with some of the other Extremist leaders, impatient idealists, whose politics seemed to him to have run away with their imagination and whose methods were better suited to the market-place than to the chamber of a legislature, or even of a lawyer. To one who had worked his way up the hard way, it was also an irritation that some of these young firebrands had no recognizable profession – except perhaps that of patriotism.

Motilal's 12,000-word presidential address at the Allahabad Conference followed the familiar Moderate lines. It contained pointed references to the words of wisdom uttered by the Hon'ble Mr. Gokhale', whom Motilal described as 'the apostle of the gospel of moderation'.[6]

Motilal acknowledged India's debt to England. She 'has fed us with the best food that her language, her literature, her science, her art and, above all, her free institutions could supply. We have lived and grown on that wholesome food for a century and are fast approaching the age of maturity. We have outgrown the baby garments supplied to us by England'. He reminded his audience that they enjoyed great blessings under the British rule, not the least of which was the right they were exercising at that very moment of assembling in a public meeting to criticize that rule itself. He paid a tribute to the Indian National Congress, 'the great University of National Politics', which had educated the people of India and secured a modicum of reform from the Government. If the gains had not been more substantial, it was entirely due to the fact that John Bull had not been sufficiently aroused. 'I firmly believe,' declared Motilal, 'that he means well – it is not in his nature to mean ill. This is a belief which is not confined to myself alone. It is shared by many of our distinguished countrymen, including past presidents of the Indian National Congress, and will be readily endorsed by those who have seen and known John Bull at home. It takes him rather long to comprehend the situation, but when he does see things plainly, he does his plain duty, and there is no power on earth – no, not even his kith and kin in this country or elsewhere – that can successfully resist his mighty will.'

On the Extremists, Motilal launched a vigorous onslaught: 'A new school of thought has lately arisen in India holding extreme political doctrines, and advocating measures of coercion and retaliation to obtain redress for their wrongs.' The repressive policy of the Government had brought people to the verge of despair 'which gave birth to that child of adversity, our good friend the Bengal Extremist'. He agreed that *Swadeshi* was an admirable doctrine. Had he not himself seen the injunction 'Patronize Home Industries' displayed at railway stations, in places of amusement and buses in England? But boycott was a different matter: although it had been given a grudging, limited and temporary acceptance by the Hon'ble Mr Gokhale at the Benares Congress as a mark of protest against the partition of

[6] Malaviya, K. D., *Pandit Motilal Nehru: His Life and Speeches*, p. 109.

Bengal, it was a negative policy and could not carry them very far: 'Not all the ill-will and vindictiveness in the world' could drive foreign manufactures out of India unless they were replaced by better and cheaper articles made in India. If India were to be industrialized, her bankers and moneylenders must provide the capital, her *talukdars* must unearth their gold and silver hoards and her ambitious young men acquire technical skill, if necessary, by visiting Europe, America or Japan.

Motilal ridiculed the Extremists' talk of extending the boycott from British goods to British institutions. 'They would have you,' he told his audience, 'make the government of the country impossible. They talk of "passive resistance" – that charming expression which means so little and suggests so much.' He deprecated unconstitutional methods: 'We are constitutional agitators and the reforms we wish to bring about must come through the medium of constituted authority.' He held no brief for the administration; nor did he deny its many shortcomings. He was too proud to recommend a policy of 'mean, cringing, fawning flattery' of those in power. 'You have grievances,' he said, 'and you must like men demand redress. Be brave, unbending, persistent in advocating and carrying out reforms.'

He ended his speech on an optimistic note, recalling Macaulay's prophecy of 'the proudest day in British history' when Indians instructed in European knowledge would 'in some future age demand European institutions'. 'That proudest day, in English history is no longer a dream. Destiny has for years been bringing us nearer to that day. Let not the bureaucracy shut their eyes to the glorious dawn that is just beginning to break. Let not our countrymen mistake the glory of that dawn for the grandeur of the noonday sun. Let both unite to dispel all passing clouds from the horizon. Let both "bow down and hail the coming morn." '

Earlier in his speech, he had deplored the fact that the subversive ideas of the Extremists had found a ready response in 'the young blood of schools and colleges in the United Provinces'. Little did he know that the contagion had travelled to England where his only son was at school at Harrow.

CHAPTER SIX

THE ONLY SON

IT is not easy to fathom the depth of the emotion which centres on an only son in a Hindu family. A male heir is necessary not only for the continuity of the family tree and the inheritance of the patrimony, but also for the performance of those rites without which the soul, after it departs from this world, cannot rest in peace. Tradition, deeply rooted in the collective unconscious of the Hindu race, has helped to heap upon the only son a degree of anxious solicitude verging on the ridiculous. He is a little idol adored by grand-parents, uncles, aunts and sisters; his wayward will is a law unto itself. His parents live in perpetual dread, as if they had staked their all on one precarious investment in a shaky market. If they could, they would wrap him in cotton wool and shelter him from the cold blasts of a cruel world. That such pampering is a poor preparation for life is proved by the melancholy annals of many an aristocratic family: it has been rare for great wealth and high position to descend in a continuous line for two, let alone three, generations.

'I knew,' Jawaharlal has written about his childhood days, 'that my mother would condone everything I did, and because of her excessive and indiscriminating love for me I tried to dominate over her a little'. Motilal was an affectionate but not indulgent father, generous but not gentle. Little Jawahar might find himself on his father's knee, if he peeped into the drawing-room in the evening when Motilal and his friends were relaxing, but in the son's earliest memories admiration for the father was mingled with awe. If the house frequently resounded with Motilal's laughter, it also shook visibly when he was provoked into one of his paroxysms of rage. The provocation usually came from the misunderstandings and bickerings inevitable in a joint family, or from a slip on the part of a servant. Hari (Motilal's personal servant), recalls that at a dinner-party, just as the guests were about to take their seats, Motilal, noticing a servant wipe a plate with the end of his sleeve, beat up the poor wretch so violently that the other servants ran for their lives and the guests – embarrassed and hungry – quietly retired. It was only after one of Motilal's old clerks, Munshi Mubarak Ali, had interceded on behalf of the erring servant, that the household, which seemed in a state of suspended animation, hummed again with activity.

Little Jawahar himself was a trembling victim of his father's wrath when he was barely six years old. One day, noticing two fountain-pens lying at his father's table, he helped himself to one. When the search was being made, he was too much afraid to confess, but his guilt was discovered and he was punished with such a thrashing that ointment had to be applied to the wounds for several days. In that pre-Freudian age, Motilal could hardly have worried about the traumatic possibilities of such incidents. In retrospect, it seems likely that, but for his iron grip, the ease and luxury of Anand Bhawan might easily have been the slippery slope to indolence and failure.

2

Motilal was resolved to give his son the best possible education. He himself had studied only Persian and Arabic in old-fashioned *maktabs* (schools) before switching on to the high school at Cawnpore and Muid Central College at Allahabad. He considered this wholly inadequate for his son. In 1896, when Motilal's elder brother, Bansi Dhar, went to Europe, his son Shridhar (who was about the same age as Jawaharlal), was left at Anand Bhawan. Motilal put both the boys in the local St Mary's Convent school. Six months later, when Shridhar left Allahabad, Jawaharlal was removed from the school: it was decided that henceforth he would receive instruction at home from English tutors. To this decision, Motilal may have been led partly by aristocratic pride, partly by pro-English prejudices and partly by the consciousness that he could afford the best – and the most expensive – education for his children. The decision had more far-reaching consequences than Motilal could have imagined. Solitary tuition at home deepened the loneliness of a boy who had been an only child for eleven years and had little opportunity to play with children of his own age. On the other hand, Jawaharlal escaped the stereotyped courses of study in Indian schools and colleges, which were suitably spaced by examinations and adorned with degrees designed not so much to release the springs of the mind and soul as to open gateways to careers under the government and in the professions.

Jawaharlal was lucky in being spared the strait-jacket of conventional education. He was luckier still in having, during the years 1902-4, Ferdinand T. Brooks, a gifted young man of mixed Irish and French extraction, as a tutor. Brooks inspired in his pupil a zest for reading and an interest in science. The miniature laboratory which he rigged up in Anand Bhawan provided a thrilling introduction to elementary science. Encouraged by his tutor, Jawaharlal read voraciously: from children's books – *Alice in Wonderland* and *Kim* – he passed on to novels of Scott, Dickens, Thackeray and H. G. Wells, Mark Twain and the Sherlock Holmes stories. *The Prisoner of Zenda* and *Three Men in a Boat* delighted him. It was varied fare, less important in itself than as a foretaste of what was to come. Many years were to pass, however, – the years of Harrow, Cambridge and prison – before his intellect was fully fledged.

Brooks was a theosophist and had been recommended to Motilal by Mrs. Annie Besant. This remarkable woman, a friend of Charles Bradlaugh and George Bernard Shaw, a born orator and a great organizer, had travelled from Christianity to theosophy via rationalism and atheism. In 1893, four years after she had joined Madame Blavatsky, the co-founder with Colonel Olcott of theosophy, Mrs Besant had landed on Indian soil. 'Though born in this life in a western land and clad in western body', she believed that she had been, in a previous incarnation, the child of Mother India. It was characteristic of this London-born lady – Annie Wood was her maiden name – that when she said 'we' in England, she meant the Indians, not the English. Long before she flashed like a meteor through the Indian political firmament during the first world war, she had devoted herself to the task of disseminating Hindu philosophy and religion. Madras was her headquarters, but her links with Motilal's home province were close. She set up at Benares the Central Hindu School, which grew into a college, and finally into the Hindu University. She became a friend of the Nehru family. Motilal admired her great work for social and educational reform, but did not take her spiritual Odyssey seriously. In his youth he had been drawn to theosophy, into which he was initiated by Madame Blavatsky herself during her visit to India. Theosophy offers a detailed plan of the universe, its origin and nature, its past and future, based not on deductions from verifiable data, but on direct revelation to the chosen few. 'Full proof is possible,' said one of Madame Balavatsky's original converts, 'to those who have full belief.' Incapable of 'full belief', Motilal had quickly outgrown his enthusiasm for the new creed.

For his son, however, the doctrines of theosophy – 'reincarnation', 'astral and supernatural bodies', 'auras' and *Karma* – had an irresistable fascination. He attended the theosophists' weekly meetings, which were usually held in his tutor's room in Anand Bhawan. Annie Besant's eloquence swept Jawaharlal off his feet. He felt the 'call' to embrace theosophy and, with becoming gravity, approached his father for permission. Motilal did not object, and indeed seemed to treat the whole thing as a joke. Evidently he saw it as an outburst of juvenile enthusiasm which would soon pass off – which is exactly what happened. Jawaharlal had the thrill of being 'initiated' by Mrs Annie Besant and of watching the magnificently bearded face of good old Colonel Olcott at a Theosophists' Convention at Benares. But his interest in theosophy departed with his tutor. The scraps of information he had picked up about the Buddhist and Hindu scriptures, the *Dhammapada*, the *Upanishads* and the *Gita* were, however, his first introduction to the religious and cultural heritage of his country: they provided the initial impulse for that long intellectual quest which culminated forty years later in the *Discovery of India*.

3

From English tutors to an English public school and university must have seemed to Motilal a natural, perhaps a necessary step. On May 13, 1905, he sailed from Bombay in the *s.s. Macedonia* along with Swarup Rani, Jawaharlal and the four-year-old Sarup (or Nanni as she was called). This was his third trip abroad after an interval of five years. In a letter[1] to his nephew Brij Lal Nehru, who was in Oxford at this time, Motilal wrote that he was suffering from 'nervous prostration, the natural consequence of five years' hard, incessant work without rest. There are two things I have to do in London; first, put Jawaharlal in a school; second, consult some specialists about the proper treatment and the most suitable watering place for [my] wife. If you have the

[1] Motilal Nehru to Brij Lal Nehru, April, 1905 (N.P.).

time, collect all the information you can on these two points. As regards Jawaharlal, I am still in the dark as to the school where he has to go. All the well-known schools have no vacancies . . . I am sorry I have delayed Jawaharlal's visit to England'.

Luckily, with the help of some English friends, Motilal managed to get his son into Harrow. The school was not to open till the end of September, but on the advice of Dr Wood, the Headmaster, the boy was left in London to learn Latin and prepare for the entrance examination. Meanwhile, on the advice of London doctors, Motilal took his wife for a few weeks' rest and treatment to watering places on the Continent.

On July 30th the Nehrus arrived at Cologne. 'It is a beautiful city,' he wrote to his son, 'Coleridge might have had some justification for the lines he wrote in his own time. The Cologne of today is quite different . . . He is, however, right about the pavements. They do consist of murderous stones. The rattling of the carriages produces a terrific noise, the stones being laid on edge and being of uneven surface.' On August 5th, he wrote from Bad Homburg, where at seven in the morning he found himself in an endless procession of 'ladies and gentlemen, proceeding glass in hand, to the particular springs which had been prescribed for them'. The tennis-courts of Homburg were 'supposed to be the best in all Europe', but Motilal gave up the idea of joining the local club, when he saw that 'not only men but girls played a much prettier game than I could ever expect to do.'

The mineral waters of Bad Homburg failed to produce the magical properties ascribed to them, so on August 17th the Nehrus moved on to Bad Ems. The four hours' train journey on the bank of the Rhine was delightful, and the scenery was 'simply perfect'. Surrounded by high hills and standing on both banks of a small river in which motor-boats were plying up and down every few minutes, Bad Ems struck Motilal as 'one of the loveliest little places' he had ever seen. He was in high good humour and arranged a tea-party for the children of local schools on his daughter's fifth birthday. As the grounds of the Hotel D'Angleterre Englishcherhof could not accommodate four hundred children at a time, they were entertained in two batches. The children enjoyed themselves immensely, and before taking their leave sang German songs. Their teachers made neat little speeches in English to which Motilal made a suitable reply.

Motilal gave a glowing account of the party in a letter to Jawaharlal:

'Nanni was literally laden with presents, large crowds assembled round the grounds, and Nanni was cheered by them. She shook hands with each guest (poor thing was quite exhausted). Besides the presents brought by the children, the proprietor of the hotel sent a beautiful birthday cake, the jeweller from whom I bought a pair of earrings for Nanni sent her a magnificent basket of flowers, and several lodgers in the hotel also sent flowers. It was the greatest birthday Nanni has ever had, or perhaps will have in future. She behaved very well indeed, and looked like a little queen in her new dress. I have come to be known at Ems as an Indian Prince. Cheap fame purchased for £15 only!'

The 'little queen' played all day in the open air, improved her appetite and learnt to pronounce new words 'with faultless accent'. A pretty child, she was (her father noted) as much admired in Ems as she had been in London. She insisted on scribbling what she thought were letters to her brother. When her father was unable to decipher 'the crooked lines and loops', she told him: 'You do not know German, this is German'. She was the only member of the family to whom the waters of Bad Ems seemed to do any good. Her mother was decidedly worse than she had been in London and her father came to the conclusion that 'the little improvement' in his health could have been achieved anywhere if he had taken the same precautions.

When the time came for Jawaharlal's admission to Harrow the family returned to London. On September 30th, after his first visit to Harrow, Motilal warned his son: 'You must really guard yourself against cold more effectively than you have been doing. You must never be in the condition in which you were when I left you . . .' Two days later he wrote: 'I hope you have been taking care of yourself, for you must understand that in taking care of yourself you do in a great measure take care of me and my happiness.' This anxiety stemmed from the fact that in all his sixteen years this was Jawaharlal's first long separation from his parents. The parting was as hard for them as for him. When Motilal reached his hotel at Marseilles on October 19, 1905, it was almost midnight. Next morning the *Macedonia* was to take him, his wife and daughter back to India. Full of emotion, he could not leave Europe without a farewell letter to his son.

'You must bear in mind,' he wrote, 'that in you we are leaving the dearest treasure we have in this world, and perhaps in other worlds to come. We are suffering the pangs of separation from you simply for your own good. It is not a question of providing for you, as I can do that perhaps in one single year's income. It is a question of making a real man of you, which you are bound to be. It would be extremely selfish – I should say sinful – to keep you with us and leave you a fortune in gold with little or no education.

'I think I can without vanity say that I am the founder of the fortunes of the Nehru family. I look upon you, my dear son, as the man who will build upon the foundations I have laid and have the satisfaction of seeing a noble structure of renown rearing up its head to the skies.

'We leave you in flesh, but will always be with you in spirit. In less than ten months I will again be with you, and in about two years you will be in a position to pass a few months among your old surroundings at Allahabad. . . I never thought I loved you so much as when I had to part with you, though for a short time only. Perhaps it is due to my weak heart. But my sense of duty to you is as strong as it ever was, and as for the poor weak heart, it is in your keeping. I have not the slightest doubt that you will rise to all my expectations and more. You have enough work to keep you engaged . . . work includes the preservation of health. Be perfect in body and mind and this is the only return we seek for tearing ourselves from you. I could write pages in this strain, but it is close upon 1 o'clock and you really need no sermon from me. I will, therefore, say farewell, mine own darling boy, take every care of yourself. In doing so you will be taking care of your parents.

Your loving, Father.'

On November 4th, Motilal, Swarup Rani and Sarup were back at Allahabad. 'Here we are at last,' he wrote to Jawaharlal two days later, 'but somehow or other Anand Bhawan does not appear to be so full of *Anand* (Happiness). There is something wanting, and that something must necessarily be yourself. I dare say we will soon be accustomed to it.' Immediately on his return, he was inundated with briefs. He had expected that it would take some time before his presence in Allahabad would become known throughout the province. But he was 'most agreeably surprised to see a large number of clients eagerly expecting me with long purses. Briefs are flowing in from all directions . . . and I find it difficult to cope with them . . . my list of cases for to-morrow has reached its climax. During the last twenty-four hours, I have been engaged in every first appeal on the list. My absence from the High Court for any length of time does not make any difference in my practice. I am taken for a magician! To my mind it is simple enough. I want money. I work for it and I get it. There are many people who want it perhaps more than I do, but they do not work and naturally enough do not get it.'

The formula of success was not so simple as Motilal made it out to be. But of his industry there could be no doubt. On November 9th he got up at four in the morning, worked away at his briefs till eight, saw new clients till nine, was in the court at ten and on his feet throughout the day. He was resolved (he wrote to his son) 'to work as hard as I can for another seven months, after which I will have the pleasure of seeing you and the benefit of another change in Europe'.

CHAPTER SEVEN

HARROW

'MY dear Mr Nehru,' wrote Dr Joseph Wood, the Head Master of Harrow, on November 1, 1905, 'I received your kind letter this morning and hasten to assure you that your dear boy shall be my special care. I have had a long talk with him, discussed the vital question of clothing, and given him my best advice. I have told him that if his present room should prove too cold for him, I will make arrangements to give him another facing south. He looks very well today, and very smart in his cadet corps uniform.' A week later Dr Wood wrote again: 'You will by this time have arrived in India, but your thoughts will, I doubt not, often travel back to England. I promised you to write now and then and let you hear something. It is now half-term and you will in due course receive the official report. Every master speaks well of your boy, both as to his work and his conduct. He has distinct ability, is already ahead of his form and will doubtless secure promotion next term. I am *fully* satisfied with him in every way . . .'

The official report for the half-term was indeed very complimentary to young Nehru. He was top in every subject. His form work and Modern Languages were 'excellent'. In Algebra he was adjudged 'good', in Geometry, 'extremely neat and painstaking'. The tutor's comment on the 'pupil room work' was: 'Excellent, has done some good history papers for me'. The House Master summed up: 'very creditable stand'.

Motilal was delighted to hear that his son was top of his form, and predicted that before long he would be top of the school:

'Did I not tell you, soon after leaving you, that there was a great and brilliant future for you? . . . I find that the Science column is left blank in the report. Perhaps you will take it up next term. As you know, I want you specially to develop a taste for Science and Mathematics. You are no doubt doing all that can be done and nothing will please me more than to have in you the first Senior Wrangler of your year . . .'

On December 18, 1905, Jawaharlal learned that he was to receive a prize. 'I had never thought of this happening,' he wrote to his father, 'and am rather nervous about it. At the most what occurred to me was that I might get a small prize in the Head Master's study privately, but not in the speech room in the midst of all the people . . .' The shy, sensitive boy from Allahabad found the ceremony something of an ordeal: 'I was not quite sure to the very end, and when Dr Wood called out my name, I felt very confused. He gave me the book in the usual formula of congratulations.' The prize was Lamb's *Essays of Elia*. 'I am not only quite satisfied with your work,' Motilal wrote, 'but really proud of you. If you only go on working steadily, as you are sure to do, the day is not far distant when your country will be proud of you.'

Lyrical though Motilal grew over his son's scholastic attainments, he had no intention of turning the boy into a bookworm. He knew only too well that Jawaharlal had had a lonely childhood and would find it hard to come out of his shell. In his first letter (September 30, 1905) to Harrow from London, he had urged his son to 'make friends with your immediate neighbours in the house – occasionally entertain them on holidays and half-holidays – in a word try to be a general favourite as you are bound to be without my telling you'. In his first letter from Allahabad (November 6) he repeated the advice to 'make many friends' and 'patronize the creameries . . . to entertain, specially the rowdier element of the school. Never mind the expenses which cannot be very great'. A few days later, after appreciating his son's exploits at the Rifle Club Range and 'sham fights', Motilal wrote that he was surprised that Jawaharlal had not yet found himself 'mixed up in some real fight with somebody or the other'. 'Please do not suppress the information,' he added, 'even if you get the worse of it. It will by no means be discouraging to me to hear about it.'

Motilal had been a keen sportsman in his youth. He asked his son to play as many games as possible, and gave him *carte blanche* to engage a professional coach for any game. The only game in which Jawaharlal had acquired some proficiency in Allahabad was tennis, but that was not of much use at Harrow.

Nevertheless, there is evidence that young Nehru took his sports as seriously as his studies. He frequented the gymnasium and joined the Rifle Club and the Cadet Corps. 'I am agreeably surprised,' wrote Motilal, 'at your passing the examination in shooting and at the progress you have made at footer. You were quite ignorant of both these things when you joined Harrow . . . At footer specially I never had any hopes for the simple reason that it is the game of rough and burly boys and not of those so delicately framed as you.' The paternal pride was, however, tempered by paternal solicitude:

'I will advise you to play [football] cautiously. Don't venture beyond your strength. It will be a bad day for us all if you came out of it with broken bones as did the younger of the two brothers in the book entitled *The Brothers.*'

On May 4th, 1906, Jawaharlal bought a cricket bat. On June 1st he reported 'a slow but steady improvement . . . I made yesterday 40 "not out", which is rather good for me. Of course this is really not much, considering the low game I am in'. The following month his description of a cricket match between Eton and Harrow would have done credit to a sports correspondent: 'It was a victory for our opponents but the rarest chance would have changed it into a defeat for them. The first day's play was interesting, but not exciting. At the end of the innings, Eton was 135 runs ahead of us. In the second innings our men got out fast and many people thought that we would be beaten by an innings. The last man, however, played well and saved our side. He got out by a most regrettable misunderstanding. The ball was in the hand of an Eton fellow quite near the wicket, but the batsman, unaware of this, started to run with the result that he was run out. As it was, he had made 79, the highest score on our side. The Etonians had now to make 95 to win, and it seemed an easy task. But it proved less easy – the first wicket fell in the first over without any runs having been made. The second followed after a few balls. You cannot imagine the excitement which prevailed at the fall of the wickets. The Etonians went on getting out till only four wickets remained. Then somehow they stuck. Two or three easy catches were missed and this gave them confidence. If the catches had not been missed, there is not a shadow of a doubt that we would have won. As it was, we did

very well. The Eton Eleven was a strong one in every point; ours
was equally strong in batting and fielding, but in bowling it was
deplorably weak.'

2

One of the most exciting days at Harrow was the Cadet Corps
field day.

Jawaharlal to his father, April 1, 1906: 'Today was a field day
and we had to do a great deal of marching . . . The field day
today was at Hatfield House, the country seat of Lord Salisbury,
against Eton. Although they are nearly twice our size, they were
the defending side and we the attacking. And so we were not
particularly successful in dislodging them out of their position,
but they too made a mess of their affairs. The umpires, instead of
praising both sides as is usual with them, blamed both, and so
equalized matters. After the operations we had tea which was
not half so good as the last field-day's, but still far better than
what we get here. We were allowed to go over the house – a
magnificent old building. The rooms were beautifully furnished.
The walls were lined with huge paintings and everything was
charming . . .'

Harrow and Eton usually found themselves in opposition in
these manoeuvres. On March 1, 1907, when Jawaharlal and his
fellow Harrovians took the train to Uxbridge and marched the
five miles to the scene of operations, they had no doubt that
the Etonians, who had suffered a defeat in a previous engagement, were burning to avenge themselves.

Jawaharlal to his father, March 1, 1907: 'Our section was
placed on the reserve and so we had a very easy time at the beginning, lounging about in the long heathers, which made a
splendid hiding place. After some time our turn came, and we
had to make up for our slackness. Our side was supposed to be
covering off the retreat of a large army, and we were to keep the
enemy in check, whilst the supposed enemy was destroying the
bridges. We were thus fighting a rearguard action, and had often
to retire. Towards the end, the fighting got quite close, and in a
thick wood the Etonians suddenly rushed up almost into our

arms. Of course no fighting could take place at such close quarters without danger, and both sides were ordered to stop. The umpires were sought after, but they could not be found anywhere . . . After a little time the [fighting] came to cease, and both sides went to the country house of an officer, who had kindly invited us to tea. Tea being over, one of the umpires made a short speech about the field day. He praised both sides and said that they equally shared the honours.'

Motilal carefully filed and preserved not only his son's letters but also the reports and bills from the headmaster; so we know a good deal about Jawaharlal's time at Harrow. We know that his father remitted £67 19s 8d on admission and £71 9s 6d for the Christmas term, and that the amount for the remaining terms ranged round £65, except for the summer term of 1906, when (because of an item of £23 for the tailor) it shot up to £88. There is a bill for £1 13s 6d from W. Hay Wood of West Street, Harrow, for a cricket bat and a pair of 'best buck pads'. The extra charge of threepence indicates how many times young Nehru was shaved at Harrow: once in the first term, twice in the succeeding terms, rising to a maximum of four times in the Christmas term of 1906. The dentist (Dr Ernest Fox) charged him £1 1s for the service of 'gold stopping and amalgam stopping' rendered on May 7, 1906. Doctors Bindloss and Lambert, the school physicians, charged 17 shillings in the Christmas term of 1905, and 5 shillings in the summer term of 1907. It was too soon for J. C. Wilbee & Co., the school booksellers, to make money out of Nehru; they only succeeded in selling text-books. Jawaharlal dutifully forwarded to his father question papers set at the terminal examination; the arithmetic papers had answers scribbled against each question. The English History paper for the Christmas term, 1906, included combustible material for a future rebel against the British Raj. One of the questions was: 'For what reasons did the American colonies revolt? Why was it impossible to subjugate them?' Another: 'Summarize the causes of the French Revolution.'

3

Work and play kept young Jawaharlal fully occupied, but there were moments, specially in the first few months, when he was homesick for Allahabad. His father had ordered a Bombay firm to send regular consignments of mangoes to Harrow, but to Jawaharlal news from India was more important than Indian luxuries. The weekly mail brought him three letters, one each from his father, mother and baby sister. Little Nanni (Sarup), the darling of the family, seemed to be doing very well in the charge of Miss Hooper, the governess whom Motilal had engaged during his visit to England in 1905. A beautiful child, high-spirited, talkative and wilful, she was a universal favourite.

Motilal to his son, December 14, 1905: 'They observed the Foundation Day at the Muir College for the first time this year. They held all sorts of sports and Lady Stanley gave away the prizes. I was called upon to subscribe to the fund as 'one of the richest Muir Collegians' and had to do so. But I was not able to go and sent Nanni with Miss Hooper. I am told by some barrister friends that Nanni was very much admired by the ladies and gentlemen present. Lady Stanley in particular did not leave her for a minute, and went on chatting with her all the time . . .'

February 15, 1906: 'You would again have disappointed dear little Nanni had it not been for my foresight. The picture post-card, I posted as from you, came in good time and she was well pleased with it. She now wants you to write to her a letter. I am afraid I am not sufficiently advanced in the fine art of forging to pass off on her a letter from me as if it were from you . . .'

March 22, 1906: '. . . Miss Hooper is thriving and the Indian climate is taking very kindly to her – she is getting fat. Dear Nanni is making rapid progress. She can speak 170 English words correctly and can repeat multiplication tables up to 3. But somehow or other she is getting very thin – just like you did at her age . . .'

Jawaharlal to Motilal, June 13, 1906: 'Nanni in spectacles! It is unthinkable. I do hope you won't follow the advice of the surgeon, however, eminent he may be. She would look perfectly absurd in them and I doubt if they do her much good either . . . I do not like at all women, and especially girls to wear spectacles . . .'

Swarup Rani's health was the subject of anxious comment on both sides of the water. She wrote to Jawaharlal every week, except when she was too ill to do so. Her letters to her son were written in colloquial Hindustani, and overflowed with emotion. On November 4, 1905, she gave birth to a son. Irrepressibly optimistic, Motilal wrote happily to Jawaharlal: 'The little stranger chose your birthday as the most fitting time to come to this world, and I cannot help attaching a significance to this circumstance.' Unhappily the coincidence had no significance. The child, who was named Ratan Lal, died when he was hardly a month old.

In Allahabad life moved along the old grooves. Occasionally there was exciting news. In February, 1906, Pandit Sunderlal was appointed the first Indian Vice-Chancellor of Allahabad University. The Vakils' Association arranged a garden party in his honour, to which the Lieutenant-Governor and his wife were invited. 'Poor Sunderlal,' wrote Motilal, 'is taking lessons from me as to how to talk to the ladies.' Early in 1906, the *Magh Mela* drew an endless stream of pilgrims to Allahabad. About a million people had assembled and thousands were pouring in daily; cholera broke out at the river-side. 'Sunday next is one of the great bathing days,' Motilal wrote to his son. I am not going to see, what my friends call, fun. It is discouraging to me to see my countrymen engage themselves in stupid things.'

Motilal included in his letters an occasional word of fatherly advice to his son, who was spending the most impressionable years of his life away from home. When Jawaharlal pleaded lack of time for the dumb-bells which his father had sent him, he was advised 'to have the things handy whenever you enter or leave the room. Do just one exercise about seven times . . . you should, of course, do a different exercise each time during the day.' In February, 1906, Jawaharlal received a picture postcard of the Hon'ble N. G. Chandavarkar; below the photograph were just two words in Motilal's own handwriting: 'Unassuming simplicity'. A few days later, the rumoured romance of a Kashmiri youth (the son of a friend of the family) in England gave Motilal an opportunity to touch on more delicate issues. 'You must not confuse real love, with a passing passion, or a feeling of pleasure in the society of a girl . . . You know all the arguments against Indians marrying English women . . . You must know that I hold you too dear to think of coming between you and real happiness . . .In everything that concerns you, you do not look upon me as your father, but your dearest friend in the world, who would do anything for you to make you happy'.

Motilal took particular care not to sermonize. His advice was tempered with an informality and good humour which were all too rare between fathers and sons in those days; it was almost as if he was already treating his young son as an adult. After discussing the possibilities of coaching for entrance to Cambridge in the context of the crowded routine at Harrow, he concluded a letter in October, 1906:

'So after all I can give you no advice in the matter and must leave you to your own resources. This is an apt illustration of the true principle of life. You may have loving and willing parents and friends to back you, but it is you, and you alone, who must fight your own battles . . .'

The flow of advice was not wholly one-sided. Writing from Harrow (October 19, 1906) Jawaharlal implored his father to be careful 'about yourself, this time for my sake, and . . . not work too hard as you unfortunately often do. You may think this boldness on my part to give you advice, but, dearest father, it comes from my heart and as such, I hope, you will receive it'. Motilal counted his friends by the dozen; he entertained them lavishly and laughed with them heartily, but he was intimate with very few of them. Swarup Rani was often ill and, in any case, her intellectual range was too limited to enable her to share all his thoughts. It was only with his son that he could think aloud, and to him, although he was still only a schoolboy, Motilal would sometimes unburden himself.

Motilal to his son, April 30, 1908: 'I was very glad to receive a very sympathising letter from you by the last mail. Sympathy is a commodity which has never been bestowed on me by those from whom it was expected in very excessive quantities, and lately it has become very rare indeed. Coming as it does from across the seas and from my own son, it has its own value for me.

'You are quite right in saying that these repeated attacks of one ailment or another are bound sooner or later to end in a complete breakdown. The last attack of lumbago has taken a lot out of me. Having been very improvident in money matters all my life, I have to thank myself if I have now to work harder than I should. You need not, however, be afraid of losing me in the near future. I have a long span of life and mean to live it . . .'

Jawaharlal to his father, May 21, 1908: '. . . My information about your being morose is, I am glad to know partially inaccurate . . . It is you who ought to influence other people, and not be influenced by them. Yours must be the stronger personality – I doubt if you meet many people, who have the advantage of you in that commodity – and I should have thought you would bring others up to your state of mind, rather than lower yourself to theirs.'

4

During the summer vacation of 1906 Jawaharlal came to India, and spent three weeks with his parents at Mussoorie. He spent Christmas in Paris, where he saw the great automobile show of 1906. There were hundreds of motor-vehicles of all kinds, from motor bicycles of 1 h.p. to racing cars of 450 h.p. He saw the motor-car – a Renault – which Motilal had ordered and which was being made ready for shipment to India.

At the end of 1906, the motor-car was ceasing to be a novelty in Europe; the air age was at hand. 'Every one seems to be cocksure,' Jawaharlal wrote to his father, 'that aeroplanes will be as common in a few years as motor-cars are now. I actually saw, the other day, an advertisement of a firm who undertook to build aeroplanes for people ! I hope you will have time to use your car before the aeroplane craze sets in. And then perhaps, when I am at the 'Varsity – it is too much to hope before then – I may have the pleasure of seeing you on week-ends.'

Motilal was thinking of more important problems than the potentialities of civil aviation. Jawaharlal's academic progress at Harrow seemed highly satisfactory. In some subjects, such as literature, history and general knowledge, he was easily ahead of the English boys. In science also, thanks to Ferdinand T. Brooks, he had an initial advantage. 'We are doing Chemistry now', he wrote in November, 1906, 'this is fairly elementary, but it is far and away better than measuring lines and cutting circles to bits, and then calling the whole thing Physics, as we did last term. Next term, I shall probably have a more advanced course'. Though he was at a slight disadvantage in Latin and French, there was every indication that he would remain at or near the top of the form. 'You have every reason to be proud of your son,' wrote Headmaster Wood to Motilal (May 19, 1906), 'who is doing excellently and making his mark in the school. Every master, who has anything to do with him, speaks in the highest terms of his ability and his industry. He is a thoroughly good fellow and ought to have a very bright future before him'.

Jawaharlal had come to Harrow in 1905 when he was nearly sixteen; to complete the school course, he needed to stay on till the autumn of 1908. Adding three years at the university, he would be more than twenty-two by the time he graduated. He would thus have little time to prepare for the competitive examination for the Indian Civil Service. Motilal had broached the subject with the Headmaster.

Motilal to his son, October 27, 1906: 'I have told Wood that I had to enter you at Trinity College as having regard to your age and the limits imposed by the I.C.S. Regulations, there was no time to lose . . .'

Dr Joseph Wood to Motilal, November 11, 1906: 'I will do what I can to carry out your wishes, though I confess that I think your boy too young to go to Cambridge. He ought to have another year at school to bring out what is best in him. Moreover, it is putting a great strain upon him to expect him to get up these subjects for Cambridge in addition to his regular work. I fear the burden may be too heavy for him. But I will consult his tutor, and we will do our best. He is very well, and looks very bright and happy.'

Jawaharlal too was ready to leave Harrow for Cambridge. Though he had plunged into the routine of work and play at Harrow, he did not find his surroundings intellectually very stimulating. 'I must confess,' he wrote to his father on March 4, 1906, 'I cannot mix properly with English boys. My tastes and inclinations are quite different. Here boys, older than me and in higher forms than me, take great interest in things which appear to me childish . . . I almost wish sometimes that I had not come to Harrow, but gone straight to the 'Varsity. I have no doubt that public schools are excellent things and their training essential to every boy, but I have come here very late to really enjoy the life.'

'I can quite appreciate your inability to enter into the spirit of Harrow life,' replied Motilal on March 29th, 'an Indian boy is generally more thoughtful than an English boy of the same age. In fact there is early development in India, which Englishmen call precocity. Whatever it is, my own experience tells me, that what we gain in the beginning, we lose at the end. You must have seen many English boys even older than you are looking perfectly blank and stupid, but have you seen any Indian of the same age as Dr Wood looking half so vivacious and full of life? This is no doubt due to our climate, but there it is. Childhood in England occupies much greater portion of life than it does in India, and so do boyhood and manhood. Old age does not properly begin till a man is three score and odd – an age very seldom reached in India. Big boys in England are, therefore, to be found committing themselves to foolish pranks, which much smaller boys in India would be ashamed of. But this is no reason why they should be despised. They afford you, who can think, an excellent opportunity to study at least one phase of human nature, and thus add to your stock of that particular branch of knowledge called experience. You seem to put very little value on English public-school life, but let me assure you that as soon as you pass on to the 'Varsity, your thoughts will fondly turn to Harrow. And when you have done with the 'Varsity, the happy reminiscences of it will cling to you throughout life.'

A striking example of this precocity of Indian boys was furnished by Jawaharlal's insatiable interest in politics.

CHAPTER EIGHT

THE YOUNG NATIONALIST

JAWAHARLAL had hardly been two months at Harrow when he asked his father to send him an Indian newspaper, 'not the *Pioneer*'.[1] In December, 1905, he was pleasantly surprised to read in *The Times* that the *Swadeshi* movement had spread to Kashmir, where the people were reported to have bought up, by public subscription, all the English sugar and burnt it. 'The movement must be very strong indeed,' he wrote to his father, 'if it reached even the Kashmiris.'

Jawaharlal read the proceedings of the Indian National Congress with particular interest. When his father wrote from Calcutta that the Moderates and the Extremists had been at loggerheads in the 1906 Congress, he was disappointed. 'I am sorry to hear,' he wrote, 'that the Congress was not a success. I am impatiently waiting for your next letter to know the result of the proceedings. I do hope the different parties worked smoothly together, and there were no dissensions among the delegates. A most foolish thing this seems to me; for not only do they do no good to themselves but they do harm to their country they both pretend to serve. There couldn't have been any great difference or disagreement among the delegates, as our friends the Anglo-Indians would hardly have failed to wire the fact over here.'

Such passionate nationalism may seem surprising in an Indian boy of seventeen studying in an English public school, whose home in Allahabad was one of the most anglicized, whose father was an admirer of British ways and British institutions and counted high British dignitaries among his friends. However, we must remember the great gulf which, at the turn of the century, divided the British and the Indian, the rulers and the ruled. Educated Indians had not forgotten the hysteria of the European community during the agitation over the Ilbert Bill, when Lord

---

[1] British owned and edited, the *Pioneer* was the organ of European opinion and was then published from Allahabad.

Ripon was ridiculed as a 'White Baboo',[2] and a correspondent of the *Englishman* could seriously assert that 'the only people who have any right to India are the British; the so-called Indians have no right whatsoever'. Not only were Indians excluded from responsible posts in the administration of their own country; they received frequent and galling reminders of their inferior status. Compartments in railway trains and benches in public parks were reserved for 'Europeans only'. Long before the word was coined, 'apartheid' was practised by the most fashionable clubs in the principal towns of India. Many of them did not admit 'natives' even as guests; in Bombay and Calcutta it was not uncommon for an Indian gentleman to wait in the carriage, while his European wife went into the club. Nevinson, the noted British journalist, wrote after his visit to India in 1907-8 that there were in every part of the country Englishmen, who 'still retained the courtesy and sensitiveness of ordinary good manners. But one's delight in finding them proved their rarity'.[3] It was a significant commentary on racial prejudice that, right through the first world war, the Baden-Powell organization refused to admit Indian children as scouts. All this deeply hurt proud and sensitive members of the intelligentsia. Intellectually, they might feel equal, or even superior, to individual Europeans, but socially they were branded as an inferior race. No wonder the western-educated middle class passionately longed for what an Australian writer[4] has called 'freedom from the white man's contempt'.

Some of the most flagrant examples of racial arrogance were seen on the railways. In 1907, Keir Hardie, the Labour M.P., boarded a train at Madras, and found two Indians in a first class compartment. As Hardie entered, one of the Indians got up and said, 'Shall we move to another compartment, sir?' Hardie stared at the man, and enquired if he had paid his fare. 'Oh, yes,' he replied, 'but English gentlemen do not as a rule like to travel with natives.'[5] Not all Indian gentlemen were equally obliging. Some of them refused to give in to the white man's bullying, and then there were 'incidents'.

One of Jawaharlal's cousins, the 'strong man' of the Nehru family, was often involved in these 'incidents' and when they

[2] Gopal, S., *The Viceroyalty of Lord Ripon*, p. 146.
[3] Nevinson, H. W., *The New Spirit in India*, p. 117.
[4] Ball, MacMahon, *Nationalism and Communism in East Asia*, p. 15.
[5] Hughes, E., *Keir Hardie*, p. 155.

were related at home, young Jawaharlal's blood boiled. He was (he wrote later) 'filled with resentment against the alien rulers of my country who misbehaved in this manner, and when an Indian hit back, I was glad'.[6] He 'dreamt of brave deeds, of how sword in hand I would fight for India and help in freeing her'.[7]

2

On the day the Nehrus arrived in London, the newspapers carried the news of the crushing defeat inflicted on the Russian fleet by the Japanese navy off Taushima. The victory of an Asian country over a great European power thrilled Jawaharlal. The transition from Allahabad to Harrow seemed to stimulate rather than suppress his interest in politics. 'The great question of the hour,' he wrote to his father on January 12, 1906, 'is of course the General Election. Everybody is excited about it, and even in the streets you see some people talking about it . . . Today is the first day of the polling.' When Campbell-Bannerman formed his ministry, Jawaharlal was the only boy in his class, who, much to the surprise of his teacher, reeled off the names of the entire cabinet. A few days later when the Headmaster's House at Harrow, of which Jawaharlal was a member, held a 'mock election' young Nehru's political instincts vibrated to the excitement:

"Great preparations were made for two days for it and all the House was busy with placards for the respective candidates. The only difficulty in the beginning was to find a Liberal candidate. Almost everybody in this House is a strong Conservative, and the remaining few are half and half. Out of the latter the Liberal was chosen, although he himself was a better Unionist. On a half-holiday afternoon the lectures took place in a room which had been provisionally turned into a Committee Room, and the same evening the polling took place. The Conservative of course won.'

Not long after his arrival at Harrow, Jawaharlal's political proclivities almost got him into trouble with the authorities. A letter addressed to 'Master Joe, Harrow' was opened by the Head-

[6] Nehru, J. L., *Toward Freedom*, p. 21 (John Day, 1941).
[7] *Ibid*, p. 30.

master, Joseph Wood, who shared the nickname of 'Joe' with
Jawaharlal. Wood was shocked at its seditious tone. 'I think you
will agree with me,' he wrote to Motilal, 'that it is not the sort
of letter for a boy to receive at an English school.' When Motilal
explained that the writer was Rameshwari Nehru, the wife of
Jawaharlal's cousin Brijlal, Dr Wood hastened to make amends:
'I am intensely amused to hear, that it was a charming young
lady who defied the British *Raj*. Give her my kind regards, and
say I hope, some day, when she knows us better, she will like
us more.'

There was no one at Harrow to whom Jawaharlal could con-
fide his inmost thoughts, but he scoured *The Times* for Indian
news, and avidly devoured the pages of the *Indian People* and
other journals mailed to him from Allahabad. Motilal's own
letters contained a good deal of information about political developments in India, although he himself during these years
hovered uncertainly on the periphery of national politics. He
was present at the Benares (1905) and Calcutta (1906) sessions
of the Indian National Congress, but more as a spectator than
as an active participant. The reasons for this are not far to seek.
For one thing, Motilal's work at the High Court continued to
make heavy demands on his time. 'My immediate surroundings
remain unchanged,' he wrote to Jawaharlal on November 23,
1905: 'Clients! Clients!! Clients!!! One small brain to cope
with half of the work of the High Court. The other half goes to
Sunderlal.' For another, he was not at all happy at the course
Indian politics had taken after the partition of Bengal. 'The
anti-partition movement,' he told his son, was 'the most stupid
and, I may add, the most dishonest thing I have ever seen . . .'
Preoccupied as he was with his heavy – and lucrative – legal
practice, and out of harmony with the prevailing current of
public opinion, Motilal had neither the time nor the inclination
to give up the comfortable position of a critical looker-on at the
political drama.

3

Early in 1907 events conspired to push Motilal to the centre
of the stage. An open rupture between the Moderates and the
Extremists had been averted at the Calcutta Congress (December,
1906), but the tension between the two wings of the Congress

had not abated. The year opened with a propaganda offensive by the Moderates. In February Gokhale visited Allahabad. Motilal was present, along with other prominent citizens, at the railway station to welcome him. As the distinguished visitor came out, a large and enthusiastic crowd of students, which had been held back outside the station limits, shouted: 'Gokhale ki Jai', and surrounded Motilal's carriage, in which Gokhale was to drive to the house of his host, Tej Bahadur Sapru. The students unhorsed the carriage and insisted on drawing it. Gokhale pleaded with them; he threatened to go back to Calcutta. But the students were adamant: amidst deafening cries of Bande Mataram, they pulled the carriage through the streets of Allahabad. Next day Gokhale delivered a lecture on 'The Work Before Us'; Motilal, who presided at the meeting, told his son that the lecture was 'a masterpiece of close reasoning and sound common-sense expressed in the best and purest English'. There were two more lectures by Gokhale on 'Swadeshi' and 'A Few Words to Students'. Motilal gave a garden party in Anand Bhawan and invited 'all the leading Indian and European ladies and gentlemen' of Allahabad to meet the distinguished leader of the Congress.

The enthusiasm which the students of Allahabad had displayed during Gokhale's visit was inspired less by his politics than by his personality. Only a few days earlier they had given a thunderous welcome to Tilak. It was obvious that Allahabad and the United Provinces were beginning to be convulsed with the Moderate-Extremist conflict, and Motilal would be drawn into it willy nilly. In January, 1907, there was a meeting of Moderate politicians in Anand Bhawan, at which the possibilities of a provincial conference were discussed; it was suggested that Motilal should preside over it. He was not at all eager to plunge into the political arena, and asked for time to consider the suggestion. The news, however, leaked to the press and it became awkward for him to withdraw. 'I have been compelled to accept it [the presidency of provincial conference],' he wrote to his son. 'It is entirely a new line for me and I have very grave doubts of being able to justify the expectations of my friends. What I am particularly afraid of is the student class. They of late have developed a remarkable aptitude for rowdyism, and no sober and serious thinker can expect to secure an uninterrupted hearing from an audience composed of this element. Tilak was here the other day specially to address the students ... He succeeded to such an extent that the students of the Muir College (specially those of the Hindu Boarding House) have assumed an attitude of open defiance to the more moderate leaders of these provinces. Sunderlal and Malaviya are openly abused. I have so far escaped, but cannot be safe much longer as my views are even more moderate than those of the so-called Moderates. At present the boys declare that they will all be happy to follow my lead, as they think I have given enough proof of my independent and fearless adherence to my own views in matters social, etc. Whether they will think so when they hear my political views is a totally different question. I have, however, courted the storm and must brave it to the best of my ability.'

Jawaharlal did not share these misgivings. He was delighted at the prospect of his father's entry into active politics. 'I am sure,' he wrote (February 19, 1907), 'you will be as successful in the new line as you have been in other fields. You have already kept away from it far too long, but that, I hope, will add a new zest to it.' He urged his father to agree to preside over the conference. 'However you disagree with the details of the Congress programme,' he argued, 'you cannot but agree with its general aim ... your (presidential) address is certain to be a brilliant one; only I hope it will not be too moderate. Indians are as a rule too much so, and require a little stirring up.' 'You may not agree with the ways of the new Extremist party,' went on young Nehru, 'but I do not think that you are such a slow and steady sort of person as you make yourself out to be.' This was an extraordinarily shrewd judgment of his father's political make-up; but many years were to pass, and much was to happen to father and son and to India, before the truth of this judgment was vindicated.

Motilal's presidential address received the qualified approval of his son:

'You are still very Moderate, but I hardly expected you to become an Extremist. I personally like to see the Government blamed and censured as much as possible ... As regards John Bull's good faith I have not so much confidence in him as you have...'[8]

[8] *Supra*, pp. 59-61.

On July 31, 1907, Jawaharlal left Harrow for Trinity College, Cambridge. From the strait-jacket of a public school, the transition to the university could not but be exhilarating. Young Nehru's nationalist ardour was immediately fanned by the freer climate of the university, the intellectual stimulus of fresh reading, discussions with fellow Indian students and, above all, by the strong breeze of discontent from the Indian sub-continent.

4

For India 1907 was a critical year. The tensions which had been accumulating since Curzon's viceroyalty had reached bursting point. The Minto-Morley partnership had not been able to assuage Indian feeling. 'You cannot enter at this date, and with public opinion, mind you, watching you, upon an era of pure repression,' Morley had publicly warned a gathering of British members of the I.C.S., 'Gentlemen, we have seen attempts in the lifetime of some of us here tonight, attempts in Continental Europe to govern by pure repression. Has any one of them really succeeded?'[9] Privately, the Secretary of State exhorted the Viceroy to curb the over-zealous bureaucracy and to keep the political temperature low.

Morley was to discover, as other Secretaries of State discovered before and after him, that India could not be governed from London. Sir Bampfylde Fuller, the Lieutenant-Governor of the newly-created province of East Bengal, had endeavoured to suppress sedition by banning public meetings, tightening espionage, prosecuting schoolboys for preaching Swadeshi, and even by playing upon the vested interests and the fanaticism of his 'favourite wife' – the Muslim community. It was, however, in the Punjab that the political cauldron boiled over in the summer of 1907. Early in May, the Government of India received a minute[10] from Sir Denzil Ibbetson, the Lieutenant-Governor of the Punjab, on the political situation in the province, which he described 'as exceedingly serious and exceedingly dangerous'. The prosecution of the editor of the Punjabi, a nationalist paper, had stirred up feeling in Lahore; tension was mounting in Rawalpindi, Ambala, Ferozepore, Multan and other towns. The most disconcerting feature of the unrest was that it had penetrated to

9 Morley, Viscount, Indian Speeches, p. 67.
10 Minute dated May 3, 1907. (N.A.I.).

the countryside, strikes of minor revenue officials and cases of withholding land revenue had been reported; carriages and other conveniences had been denied to officers on tour; policemen were being pilloried and adjured to quit the service of an alien Government. 'Everywhere people are sensible of a change, of a new air, a *nai hawa*, which is blowing through men's minds,' wrote Sir Denzil, 'the well-disposed classes stand aghast at our inaction and wonder whether the gods, wishing to destroy us, have made us mad. And their astonishment will, before long, inevitably turn into contempt for a Government, which can (as they regard the matter) so abrogate its functions, as to permit sedition to flourish unrebuked, and for a ruling race who tamely submit to open and organized insult. It is difficult to say what their (agitators') precise object is, and probably a good many of them hardly know themselves . . . Some of them no doubt, look to driving us out of the country, at any rate from power, either by force, or by the passive resistance of the people as a whole. But the immediate object of all seems to be to make our government of the country impossible; and probably the idea of the greater number is that we shall, then, in order to escape from an *impasse*, be compelled to give them a larger share of power and of appointments, and to introduce the changes which they desire.'

Sir Denzil was convinced that the brain behind the agitation was Lajpat Rai, a leader of the Arya Samaj, a religious body which in his opinion had a strong political bias in the Punjab. He did not favour the prosecution of Lajpat Rai nor of his chief lieutenant Ajit Singh: if it succeeded it would make martyrs of them; if it failed it would be a disastrous blunder. He demanded their immediate deportation, and asked for special powers for 'strong executive action' to suppress political meetings and newspapers.

Sir Denzil's minute was received in Simla on May 3, 1907. Within ten days, Regulation III of 1818 had been resurrected from the dusty state archives and applied to the 'dangerous revolutionary Lajpat Rai', who was taken in a special train (by-passing Calcutta) to Diamond Harbour, where the steamer *Guide* was waiting to carry him to his ultimate destination – Mandalay gaol in Burma.

'I was astounded to read the news from India,' Jawaharlal wrote on May 17th. The same day Motilal included in his weekly

letter from Allahabad a trenchant résumé of the political situation in which neither the Government nor the Extremists were
spared. 'The whole position can be summed up in a very few
words. A set of moral cowards has been placed at the head of an
administration which is to govern a people who are both moral
and physical cowards. The latter kicked up a row in the hope of
impressing the former with their power and importance. The
former got frightened, and, not knowing exactly what to do,
laid their hands on the most prominent man in the Punjab
simply with the object of overawing the people. This has had
the desired effect . . . The arrest and deportation of Lajpat Rai,
unjustifiable and inexcusable as it is, has shown what stuff our
countrymen are made of. It is nothing but a storm in a tea-cup,
and it is all over now – only we are put back half a century. The
forces which were slowly and silently working for the good of
the country have received a sudden check.' He cautioned his son
not to be unduly alarmed by the news from India: 'It is in the
interest of both Government and the people to exaggerate. Each
has to justify its action . . .'

Perhaps these strictures on the Extremists were made for the
benefit of his son, whose political consciousness was sharpening
fast. 'Do not go near the Majlis or the Native club or whatever
it is called,' Motilal warned Jawaharlal when he went up to
Cambridge. The warning was not heeded. 'I went the other day
to a meeting of the Majlis here,' came the answer, 'just to see if
they were as bad as they were painted. I failed to discover anything reprehensible in it.' And as for the 'Native Club', Jawaharlal reported that there was one in Cambridge, 'but it was for
eating natives'.

A few weeks earlier, Motilal had a twinge of anxiety on
reading in the newspapers that there had been disturbances in
Ireland where his son was holidaying. 'In your last letter,'
Jawaharlal wrote from Dublin on September 12, 1907, 'you
asked me not to go near Belfast on account of the riots, but I
would have dearly liked to have been there for them. About a
fortnight ago, there was a chance of our having similar scenes
here, but to my mortification the whole thing ended in a fiasco.
The tramway employees were on the point of striking, and if
they had done so, there would have been a little fighting in the
streets of Dublin.'

The visit to Ireland had put new ideas into the head of the young nationalist. 'Have you heard of the Sinn Fein in Ireland?,' he asked his father, 'it is a most interesting movement and resembles very closely the so-called Extremist movement in India. Their policy is not to beg for favours but to wrest them. They do not want to fight England by arms, but "to ignore her, boycott her, and quietly assume the administration of Irish affairs" . . . Among people, who ought to know, this movement is causing . . . consternation. They say that if its policy is adopted by the bulk of the country, English rule will be a thing of the past.'

5

The militant nationalism of his eighteen years old son did not please his father who, in his forty-seventh year, was making a cautious, almost tentative, entry into active politics on the side of a party wedded to slow and ordered progress. As the tension between the two wings of the Congress mounted, Motilal became, along with Malaviya and Sunderlal, the target of the Extremist press in his own province. He retaliated with a hard-hitting article in the *Pioneer* and sent the extract to his son. Jawaharlal's reactions were sharply critical: 'I had till now an idea that you were not so very moderate as you would have me believe. The article almost makes me think that you are 'immoderately Moderate'. I would have said that the article had been written by a person with strong loyalist tendencies if I had not known you better . . .' Having overshot his mark, Jawaharlal received an immediate reproof. 'You know me and my views well enough,' Motilal wrote (January 10, 1908), 'to understand that I do not approve of opinions expressed by you, but boys must be boys . . . We are living in very critical times and events are crowding so fast that the present situation cannot last very long . . . It is unnecessary to enter into any discussion on this subject. Within a year or two, there will be no doubt left in the mind of anyone as to the correctness and otherwise of the attitude of the various so-called political parties in India'.

Events had indeed already moved to a dramatic climax at Surat, where the Indian National Congress met for its twenty-third session in December, 1907. Motilal had been reluctant to attend the session; he was not well and feared that the long train journey would aggravate his asthma. But his Moderate friends in Allahabad were insistent and Gokhale telegraphed him to come without fail.

It is hardly necessary to recapitulate the oft-told story of the Surat Congress: the bitter controversies surrounding the choice of the president and the place for the session; the manoeuvres of the Moderates for the election of Dr Rash Behari Ghose; the fears of the Extremists that they were being elbowed out of the Congress and that the programme of *Swadeshi* and boycott adopted by the Calcutta Congress was being jettisoned; the abortive efforts at mediation behind the scenes; the ominous adjournment of the session on the opening day; the stormy scenes on the following day with Tilak on the platform; the flying missile – the fateful shoe – which touched off the unseemly scuffle; the brandishing of sticks, the unrolling of turbans, the broken chairs and the bruised heads; and finally the crowning humiliation when the police arrived to clear the hall. Motilal was one of the prominent Moderate delegates and had been called upon to second the proposal for the election of Dr Rash Behari Ghose as president just before the last tumultous scenes; he returned from Surat with redoubled dislike of Extremist policies and tactics. The reactions of his son (who had not yet received the freezing dose his father had administered in the letter dated January 10th), were just the opposite.

Jawaharlal to Motilal, January 2, 1908: 'We expected lively things at Surat and our expectations were more than fulfilled. It is of course a great pity that such a split should have occurred. But it was sure to come and the sooner we have it, the better. You will most probably throw all the blame on Tilak and the Extremists. They may have been to blame for it, but the Moderates had certainly a lot to do with it. I do not at all object to Rash Behari Ghose being president, but the manner in which he was declared president in the face of opposition can hardly be defended from any point of view. The Moderates may represent part of the country, but they seem to think, or at any rate try to make others believe, that they are the "natural leaders" and representatives of the whole country. The manner in which some of them try to ignore and belittle all those who differ from them would be annoying, if it was not ridiculous.' 'I firmly believe,' Jawaharlal concluded, 'that there will hardly be any so-called Moderates left in a very few years' time. By the methods they are following at present, they are simply hastening the doom of their party.'

Though he had only the reports in the British press and his own Extremist sympathies to guide him, young Nehru's analysis of the Surat fiasco was remarkably near the truth, and his forecast of the future of the Moderate party was almost prophetic. But if he expected his father to swallow these pronouncements, he had made a serious miscalculation. There was a touch of irony in Motilal's reply (January 24th):

'I am favoured with your views as to the conduct of the Moderates and Extremists at Surat in December last, and feel flattered by the compliment you have paid to the Moderates, knowing of course that your father is one.' 'I am sorry,' Jawaharlal wrote back, 'you don't approve of my opinions, but really I can't help holding them in the present state of affairs . . . anyhow I have not the presumption of imagining that my opinions are infallible.' After this half-hearted apology, he was tempted into a thoughtless witticism: 'The Government must be feeling very pleased with you at your attitude. I wonder if the insulting offer of a *Rai Bahadurship*, or something equivalent, would make you less of a Moderate than you are.'

Motilal was furious, but he did not refer to this subject in his weekly letters. From a number of sources, however, Jawaharlal was left in no doubt of the mood of his father, who even talked of fetching the young hothead home. It was not until April, 1908, that the storm blew over, when Jawaharlal begged to be pardoned for an offence, which 'I did not intend to commit', and Motilal closed the controversy with a confession:

'I do not of course approve of your politics and have on certain occasions expressed myself very strongly, as you know, I can, when I wish to. This is, however, neither here nor there. My love for you knows no bounds, and unless there is some very remarkable change in me, I do not see how it can be affected.'

One wonders whether Motilal realized his own responsibility for the political precocity of his son. His letters to Harrow covered the political scene almost as fully as the domestic. He could, if he had wished, have avoided the subject altogether. Perhaps he thought it was safer to allow the boy to let off steam and to channel his interest along prudent lines. Jawaharlal, for his part, had shrewdly discerned a deep vein of defiance in his father beneath the placid surface of Moderate politics. Cautious as he was in advocating political changes, Motilal exhibited a prickly intolerance of bureaucratic or racial arrogance. 'Our Chief Justice is developing a temper,' he wrote in one of his letters. 'I was surprised to see Sunderlal and Chaudhuri submitting to it. Encouraged by their example, he tried to be nasty to me. I paid him back in his own coin, and he is now milk and honey with me.' And when the Prince of Wales laid the foundation stone of the Medical College at Lucknow in December, 1905, Motilal was almost apologetic about his presence at the ceremony: 'As I have subscribed Rs. 1,000, I am on the Central Committee and as such have to be present. Otherwise there is no charm for me in such gatherings.'

The father's avowed displeasure did not moderate the son's radicalism. As we shall see later, Jawaharlal's political consciousness – academic as it was at this time – was further sharpened on the intellectual grindstone of Cambridge. There are signs that from 1908 onwards, Motilal himself began to drift from his Moderate moorings. How far he was influenced by the views of his son it is difficult to say, as his own pride and the compulsion of events were also factors to be reckoned with.

This was the first political clash between father and son, but already it is possible faintly to trace the pattern of the future. Towards the ever-growing radicalism of his son, Motilal's attitude was successively to be one of indignation, opposition, conflict, conversion and, finally, championship.

CHAPTER NINE

FATEFUL CHOICE

THE fears of Headmaster Wood proved groundless. Jawaharlal was able to cope with the school routine at Harrow and also to pass into Trinity College, Cambridge. Five days before his departure from Harrow, he received his father's congratulations and good wishes.

Motilal to Jawaharlal, July 26, 1907: I was delighted to hear from your last letter that you had done so well at Part II of the Previous. You have thus closed your career at school with every success and credit that we could possibly expect. Need I tell you how happy and proud I feel?

'Your admission to Trinity now being assured, you enter on the second stage of your education which promises to be even more successful than the first. It was lucky that you could get into Harrow, one of the premier schools of England, and it is equally lucky that you could get admission into Trinity, a college with a great name and a great history. It would be something for any man to speak about his connections with these great institutions, but in your case it will be the institutions who will own you with pride as one of their brightest jewels. I am sure they will profit as much as you will by your connection with them. Go on working, my dear boy, as you have been – good, solid, steady work, interspersed with a fair amount of recreation, amusement and exercise – and you will shine out as one of the leading lights of your time . . .'

Though Motilal's optimism was racing rather ahead of events, it was certainly backed by the boy's creditable record in Harrow. But already, it was possible to detect signs of boredom, if not fatigue, in Jawaharlal's approach to the scholastic tournament. In November, 1906, he was writing:

'I think I can easily come out third, and perhaps second, in the form but of coming out on top I have no hope . . . And even if I come out on top, it would not do me much good. I would get a prize and that would be the end of it . . .'

Two weeks before the Trinity entrance examination he confessed he had not started working for it:

'Even now there is time for me to get up the books if I go to work seriously, but it is doubtful if I can manage to drag myself from a good cricket match to work.'

Academic laurels did not lure him. The love of reading which his tutor F. T. Brooks had inculcated never left him, but he would rather read two books than read a book twice. He had no stomach for cramming. Nor did he know the fine art of the examinee – the art of making a little go far. Books could, however, make a strong impact on him. By a curious oversight on the part of the school authorities, one of Trevelyan's books on Garibaldi was given to young Nehru as a prize. He bought the remaining two books in the series, and read the exciting story of Italy's struggle for freedom and unity. Italy and India got inextricably mixed up in his mind, and he dreamed of heroic deeds to liberate India from the foreign yoke.

The public schools of England have traditionally been the nurseries of her governing classes; they have supplied cabinet ministers, commanders on land and sea, and proconsuls for the British Empire. All the Viceroys of India from 1884 to 1947 went either to Harrow or Eton, with the exception of Chelmsford and Wavell who went to Winchester, and of Mountbatten who went to Osborne. It is true that the son of an Indian lawyer, entering Harrow in the first decade of the twentieth century, could not aspire to be a cabinet minister, a proconsul or a general. Nevertheless, the fact remains that English public schools produced or were designed to produce (in Patrick Geddes' words) 'a courage caste with its ambitions turned from gain or learning towards an ideal of rule'. The qualities which went to the making of the 'guardians' of the Empire were equally serviceable in hardening the fibre of the future rebel against the British Raj. If the battle of Waterloo was won on the playing fields of Eton, the battle of the British Empire was lost in the class-rooms and playing fields of Harrow.

2

Motilal wanted his son 'to be the most popular young fellow and the most distinguished graduate of Cambridge', but it is doubtful if these struck Jawaharlal as sufficiently exciting goals. His reading was too catholic and desultory for the former; his innate reserve and loneliness militated against the latter. He was, however, in high good humour and glad to enjoy 'a good deal of freedom, compared to the school', to do what he chose. With a self-conscious air, he sauntered about the big courts and narrow streets of Cambridge, delighted when he met someone he knew. He discussed literature, history, politics and economics and became sensitive to new intellectual stimuli. 'I have just come back,' he wrote to his father late on the evening of October 24, 1907, 'from a lecture on "Socialism and the University Man" which lasted quite two hours . . . The lecturer was George Bernard Shaw, about whom you must have heard a good deal. I was more interested in the man than in the subject of the lecture, and that was the reason of my going there. George Bernard Shaw is a very able speaker and he gave a very interesting lecture.'

Cambridge gave a keener edge to Jawaharlal's political thinking. Unlike Harrow, it had a number of Indian students with whom he could share his boyish hopes and fears for the future of his country. The *Majlis* was a useful forum for Indian students, not only for playing at parliamentary technique, but also for earnest discussion of political issues. Though he could not screw up his courage to speak at these gatherings, Jawaharlal was an interested listener, particularly when an eminent Indian leader addressed them. In November, 1908, Lajpat Rai visited Cambridge and spoke at the *Majlis*. 'Lajpat Rai read a most interesting paper,' he wrote to his father, 'he didn't at all like the idea of Indians going into the C.S. (Civil Service) or the Bar. He told me that as I had taken science, I might go in for manufacturing various things.' B. C. Pal, who came a few days later, created a less favourable impression. For one thing, he thundered in a Cambridge sitting-room before an audience of ten students as if he were addressing a crowd of ten thousand in Calcutta. For another, young Nehru detected traces of Hindu revivalism and narrowness in Pal, who 'did not take the Muslims into account. Once or twice he referred to them, but he was not very complimentary'.

Despite Motilal's disapproval of his son's radicalism in 1908, Jawaharlal's letters from Cambridge continued to breathe the same nationalist fervour; if anything, they revealed a deeper distrust of British intentions and a greater cynicism about British professions. 'The Saturday Review,' he wrote to his father (June 4, 1908), 'by the way, made a very wise remark a few weeks ago. It said that Indians were bound to have self-government but – and herein lies the difficulty – not before a few aeons of geological time! This may mean anything between a few million years and a wholly incomprehensible period. The chief difficulty was the want of education and some million generations will be required to educate them [Indians] up to the Colonial standard.' When the Minto-Morley reforms were announced in December, 1908, Jawaharlal's only comment to his father was: 'Do you not think he [Morley] has got a strange sense of humour?' Morley became the *bête noire* first of the son, and then of the father, an irritating image of British bad faith towards nationalist India.

Jawaharlal to Motilal, November 19, 1908: '. . . I am told that Morley has shown him [Gokhale] a draft of the reform proposals and asked him to criticise them. He has been busy doing this for the last month. He thinks that they are fairly liberal. This evidently is not the opinion of the Government of India, who think that they are far and away too liberal. Great pressure is being brought to bear on Lord Morley, and Gokhale seems to think that he may yet succumb to Anglo-India and drop the more drastic proposals.'

December 3, 1908: '. . . I was much amused to learn that the C.I.D. had interested themselves in such an unimportant person as I am. If this was due to a letter being opened, I am very curious to know who wrote that letter . . .'

March 12, 1909: '. . . Morley is coming up to Cambridge today, presumably to confer with the dons on the Indian question. There was a meeting here a few days ago of Masters of colleges and others to discuss the same question. Various resolutions were passed which, I am told, were to the effect that no other college should take in an Indian who had been forcibly made to leave his college. The Master of Downing was the only person who objected to this. He told them plainly that if an Indian was expelled through spite and without sufficient reason from the college, he would take him.

'Morley was asked to come to the Indian *Majlis* dinner here which takes place tonight. His answer, of course, was that he was too busy . . .'

It would almost seem as if Jawaharlal, young though he was, was holding a watching brief for his country in England. After hearing Haldane, the British Secretary of State for War, on the new Officers' Training Corps, Jawaharlal wrote home:

'If I were an Englishman, I should certainly take advantage of it [The Officers' Training Corps]. At the end of his speech [Haldane] was asked a number of questions, among them being one concerning Indians. The question was whether Indians could join the Officers' Training Corps and, at the end of their 'Varsity life, go out to India as officers. His answer to this was rather evasive. He said that it was an excellent idea . . . but, as the Indian army was quite separate from the English army, he could not say anything definite about it. The Corps here, as you know, does not take Indians in.'

At a ceremonial function held at Cambridge to award honorary degrees to a number of distinguished persons, including the Aga Khan and the Maharaja of Bikaner, young Nehru's sharp eyes noted that the Vice-Chancellor did not deign to get up from his chair when giving the degrees to the Indians, although he had stood up for everyone else.

The General Election of 1905 had roused Jawaharlal's curiosity during his first term at Harrow; that of 1910 excited him. 'The party moves are most interesting to watch for an outsider. The betting was, I think, 5 to 1 in favour of the Liberals a few days ago. Since Mr. Balfour's declaration about the Referendum it has practically become level. The first results will be announced tomorrow evening, and I hope to be in Fleet Street or near at the time.'

Indian politics continued to bulk large in the letters exchanged between Allahabad and Cambridge. Motilal now seemed less ruffled by Jawaharlal's unabashed extremism, partly because he had got used to it, and partly because his own faith in the British Government and in the Moderate leadership in India was weakening under the impact of events.

Motilal to Jawaharlal, November 6, 1908: 'Reuter says that the English papers are all full of the highest appreciation of the King's (or rather Morley's) Proclamation. The whole Indian and Anglo-Indian Press, however, has condemned it as a weak and spiritless document, ill-conceived and badly expressed . . . The wonder is that it has not even literary merit to recommend itself. The *Statesman* has brought out clearly all the lies it conceals under verbosity. Fancy "equal treatment of Indian and other subjects", after what is going on in South Africa and India itself. It is almost certain that Morley's reforms will be as disappointing as his Proclamation has been . . .'

January 3, 1909: '. . . I was not at all satisfied with the proceedings of the Congress of which I made a special study in order to decide upon my own attitude towards it in future. I must say that I am not very much in sympathy with the *modus operandi* of my friends of the Congress . . .
'Pandit Sunderlal has been made a C.I.E. This was La Touche's[1] parting present to him for his weak submission to the powers that be.'

The political gulf between father and son was beginning to narrow, but it would be wrong to infer that their attitude towards England or individual Englishmen was in any way coloured by political developments. 'The mail boat which will carry this letter,' Motilal told his son (April 22, 1909), 'will also carry Mr Aikman, his wife and daughter. He was a good judge and a perfect gentleman and we gave him a splendid send-off.' And Jawaharlal confessed to a feeling, 'akin to that of homecoming', when in October, 1908, he returned to England after a brief vacation in India. 'The familiar sights and sounds had quite an exhilarating effect on me,' he wrote, 'and what a strange home-coming it was, with no one to welcome us after our long voyage. For everyone else there was a friend or relation to bid him welcome, and I stood there with a heavy heart thinking that

[1] Sir J. J. D. La Touche, Lieutenant-Governor of the U.P.

that was not for such as us. It is strange that in spite of the homelike feeling, I am constantly reminded of the fact that I am a foreigner, an intruder here.'

3

In the autumn of 1906 Jawaharlal spent a few weeks with his parents at Mussoorie. Professional and domestic preoccupations made it impossible for Motilal to leave India in 1907 and 1908, but in the summer of 1909 he took a few months off for a holiday in Europe. Father and son saw Count Zeppelin arrive in his new airship amid thunderous cheers from millions of Berliners. Two months later, they were in Paris, when the Comte de Lambert flew over the city and circled round the Eiffel Tower. Two years later, in September, 1911, Jawaharlal had the thrill of writing home on an 'aerial postcard' issued to commemorate the coronation of King George V. The success of the venture was by no means a foregone conclusion. 'The experiment has not met with very great success so far,' Jawaharlal informed his father, 'two aviators have maimed themselves and are lying in hospital.'

Though optimistic by temperament, Motilal found it hard not to worry about his son. On reading in the papers of 'a spate of accidents in England and the continent', he wrote:

'[The news] makes me shudder to think of you travelling about. Your mother would kill herself if I were to tell her these things. As it is, she remains in blissful ignorance while the anxiety is all my own. But I am strong enough for it, while she is not.'

While at Cambridge Jawaharlal expressed a wish to buy a motor-car. Motilal turned down the suggestion, not because of the expense involved, but because he feared motoring would distract the boy from his studies and keep his parents in 'perpetual dread of accidents'.

The parental fears were not altogether groundless. In the summer of 1910 Jawaharlal had the narrowest of escapes in the course of a holiday cruise to Norway. One day the party left the boat for an overland excursion; Jawaharlal and an Englishman, more energetic than the rest, were the first to reach a small hotel where the party was to spend the night. Feeling tired and hot after the stiff climb – the hotel was nearly five thousand feet above the sea level – they expressed a wish for a bath. Somewhat bewildered by this unusual request, the hotel staff directed them to a river near by – a shallow but wild mountain torrent fed by a glacier. As they plunged in the ice-cold water their limbs were nearly numbed; but worse was to follow. Jawaharlal's foot slipped, he lost control and began helplessly to drift with the current. Fortunately, his English companion managed to get out on to the bank, run along it, catch hold of his legs and pull him out. 'The exciting part of it,' Jawaharlal informed his father, 'lies in the fact that there was a mighty waterfall of about 400 ft. quite near.' To Motilal there was nothing 'exciting' in the incident: it is difficult to say whether he was more indignant at his son's recklessness or relieved at his miraculous escape. Jawaharlal was unrepentant; though the accident had not been of his seeking, he was highly pleased with the 'adventure and would not have missed it for a lot'. He protested that he was fit as a fiddle:

'At one time over fifty of our fellow passengers were unwell owing to the rough sea. I need hardly say that I was not one of these unhappy people. You need never have any anxiety about my health. I am one of the most violently healthy persons I have come across.'

Jawaharlal's three years at Cambridge were 'three quiet years with little of disturbance in them, moving slowly like the sluggish Cam. They were pleasant years, with many friends and some work and some play and a gradual widening of the intellectual horizon'.[2] His interest in science, stimulated by his tutor, F. T. Brooks, and encouraged by his father, led him to the Natural Sciences Tripos. He took chemistry, geology and physics; after nearly a year and a half he substituted botany for physics. His letters do not betray any feverish resolve to climb to the top of the academic tree.

He noted the probability of the grandson of Charles Darwin, who was at Trinity College at the time, being the last of the Senior Wranglers, but discounted his father's forecast that he (Jawaharlal) would also reach 'these Olympian heights'. 'You

[2] Nehru, J. L., *Toward Freedom*, p. 33.

are apt to underrate yourself,' complained Motilal. 'I mentioned the scholarship and the prize to put some stimulus in you and to show that I thought more of you than you do.'

Untroubled by ambition, unruffled by competition, and un-inhibited by religion, Jawaharlal had enough time – and money – to enjoy life at Cambridge. The aesthetic side of life appealed to him and 'the idea of going through life worthily, not in-dulging it in the vulgar way, but still making the most of it and living a full and many-sided life'.[3] The days were taken up with work and play, the long winter evenings whiled away in inter-minable discussions with his friends on life, literature, politics, ethics, sex and people, until, long after midnight, the dying fires sent them shivering to their beds.

These were the years before the Great War, when Europe was at the zenith of its prestige and power. Science was on the march, and unlike the science of the mid-twentieth century, it was con-fident, almost cocksure within the mechanical universe of forces, pressures, oscillations and waves all explicable in terms of their 'laws'. The practical applications of science – electric light and heat, telegraph and telephone, bicycle and cinema, motor-car and aeroplane – were rapidly transforming European society. A new and more hopeful era seemed to be dawning for the common man. Standards of public health were rising; preventive medicine was prolonging life; penal codes were being humanized; the penny newspapers, the public libraries, light opera and the music-halls were bringing recreation within the reach of the masses. But for the stray clouds which occasionally hung over its chan-celleries, the future of Europe seemed wholly bright, and nowhere brighter than in Great Britain. The soundness of her economic structure, the stability of her Empire and the proven wisdom of her ancient institutions seemed axiomatic.

To Campbell-Bannerman, the Liberal Prime Minister, whose term coincided with Jawaharlal's time at Harrow, there were no evils, 'except, of course, natural evils that cannot be remedied by freedom, self-government and English institutions'.[4] Yet even on the placid stream of British life there were ripples caused by Fabian-Socialists, English suffragettes and Irish nationalists. Strikes were becoming disconcertingly frequent; they accounted for the annual loss of no less than eleven million working days

[3] Nehru, J. L., *ibid.*, pp. 33-34.
[4] Brogan, D. W., *The Price of Revolution*, p. 64.

during the years 1906-14. The Victorian doctrine of *laissez-faire* was going by the board; statutory provision was being made for insurance against sickness, accidents and (to some extent) against unemployment, for old age pensions, minimum wages in 'sweated' industries, regulation of housing and town-planning. Symbolic of the new forces which were to shape the future of Europe and the world were the advent of a Labour Government in Australia, the growing strength of the socialist and syndicalist movements on the continent of Europe and the struggle between the Tsarist autocracy and its enemies in Russia.

What could be more bracing for a precocious young Indian at Cambridge than this climate of scientific and economic progress, social flux and nationalist discontent? We must remember, however, that it was not uncommon for Indian students in England to go through a passing phase of intellectual and political ferment. When they returned home to coveted posts in the Indian Civil Service or joined in the frantic race for professional success, the fireside arguments at Cambridge or Oxford became no more than dim memories of exuberant youth. This was the experience of the majority of Jawaharlal's contemporaries; it could have been his as well.

4

'It is curious,' Jawaharlal writes in his autobiography, 'that in spite of my growing extremism in politics, I did not then view with any strong disfavour the idea of joining the I.C.S.' The choice was not half as obvious in 1908-9 as it appeared a quarter of a century later. Satyendranath Tagore was the first Indian to win his way into the Indian Civil Service in 1863, ten years after entry had been thrown open to a competitive examination. In 1869 four Indians passed in – R. C. Dutt, S. N. Banerjea, B. L. Gupta and S. B. Thakur. On their return to India they were feted and lionized; at Howrah railway station the great Keshub Chander Sen welcomed them in person. Europeans, officials and non-officials, whose minds had been baked by the Indian sun, looked askance at these intruders into the higher levels of administration. S. N. Banerjea indeed soon became a victim of race prejudice: he was dismissed from the service for an offence

for which a young English officer would have received no more
than a 'friendly reproof'.[5]

The fact that the entry of these Indians into the I.C.S. was
the first dent in the armour of the British Raj was clearly recognized at the time by both sides. In 1877-8, the reduction of the
age-limit for the I.C.S. (which handicapped Indian entrants) led
to a country-wide agitation in which Banerjea took a prominent
part. This agitation heightened the national self-consciousness of
the intelligentsia, and helped to crystallize forces which brought
into being the Indian National Congress in December, 1885.
When R. C. Dutt was appointed Magistrate of Balasore district
in 1882, the *Pioneer*[6] of Allahabad lamented:

'We believe this is the first occasion on which a native of
India has held executive charge of a district . . . The administration of districts means the government of the country . . .
People have pleaded for employment of natives . . . but the
warmest partisans of the movement have generally conceded
that it would be premature to put natives in charge of
districts . . .'

It was an Indian colleague of R. C. Dutt – Bihari Lal Gupta –
who raised the question of jurisdiction of Indian judges over
Europeans, which touched off the famous Ilbert Bill agitation.

In March, 1907, Motilal publicly described the I.C.S. as 'the
greatest of the services in the world which has produced some
of the most distinguished builders of the British Empire'. A few
months later he made his son leave Harrow early to go up to
Cambridge so that he might have enough time left after taking
his degree to prepare for the I.C.S. examination. As the tempo
of nationalist discontent rose in India during the next two years,
Motilal began to suspect that the Civil Service Commissioners
were biased against Indian candidates. He voiced this suspicion
in a letter to his brother Bansi Dhar when the latter's son
Shridhar Nehru failed in his first attempt at the I.C.S. in 1910.
There is no doubt, however, that the final decision against Jawaharlal joining the I.C.S. was based not on the merits of the
service but on sentimental grounds.

If Jawaharlal joined the I.C.S., his return to India would be

5 Woodruff, Philip, *The Guardians*, p. 170.
6 *Pioneer*, October 20, 1882.

delayed by at least two years, and if he became a district officer, he could be posted anywhere in India. These were chilling prospects for his parents, to whom the idea of being parted from their only son for the rest of their lives was intolerable. It was therefore finally decided that Jawaharlal should follow in his father's footsteps, become a barrister and practise at Allahabad.

Looking back we can see how effectively the I.C.S. absorbed the energy of India's talented young men. One has only to think of the damage done to the Empire by those who left the Service or who just failed to get in – Surendranath Banerjea, Aurobindo Ghose, Subhas Chandra Bose. It is tempting to conjecture what might have happened if Jawaharlal had slid into the comfortable anonymity of a civil servant. With his tremendous capacity for work, his iron constitution and his love of outdoor life, he would doubtless have made an excellent officer in the field; his attention to detail and fluency of expression would have made it equally easy for him to make a mark in the secretariat. His literary ability might have found expression in a handy manual on the 'Land Revenue Problems of Mirzapur District', in a standard work on the 'Flora of Kumaon Hills', in revised gazetteers of the districts in which he served, or even in a fascinating travel book entitled 'Trekking in the Kulu Valley'. And provided he had not ruined his chances by being too outspoken to a choleric superior, he might have risen to the dizzy heights of the Board of Revenue or the Bench of a High Court, and retired with a C.I.E. to Anand Bhawan, to grow the finest roses and browse on the largest private library in northern India. Not only his own life, but that of his father, mother, wife, daughter and sisters would then have run in less turbulent, albeit obscurer, channels, and the history of India, Asia, Africa – and indeed, the whole world – might have been changed for good or ill. All this was not to be, because he was the only son.

CHAPTER TEN

POLITICS CALLING

'I AM sure,' Jawaharlal had written in January, 1907, when Motilal was wondering whether he should agree to preside over the U.P. Provincial Conference, 'you will be as successful in the new line as you have been in other fields.' During the next three years, Motilal was drawn willy nilly into the vortex of public life. Admiration for Gokhale and old associations with his colleagues in the legal profession and in the Congress had led him into the Moderate camp. But though political moderation seemed to him to be founded on the hard realities of the Indian situation, the second thoughts, the half-measures and the compromises of the Moderate party ran counter to a strong vein of pride in his character – pride in his noble ancestry, pride in his country, pride in his own powers – and later, pride in his son. Submission, whether to priestly pretensions or to bureaucratic arrogance, went against the grain. The champions of orthodoxy received no quarter from Motilal when he presided in April, 1909, over the third United Provinces Social Conference at Agra.

His presidential speech, delivered extempore, was remarkably eloquent and forthright. 'As I stand before you in this beautiful and historic city of yours,' he began, 'abounding in magnificent monuments of a glorious past, I feel more like an object of pity than of envy. For was it not here that the greatest of the Moghal Emperors engaged himself in· nightly debates in Council and silent meditations in the loneliness of early dawn on the problems we have met to discuss?' Three hundred years had rolled by since the reign of Akbar, but the problems which he was supposed to tackle and solve remained as intractable as ever. A century of *Pax Britannica* had not destroyed 'the canker-worm of caste' which was eating into the vitals of India's social structure; her womanhood was groaning under the combined weight of forced seclusion, illiteracy, and early marriage. These evils continued to thrive, all the eloquent speeches and learned treatises on social reform notwithstanding. Quoting Ranade, the great judge and reformer who had once described the Social Conference as 'an humble sister' of the National Congress, Motilal affirmed:

'Social reform in my opinion, is the much despised parent of political reform and not merely its humble sister. It is impossible for any community of men, however large and influential it may be, to obtain political emancipation before it has attained that height of political elevation which compels the respect of the best-ordered, highly civilized and self-respecting communities of the time. Our great ambition is to build a united Indian Nation. Can we expect to achieve that ambition by obtaining political concessions alone? There is no process of legislation or diplomacy by which these millions with all their diversities of caste and creed could be fused into a harmonious whole . . . Now let us assume the converse case . . . Imagine for a moment that there was no caste system in India, that Hindus and Musalmans, and the numerous sub-divisions of these two great communities sank their differences and met together as children of a common mother; that the ladies of India instead of being shut behind the prison walls of the *zenana* were properly educated; that there were no longer in the population of India the children of premature mothers and under-developed fathers. Suppose we reached such a social, moral and physical perfection, could any power on earth keep us from obtaining the fullest political privileges enjoyed by the most advanced nations of the world?'

He then attacked the two villains of the piece:

'Let us, therefore, begin at once, and in all earnestness, to remove the two ugliest blots on our social system – caste and *purdah*. These are the two evils which have dragged us down the social scale and made us the laughing-stock of modern civilization.'

The conference had to put up with more plain speaking from its President than it may have bargained for. 'I beseech you,' he said, 'not merely to confine yourself to passing resolutions . . . it is high time that we ceased to be a mere post office and did something practical.' He declared that he himself was an Indian first and a Brahmin afterwards and would not follow any custom or usage of the Brahmins, however sanctified by age or authority, if it came in the way of his duties as a true Indian. He was convinced that the days of orthodoxy were numbered, and recalled 'the tea-pot storms' raised twenty years earlier over foreign travel, which had not prevented 'the more daring souls amongst us to go or send their sons to foreign countries'.

Such candour was unusual at social conferences. The *Indian Social Reformer* described Motilal's speech as 'vigorous'; the *Indian Mirror* called it 'outspoken' and the *Wednesday Review* praised its 'manly tone'. Jawaharlal was delighted when he read the extracts his father had sent him:

'It was quite characteristic of you, and I could have guessed as much as I have often heard you talking in the same strain. But I was rather afraid that you might respect the feelings of the more conservative people and not be so explicit. Not that you generally do so, but the draft resolutions led me to think that it would be a tame affair.'

Among those who wrote to Motilal complimenting him on his excellent speech was Sir J. P. Hewett, the Lieutenant-Governor of the United Provinces. If His Honour derived a secret satisfaction from Motilal's emphasis on social vis-à-vis political reform, he was soon to discover that the enemy of social obscurantism was no friend of political status quo.

2

Like other leaders of the Moderate party, Motilal had set much store by Secretary of State Morley's desire and ability to inaugurate a new chapter in Indo-British relations. He had telegraphed his congratulations to Morley on the appointment of an Indian – Sir S. P. Sinha – to the Viceroy's Executive Council in the teeth of opposition from influential quarters in India and England. The Secretary of State's stock with the Nehrus was soon to slump. During the spring and summer of 1909 while the reforms were on the anvil in England, the excitement in Allahabad was intense. 'We simply live for half the day in expectation of the *Pioneer*,' Motilal wrote, 'and spend the other half in discussing the news which it brings.' However, the publication of the reform proposals was something of an anti-climax. The image of Morley as a friend of India fell from its high pedestal and broke in pieces.

Motilal to Jawaharlal, August 30, 1909: 'Morley's long-promised reforms have at last been published. They are . . . just the opposite of reforms. His advisory Council of Noodles (I beg your pardon . . . I mean Notables) will be a huge farce, and the enlarged Legislative Council will be no more than a collection of *Ji Hazoors* (yes-men) where the opinion of the Chairman (who is always the Collector of the district) is dittoed by every member. The avowed object of the so-called reforms is to destroy the influence of the educated classes, but the law of the survival of the fittest is too strong even for Morley.'

It was not only the slow and halting measure of constitutional proposals which had shaken Motilal's robust faith in the sincerity of John Bull. He was disgusted at the way some of the British officials and their *protégés* were playing up the differences between Hindus and Muslims: democracy was being made to wither at the roots before it had even sprouted.

Motilal to Jawaharlal, March 25, 1909: 'An open rupture between the leaders of the two communities is imminent. Nothing short of a miracle can save it. I do not attach much importance to the differences of opinion among the leaders as there has never been much love lost between the two. The masses of both communities have, however, always been good friends and neighbours, and what I dread is the day when the tension of feeling filters down to the lower classes. Nation-building will then be a thing of the past . . . Our Anglo-Indian friends have distinctly scored in this matter and no amount of Council reforms will repair the mischief.'

Motilal to Jawaharlal, April 29, 1909: 'The Hindu-Muhammadan question is the talk of the day. They [Muslims] have insulted us so often and so grossly that we are seriously thinking of breaking off with them . . . Amir Ali and others are being put up not by the fifty-three millions of Indian Muslims, but by a few Anglo-Indians who see their only chance in setting Hindus against Muslims. The Hindus were actuated by the best feelings for what they are now being discredited everywhere.'

In spite of his avowed disappointment with the reforms, Motilal contested a seat in the enlarged provincial council under the 'reformed' constitution and was elected. Endowed with limited and wholly advisory functions, packed with British officials and titled Indian gentry, presided over by the Lieutenant-Governor, the council was an obsequious body. Friendly relations with many of those who sat on the Government benches did not prevent Motilal from assuming from the first the role of a fearless critic of the official policies. He was sworn in on February 7, 1910. On the same day he asked his first question: 'Will the Government be pleased to state whether it contemplates to confer upon graduates of the Allahabad University the right of electing Fellows to the University?' On the following days he asked more questions: 'What were the qualifications of the prosecuting inspectors attached to the courts of the magistrates? How many police reporters sent to political gatherings knew shorthand?' He was often on his feet during question time goading the executive, but it was not until April 25th that he delivered his maiden speech. He criticized the financial arrangements with the Government of India. 'Provincial Governments in matters of finance have been likened by some to shorn sheep left out in the cold, and by others to fat sheep, who having eaten too much, have rolled on their backs and are unable to stand on their legs. But whether as a class they are the one or the other, there is no doubt that this province is treated as the black sheep of the flock under the Government of India.'

He criticized the small allocations for sanitation and education: 'There is so much wanted and so little done in these directions.' He felt that the United Provinces were 'over-policed': 'We spend more on the police than any other province except Burma, though ours is the most well-behaved of all provinces in India.'[1]

Motilal to Jawaharlal, April 29, 1910: 'I had the first experience of the Provincial Budget debate at the last meeting of the Council. It was quite a farce and could hardly be described a debate. The Lieutenant-Governor began by calling upon non-official members one after the other to address the Council. Each member rose at a sign from the Governor and, with a few exceptions, complimented him for his successful rule. The Moham-

[1] *U.P. Council Debates*, 1910, pp. 165-69.

madens in a body adopted this attitude. I was the first to be
called upon to speak, the idea being, as I afterwards learnt, that
the Governor expected I would be nasty, and he wanted to give
the officials as much time as was possible to prepare their reply.
I only made a few general observations. They were not complimentary to Government: I admit there was nothing so dread-
ful in them to excite the anger of the "Gods". Malaviya and
Ganga Prasad Varma followed on the same lines. They in their
turn were followed by the loyalists. This is what happened on
the first day.

'The next day, having a whole night to prepare themselves,
the officials got up one after another, and Malaviya, Ganga
Prasad and myself, came in for a lot of abuse from each of them.
We had no right of reply and the important debate was wound
up by the Governor who patted (on the back) the *khushamdis*
(sycophants) and the officials.'

Politics have a seductive logic of their own; one thing leads to
another. Since March, 1907, when he had made his reluctant
début in the Allahabad Conference, Motilal had been drawn into
militant advocacy of social reform, into active political agitation
and finally into the arena of the provincial legislature itself.
From politics to journalism was a short, almost an inevitable
step. The urban intelligentsia which formed Indian public
opinion at the time could be reached only by the English press,
but the only English daily newspaper in the province was the
Pioneer – the spokesman of official and non-official European
interests. Indian ventures into English journalism had met with
little success in the United Provinces. The *Advocate* of Lucknow
and the *Indian Opinion* of Allahabad were weekly papers. The
launching of the *Leader* in October, 1909, was therefore an important event. The first editor was Madan Mohan Malaviya, who
was assisted by Nagendra Nath Gupta and C. Y. Chintamani.
Gupta's weekly paper, *Indian Opinion*, (which Jawaharlal had
been reading at Harrow) was merged in the *Leader*. Motilal was
the first Chairman of the Board of Directors and in this capacity
had his first experience of the pleasures and pains of newspaper
proprietorship, of which he was to have more than his share ten
years later.

Motilal to Jawaharlal, June 3, 1910: 'A great difficulty arose in

connection with the *Leader*. One of the editors (Chintamani)
took seriously ill . . . Tej Bahadur (Sapru) and Ishwar Saran,
Shamji Mushran and other young fellows were commandeered
and it was with the utmost difficulty that the paper could be
issued every morning. As Chintamani had worked very hard
indeed, the Directors . . . increased his salary by Rs. 50 last
month . . . Mr Gupta, the other editor, seeing that preference
was shown to Chintamani over him, got very angry and yesterday morning handed in his resignation. Till about eight last
night there was no leading article for this morning's issue . . .
Gupta never worked beyond the usual office hours, while Chintamani besides his own work did duty for a night editor as well,
and often went on without any sleep at night . . .'

From the humble position of a struggling journalist, Chintamani was within a decade to establish himself as one of the
eminent editors in the land, sparing neither the Government nor
the Congress. The *Leader* soon became a thorn in the side of a
bureaucracy which was unaccustomed to criticism. Apropos of
an article by Bishan Narayan Dhar, the paper was warned and
threatened with prosecution. Motilal and his friends did not take
the threat lying down. They consulted two eminent lawyers in
England – Sir Edward Carson and Sir Horace Avery – who
certified the article as innocent of sedition.[2] This opinion was discreetly conveyed to the authorities. No more was heard of the
threatened prosecution. Throughout the crisis Motilal had stood
like a rock. 'So long as a single brick is left on top of another in
my house,' he told St Nihal Singh an Indian journalist, 'I will
defend the right of the *Leader* to fight in the cause of freedom.'
St Nihal Singh, who had just returned from a visit to the
United States via Britain and spent ten days in Anand Bhawan
in 1910, has left a graphic pen-picture of his host:

'A tall slender man . . . A head crowned with coal-black locks,
carefully cut and pomaded, surmounted an erect, lithe figure.
His forehead was broad and lofty. Time had lightly pencilled a
few lines across it. From under arched brows shone two dark
eyes aglow with some fire hidden away back in his brain. The
expression changed constantly. Now mirth entered them, and
they fairly danced with the joy of life. Again, seriousness crept

---

[2] Natarajan, J., *History of Indian Journalism*, p. 141.

into them, or, they would become suddenly ablaze with righteous indignation. The nose was perfectly modelled. It nevertheless conveyed a suggestion of strength. The lips were thin. A slight curve betokened that they could utter sharp remarks. They were, however, more often parted in a good-natured repartee. The chin was in harmony with the almost Grecian purity of the other features, but gave an impression of combativeness.'

St Nihal Singh found Motilal's hospitality overwhelming:

'The meals were good enough to be placed before royalty. Wine flowed liberally – wine of many kinds. With the dessert were brought boxes of cigars and cigarettes and liqueurs. A fair-sized bar could have been opened with the decanters placed in front of us . . . The intellectual feasts served in the evening and on holidays were stimulating . . .'

3

The twenty-sixth session of the Indian National Congress was held at Allahabad during Christmas week, 1910. Motilal was one of the prominent citizens who had invited the Congress to meet at Allahabad, and Vice-Chairman of the Reception Committee. The president of the session was Sir William Wedderburn, a former Civilian, an associate of Hume, a confidant of Gokhale and an ardent champion of Indian aspirations in and outside the British Parliament. Motilal did not find the proceedings of the Congress very inspiring. The timorous politics of some of his Moderate colleagues, no less than the irrational conservatism of others, had begun to jar upon him. One of his guests, Mrs Sarla Chaudhrani, who played a notable part in the politics of the Punjab ten years later, had at his instance set a few Vedic verses to music and trained a group of little children, including his elder daughter Sarup, for a performance on the opening day. After the children had practised for a week, Pandit Madan Mohan Malaviya forbade the recitation on the ground that to chant the Vedic *mantras* (verses) in the hearing of non-Hindus was a sacrilege. 'I am so disgusted,' Motilal wrote to his son, 'that I would have chucked the Congress . . . As it is, I take a lukewarm interest in it.'

A notable feature of the Allahabad Congress was the initiative

taken by its president, Sir William Wedderburn, in convening a
Hindu-Muslim conference, probably the first of a series of conferences on unity, which during the next thirty years produced
a harmony of phrases rather than of minds and hearts. It was
also at this Congress that a number of Hindu leaders conceived
the Hindu Mahasabha, as a communal counter-blast to the All
India Muslim League. To Motilal, whose good-humoured agnosticism set him above the storms of religious passion,[3] the emergence of the new organization was a bad omen.

Motilal to Jawaharlal, January 6, 1911: 'They [in the Hindu-
Muslim Conference] called each other brothers, "cousins". A
Committee of 8 Hindus and 8 Mohammedans with Gokhale
as the 17th Member, was nominated by the Aga Khan. It is
certain that this committee will never meet or come to no conclusions whatsoever.

'Another new feature of the Congress has been that it has
given birth to an All India Hindu Mahasabha, which in my
opinion will not only minimize the chance of the Hindu-Muslim
Committee doing any good, but sap the foundation of the Congress itself. I opposed the formation of this Sabha, brought round
Surendranath Banerjea and Bhupendra Basu, but the great
majority of the so-called leaders of upper India, specially those
of the Punjab, had worked themselves to a high pitch and could
not be made to listen to reason . . .'

The fires of Muslim communalism were to be stoked for the
next thirty years by British reactionaries on the one hand and
Hindu partisans on the other.

In one of its resolutions, the Allahabad Congress offered its
'humble homage' and expressed its 'deep and heartfelt joy' at the
(expected) visit in 1911 of their Most Gracious Majesties King
George and Queen Mary to India.

---

[3] In 1916, Motilal was violently criticized by the Hindu press and politicians
in the U.P. for taking an independent line on what was known as the
Jehangirabad amendment to the Municipal Bill, which was alleged to be a
surrender to Muslims.

CHAPTER ELEVEN

HALCYON DAYS

'I HAVE received the command of His Gracious Majesty King-Emperor George V,' Motilal wrote on July 28, 1911, 'to be in attendance at Delhi, a funny way of inviting a gentleman. This is accompanied by a letter saying that the Lieutenant-Governor and Mrs Porter will be pleased to accommodate me and Mrs Nehru in their own camp.' A few weeks later, when Motilal received dress regulations 'for English civil officers and English gentlemen', he instructed his son to place orders for a complete outfit in London and to arrange to despatch it by parcel post. For several weeks the court dress bulked large in the correspondence between father and son.

Jawaharlal to Motilal, October 12, 1911: 'I got your cable day before yesterday and have ordered the court dress and the other clothes you require at Poole's. I suppose you want the ordinary levee dress with sword and everything complete. The shoes for the court dress will be made at Knighton's and the gloves at Travellette's . . . the hats I am sending ought to fit you. Heath's man has managed to fish out your old measures and cast, and he will shape your hats accordingly.'

The Durbar of 1911 was a splendid spectacle. A new city of tents covering twenty square miles and housing nearly a quarter million people was erected in Delhi; it was served by a network of railway stations, post offices, banks and bazaars and was illuminated by electric light, which was then a novelty in India.

Motilal, Swarup Rani and their daughters Sarup and Krishna travelled to Delhi in the special train which carried Lieutenant-Governor Leslie Porter and the official and non-official guests from the United Provinces. The Governor and his wife were very cordial to the Nehrus. 'They have lately become very friendly with us,' Motilal informed his son in January, 1911, 'dinners and teas have been exchanged and Mrs Porter has been very gushing

in her treatment of your mother and myself.' Later in the year
when the Nehrus visited Naini Tal, they dined at the Government House. There were about thirty guests, mostly senior
British officers. 'It was rather nice of Porter,' Motilal wrote soon
afterwards, 'to give us the position of the chief guests of the
evening – he taking in your mother to dinner, and I, Mrs Porter.
We spent a very pleasant evening.'

At Delhi, the Nehrus were given every possible consideration
and courtesy. They were lodged in the Lieutenant-Governor's
special camp; their tent was between those of Sir A. McRobert
and an I.C.S. Officer, Mr Tweedy. There were only two Indian
ladies in the United Provinces camp; Swarup Rani was one of
them.

Except for the State Dinner, to which no practising lawyer
was invited, Motilal and his wife received invitations to all important functions, and were given (he recorded) 'the most
prominent places and received special bows from the King and
the Queen'. Their eleven years old daughter Sarup (or 'Nan', as
she was called in the family) who was one day to represent independent India in the principal capitals of the world, and to
preside over the United Nations Assembly, had her first introduction to protocol: 'Nan received special attention from the
Queen, who would certainly have spoken to her, had it not been
for the stiff formality of the occasion.'

A first-hand version of the 'Gaekwad incident' during the
Durbar, which horrified that august assembly, is preserved in a
letter written by Motilal, who knew the Gaekwad (The Maharaja
of Baroda) rather well and earlier in the year had entertained
him at Anand Bhawan.

Motilal to Jawaharlal, December 22, 1911: 'I was not quite un-
prepared for something silly on his (Gaekwad's) part. My seat at
the Durbar was not far from his and we were chatting away
before the arrival of the King. He asked me what I thought of
the show and on my saying that it was the grandest *tamasha*
(show) I had seen, remarked that it would have been all right if
we had not to act in it like animals in a circus . . . He went
straight to the dais, made a slight bow, and at once turned his
back on the King and the Queen, walking away (rather saunter-
ing away) with one hand in his pocket, and turning his stick
round and round with the other. Where was the necessity for

all this, if it was all to end in the abject apology you must have seen?'

A few days before the investiture, which was to be held during the Durbar, rumours were afloat that Motilal would receive a decoration from the King. 'I was rather surprised to know,' wrote Jawaharlal, 'that people expected you to be knighted. Knighthood in India is more or less an uncommon distinction, in England it is nowadays not worth very much. For the matter of that even a peerage is now hardly a thing to shout about. I do not suppose you are disappointed at the absence of your name from the Honours List.' Motilal hastened to clear up the misunderstanding. 'I do not intend to give you the impression,' he wrote, 'that I cared for a title. It is the last thing in the world that I can expect after the attitude I have adopted towards government officials. It is only men of the type of Leslie Porter, who do not allow their heads to be swollen by high official position, and can appreciate criticism of their official acts that I can pull on with. Such men are scarce.'

Motilal had received invitations to a number of functions at Calcutta, where the King and the Queen were spending Christmas, but he decided to return to Allahabad. 'I have had enough of royalty,' he wrote, 'and have a lot to do at home.' The ten days under canvas in the bracing winter of Delhi turned out to be a perfect holiday. He had left Allahabad with a 'hacking cough and carried a number of medicines to avoid coughing in the presence of the King,' but, fortunately, there had been no occasion to use the medicines. Swarup Rani and the two girls also visibly benefited from the change.

2

For many years Motilal had been a victim of asthma. The six months in Europe in 1905 had given him little relief. During his visit to Europe in 1909, he consulted Professor Kilian, the best-known specialist on throat and chest diseases in Germany, but the learned professor had nothing to add to the remedies which had already been tried and found wanting; all that he could recommend was (Motilal wrote) 'a change to the most impossible places for impossible lengths of time'. While in Germany, Motilal had received a cable from Pandit Prithinath, (the lawyer friend under whose aegis he had embarked on his career as a lawyer in 1883) urging him to consult a homoeopath, but he was sceptical and ignored his advice. But when on returning to India he visited Calcutta, where Prithinath was lying seriously ill, he was persuaded to try a homoeopathic remedy. The results were miraculous. 'My cough and I have at last parted,' he triumphantly informed his son. Homoeopathy had won an enthusiastic convert. From that time he was never without homoeopathic books and medicines and even learned to prescribe and dispense medicines for ordinary family ailments.

With his health restored, his son's future settled and politics at a low ebb, Motilal's life flowed placidly. At the High Court his pre-eminence was unquestioned. In the provincial council he commanded the respect of Indians and Britons alike. In Allahabad his house was at once the hub of social life and the nerve centre of politics. He continued to earn enormous sums and at the same time to display a curious, aristocratic disdain of money. One of his clients, the Raja of Amethi, was so grateful to him for winning an important suit that he offered him a lakh of rupees. Motilal, however, advised the Raja not to be hasty but to defer payment till after the first flush of victory. On second thoughts, the Raja, to Motilal's chagrin, reduced the offer to Rs. 25,000; he was, however, prepared to settle on Jawaharlal a few villages with an annual income of Rs. 6,000. This tempting proposal, which ironically enough would have turned young Nehru into a landlord, was not accepted by his father, who feared that it might be misconstrued. 'I would have been condemned,' he told his son, 'in drawing-rooms and at dinner tables behind my back, and my reputation (which I value at more than a hundred lakhs) would have suffered.'

There was only one thing wanting during these years to complete Motilal's happiness – the presence of his son. 'Your birthday comes and goes,' he wrote. 'Your account of my birthday parties,' wrote Jawaharlal, 'makes me feel quite envious. My "twenty-firster" was observed here with marked simplicity; in other words, I almost forgot all about it till the last moment.'

In spite of the strong emotional bonds between father and son, their temperamental and intellectual differences were already apparent. Motilal was practical, confident, optimistic; Jawaharlal was academic, introspective, diffident. Motilal saw the world as it was without any illusions; Jawaharlal had a tendency towards abstraction, a disposition to seek a shape for life from within himself. Motilal's reading was utilitarian, usually related to the job in hand: he had one of the largest private libraries of law-books in India. To Jawaharlal, reading was not only an ex-quisite pleasure, but a key to those immeasurable realms of know-ledge the existence of which he dimly perceived; his intellectual appetite was insatiable. Once he made the curious suggestion that he should take the I.C.S. course, not to sit for the examina-tion but to widen his knowledge. Occasionally, he gave vent to his literary enthusiasm in letters to his father.

Jawaharlal to Motilal, March 9, 1911: '. . . The edition of Mere-dith, which started coming out when you were here last, has just been completed. I should like to send it to you together with some other books which, I am sure, would please you. Some new editions of old authors have just come out, and they are very good indeed and would delight the heart of anyone who at all cares for books. A twenty-volume edition of Thackeray proved too great an attraction for me, and I could not resist ordering it. . . . A charming edition of Dickens is out too. It runs into forty volumes . . . The author I am very keen on getting is Oscar Wilde . . .

'I think it will be a rather good idea if you opened an account at one of the book-sellers here – The Times Book Club for preference . . .'

The last suggestion led to a curious misunderstanding. Motilal told his son that he could not give him 'a *carte-blanche* to buy up the Times Book Library'. 'The Times Book Library,' wrote back Jawaharlal, 'would take a lot of buying, and even if it could be bought, I don't think many persons would be foolish enough to invest in it . . . A library should in my opinion be built up gradually and with care, and it was in order to do this that I asked you to have an account with the Book Club . . .'

In June, 1910, Jawaharlal graduated from Cambridge with a second class Honours degree. In July, he was urging his father to let him go to Oxford instead of London to study law. This was not because he wanted a degree, but because he wanted to study something besides law. 'Law and Science are all very well in their own way,' he wrote, 'but no man, however great a lawyer he may be, will or should be excused for his want of

knowledge in certain other subjects. I would much rather risk
my success at the Bar than go through life as a mere lawyer
with no interest in anything save the technicalities and trivialities of law'. Motilal was rather taken aback by this superior,
almost supercilious attitude of his son's towards the profession
from which he was to earn his bread and butter. 'I am dense
enough,' he wrote dryly, 'not to be able to guess what that
branch of knowledge is to which the unfortunate lawyer is or
should be a stranger. I may, however, tell you that a mere
lawyer has not yet been known to succeed in his own profession,
and that the lawyers who have succeeded and will succeed have
generally something more than mere law to draw upon. Please
do not judge the profession by the bad example of your father
who is not even well-versed in law.'

It would seem that Jawaharlal was confusing the spheres of
literature and law: a successful lawyer did not have to be a
learned don. Jawaharlal's criticisms of 'the technicalities and
trivialities of law' were a sign of his own inner conflict, rather
than a valid criticism of the legal profession. Having already
decided not to compete for the I.C.S., he could not turn away
from the law, but he hated the idea of narrow specialization. He
felt the pangs of intellectual hunger. For his Natural Sciences
Tripos he had studied rocks, plants and the physical structure of
universe. He was now eager to learn something about the social,
economic and political forces which were shaping the modern
world. This was why he preferred Oxford to London for the
study of law, and why, when in deference to his father's wishes
he finally joined the Inner Temple, he wanted also to enrol at
the London School of Economics.

Motilal did not deny the usefulness of the study of economics,
but feared that it might distract Jawaharlal from his legal curri-
culum. In actual fact London had a softening influence on young
Nehru. He found some old friends from Harrow, scions of aristocratic families, developed expensive habits, took rooms in
Holland Park in the West End, joined the Queen's Club and tried
to 'ape the prosperous and somewhat empty-headed Englishman
who is called a man about town'. His requests for funds became
more frequent and insistent; sometimes a cable would arrive at
Allahabad with just one expressive word: 'Money'. Motilal did
not mind the extravagance, but was irritated by his son's hints
he might not be able to scrape through the law examination.

Jawaharlal's diffidence stemmed partly from his resistance to cramming and partly from what his father had once described as his habit of underrating himself. He did get through the Law Finals, but in the meantime he had incurred his father's wrath. The immediate provocation was the loss of £40 lent by young Nehru to a friend. 'I do not think', Motilal wrote on May 30, 1912, 'there are many fathers in the world who are more indulgent than I am, but however indulgent I may be, I am not the man to stand nonsense . . . What am I to think when you tell me seriously that there is a chance of your being put back [in the law examination] . . .? Again, the idea of throwing away £40 in the way you did, does not commend itself to me . . . I am afraid that you have managed to fall in with a set of people, not always desirable for the son of a father of my means . . . You cannot imagine how grieved I am to say all this but things have come to a pass when I must cry halt'. Motilal went on to ask his son to render an account of the money spent by him during the preceding six months. Jawaharlal replied with a reasoned and dignified explanation, which concluded on a point of principle. The father thus received a foretaste of that peculiar blend of logic and ethics, which many years later was to fascinate his son's admirers as much as it was to exasperate his critics.

Jawaharlal to Motilal, June 21, 1912: '. . . Your last letter pained and surprised me very much. I am fully aware of the fact that I have lately spent far too much money and have not given attention to my studies, which I should or might have given. The latter did not have as disastrous results as it might have had, the former I could not very well help after I had decided to live in such expensive surroundings. As for the £40, I could not very well refuse. I suffered enough for my folly later on; I was driven to such straits that for the first time in my life I had to pawn my watch . . .

'You ask me to send you an account of expenditure. . . . May I know if I am supposed to keep you informed of every penny I spend on a bus fare or a stamp? Either you trust me or you do not. If you do then surely no accounts are necessary. If you do not, then the accounts I send you are not to be relied upon. To me the very idea of furnishing accounts is anathema and suggests my being on ticket-of-leave. I am not desirous of staying in England or any where else under these conditions. I think it will be best for me to return home at once . . .'

This long explanation had become unnecessary even before it reached Allahabad. After posting his caustic letter of May 30th Motilal admitted that he would 'have given anything in the world to recall the letter and destroy it'. He felt that in a fit of temper he had been unjust to his son and he hastened to make up the quarrel: 'You know as well as anyone else does that, whatever my shortcomings may be, and I know there are many, I cannot be guilty of either love of money or want of love for you.'

3

The incident was soon forgotten. Motilal was already busy preparing an album of photographs of his son from 'The Cradle to the Bar', and planning another: 'From the Bar to . . .' He gave orders for Anand Bhawan to be redecorated and two new rooms to be built on the first floor to make the house 'at least tolerable to one whose head is full of palatial buildings'. From a letter to his brother it appears that he had toyed with the idea of visiting Europe to fetch his son.

Motilal to Bansi Dhar, June 28, 1912: '. . . The idea was that I would go to Europe and take [Jawaharlal] to places he has not yet seen before he finally came back. But my engagements did not permit of my leaving India . . . It must be a great disappointment to Jawaharlal, as it certainly is to me, but it is in his own interest that I should keep up my practice in its various branches in India eventually to be able to hand at least some of it to him. The competition for a beginner is at present very keen . . . The one object of my life, after his return, will be to push him on and, if within the next four years he can manage to be independent of me, I shall retire in peace and comfort after a most strenuous life of active work extending over thirty-five years.'

The family reunion took place at Mussoorie in August, 1912. Swarup Rani was beside herself with joy – her sickness had miraculously vanished; Motilal was proud and happy; the twelve-year-old Sarup was agog with excitement, while her baby sister Krishna, who had been born while her brother was in England,

wondered what all the fuss was about. A few weeks later, while
Motilal was in Allahabad attending to his legal work and the
rest of the family was holidaying at Mussoorie, he received a
money order for Rs. 500 from a client named Rao Maharaj Singh
who wished to engage young Nehru as a counsel. 'The first fee
your father got,' Motilal wrote to his son, 'was Rs. 5 (five) only.
You are evidently a hundred times better than your father. I
wish I was my son instead of being myself . . . Your mother will
be delighted to hear that you got it as your first fee. So there
is the double pleasure for the man who started on Rs. 5 only'.

Rao Maharaj Singh blazed a trail which other clients were
rather slow in following. Motilal was of course very anxious to
pass on at least part of his vast clientele to his son. Legal practice
is not usually a heritable commodity, but it is important to remember that Jawaharlal had assets of his own for the profession
he was entering. 'He is a son to be proud of, such perfect manners!', wrote Sir Robert Aikman, a friend of Motilal and a retired judge of Allahabad High Court, who had met Jawaharlal
in London towards the end of 1911. To personal charm, young
Nehru added an earnestness of purpose and a capacity for hard
work even in those early years, which belie his description of
himself as 'a bit of a prig with little to commend me.'[1] His cousin
Shridhar Nehru of the Indian Civil Service, who was in Allahabad during the years 1913-15 and shared a room with him in
Anand Bhawan, recalls that Jawaharlal's dinner often went cold
while he was poring over his law books. Against these assets
must be set certain limitations. The stage-fright which had
troubled Jawaharlal at Harrow and Cambridge died hard. 'At
the present moment,' he had written to his father from London
in August, 1911, 'I can imagine nothing more terrifying than
having to speak in public.' His long stay in England had served
not only to deepen the loneliness from which he had suffered
since his childhood, but also to make him a stranger to the
seamy side of life in his own country. His sensitive spirit found
the heavy odour of cynical self-interest and calculated rapacity
which overhung the Indian courts unbearably oppressive. And
unlike his father thirty years earlier, he lacked the spur of
necessity to goad him into a profession in which total absorption
was the price of total success. It was not easy for young Nehru
to pay this price. During the years 1913-14, among the books he

[1] Nehru, J., *Toward Freedom*, p. 39.

read were Addington Symond's *Renaissance in Italy*, John Drink-water's *Swinburne*, Norman Angell's *The Great Illusion* and John Morley's *Notes on History and Politics*. He could not find time for all the reading he wanted to do. Deep down in him there was a vacuum which needed filling with something more than personal and professional ambition. He took to Red Cross work and with Mr Knox of the I.C.S., who was later to try him for sedition, became the joint secretary of the Allahabad branch of the St John Ambulance Brigade. He seriously thought of joining the Servants of India Society founded by Gokhale, whose person-ality and patriotism attracted him as much as his Moderate politics repelled him. When Gokhale appealed for help for Gandhi's South African struggle, Jawaharlal threw himself wholeheartedly into the campaign and became the secretary of the organization set up at Allahabad for the collection of funds. It was politics which seemed to strike the vital chord in him.

4

In December, 1912, within four months of his return from England, Jawaharlal attended the Bankipore Congress with his father. They found the proceedings rather tame. The political temperature had dropped even before the reversal of the partition of Bengal removed the running sore in Indo-British relations. The Congress had not yet recovered from the shock of the Surat split. The Moderates, who were in possession of the party machine, had slammed and bolted the door against the Ex-tremists, whose leader Tilak had been clapped into prison. Be-tween the caution of the Moderates and the complacency of the authorities, political life was in the doldrums. Discontent had been driven into the subterranean channels of violence. The average number of political murders during the years 1910-11 was one a fortnight.[2] Terrorism was, however, a two-edged weapon; it threw the official world into panic, and provided specious pleas for repressive legislation and strong-arm methods which had the effect of emasculating even normal political life.

The outbreak of the world war in 1914 seemed momentarily to bridge the gulf between India and Britain. The East, said Lord Curzon, was 'sending out civilized soldiers to save Europe from the modern Huns'. It was clear, said Charles Roberts, that 'India

[2] Lord Hardinge of Penshurst, *My Indian Years*, p. 79.

claimed to be not a mere dependent of, but a partner in the Empire, and her partnership with us in spirit and the battlefield could not but alter the angle from which we should all henceforward look at the problems of the Government of India Act'. The political implications of the war were well summed up by Surendranath Banerjea at the Lucknow Congress: 'The object of the war is to vindicate the sanctity of treaty obligations – to uphold the sacredness of scraps and bits of paper . . . In the same spirit the Royal Proclamation and Charters to India should be redeemed. The moral law does not work by latitudes and longitudes.' It was a sign of the new spirit that the Imperial Legislative Council unanimously passed the Defence of India Act, despite its drastic provisions, and large sums were voted as grants to Britain in her hour of trial. Unfortunately, the generous impulses generated by the German peril soon spent themselves, and were succeeded by cynicism and doubt. There were insinuations in the Anglo-Indian press that the Indian soldier was unable to adapt himself to winter warfare on the battle-fronts of Europe, that the Indian politician was doing nothing to win the war. Misgivings and impatience grew on the Indian side as well: the near-success of the German challenge had exploded the myth of the invincibility of British arms. There were complaints that the special powers conferred by the Defence of India Act were being abused to crush normal political activity. The internment of the Ali Brothers – Maulanas Mohammed and Shaukat Ali – became a sore point with the Muslim intelligentsia. 'Never before,' wrote Valentine Chirol in 1910, 'have the Muslims of India as a whole identified their interests and their aspirations with the consolidation and permanence of British Rule.' Events in South-Eastern Europe and the Middle East soon made nonsense of this estimate. After the Mutiny had shattered their imperial day-dreams, the Indian Muslims had looked increasingly for inspiration to the Muslim states beyond the Indian border. They saw the Balkan Wars not as a conflict between the outmoded Turkish imperialism and the resurgent forces of nationalism, but as a hopeless struggle of Islam against the superior might of Christendom. Poets such as Iqbal and Shibli, publicists such as Abul Kalam Azad and Mohammed Ali, dwelt on the many dangers which beset Islam in the world. The professions of Muslim loyalty to the British Crown began to wear thin. In 1913, the goal of the Muslim League – which had been brought into being in 1906 as

a counter-blast to the Congress and as an avowed organ of
Muslim sectional interests – was enlarged to include the attainment of self-government. The outbreak in 1914 of a war in
which Turkey was ranged on the side of Germany created a
painful dilemma for the devout: as a Muslim leader put it, 'the
Government of our Caliph is at war with the Government of
our King-Emperor'.

The political consciousness of the Muslim middle class was
thus heightened by events abroad. The Hindu middle class had
already been made sensitive by bureaucratic sins of omission and
commission at home. The two streams of discontent converged
at Lucknow, where the Congress and the League held their
annual sessions in December, 1916. M. A. Jinnah, who presided
over the League, spoke of a new India under the influence of
Western education fast 'growing in identity of thought, purpose
and outlook'. 'We have found luck in Lucknow,' declared Tilak,
'we are now united in every way in the United Provinces.'
History was to make a mockery of this optimism. The Lucknow
Pact did not prove the turning point in the nationalist movement it was expected to be. Separate electorates failed to win
lasting adherence of the Muslim middle class to Indian nationalism and in fact turned out to be the thin end of the wedge
which was to split India apart thirty years later. And ironically
enough, Jinnah, one of the chief architects of the Lucknow Pact,
was to become the prophet of Muslim separatism. All this was
of course in the womb of the future. In 1916 the fraternization
between Moderates and the Extremists as well as between
Muslims and Hindus warmed the hearts of all patriotic Indians.
In these stirring events Motilal also played his part, though he
did not yet occupy the centre of the stage. The details of the
Congress-League compromise, of which Lucknow Pact was a
part, were indeed hammered out at a meeting in his house in
Allahabad.

The war years made their impact on the Nehrus. They
earnestly followed and discussed the news from the war-fronts;
Swarup Rani joined groups of European and Indian ladies in
knitting and collecting woollen garments for the soldiers. These
preoccupations did not, however, dim the flame of their
patriotism. The girls of the Nehru family formed an association
– the Kumari Sabha – whose meetings in Anand Bhawan were
enlivened by national songs and patriotic plays and debates. The

Leader continued to ventilate grievances, national and local; in the Provincial Council Motilal continued to hold a watching brief for the nationalist cause. The meetings of the U.P. Congress, the visits of prominent political leaders to Allahabad and the annual sessions of the Congress provided occasional diversions. At home, there were long and sometimes heated discussions between father and son; it was as if they had picked up the threads of the argument which had continued by letter for the seven long years of Jawaharlal's stay in England. Jawaharlal vehemently denounced the feebleness of Moderate politics and the futility of their tactics. It was foolish, he argued, to take British professions at their face value: Great Britain could never be talked out of her imperial position. Motilal acknowledged the limitations of constitutional agitation, but saw no practical alternative to it. He knew something of the game of politics; he had played it, albeit intermittently, for more than a quarter of a century; it required much patience and skill. He was suspicious of the emotional approach. As he listened to his son's ceaseless stream of passionate argument, he wondered how badly the boy had been bitten by the patriotic bug. He shuddered to think that the impulsive youth might be drawn into a gang of revolutionaries and end his career in jail, if not on the gallows.

5

To put the events of these years in perspective, it is important to remember that politics were not yet the dominant interest of the Nehru family, but in the nature of a diversion for the weekend or for the dinner table. Domestic and professional activities continued to absorb the energies of both father and son.

The most important event of these years was Jawaharlal's marriage. Curiously enough, the subject had cropped up while he was at Harrow. Motilal did not of course contemplate an early marriage, but he favoured an early engagement on the ground that the choice in the small Kashmiri community was limited, and the couple of eligible girls were likely to be 'booked' by the time Jawaharlal returned to India. The parents were naturally anxious to find an ideal girl for their only son, but they came up against the not uncommon difficulty that beauty and education were hard to come by in the same person. However, while good looks could not be conferred, it seemed quite possible to cultivate the mind of a good-looking girl. An unusual candour marked the debate between father and son on every aspect of matrimony. 'As for looks,' Jawaharlal wrote from Harrow, 'who can help feeling keen enjoyment at the sight of a beautiful creature? And I think you are quite right in saying that the outer features generally take after the inner person. And yet sometimes this is not the case. Beauty is after all skin deep . . .' Jawaharlal's pleas that the engagement should await his return to India finally prevailed.

The final choice fell on Kamala Kaul, daughter of Pandit Jawaharmul, a Delhi business man. Kamala, who was born on August 1, 1899, was tall, slim, pretty and healthy. Her home was less westernized than that of the Nehrus, but during her engagement, while she was staying with some of her relations in Allahabad, she was turned over for grooming to the European governesses of her fiancé's sisters.

The marriage took place at Delhi on February 8, 1916, the *Vasanta Panchami* day, the Hindu festival which heralds the coming of spring. A special train took Motilal's numerous friends and relatives to Delhi, where the Nehru Wedding Camp was the centre of festivities for a week. On the return to Allahabad, the entertainments continued for several weeks: Indian and European friends of the Nehrus were invited to teas and dinners, badminton and tennis parties, poetical recitations and musical concerts. To Motilal, at the age of fifty-five, the marriage of his only son was a joyous consummation of his life.

That summer, the whole family had a holiday in Kashmir. After spending a few days in the valley, Jawaharlal, with a cousin, went on a mountain expedition beyond Zoji-la pass. It was a perilous venture; the two young men had neither the experience nor the equipment necessary for climbing high peaks. Once, stepping on fresh snow, Jawaharlal slipped down a steep gorge. For a critical moment his life trembled in the balance, as it had done in that mountain torrent in Norway six years before. Now, as then, fate in the person of his companion pulled him back from the brink of death.

It may seem odd that Jawaharlal should have left his wife and mother to go off on a hazardous mountain expedition at such a time. But his spirit was too restless to take kindly to the pleasant but rather pointless routine of many of his contemporaries – the strenuous day at the desk and in the court relieved by gossip in the Bar Library, chatter of women and children at home, the daily drink and rubber of bridge at the club, the glossy magazines on Sunday mornings. Born thirty years earlier, Jawaharlal might have been one of Vivekananda's faithful apostles of re-awakened Hinduism; thirty years later, he might have led an expedition to Mount Everest. In his forties, while in jail, he wistfully recalled Walter de la Mare's lines:

> 'Yea, in my mind these mountains rise,
> Their perils dyed with evening's rose;
> And still my ghost sits at my eyes
> And thirsts for their untroubled snows.'

For an Indian youth, in the stirring years of the first world war, the path of adventure led not to the solitudes of a monastery, nor to the slopes of unconquered peaks, but to the struggle against foreign rule.

After Jawaharlal's return to Allahabad, Motilal took a few weeks off in Kashmir. It was a holiday on the grand scale, with a fleet of houseboats and cars and a retinue of servants. He could not, however, be away very long. His cough grew worse, his professional work was waiting, and he was missing (he wrote to his son) 'the pleasure of seeing you which is never expressed in words but felt and felt as any pleasure has been or will be felt.'

The holiday over, the family came back to Allahabad. Jawaharlal returned to his desk in Anand Bhawan as his father's junior, to the banal round of the court-room, the Bar Library and the club, relieved by such tepid politics as Allahabad had to offer.

Fortunately for young Nehru, local and national politics soon warmed up to fever heat.

CHAPTER TWELVE

HOME RULE

'HOME Rule.' 1917 opened and closed with these magic words which echoed in a million Indian homes, spelling patriotism and hope to nationalist India, sedition and anarchy to her rulers.

The high-priestess of Home Rule was the London-born sixty-nine-year-old Mrs Annie Besant, who had adopted India as her home. In the words of an eminent contemporary, Srinivasa Sastri, who knew her well, she believed 'that she belonged in her spirit, and by her soul to this country, that its culture, religion and philosophy belonged to her, and that in future lives she would be born in this country to learn that culture, to spread that philosophy, to teach that religion'. With her snow-white hair, beautiful voice and immaculately white *sari*, the venerable Mrs Besant was a well known and well-loved figure in Allahabad, and particularly in Anand Bhawan. Ferdinand T. Brooks, Jawaharlal's tutor, had been appointed on her recommendation, and she had personally officiated at the initiation of the thirteen-year-old Nehru into theosophy.

Mrs Besant's dramatic entrance on the Indian political stage during the years 1916-7 astonished friends and enemies alike. In her youth she had followed her friends Bradlaugh and George Bernard Shaw into many a political skirmish, but after her arrival in India she seemed for many years wholly immersed in the affairs of the Theosophical Society, of which she became the head, and in social and educational reforms. In an article published in 1894, she had declared that her work in the sphere of politics was over; that India would rise again not through political methods but through the renewal of her ancient religion and philosophy. Nevertheless, over the years there was a perceptible shift in her activities from the occult to the spiritual, from the spiritual to the social, and finally to the political. This shift was hastened by the unseemly controversies which raged round the Leadbeater case and the Krishnamurti incarnation. Her prestige with the Hindu intelligentsia was waning, her educational institutions passed into other hands, but she was able to stage a spectacular comeback.

In January, 1914, she started a weekly paper, the *Common-weal*, from Madras. Six months later she bought a daily paper and renamed it *New India*; the first issue appeared on July 14th, the anniversary of the fall of Bastille. She conceived a movement for India on the lines of Redmond's Home Rule League. 'I am an Indian tom-tom,' she declared, 'waking up all sleepers so that they may wake and work for their motherland.' She tried to 'sell' the idea of her Home Rule League to the Indian National Congress, and to unite that body by the re-admission of Extremists who had been expelled after the 'Surat Split'. The Moderate faction led by Pherozeshah Mehta, which controlled the Congress, was as reluctant to embrace the Extremists as it was to embarrass the Government; it feared that a new organization would divide and weaken the Indian National Congress; it was suspicious of the dynamic old lady, who neither rested herself nor let others rest. When Dadabhai Naoroji accepted the presidency of Mrs Besant's Home Rule League, he received an immediate protest from Dinshaw Wacha, a prominent Moderate and a lifelong lieutenant of Pherozeshah Mehta. 'We do not approve of the methods of Mrs Besant,' wrote Wacha, 'who late in the day has come forward to support the Congress movement . . . We are alarmed at the way in which she is going about on her own responsibility, supported from behind by the Extremists . . . [it] is a distinct menace to the peaceful progress of the country.'[1]

Distrusted and discouraged by the Old Guard of the Congress, which was weakened by the deaths in 1915 of Pherozeshah Mehta and Gokhale, Mrs Besant decided to take the plunge alone. In September, 1916, she founded her All India Home Rule League. An experienced campaigner, a tireless organizer, an eloquent speaker and a facile editor, she knew something of the tactics of Irish nationalists and English suffragettes. All these assets, however, could hardly have won her an immediate and spectacular success, but for the fact that her movement was exquisitely timed to focus and express the vague fears and hopes which a global war had generated in the politically-conscious classes. Her words spoke to the heart of India's youth: 'Let India remember what she was and realize what she may be; then shall

[1] Masani, R. P., *Dadabhai Naoroji*, p. 531.

the sun rise once more in the East and fill the western lands with
light.' She conceded that British rule in India was efficient, 'as
German rule in Germany was efficient', but asked whether any
Englishman desired to see the Germans occupying the highest
positions in England. India preferred, she declared, her 'bullock
carts with freedom to a train *de luxe* with subjection; . . . India
no longer wants your boons, your concessions and those offers
you make; India wants to be mistress in her own house . . .
Autocracy is destroyed in Russia, tottering in Germany; only
under England's flag it is rampant . . .'

The Home Rule movement made a swift and strong impression on the country. Mrs Besant's Home Rule League was
founded in September, 1916; in April of the same year Tilak
had already started a Home Rule League in Poona. There was
no rivalry between the two organizations and their leaders
worked in harmony. In May, 1916, Mrs Besant came to Poona
and, with Tilak in the chair, delivered a lecture on Home Rule.
Tilak deliberately confined the activity of his Home Rule League
to western and central India, and let Mrs Besant operate freely
in the rest of the country.

The Home Rule movement made an instantaneous appeal to
Jawaharlal. 'The atmosphere became electric,' he wrote many
years later, 'and most of us young men expected big things in
the near future.' He joined both Home Rule Leagues, but worked
mostly for Mrs Besant's. Motilal had a high regard for Mrs
Besant, but was too seasoned a lawyer and politician to be swept
off his feet. Home Rule was a new slogan but not a new doctrine:
self-government had been the avowed aim of the Indian National
Congress for the thirty-odd years of its existence and there did
not seem to be any need for another organization with the same
aim. Not all his son's arguments could persuade Motilal to join
Mrs Besant's movement; these arguments were, however, soon
powerfully reinforced from an unexpected quarter.

2

The Government's reaction to the Home Rule Movement
quickly changed from derision to bewilderment, and from bewilderment to alarm. Mrs Besant's aim – self government within
the British Empire – was modest enough, but her advocacy was
militant. She set up a branch of her Home Rule League in

England; it published one of her booklets, *India, A Nation*, which the publishers withdrew from circulation under official pressure. 'Obstreperous old harridan' – this is how Geoffrey Dawson, the Editor of *The Times*, referred to Mrs Besant in a private letter to the Viceroy.[2] 'A vain old lady influenced by a passionate desire to be a leader of movements' – this was the verdict of Sir Reginald Craddock, the Home Member of the Government of India. There was, however, no denying the fact that her movement was spreading like a prairie fire. Craddock summed up the political situation:[3]

'The position is one of great difficulty, the Moderate leaders can command no support among the vocal classes who are being led at the heels of Tilak and Besant. The great figures among the Moderates have passed away and so far they have no successors. Home Rule is pressed for not so much as constitutional reform now becoming due, but as the only salvation from innumerable wrongs and grievances under which India is suffering . . . under cover of constitutional agitation, the minds of the people who read newspapers are being poisoned against·the British Government . . .'

'Sedition in India,' Craddock wrote a month later, 'is like the tides which erode a coastline as the sea encroaches. The last high tide was in 1907-8. The tide then went out, but it is flowing in now rapidly, and it will reach a point now higher than it ever reached before. We must have our dam in order lest it inundate sound land'.[4]

The projected dam against the seditious flood was a declaration of policy. In a series of 'Clear-the-Line' telegrams the Viceroy, Lord Chelmsford, urged the Secretary of State, Austen Chamberlain, to hasten an announcement by His Majesty's Government on post-war constitutional and administrative changes in India. While the contents of this declaration were being debated between Delhi and London, the Viceroy was being pressed by the provincial governments to give a clear lead on

[2] *The History of The Times, The 150th Anniversary and Beyond*, Part II, p. 841.
[3] Minute January 17, 1917. (N.A.I.).
[4] Minute February 19, 1917. (N.A.I.).

the policy to be adopted towards Home Rule. This Lord Chelmsford declined to do. The policy of the Government of India, he
wrote[5] 'has been that local Governments should have a free
hand to take such measures as they, with their local knowledge,
deem to be necessary . . . with the assurance that the Government of India will support them in any action . . . Lord Willingdon[6] thought it advisable to restrain Mrs Besant from entering
the Presidency of Bombay. We supported him. Sir Benjamin
Robertson,[7] on similar grounds, took a like step in Central
Provinces and we supported him. Sir James Meston, however,
felt that such action was inadvisable in the United Provinces.
We supported him'.

This policy, or rather the lack of a policy, was to lead the
Government of India into deep waters at the heels of Lord Pentland, the Governor of Madras. 'Thin, whiskered, in tightly-
buttoned frock-coat, large gardenia flower in his button-hole . . .
looking what he is – an early Victorian Governor in post-war
India'—this is how Lord Pentland appeared to a visiting Secretary of State.[8] Pentland decided to silence Mrs Besant by demanding and forfeiting securities from her journals, by imposing restrictions on the movements of her lieutenants and finally by
issuing orders under the Defence of India Rules (June 16, 1917)
for her internment in Ootacamund and Coimbatore along with
B. P. Wadia, the Assistant Editor of New India, and G. S.
Arundale, a popular contributor to that paper.

The news of Mrs Besant's internment came as a bombshell to
the Indian intelligentsia, who saw it, not as an ordinary miscalculation by the Government, but as another link in the chain of a
reactionary conspiracy to stifle Indian political aspirations. Had
not the Defence of India Act been misused to suppress normal
political life in the country? Was not Lord Sydenham, a retired
Governor, publicly advocating in England the pernicious doctrine
that there could never be a diminution of British authority in
India? Had not Sir Michael O'Dwyer, the Lieutenant-Governor
of the Punjab, suggested that municipal work was good enough
for Indian politicians for many years to come? Had not Lord
Pentland told the Madras Legislative Council that 'the placing
of executive government under the direct control of the legis-

---

[5] Minute February 1, 1917. (N.A.I.).   [6] Governor of Bombay.
[7] Chief Commissioner Central Provinces.
[8] Montagu, E. S., An Indian Diary, pp. 135-6.

lature was outside the range of politics'? Had not the Viceroy himself warned his Legislative Council against expecting 'catastrophic changes' in the near future?

'Who would have thought,' a high official was reported to have said, that 'there would have been such a fuss about an old woman.' To Indian nationalists, however, nothing could be more pusillanimous and unchivalrous than to sit back with folded hands while an aged English lady went to prison for declaring that self-government was India's birthright. The repercussions of Mrs Besant's internment were shrewdly summed up in a letter to the Viceroy by Gandhi, who was at this time conscientiously trying to keep out of controversial politics.

M. K. Gandhi to J. L. Maffey, Private Secretary to the Viceroy, July 10, 1917: '. . . In my humble opinion the internments are a big blunder. Madras was absolutely calm before then, now it is badly disturbed. India as a whole had not made common cause with Mrs Besant, but now she is in a fair way towards commanding India's identity with her methods . . . I myself do not like much in Mrs Besant's methods. I have not liked the idea of political propaganda being carried on during the war. In my opinion our restraint will have been the best propaganda. And no one could deny Mrs Besant's great sacrifice and love for India or desire to be strictly constitutional. But the whole country was against me . . . The Congress was trying to capture Mrs Besant. The latter was trying to capture the former. Now they have almost become one . . .'[9]

3

During the week following the arrest of Mrs. Besant, events in Allahabad moved with unwonted rapidity. Lord Pentland succeeded where Jawaharlal had failed. On June 20, 1917, the *Leader* announced:

'The Hon'ble Pandit Motilal Nehru, the Hon'ble Dr Tej Bahadur Sapru, the Hon'ble Munshi Narayan Prasad Asthana, the Hon'ble C. Y. Chintamani . . . and a number of others have joined the Home Rule League as a protest against the arbitrary action of the Madras Government.'

[9] Unpublished (G.S.N.).

The same issue of the *Leader* carried a notice of a public meeting of 'the Indian citizens of Allahabad' on June 22nd over
which Motilal was to preside. The forty-four signatories to this
notice included almost all the prominent citizens of the town,
headed by Tej Bahadur Sapru; they included, besides Jawaharlal,
Motilal's nephews Sham Lal Nehru and Ladli Prasad Zutshi.
Even though the summer vacation had emptied Allahabad of its
student population, which bulked large in political gatherings,
no less than four thousand people gathered in Munshi Ram
Prasad's gardens on the evening of June 22nd. 'The country is
in the midst of a crisis,' Motilal declared, 'The Government has
openly declared a crusade against our national aims . . . Are
we going to succumb to these official frowns? . . . Let us raise
aloft the banner of Home Rule League and 330 million throats
voice forth the motto of Home Rule. The bureaucracy is preparing a coffin for Home Rule before its birth . . . Let us advance
with stout hearts saying with the poet: "Come what may, we
have launched our boat into the sea.". . . .'

Next day at a meeting of the Allahabad Home Rule League,
Motilal was elected president and his son one of the joint secretaries. On June 25th, Motilal cabled to Lloyd George, the British
Premier, appealing to 'constitutional England against unconstitutional methods of repression in India'.

An interesting sequel to this crisis was that Jawaharlal Nehru
missed a King's Commission. The exclusion of Indians from the
officers' cadre of the British Indian army was, to sensitive Indians,
one of the most galling humiliations of foreign subjection. We
have already seen[10] how bitterly Jawaharlal had resented the exclusion of Indian students from the Officers' Training Corps at
Cambridge. In response to persistent agitation, in which Tilak
had played a notable part, the Government of India at last agreed
in 1917 to· raise a volunteer force – the Indian Defence Force –
which educated Indians could join. 'The emergencies of a great
war', so ran the official resolution, 'cannot justify the hurried
determination of so important and difficult a question.' It was a
half-hearted concession hedged by quite a few ambiguities and
reservations. Nevertheless, Jawaharlal applied for a commission,
and both he and his father agreed to serve on a six-man committee whose aims were to popularize the scheme with educated

[10] *Supra*, p. 98.

young men, and at the same time to try to rid it of some of its
objectionable features. A meeting of the committee was to be
held in Anand Bhawan on June 23rd, but when the news of
Mrs Besant's internment came through, Jawaharlal persuaded
the committee to cancel the meeting and disband itself.

'The Hon'ble Dr Tej Bahadur Sapru and the Hon'ble
Pt Motilal Nehru have ostentatiously withdrawn from the
Indian Defence Force,' the U.P. Government reported to the
Government of India, 'Talk in Allahabad indicates that they
were not sorry for an excuse to get out of a difficult task.'[11] The
Pioneer of June 25th made a scurrilous attack on the 'political
puerility' of the Indian politician. Motilal promptly retorted in a
letter to the *Leader*:[12]

'Sir, it is not often that I am tempted to take any notice of
what is said by the section of the Anglo-Indian Press which de-
lights in running down Indians in every conceivable manner . . .
Life is too short to deal with the volume of contempt and
calumny it pours over the people of the country from day to day.
A scheme [of Indian Defence Force] bearing such objectionable
features was not likely to meet with an enthusiastic response. It
was decided at an informal conference that committees be established in Allahabad and Lucknow which were to perform more
or less the part of intermediaries between the Government and
young men eligible for enrolment, and that while on the one
hand they were to influence the young men to put up with
certain defects [of the scheme], they were on the other hand
to approach the Government – to secure the removal of certain
drawbacks – without affecting the emergencies of the Great War
. . . [After the arrest of Mrs Besant] it was quite obvious that
we could not approach either the Government or the young men
concerned with any reasonable hope of success . . .'

The Lieutenant-Governor of the United Provinces at this time
was Sir James Meston. His political instincts were better trained
than those of his opposite number in Madras and of his superiors
in Simla. In December, 1916, he had paid a courtesy visit to the
Indian National Congress when it met in Lucknow. He had discreetly refrained from restricting Mrs Besant's movements in the

[11] Chief Secretary U.P. Government to Government of India.
[12] June 28, 1917.

United Provinces. Early in July, 1917, he felt greatly perturbed at the sharp edge politics were developing. At first he thought of meeting the leading politicians, but 'in order not to run the risk of too direct a rebuff' he left the task to the Commissioners of Allahabad and Lucknow. The result of the interviews was communicated by him in a confidential letter to the Viceroy: [13]

'They both report that there was a disposition to be reasonable, to disavow any intention of stirring up racial animosities . . . They both, however, felt – and they are quite capable judges of the Indian mind – that there is a genuine suspicion even among the agitators that the Government is contemplating a reactionary policy . . . I wish it were possible for the Home Government to realize how full of nerves the country is at present, and how eagerly the vast majority of thinking people would welcome any declaration . . .'

Sir James Meston's letter was dated July 7th. During the succeeding month Motilal, assisted by his son, put new life into the local Home Rule League. 'Capable and energetic' . . . this was how the U.P. Government described[14] the Allahabad branch of the League in a report to the Government of India. 'The chief political event of the fortnight,' the report continued, 'has been the special meeting of the Provincial Congress at Lucknow on August 10th.' The conference which was presided over by Motilal was attended by 548 delegates from the various districts of the U.P., Delhi and Agra. It was a motley crowd, which included Moderates, Extremists, lawyers, doctors, businessmen, zamindars and many others who had so far taken little part in politics. The choice of Motilal as president of the conference evoked an editorial comment from the Leader: [15]

'Pandit Motilal Nehru cannot be dismissed as a prentice hand, an amateur politician, a hot-headed youth or an unquestioning follower of Mrs Besant. Fifty-six years of age, talented and thoughtful, sober and independent, dignified and manly, he speaks and acts with a proper sense of responsibility, and is ad-

[13] Sir James Meston to the Viceroy: July 7, 1917. (N.A.I.).
[14] R. Burn, Chief Secretary U.P. Government to Du Boulay. Home Secretary Government of India, August 17, 1917. (N.A.I.).
[15] August 13, 1917.

mired, trusted and respected by his countrymen . . . He can be equally trusted even by the bureaucracy to see that any organization or movement, with which he is associated, always conducts itself in the most becoming manner. He has both tact and courage, and is inspired equally by loyalty and patriotism.'

'Studiously moderate,' was the official verdict on Motilal's presidential address. The moderation was apparent more in the language than in the contents of a speech, which was a sharp though closely reasoned indictment of official policies since the outbreak of the war. The bureaucracy, Motilal argued, suffered from the obsession that the root of the trouble lay not in its policies, but in the people themselves. He contrasted the rashness of Lord Pentland with the restraint of Sir James Meston. He drew pointed attention to the freedom of discussion in Britain and the Dominions during the war and deplored the irksome restrictions imposed in India. 'These bureaucratic rulers of ours,' said Motilal, 'are almost completely lacking in imaginative conception, sympathetic understanding and intelligent enterprise. They fail to realize how deeply interested we are in the maintenance and permanence of the British connection in India.' He appealed to 'British Democracy, the sole tribunal appointed by Providence – to decide between us and the bureaucracy'. At this point someone from the audience shouted: 'Question.' The sequel to this interruption may be described in the words of an eye-witness: [16]

'Mr Nehru flared up, violently tapped the table before him, angrily threw over the papers in his hands and hastily put off the spectacles . . . he challenged the sceptical intruder to come out in the open and disprove his contention. There was complete silence. Pandit Motilal so completely overpowered the assembly, that not a word was breathed in defiance or disagreement while he was on his legs . . .'

Such was the excitement at this conference that a vocal section advocated the adoption of passive resistance to bring the Government to heel. Motilal steered the proceedings skilfully, holding the conference to its original aim of protesting against the internment of Mrs Besant and her colleagues and demanding a new political deal for India.

[16] Malaviya, K. D., *Pandit Motilal Nehru: His Life and Speeches*, p. 10.

Within ten days of the conference came Montagu's declaration of August 20, 1917: 'The policy of His Majesty's Government . . . is that of increasing association of Indians in every branch of the administration, and gradual development of self-governing institutions with a view to the progressive realization of responsible government in India as an integral part of the British Empire.' The declaration came as gentle rain on parched earth. Though trust in Montagu and the British Government was partly offset by suspicions of their agents in India, there was an immediate relaxation in the political atmosphere. On September 17th, Mrs. Besant was released. On October 5th, she arrived at Allahabad. Among those who received her at the railway station were Tilak, Motilal, Sarojini Naidu and Jawaharlal Nehru. The carriage in which Mrs Besant was to be driven in the company of Tilak and Motilal to Anand Bhawan, was unhorsed and dragged by a party of young men through the streets of Allahabad, which were decorated with Home Rule flags, bunting and floral arches. Along the route resounded cries of 'Bande Mataram' and 'Besant Mata Ki Jai' ('victory to Mother Besant'), and flower petals rained from housetops. When the procession reached the office of the Allahabad Home Rule League, Motilal presented an address to Mrs Besant. 'Two years ago,' he said, 'you saw with the clear intuition of genius what the motherland needed . . . You saw the inner hopes and aspirations in the hearts of the dumb, inarticulate millions of the people of this country . . .'

Mrs Besant replied briefly. Indian blood, she said, had soaked the soil of Flanders, Gallipoli, Egypt and Mesopotamia. The land that had welcomed Garibaldi, the land that had sheltered Mazzini, could not but give the same welcome to Indians who had fought for the same cause . . . 'We shall join together under a free crown in a free commonwealth of nations in which India shall shine as the sunshine in the East.'

This was Mrs Besant's glorious hour, even though the glory was to prove evanescent. Lord Pentland had given a tremendous impetus to her swift triumphal progress from Madras to the prison in Nilgiri Hills and finally to the presidency of the Calcutta Congress in December, 1917. In the ensuing dust and heat, Motilal, Tej Bahadur Sapru, C. Y. Chintamani and others – once picturesquely lumped together by the U.P. Government as 'the Brahmin clique of Allahabad' – had taken a fateful step

away from Moderate politics. While most of his colleagues were
to have second thoughts, for Motilal there was to be no turning
back.

CHAPTER THIRTEEN

REFORMS ON THE ANVIL

On November 27th, 1917, a group of U.P. politicians, including Motilal Nehru, Gokran Nath Misra and Tej Bahadur Sapru, had an interview with Edwin S. Montagu, the Secretary of State for India, at Delhi. Montagu had joined the British Cabinet in July, 1917, made his famous declaration on the political future of India in August and landed at Bombay early in November. That a member of the British Cabinet should, in the midst of a global war, have found it necessary to visit India was an event of great significance, without precedent in the history of the Indian Empire.

The August declaration, with which Montagu's name is associated, was in fact the handiwork of his predecessor Austen Chamberlain, who would have made it if the 'Mesopotamia Muddle' had not led to his resignation. And paradoxically enough, the main impulse for the declaration came from Lord Chelmsford and his Executive Council. By the beginning of 1917, even the blinkered bureaucrats of Delhi could see that not all the ills of the body politic could be attributed to the 'machinations' of Tilak and the 'demagogy' of Mrs Besant. There were other forces at work. As Austen Chamberlain told the Viceroy:[1]

'After all, we must take into account the changes produced by this war, of the constant emphasis laid upon the fact that the Allies are fighting for freedom and nationality, of the revolution in Russia, and the way it has been hailed throughout Europe, and of the effect of all these things on Indian opinion and on our own attitude to Indian questions. What would have seemed a great advance a little time ago, would now satisfy no one and we should, I think, be prepared for bold and radical measures.'

A similar conclusion was reached by an experienced adminis-

[1] Telegram dated March 29, 1917, From Secretary of State to the Viceroy. (N.A.I.).

trator, Sir James Meston, the Lieutenant-Governor of the United Provinces, who said that the strength of nationalist feeling was 'greater than it has ever been in our time . . . The Christmas meetings at Lucknow[2] caught up and consolidated popular sentiment as few political events have done. Extremists and Moderates had united after years of misunderstanding; and, greatest marvel of all, the Muhammadens also had come into the fold. A few Moderates may grumble here and there; and a few conservative Muhammadens may urge that the [Muslim] League does not really represent their community. But they do nothing. They are voiceless . . . The resultant union of all voices has filled educated India with a pride and a feeling of nationality which is impossible to ignore'. Sir James Meston felt that the time had come for a gesture which would strike the imagination of the people of India, and suggested frank discussions between 'the chosen of the Government' and the 'chosen of the people'. By the latter, he meant the representatives of the Indian National Congress and the Muslim League.

Sir James' diagnosis was too blunt, his prescription too bold to find favour with his superiors in Simla. True, Lord Chelmsford and his council were pressing the home government for a new declaration of policy to define the goal and pace of constitutional evolution in India; but this declaration was intended not so much to bring about major political changes as to set a limit for the Extremists in India and to restrain a post-war radical ministry at home which might be swept into office in the first flush of victory. The latter danger was described in a minute by Sir R. H. Craddock, the Home Member of the Viceroy's Council:

'It is at least a possibility that the views of the Government of India and of the Secretary of State may be swept aside in a fit of generosity and gratitude on the conclusion of peace by a nation which is daily becoming more democratic . . . the United Kingdom [is] now ruled by a dictator[3] who is a great believer in democracy. Such a politician is likely to be moved more by theoretical, plausible arguments of a number of Congress emissaries [in England] than by the cautious and cold reasoning of a bureaucracy.'

[2] Annual sessions of Indian National Congress and All India Muslim League at Lucknow in December, 1916.
[3] Lloyd George.

It is obvious that Lord Chelmsford and his Executive Council did not contemplate any considerable devolution of authority, for they could hardly conceal their consternation when Austen Chamberlain, prodded by Sir William Wedderburn and the pro-Congress element in the House of Commons, proposed a non-official committee consisting of members of the British Parliament and a few eminent Indians to suggest the outlines of a new scheme of reforms. This attitude called forth a rebuke from Austen Chamberlain.

Secretary of State to Viceroy, May 15, 1917: 'I can see no use in multiplying elected representatives until we are prepared to entrust them with some degree of responsibility in financial or administrative matters . . . nor do I think it is possible to leave the question to be settled by a Government [of India] whose members are drawn from a great service – but who are yet necessarily steeped in traditions of bureaucracy, and are therefore likely to be critical and impatient of the faults and defects which any approximation to a parliamentary or self-governing system involves. No bureaucracy in the world will ever transform itself into self-government. The motive power must come from outside. Their very virtues are inimical to a parliamentary system, and it is inevitable that they should magnify the difficulty and dangers of any change . . .'[4]

Montagu, who joined Lloyd George's cabinet on the understanding that he would go to the India Office, saw as clearly as his predecessor that a specious declaration, unless followed up by concrete concessions, would only add fuel to the flames of Indian discontent. Accepting an invitation from the Viceroy originally intended for his predecessor, Montagu sailed for India with a small team of advisers, including Bhupendranath Basu, a member of his council and a former president of the Indian National Congress. 'My visit to India,' Montagu wrote in his diary soon after setting foot on Indian soil, 'means that we are going to do something big . . . it must be epoch-making or it is a failure.'[5] For this self-imposed mission, he had unusual qualifications. He was singularly free from the pride of race or office. Invited to a luncheon party at Bhupendranath Basu's house in Calcutta, he

[4] Unpublished. (N.A.I.).
[5] Montagu, Edwin S., *An Indian Diary*, p. 8.

cheerfully stood up with his fellow guests during the singing of
'Bande Mataram', the song of Indian nationalism and the symbol
of sedition in official circles. Montagu had something of the
sincerity of a Pethick-Lawrence, the subtlety of a Stafford Cripps,
the courage of a Clement Attlee and the drive of a Louis Mountbatten. These were too many roles for one man who had come
to India thirty years too soon. Nevertheless, during the next five
months Montagu applied himself to the task of outlining a new
constitution which would set India on the road to self-government.

2

On November 26, 1917, the Viceroy and the Secretary of State
received the deputations of the Congress and the Muslim League.
These were, as Montagu said, 'the real giants of the Indian
political world', including as they did Mrs Besant, Hasan Imam,
Vesan Pillai, Mazhar-ul-Huq, Jinnah and Gandhi. Next day,
they received Madan Mohan Malaviya alone, and then came, to
quote again from Montagu's diary, 'four men from the United
Provinces . . . Motilal Nehru has been a great firebrand to
Meston, but even he, and more particularly Sapru, and the old
Pandit Misra seemed to be quite willing to consider something
less than [the Congress League] scheme . . . if only they were
satisfied that we meant business and that they could get responsible government in, say, twenty years. It seems to me . . . it is
useless to count upon these lesser men who will be swept off their
feet when their leaders start agitation again . . .'
The inclusion of Motilal among the 'lesser men' may sound
incongruous in the light of later history, but in November, 1917,
the description was not inappropriate. He had presided over two
'special' political conferences, at Allahabad in 1907, and at Lucknow in 1917; he had been a member of the provincial legislature since 1909; he had been the president of the Social Conference at Agra, of the U.P. Congress, of the Vakils Association
and of the Home Rule League at Allahabad. But he was only
distinguished in his own province and more particularly in his
home town of Allahabad. Though he had served as a member of
the All India Congress Committee and, since the return of his
son from England, had attended all its annual sessions, he was
still very much a provincial leader – one of the 'lesser men'. In

less than two years, he was to tower head and shoulders above most of the 'giants of Indian politics'.

In his interview with the Viceroy and the Secretary of State, Motilal pleaded for the acceptance of the Congress-League scheme, which had been approved at Lucknow in December, 1916. Designed as a compromise between Indian aspirations and British objections, between Hindu nationalism and Muslim communalism, the Congress-League Scheme included a series of checks and balances. It sought to place the Secretary of State for India on a par with the Colonial Secretary. The control of defence and foreign affairs was to be reserved to the Imperial Government. Fiscal and administrative autonomy was to be granted to the provinces. The executive councils at the centre as well as in the provinces were to include more Indians, and become responsible to legislatures four-fifths of which were to be elected. The bills passed by the legislatures could be vetoed by the Viceroy or the Governor as the case might be, but if passed again after a year, were to be enforced.

In retrospect, the Congress-League scheme seems modest enough; in 1917 it sounded revolutionary. Even Montagu, sympathetic as he was to Indian aspirations, was unable to see how the control of the executive – and of the purse – could be transferred at one blow to newly-elected and inexperienced legislators. Was India to have no intermediate stage between complete irresponsibility and fully responsible government? Was it possible to transplant British institutions into the soil of India without giving her people time to master 'those customs, conventions and traditions which could not be embodied in an Act of Parliament'? Could democracy work without training ministers, legislators and voters? 'Do not be in a hurry,' Montagu had begged old Motilal Ghose, the editor of *Amrit Bazar Patrika*, 'ten years is a long stretch in the life of a man, but very little in the life of a nation'.

Left to himself, Montagu might have taken a long stride forward. But he found in high officials in Delhi and the provincial capitals a deep distrust of the Indian politician. He had also to reckon with the diehards in the Cabinet, Parliament and the press and above all, the powerful Anglo-India lobby in Britain. 'Why is it necessary to proceed at a breakneck speed,' Curzon remonstrated[6] with Montagu when the reforms came up before

---

[6] Ronaldshay, Earl of, *The Life of Lord Curzon*, vol. III, p. 172.

the Cabinet, 'in a case that constitutes a revolution, of which not one person in a thousand in this country [Britain] realizes the magnitude, and which will probably lead by stages of increasing speed to the ultimate disruption of the Empire . . . shake the foundations of the entire structure both of Indian society and of British rule.'

It was not easy to evolve a scheme which would give a modicum of satisfaction to the Indian intelligentsia without antagonizing the I.C.S. and the Tory politicians. But Montagu decided to take the risk and to begin the experiment at the provincial level. He seized on Lionel Curtis' formula of 'dyarchy', modified it, and proposed the bifurcation of the provincial executive into two parts, one to be responsible to the Indian electorate through the legislature, and the other to the Governor. The Imperial Legislative Council was to be enlarged and given wider powers of interpellation and discussion, but it was not to control the central executive.

Even these proposals, conceived as a cautious first step, filled the older members of the I.C.S. with deep foreboding. 'I had a talk with Marris,'[7] Montagu noted in his diary on January 31, 1918, 'who is rather upset about the civil service, who fear that everything is crumbling under them.'

3

The Montagu-Chelmsford Report was published in July, 1918. It was not enthusiastically received in India. Tilak dismissed it as 'entirely unacceptable'. 'Unworthy to be offered by England or to be accepted by India', was the verdict of Mrs. Annie Besant, the president of the Congress. Most of the Moderate leaders, while acknowledging the defects of the report, sprang to Montagu's defence. The cracks in the Congress organization, which had been plastered over at Lucknow barely two years before, reappeared and widened beyond repair.

In the United Provinces, the split between the Moderates and the Extremists was immediately reflected in and outside the legislature. On August 12th, Motilal rose from his seat in the provincial council to oppose a resolution welcoming the Montagu-Chelmsford Report. 'To express gratitude for all official acts, whatever their character,' said Motilal, 'is the natural out-

[7] Sir W. D. Marris, K.C.I.E., C.S.I. (later Governor of U.P. 1922-8).

come of centuries of bureaucratic rule.' He conceded the good points of the report: its masterly treatment of the subject, its clear reasoning, its sound principles. But before he could express his gratitude, he wanted 'an honest answer to an honest question'. What had they (Montagu and Chelmsford) actually done? Had they redeemed the pledges implicit in the 1917 declaration? Was not the authority of the legislatures hedged by too many 'reservations' and safeguards? It looked as if what was being given with one hand was being taken away with the other. He went on to quote from a speech of Sir James Meston (who as Lieutenant-Governor was presiding over the deliberations of the Council): 'There is a canon of moral strategy that reform must not be afraid of itself.'

On the following day, August 13th, Motilal moved a resolution recommending that all departments, except those of the police, law and justice, should be transferred to ministers responsible to the provincial legislature. The Montagu-Chelmsford Report had vested the control of the army and the navy, foreign affairs and relations with Indian States in the Government of India. 'What catastrophe would befall the Empire,' asked Motilal, 'if popular ministers controlled all provincial departments except those concerned with law and order?' He ridiculed the timid counsels of Chintamani and other Moderate members of the council who had endorsed the official line that Indians must learn to stand before they could walk. 'We cannot learn to walk,' he said, 'unless you give us the opportunity to exercise the function. If we keep lying down all the time, then goodbye to all benefits of the exercise.'

While the U.P. Council was in session, the Moderate party suffered a serious reverse at a political conference at Lucknow at which Motilal had presided. A number of his Moderate friends – Sapru, Jagat Narayan, Chintamani and others – declared themselves in favour of the Montagu-Chelmsford report. Some of them stayed away from the conference, others found themselves in a hopeless minority.

An important consequence of Motilal's break with his Moderate friends was his incursion into journalism. He had been associated with the *Leader* since its inception in 1909 as an organ of nationalist opinion in the United Provinces. He was indeed the first Chairman of the Board of Directors of 'Newspapers Limited' which owned the *Leader*, and had valiantly resisted early official attempts to muzzle the paper. Chintamani, the young and enthusiastic journalist from Andhra – whose salary Motilal had increased in 1910[8] – had within a decade made the *Leader* a power in the land, and himself a power in the *Leader*. In the summer of 1917 Motilal and Chintamani had pulled together over the aftermath of Mrs Besant's internment. But Montagu's visit at the end of the year proved decisive in Chintamani's final conversion to the idea of constitutional advance by measured stages. At the same time forces at home and in the country were driving Motilal in the opposite direction. He pressed for a more forward editorial policy; but in Chintamani he met a Tartar. At a meeting of the shareholders Chintamani silenced the elder Nehru by producing a majority of proxies. Motilal did not admit defeat, and decided to launch a daily paper of his own; the *Independent* appeared on February 5, 1919.

In the last week of August, 1918, Motilal and his son were in Bombay for the special session of the Indian National Congress, which had been convened to consider the Montagu-Chelmsford Report. Besides asking for greater powers for ministers in the provinces – somewhat on the lines of Motilal's resolution in the U.P. Council – the Bombay Congress demanded dyarchy at the centre as a first step in the process of making the Government of India fully responsible to the legislature within fifteen years. It was an indication of Motilal's rising stature in national politics that he was called upon to speak on the main resolution at the plenary session. Referring to the charge that there was no parallel in history for the Congress-League scheme, he said: 'I plead guilty to the charge, but I say, are you able to point out a parallel in history for the conditions under which we live and have lived for a hundred and fifty years and more? While we cannot find an exact parallel in history to our case, you are acting in the teeth of the lessons of history.'[9]

The Bombay session was remarkable for the absence of Moderate leaders, who seceded from the Congress and formed a separate body – the National Liberal Federation. The wheel had come full circle: the Moderates, who had expelled the Extremists in 1908, found themselves edged out of the Congress ten years later and suffered a sudden slump in prestige and popularity. Henceforth they were ridiculed by those who sup-

---

[8] *Supra*, p. 112.
[9] Indian National Congress, Report of the Special Session 1918.

planted them in popular esteem as fossils incapable of registering the vital currents of national feeling; their policies were denounced as craven, even corrupt. The verdict was unjust to some of these veterans who had spent their lives in the nationalist cause. Among them was Surendranath Banerjea – the 'Surrender-Not' of the partition of Bengal – who had attended every Congress session from 1886 to 1917 and enthralled the delegates with his sonorous eloquence. Then there was old Dinshaw Wacha, who as a little boy had sat on the steps of the Bombay Town Hall and heard the reading of Queen Victoria's Proclamation of 1858. Wacha had faithfully backed Pherozeshah Mehta's long sway over the Bombay Corporation and the Indian National Congress, and ceaselessly bombarded the Government in and outside the legislature with a volley of facts and figures on Indian grievances. Banerjea and Wacha were the last survivors of a fast diminishing band, which had included Dadabhai Naoroji, and Badruddin Tyabji, Hume, and Wedderburn, W. C. Bonnerjee and R. C. Dutt, Gokhale and Ambika Charan Mazumdar, and which had sown and nurtured the seed of Indian nationalism.

'What a wonderful revolution have we seen within the lifetime of a generation?' R. C. Dutt wrote just before his death in 1909 to S. N. Banerjea.[10] Of the magnitude of this revolution there was no doubt. The founding fathers of the Congress had been born into an inert society which needed to be prodded into vigour with western education and social reform. It was a society in which political aspiration, let alone political agitation, was unknown, the sense of Indian nationality was submerged under the confusion of sectarian and regional loyalties, the press was neither vocal nor free, there was a handful of Indians in the civil service, and none in the provincial and central executives; municipal bodies were run by officials; and the so-called legislative councils – packed with British officials and the Indian titled gentry – resembled the *durbar* of an Indian prince. In less than fifty years the scene had been completely transformed. National consciousness had come to be recognized by the rulers and the ruled as the strongest force in the land; the press had become a power to be reckoned with; the proportion of Indians in the superior ranks of the civil service had risen, and some of them sat even in the executive councils of the Governors and

10 Gupta, J. N., *Life and Work of R. C. Dutt*, p. 394.

the Viceroy; the local bodies had been reorganized on a popular basis; and, above all, a beginning had been made with parliamentary institutions. The declaration of August 20, 1917, infused new life into the ageing arteries of the Moderate veterans, who read into it the consummation of their life-mission, a tangible proof that their patient pleading at the bar of British justice had borne fruit. The Montagu-Chelmsford scheme seemed to them a promise of better things to come. Was it not foolish, they argued, to oppose the scheme and play into the hands of its Tory critics in England who were in any case bent upon wrecking it?

A vocal section in the Congress – a new generation of leaders, egged on by new politicians in the country at large – feared that the Moderate veterans were confusing the beginning of the journey with its end, the promise with the fulfilment. The declaration of 1917 might be a charter of liberty but it was not liberty itself. That the Congress leaders should have divided into two camps at this critical juncture in the national movement is not surprising. What is surprising is that Motilal, in his fifty-eighth year, should have walked into the Extremist camp. 'The Extremist of today,' Tilak had said at Calcutta in December, 1906, 'will be the Moderate of tomorrow just as the Moderates of today were the Extremists of yesterday.'[11] This normal sequence of political evolution was to be reversed by Motilal; he began as an 'immoderate Moderate', and ended in the van of militant nationalism.

In the autumn of 1918, Motilal's path had diverged from that of his old colleagues, but no one could have foreseen how far and fast he would travel. That was to be decided by the emergence of a new leader on the Indian stage, who was to make in 1919 one of the most spectacular political conquests in history. Among Gandhi's earliest and most fateful annexations was Allahabad's Anand Bhawan.

[11] Parvate, T. V., *Gopal Krishna Gokhale*, p. 228.

CHAPTER FOURTEEN

EMERGENCE OF GANDHI

IN the early nineties, when Motilal had already forged his way to the forefront of the Allahabad Bar, M. K. Gandhi, a young Gujarati lawyer, was floundering hopelessly in the courts of Bombay. Tongue-tied, diffident and self-conscious, Gandhi had perforce to retire to the small town of Rajkot to make a modest living from petition-writing. He could not carry on for long even as a barrister-scribe, as he fell foul of the local British officer in whose court most of his work lay. In 1893 he was glad to accept a year's contract from an Indian firm in Durban, even though the fee was modest and it was not quite clear whether he was being engaged as counsel or as a clerk.

From the day of his arrival in the Dark Continent, Gandhi was made sharply aware of the humiliating conditions under which his countrymen had to live. In a Durban court he was ordered to take off his turban; and in the course of a harrowing journey by rail and road to Pretoria he was thrown out of a first class compartment, mercilessly beaten up by an arrogant white and refused admission into the best hotels. There was nothing new in these humiliations; Indian merchants had learnt to pocket them, as they pocketed their daily earnings. What was new was Gandhi's reaction: he did not give in to those who abused and assaulted him, nor did he retaliate in kind. He observed that the Indian immigrants had few rights, and did not know how to assert even the rights they had. The helplessness of his fellow-countrymen in a hostile environment had the miraculous effect of dissipating his own pathological shyness. Though barely twenty-five, Gandhi quickly blossomed into a successful lawyer and an astute politician. He organized the Indians in Natal – and later in the Transvaal – against a racial tyranny which not only denied them elementary civic rights but threatened to undermine the position they had built by dint of hard work in the economy of South Africa. He was able to infuse a spirit of solidarity among his compatriots, although they came from different provinces, faiths and strata of society. He appealed to the conscience of the saner section of the European community in South Africa; he sought the sympathy of Indians and Englishmen whose moral sense had not been blunted by race prejudice.

It was a measure of Gandhi's success that the Indian National Congress repeatedly passed resolutions and the London *Times* commented editorially in favour of the cause he championed. But in South Africa itself he made little headway. Except for a handful of Christian missionaries and youthful idealists bewitched by Gandhi, the Europeans of South Africa tended to view the 'Indian Question' not so much as a matter of political ethics as a question of their own bread and butter and that of their children. The logic of colonial self-government prevented the Imperial Government in London from effectively interceding on behalf of the Indian settlers. Gandhi made some fine gestures: he led ambulance units composed of Indian volunteers during the Boer War and the 'Zulu Rebellion', but these gestures were wasted on his opponents. Nor did the British victory in the Boer War bring any relief; it resulted in a new partnership between Boer and Briton, but the brown, black and yellow races had no place in it. Gandhi's patience was finally exhausted in 1906 when the Transvaal Government proposed to enact an irksome, humiliating and wholly unnecessary law for the registration of the Indian population. 'There is only one course open to those like me,' he told a meeting of his fellow-countrymen in Johannesburg, 'to die but not to submit to this law.' To die, not to kill: thus was born *Satyagraha*, a new technique for fighting political and social injustice. It was not the product of a sudden impulse; behind it lay a lifelong discipline, in which the austere background of Gandi's home, the influence of his devout mother, the impact of the Sermon on the Mount, the daily meditation on the *Bhagavad Gita*, the inspiring words of Tolstoy and the harsh realities of South African politics had all played their part.

For eight years – from 1906 to 1914 – Gandhi waged a seemingly unequal struggle against the Government of South Africa. The Indians lacked the right to vote or to be represented in the local legislatures and were exposed to economic pressures from the dominant European community. Nevertheless they refused to submit to unjust laws, though they refrained from hatred or violence against those whom they regarded as their oppressors.

Under Gandhi's leadership, hundreds of Indians cheerfully faced impoverishment, imprisonment, flogging and even shooting. Gandhi tried, with great success, to keep his agitation from passing from the realm of conscience to the realm of force. Public opinion in India and Britain – and indeed throughout the world – was deeply stirred and impelled the South African Government to a compromise in 1914. Not all Indian grievances were redressed, but General Smuts, who negotiated with Gandhi on behalf of the South African Government, recalled many years later that the compromise was 'a successful *coup* for Gandhi'. 'It was my fate,' added Smuts, 'to be the antagonist of a man for whom even then I had the highest respect.'[1]

2

In January, 1915, the Government of India joined the people of India in welcoming Gandhi home. The New Year Honours' list included a *Kaiser-i-Hind* medal for him. His fame had long preceded his return to the homeland. Gokhole, whom he acknowledged as his political mentor, had paid a tribute to his 'marvellous spiritual power to turn ordinary men into heroes and martyrs'.

Early in 1915 Gandhi was in no great hurry to plunge into public life. For one thing, he had promised Gokhale that he would watch and wait for a year before irrevocably committing himself. For another, he was convinced that it did not become a votary of *Satyagraha* to embarrass the Government so long as the war lasted. During his stay in England *en route* to India, he had organized an ambulance unit from among Indian students. Had it not been for a severe attack of pleurisy, which compelled him to return home, Gandhi might have served in the battlefields of Europe and the Middle East, and possibly lost his life in the defence of an Empire which he was destined to shake to its foundations.

For the first few years after his return from South Africa, Gandhi was a strangely enigmatic figure hovering uncertainly on the periphery of Indian politics, 'rather an eccentric specimen of an England-returned-educated Indian'.[2] He avowed his political creed in a speech he delivered at the annual law dinner at Madras

---

[1] Radhakrishnan, S. (Ed.), *Mahatma Gandhi Essays and Reflections*, pp. 277-8.
[2] J. B. Kripalani in *Incidents of Gandhiji's Life (Edited by Shukla)*, p. 118.

in April, 1915. 'It gives me the greatest pleasure this evening,' he said, 'to re-declare my loyalty to the British Empire. I discovered that the British Empire had certain ideals with which I have fallen in love and one of those ideals is that every subject of the British Empire has the freest scope for his energies and honour whatever he thinks is due to his conscience.'[3] His tributes to the British Empire, his criticisms of western civilization and modern science, his use of religious jargon to describe social and political problems, his crusade against child marriage and untouchability, his pleas for revival of handloom industry, the *ashram* he set up to practise voluntary poverty – all these seemed to mark him out as a visionary, strangely unpolitical and otherworldly, whose energies were likely to be drained off in innocuous channels of social and religious reform.

Gandhi did not make a sharp demarcation between religion and politics. His technique of *Satyagraha* sought to introduce the spirit of religion into politics. He was eager, almost impatient, to apply this technique to cure his motherland of the many ills from which she suffered. It was, however, part of the strategy of *Satyagraha* not to take advantage of the difficulties of the opponent; this self-denying ordinance determined Gandhi's attitude to the Government during the war, which he explained in a letter to the Viceroy.

Gandhi to the Viceroy, April 29, 1918: 'I recognize that, in the hour of its danger we must give – as we have decided to give – ungrudging and unequivocal support to the Empire, of which we aspire in the near future to be partners in the same sense as the Dominions overseas . . . If I could make my countrymen retrace their steps, I would make them withdraw all the Congress resolutions and not whisper "Home Rule" during the pendency of the war. I would make India offer all her able-bodied sons as a sacrifice to the Empire at this critical moment, and I know that India by this very act would become the most favoured partner in the Empire and racial distinctions would become a thing of the past . . .'[4]

So remote was this romantic idealism from *real-politik* that it carried conviction neither to the nationalist leaders nor to the

---

[3] Natesan, G. A. (Editor), *Speeches and Writings of Mahatma Gandhi*, p. 310.
[4] Unpublished. (G.S.N.).

Government of India. Tilak and Mrs. Besant saw (as the Irish nationalists had seen) that 'the price of India's loyalty was India's freedom'. The Government soon discovered that Gandhi was no honeyed loyalist and Satyagraha was no passive doctrine. When Lord Chelmsford appealed for 'domestic differences' to be sunk during the crisis of war. Gandhi answered, 'If the appeal involves the toleration of tyranny and wrong-doing on the part of officials, I am powerless to respond . . . I shall resist tyranny to the utmost . . . Ask me to suspend my activities in that direction, and you ask me to suspend life. If I could popularize the use of soul-force which is another name for love-force, in the place of brute force, I know I could present you with an India that could defy the whole world to do its worst . . . In season and out of season, therefore, I shall discipline myself, to express in my life this eternal law of suffering . . . And if I take part in any other activity, the motive is to show the matchless superiority of that law . . . I write this because I love the English nation, and I wish to evoke in every Indian the loyalty of the Englishman'.

It is doubtful if the Viceroy and his advisers understood or cared for the moral superiority of Satyagraha. If they were ostentatiously courteous, almost respectful to Gandhi, it was because they knew what a nuisance he had been to authority in South Africa. They did not mind his advice on the problems of Indians overseas – a subject on which he was acknowledged as an expert. But when he went on to comment on such delicate issues as the internment of the Ali Brothers or Mrs Besant, or to champion agrarian grievances in Bihar and Bombay, their esteem turned to suspicion, and finally to indignation. They tended to see Gandhi not (as he saw himself) in the role of a bridge-builder, but as a busy-body who was exaggerating and even inventing grievances. In April, 1918, Home Member Vincent suggested to the Viceroy that 'it would save a lot of trouble if Mr Gandhi's offer of serving in the battlefields of France or Mesopotamia were accepted'.

Gandhi did not go to Mesopotamia. He spent the closing months of the war touring his native province of Gujarat to collect recruits for the British Indian Army. Prostrated by the strain of this tour followed by an acute attack of dysentery, he lost interest in life and seemed to be at death's door. The publication of the Rowlatt Bills, however, stirred him to the depths and gave him a fresh incentive to go on living. The scales fell from his eyes: the fanciful image of the Empire which he had cherished so long crumbled in a moment. Throughout the war, he had struggled hard to keep out of political agitation; now he felt an irresistible call to fight a wrong perpetrated in peace.

The Rowlatt Bills sought to arm the executive with special powers to suppress political violence. They could not have been more ill-timed. To the Indian intelligentsia looking for a generous gesture from Britain after the war, a measure curtailing civil liberties came as a bolt from the blue. 'Wrong in principle, unsound in operation and too sweeping,' was the comment of Tej Bahadur Sapru. Another Moderate leader, Jinnah, declared that a government which enacted such a law in peace-time forfeited its claim to be called a civilized government. 'Though I have not left my bed,' Gandhi wrote to Srinivasa Sastri, 'I feel I can no longer watch the progress of the Bills lying in bed. To me the Bills are the aggravated symptoms of the deep-seated disease. They are a striking demonstration of the determination of the Civil Service to retain its grip of our necks . . . I consider the Bills to be an open challenge to us . . .'[5]

The tenacity of the Government in pushing the measure through the Imperial Legislative Council in the teeth of the unanimous opposition of the Indian members shocked Gandhi. Constitutional opposition having failed, he thought recourse to Satyagraha was the only alternative. He set up a new organiza-tion – the Satyagraha Sabha – and published a Satyagraha Pledge: 'Being conscientiously of opinion that [the Rowlett Bills] . . . are unjust, subversive of the principle of liberty and justice and destructive of the elementary rights of individuals on which the safety of the community as a whole, and the State itself is based, we solemnly affirm that . . . we shall refuse civilly to obey these laws and such other laws as a Committee to be hereafter appointed may think fit, and further affirm, that in this struggle we will faithfully follow truth and refrain from violence to life, person or property.'

It is not easy to understand the policy of the Government of India at this time, if indeed it had a policy at all. In Britain Montagu had been endeavouring to create a favourable climate for the next instalment of constitutional reforms. If he had had his way, an Indian – Sir S. P. Sinha – would have become the

[5] February 9, 1919. (G.S.N.).

Secretary of State for India, with Montagu as his deputy. This was too bold and statesmanlike a proposal to go through, but early in 1919 Sinha was raised to the peerage and appointed Under-Secretary of State for India. In April, 1918, before leaving India, Montagu had advised Chelmsford 'to lead and not to follow the administration over which he presided'. This was excellent advice, but it was wasted on a Viceroy who was (Montagu noted in his diary) 'cold, aloof, reserved, strongly holding views collected from his surroundings'. A kindly and well-meaning man, who daily struggled to the best of his ability through the mounds of files and the exacting Viceregal ceremonial, Chelmsford was overtaken by events which he could neither foresee nor control.

3

The Rowlatt Bills and Gandhi's appearance on the political stage were to exercise a profound influence on the fortunes of the Nehru family. Motilal had followed with interest and admiration the course of Gandhi's valiant struggle on behalf of Indians overseas. In 1913 Jawaharlal had collected funds in Allahabad to assist the Satyagraha struggle in South Africa. Lord Hardinge's strictures on the policies of the South African Government, which nearly led to his dismissal,[6] seemed too mild to Jawaharlal. When one of the young ladies of the family, Uma Nehru, criticized the Viceroy in a public speech and Jawaharlal concurred in her sentiments, Motilal wrote: 'Uma's speech is a very creditable one, coming as it does from the heart. The heart, however, is always a fool whoever it belongs to. The only safe guide is the head and I must say there is little of it in the speech . . . the Viceroy is as helpless in the matter as any of us . . . it was impossible for him to declare war on the Union Government . . . [he] went much further than he was justified, having regard to the peculiar relationship which exists between the Indian and the Imperial Governments.'[7]

Jawaharlal had first seen Gandhi at the Bombay Congress in December, 1915; the following year during the Lucknow session they met. Gandhi still had some of the halo of the South African struggle, but his politics seemed a strange mixture. If he avowed

---

[6] Hardinge of Penshurst, *My Indian Years*, p. 91.

[7] December 21, 1913. (N.P.).

loyalty to the British throne and deprecated controversial politics for the duration of the war, he also venerated Tilak, pleaded for the release of Ali Brothers and Mrs Besant, led agrarian agitations and conducted himself like a knight-errant of truth, ever ready to take up the 'sword' of Satyagraha against injustice. Jawaharlal was puzzled by Gandhi's politics but captivated by his personality, finding him 'humble and clear-cut and hard as a diamond, pleasant and soft-spoken, but inflexible and terribly earnest. His eyes were mild and deep, yet out of them blazed out a fierce fire . . . this little man of poor physique had something of steel in him, something rock-like which did not yield to physical powers, however great they might be. And in spite of his unimpressive features, his loin-cloth and bare body, there was a royalty and a kingliness in him which compelled a willing obeisance from others . . . It was the utter sincerity of the man and his personality that gripped; he gave the impression of tremendous inner reserves of power'.

The Champaran agitation had shown that the quaint little man, seemingly so unworldly, possessed a keen political acumen and a formidable political weapon. The publication of the 'Satyagraha Pledge' made an immediate impact on young Nehru; it filled a void in his soul which the arm-chair politics of Allahabad had failed to do. The vague nationalism of his childhood, nourished by the self-imposed exile at Harrow and Cambridge at last found a focus.

Motilal was astounded when Jawaharlal told him that he intended to join the Satyagraha Sabha. The elder Nehru held Gandhi in high esteem and was second to none in denouncing the Rowlatt Acts. But the idea of an extra-constitutional agitation seemed to him preposterous. His entire career as a lawyer, legislator and Congressman strongly predisposed him against civil disobedience. In his presidential address to the Allahabad Provincial Conference in 1907, he had ridiculed passive resistance as a 'charming expression which means so little and suggests so much', and pictured the results of such an agitation. 'I for one tremble to think,' he had said, 'of the condition of things which would prevail if all our Government and 'aided' schools and colleges were to be closed, all municipal and district boards abolished, and the elected element of the legislatures done away with. Where shall we be? The answer is plain enough: nowhere. We cannot even occupy the position we did at the beginning of the British rule, when the institutions, I have just mentioned, did not exist. Remember the price you have been paying upwards of a century for the few blessings that you enjoy. Remember the greater price you will have to pay if you throw away these blessings.'

Twelve years later, Motilal's faith in the sincerity of John Bull had visibly declined, but his faith in constitutional methods remained intact: unconstitutional agitation struck him not only as foolish but futile: breaking the law could land a few hundred people in gaol, but hardly affect the apparatus of the administration. 'The heart is a fool, the only safe guide is the head.' It was all very well for Jawaharlal to say that he was going to gaol, but did he realize the repercussions of this step on the health of his ailing mother, the professional fortunes of his old father, the happiness of his young wife and the future of his baby daughter?[8]

These misgivings were the more natural in the spring of 1919 when Gandhi was an unknown quantity in Indian politics. The publication of the Satyagraha pledge had instantly provoked a 'manifesto' of protest signed by a galaxy of senior politicians, who feared that civil disobedience would undermine the stability of the society and the state. There were strong reasons, personal as well as political, for Jawaharlal to pause and think before taking the plunge. What seemed 'a tryst with destiny' in 1947[9] was, twenty-eight years earlier, a leap in the dark.

Father and son realized that they were at the cross-roads. Night after night, Jawaharlal 'wandered about alone, tortured in mind and trying to grope' his way about, torn by the conflict between his political convictions and family affections, tormented by the feeling that he was not requiting his parents' lifelong love and care. For once, Motilal found that the crisis was too serious to be resolved by the exercise of the paternal prerogative of an angry explosion; secretly he tried sleeping on the floor to get an idea of what his son would have to go through in gaol.

Having failed to wean his son from Satyagraha, Motilal sought Gandhi's intervention. The Mahatma came to Allahabad in the second week of March and advised Jawaharlal to be

[8] Their only child Indira was born on November 19, 1917.

[9] On midnight of August 14, 1947, Jawaharlal Nehru told the Constituent Assembly: 'Long years ago, we made a tryst with destiny and now the time comes, when we shall redeem our pledge.'

patient awhile and not to do anything which was likely to upset his father. The domestic crisis was postponed rather than resolved; soon it was overshadowed by a catastrophe which shook the Indian sub-continent, and incidentally brought father and son into political alignment.

CHAPTER FIFTEEN

AMRITSAR

'THE people of India,' wrote Ramsay MacDonald, after a visit to India in 1909, 'are like the aged Simeon and Anna, the prophetess who watched by the temple for the Messiah. Every year prophets arise who blaze across the religious firmament like a comet, and palpitating hearts are drawn to them.'

Early in 1919, the Government of India was as slow to recognize the political Messiah as 'the giants of Indian politics' who had rushed to the press with a joint manifesto denouncing Satyagraha. From Allahabad, where he had gone to see Motilal Nehru, Gandhi sent another telegram to the Viceroy on March 12th: 'Even at this eleventh hour, I respectfully ask H.E. and his Government to pause and consider before passing the Rowlatt Bills.' Whether justified or not there is no mistaking the strength of public opinion on [these] measures.' The Viceroy and his advisers remained unmoved by Gandhi's appeals. They were convinced that the bills were necessary 'in the public interest'; they dared not risk the loss of face in bowing before Indian opinion; and they tended to underrate (just as a little later they were to exaggerate) the risks of Satyagraha.

Gandhi launched his movement with a day of *hartal* when business was to be suspended and the people were to fast and pray. As a token of anger or mourning, the *hartal* was not unknown in India's villages and towns, but as a national strike in a political campaign it was a novel idea. 'When I suggested the Sunday demonstration and fast,' Gandhi confessed[1] later, 'I thought I would be laughed at by most people as a lunatic. But the idea struck the imagination of an angry people.' If the enthusiastic response to his appeal surprised Gandhi, it alarmed the Government. At Delhi, where owing to a misunderstanding the *hartal* was observed on March 30th, the police opened fire to disperse a crowd; Gandhi described the firing as 'a sledge-hammer to crush a fly'. The country-wide demonstrations on April 6th

[1] Gandhi to Montagu, June 14, 1920. (G.S.N.).

unhinged the authorities. The mighty imperial edifice was shaken by a political earthquake the tremors of which pervade the secret telegrams exchanged between the Government of India and the Provincial Governments.

Governor of Bombay to the Viceroy, April 7/8, 1919: 'Yesterday's demonstrations were large. Owing, however, to the knowledge of the presence of a military force they passed off quietly ... it will almost certainly be necessary for me to proceed against Gandhi and others ... but in view of the fact that such action may result in considerable disturbance here and possibly elsewhere, I consider it proper to inform you immediately and to defer taking action until I receive telegraphic intimation of the receipt of this telegram by you.'

Viceroy to Secretary Home Department, Government of India, April 8, 1919: 'Please see "clear the line" telegram from H.E. the Governor of Bombay dated the 7th April, 1919. I think it important that in order to deal with the possible development of the passive resistance movement a definite plan of action should be prepared at once ...'

Secretary Home Department to Private Secretary to the Viceroy, April 9, 1919: '... In the opinion of O'Dwyer,[2] the situation is now so serious that it is desirable that Gandhi should, under Regulation III of 1818, be deported to Burma. Vincent[3] at any rate does not agree with O'Dwyer as to the expediency of deportation ... In Egypt recent doings show deportation might cause general conflagration ... After consulting Sir James Meston and Sir George Lowndes,[4] the Home Member has telegraphed to the Punjab and the United Provinces Governments and the Chief Commissioner Delhi sanctioning the issue by them of an order directing Gandhi to remain in Bombay Presidency ...'

Secretary Home Department to Chief Secretary Bombay Government, April 12: 'In connection with His Excellency the Governor's [Sir George Lloyd's][5] conversation with His Excel-

[2] Governor of the Punjab.
[3] Home Member of the Viceroy's Council.
[4] Law Member of the Viceroy's Council.
[5] Governor of Bombay.

lency the Viceroy regarding the deportation of Horniman,[6] Jamnadas Dwarkadas, Sobhani, Mrs Naidu, Sethe, Banker, Jinnah and Gandhi . . . If however they [the Government of Bombay] consider this action to be essential for peace and safety of the Bombay Presidency, the Government of India will support them. Government of India doubt the expediency of including Jinnah and they think that Gandhi should not be deported unless some further occurrences take place which render it unavoidable . . .'

Viceroy to Governor of Burma, April 12: 'It is probable that I shall deport in the immediate future some six persons from Bombay area. I hope you will assist us by accepting charge of them . . .'

Of the Bombay politicians only Horniman was actually deported to England. Jinnah soon ceased to be *persona non grata* by showing that he was immune to the Gandhian virus. Gandhi himself was arrested on the night of April 9th, while he was on his way to Delhi, taken by train to Bombay and set free. He would have again courted arrest by leaving for Delhi, were it not for the fact that the news of his arrest had provoked serious disturbances in Bombay, Ahmedabad, Nadiad and other places in his own province which was the least expected to forget his fundamental principle of non-violence. He observed a three-day fast to expiate his 'Himalayan miscalculation' in launching a mass-movement without making sure that the people were ready for it. He was as unsparing in his denunciations of mob violence as of official excesses. Though he decided to restrict and finally to suspend civil disobedience, his faith in Satyagraha did not falter. He argued that Satyagraha had not caused violence but only brought it to the surface, curbed it and channelled it along less harmful lines. 'In spite of the indications, which to superficial observers may appear to the contrary,' he wrote to Maffey, Private Secretary to Lord Chelmsford, 'Satyagraha alone can smooth the relations between Englishmen and Indians.' Gandhi renewed his appeals to the Viceroy to repeal the Rowlatt Act, conciliate Muslim sentiment on Khilafat and grant constitutional reforms 'in a liberal and trusting spirit'.

[6] Editor of the *Bombay Chronicle.*

2

Gandhi's appeals to the Viceroy went unheeded. Lord Chelms-ford did not seem to have a policy of his own. In June, 1917, Lord Pentland, the Governor of Madras, had led him up the garden path over Mrs Besant's internment; in April, 1919, another satrap, Sir Michael O'Dwyer, was to push him into the gravest crisis in Indo-British relations since the Mutiny. Montagu had noted in his diary (January, 1918) that O'Dwyer was 'deter-mined to maintain his position as the idol of the reactionary forces and to try and govern by the iron hand'.[7] On September 13, 1917, an outburst by O'Dwyer rubbed salt into wounds which the Viceroy had been striving to heal. 'O'Dwyer undid my work in a minute,' Chelmsford complained[8] to Geoffrey Dawson. On the afternoon of April 13, 1919, a British general backed by O'Dwyer was to undo the work of many more people and bedevil Indo-British relations for a generation.

The hartal and demonstrations on April 6th against the Rowlatt Act, alarmed the authorities in the Punjab, who read into them not the emergence of the Mahatma, but the recrudes-cence of the Mutiny. 'The British Government', thundered Sir Michael, 'which has crushed foreign foes and quelled internal rebellion could afford to despise these agitators.' On April 9th, the day of the *Rama Naumi*, the anniversary of the birth of Lord Rama, Amritsar, the second largest town in the Punjab, witnessed extraordinary scenes of fraternization between Hindus and Muslims. A huge procession formed, but it was peaceful and good-humoured; the brass bands leading it struck up 'God save the King' while marching in front of the (British) Deputy Com-missioner. On April 10th, another procession, protesting against the arrest of two local leaders, was fired upon, ran amuck, com-mitted acts of arson and assaulted a few Europeans, including two women. On April 11th, troops under the command of Brigadier-General Dyer were drafted into the city, which was quiet for the next two days.

On the afternoon of April 13th, which happened to be the festival of *Baisakhi*, a public meeting was held in Jallianwala Bagh, despite a ban on meetings of which many people in the town were not aware. General Dyer marched his troops to the

[7] Montagu, E. S., *An Indian Diary*, p. 207.
[8] *The History of the Times: 150th Anniversary and Beyond*, Part II, p. 844.

place where the meeting was being held, and ordered firing which lasted for ten minutes until the ammunition was exhausted. The Jallianwala Bagh, with its high-walled enclosure and one narrow entrance, proved a virtual rat-trap for the hundreds of men, women and children who had assembled there.

Tragic as this massacre was, worse was to follow. Martial law was declared in Amritsar, Lahore and several districts of the Punjab. O'Dwyer and his civilian and military advisers made themselves believe that by ruthless action they were nipping an incipient rebellion and saving the Punjab for the Empire. All was certainly not well with that unhappy province of which the war and influenza had taken a heavy toll; there was real social and economic discontent which German, Afghan and Pan-Islamic agents had been trying to exploit. However, all this had nothing to do with the demonstrations against the Rowlatt Act. That the theory of a conspiracy had no basis in fact is proved by secret letters exchanged between M. L. Robertson, Bombay's Inspector-General of Police, and Sir C. R. Cleveland, the Director of the Government of India's Intelligence Bureau – the two officers who should have been best informed on the political situation. 'It is difficult to understand the position in the Punjab fully,' wrote Robertson on May 19, 1919. 'Have you been able to trace any organized conspiracy? We have not yet succeeded in doing so in respect of Ahmedabad.' Cleveland replied on May 23rd: 'So far no traces of organized conspiracy have been found in the Punjab. There was organized agitation, and then in particular places the people went mad ... I am sorry to see that the *Times of India* and *The Pioneer* have committed themselves to the theory of Bolshevism or Egyptian instigation for our Indian troubles. I have satisfied myself that they have no evidence worth the name to support the theory.'

This 'mutiny-complex' explains, even though it cannot excuse, the draconian punishments and nameless indignities indiscriminately meted out to the Indian population by trigger-happy majors and tense magistrates. 'For me,' General Dyer had bluntly told the people of Amritsar on the morrow of the Jallianwala Bagh tragedy, 'the battlefield of Amritsar or Flanders is the same.' Blind anger and fear alone could have prompted bombing and machine-gunning of villages from the air, and created under the martial law regime a number of ingenious and indeed fantastic offences. It became for example an offence for two Indians

Father and son before the
plunge into politics

Father and son after the
plunge into politics

Motilal Nehru, the Leader of the Opposition in the Central
Legislative Assembly

to walk abreast, or for a Hindu and a Muslim to fraternize in public. In Lahore, the capital of the province, college students were made to march sixteen miles in the scorching summer sun to salute the Union Jack, and a marriage party which numbered more than ten was arrested, the bridegroom detained, the priest and the others whipped. Hundreds of persons were rounded up all over the province and tried by summary courts set up under martial law.

Motilal's links with Lahore were close: it was his wife's home town. One of the victims of martial law was his friend Harkishenlal, a prominent Congressman, who was charged with 'waging war against the King'. Motilal applied for permission to defend him, but was not allowed to enter the Punjab. He addressed a long telegram to the Home Member at Simla and sent copies to Montagu and Sinha in London. Montagu, probably goaded by Sinha, reacted quickly, called for the Viceroy's explanation and then, without waiting for it, cabled on June 4th:

'The reasons why advocates from other provinces are being prevented from appearing should please be communicated to me. It is considered by my council that unless special strong reasons exist, the prohibition is improper.'

The Viceroy dutifully defended the action of the local authorities as being 'legal' and 'within the jurisdiction of the Military Administrator', but added that lawyers from outside the province would be admitted after June 11th when martial law was expected to be withdrawn. Not satisfied with this assurance, Montagu telegraphed again on June 9th:

'I presume that there is no probability of proceedings against Harkishenlal and other accused being disposed of before counsel from outside provinces have opportunity of appearing. If there is any doubt, kindly arrange for postponement of proceedings.'[9]

Motilal's strategy in appealing to Montagu and Sinha above the heads of O'Dwyer and Chelmsford was shrewd and successful. He was able not only to save Harkishenlal, but also perhaps to shorten the duration of martial law. But for Montagu's inter-

[9] Telegram Secretary of State to Viceroy. (N.A.I.).

vention, the Government of India would have let things slide
and the Punjab Government would have been in no hurry to
restore civil liberties. Unlike many lawyers in Lahore and outside, Motilal refused to make money out of the distress of the
Punjab. He neglected his own practice, visited Lahore at the
earliest opportunity and took in hand the appeals of several unfortunate persons who had been condemned by the martial law
courts. In London the appeals to the Privy Council were handled
by his own solicitors, Barrow Rogers and Nevill.

3

The Punjab tragedy had a strong, almost a traumatic, impact
on a generation whose sensitivity had not been blunted by the
purges, firing squads, pogroms and gas chambers of our own
times. 'The time has come,' Rabindranath Tagore wrote to the
Viceroy while renouncing his knighthood, 'when badges of
honour make our shame glaring in their incongruous context of
humiliation.'[10] C. F. Andrews, a friend of Tagore, Gandhi and
the Nehrus, wrote to Mahadev Desai after a visit to Amritsar:

'It was a massacre, a butchery . . . I feel that if only I could
take each single Englishman and show him out of my eyes what
I have seen, he would feel the same as I. English honour has
departed . . .'[11]

More disastrous for Indo-British relations than these tragic
happenings was the way the official world reacted to them. Sir
Michael O'Dwyer and his advisers were, of course, the victims
of their own 'mutiny complex'. But even Lord Chelmsford was
content gallantly to defend the actions of the local officials. Only
rarely did the Government of India put its foot down, for
example, when the Punjab Government proposed to recover from
the unfortunate local population the cost not only of the
punitive forces stationed there while martial law was in force,
but also of removing European women and children to the hills.
As for Montagu, it could fairly be said that he was no less a
victim of General Dyer's firing than the hundreds whose blood
had soaked the stricken field of Jallianwala Bagh. The turn of

[10] Thompson, Edward, *Rabindranath Tagore*, p. 259.
[11] G.S.N. Papers.

the wheel which the Amritsar tragedy set into motion was to spin Montagu from one crisis to another, wreck his patient work for conciliation and co-operation on both sides of the water and deny any chance of success to the constitutional reforms on which he had laboured so long and hard. He felt in duty bound to defend the men on the spot, but he used his influence, whenever he could, on the side of restraint and moderation. We have already seen how readily he responded to Motilal's appeal on behalf of Harkishenlal. Sensing the depth of Indian feeling, he advocated a judicial and public inquiry into the Punjab disturbances in preference to the departmental inquiry recommended by the Government of India.

Unfortunately, Montagu's sympathy and generosity were not emulated by those who occupied the seats of power in Simla and the provincial capitals. The Government of India brought forward and pushed through the Imperial Legislative Council an Indemnity Bill designed 'to protect' officers who had acted 'in good faith' in the recent disturbances. There were of course precedents for an indemnity bill following a period of martial law, but those were cases in which the *raison d'être* of martial law was not in question. The enactment of an Indemnity Act, even before the official enquiry committee headed by Lord Hunter began its work, sounded frankly cynical. The 'whitewashing bill' formed the subject of a speech by Motilal at a public meeting at Allahabad on September 17, 1919. 'I maintain,' he said, 'that the Government of India is not only the most interested party in this matter . . . but a very unfair party . . . Indeed the way the Government of India has behaved would do little credit even to an ordinary litigant in a court.'

On October 8th, Malaviya, the Congress President, informed the Government of India that a Congress sub-committee had been constituted to collect and produce evidence before the Hunter Committee. On October 24th, Gandhi arrived in Lahore; three days later he met O'Dwyer's successor, Sir Edward Maclagan, 'a true gentleman loved by all'.[12] The Governor was impressed by the conciliatory attitude of the Mahatma. 'Mr Gandhi evidently does not take the intractable attitude as Pandit Malaviya,' Sir Edward informed the Government of India, 'he appears sincerely anxious to get matters settled as soon as

[12] Chaturvedi, Benarsidas and Sykes, Marjorie, *Charles Freer Andrews*, p. 131.

possible.' Gandhi suggested that Rauf, one of the High Court Judges, appointed to review the martial law cases, should be replaced by a judge from another province; that Congress representatives should be permitted to suggest questions when witnesses were examined by the Hunter Committee; that some of the gaoled Punjab leaders, who were conversant with the subject of the inquiry should be temporarily released. The Punjab Government (backed by Government of India) was prepared to accommodate Gandhi on the first two suggestions, but declined to release the Punjab leaders; the farthest the Government could go was to release each of the leaders on parole on the day his evidence was to be recorded. The gulf was narrowed but not bridged, and the Congress announced that it would boycott the Hunter Committee and conduct a parallel inquiry of its own. 'The public effect of the [Hunter] Inquiry Committee,' Sir Edward Maclagan wrote, 'would be weakened by the absence of the other side.'

However unfortunate the breach on this issue, it had far-reaching consequences. Motilal was appointed a member of the Congress Inquiry Committee; his colleagues were Gandhi, C. R. Das, M. R. Jayakar and Abbas Tayabji. 'This was the first occasion,' Gandhi recorded many years later, 'on which I came in close personal contact with Motilalji.'[13] A pen-picture of the committee at work has been left by Jayakar: 'Gandhi invariably assumed the role of the stern judge in sifting the chaff from the substance. He took infinite pains to see that what was to be put before the public was the quintessence of truth. The occasions were not infrequent when we differed violently as to what was the truth . . . Das and I often advocated our view with great insistence; Das often thumped the table with a vigorous gesture, which was his favourite habit when putting forward his point of view. Motilal did the same but with great restraint. Gandhi often stood alone against all this fusillade.' Jayakar adds that Gandhi's weak voice and irresistible logic finally prevailed, and at the end of the day Das would leave the discussion with the remark: 'Damn it all, Gandhi. You are right and we are wrong.'[14]

For Motilal, as for other members of the committee, this close association with Gandhi was an instructive experience. The

13 Gandhi, M. K., *My Experiments with Truth*, p. 583.
14 Jayakar, M. R., *The Story of My Life*, vol. 1, p. 322.

Mahatma's incisive intellect, moral sensitivity, passion for justice, rock-like will, conscious humility, flair for polemics and publicity, were a strange but effective mixture. No longer was it possible to dismiss him as a starry-eyed visionary: it seemed as if his practical sense had been strengthened rather than weakened by the religious cast of his mind. Jawaharlal had already fallen under the Mahatma's spell early in 1919; by the end of the year his father had developed a wholesome respect for Gandhi which was to survive basic temperamental differences as well as the vicissitudes of politics.

An important consequence of Motilal's legal and political work for the Punjab was his election as president of the Amritsar Congress. The Amritsar railway station was 'a seething mass of humanity' when he arrived from Lahore on the afternoon of 25th December. He was escorted by a huge procession amidst scenes of great enthusiasm. It was a sign of the times that Motilal and Ajmal Khan (the President of the annual session of the Muslim League which was also meeting in Amritsar) together visited and offered prayers at the Golden Temple, the holy shrine of the Sikhs.

The Amritsar Congress was attended by a galaxy of nationalist leaders, including Tilak and Annie Besant, B. C. Pal and C. R. Das, Malaviya and Gandhi, Srinivasa Sastri and Jinnah. Motilal's presidential speech took three hours. His voice was faint from a recent illness; the audience was in an excitable mood, but he wittily headed off hecklers, who objected to his speaking in English, by 'begging as a Brahmin' for silence to enable his weak voice to reach the ends of the hall. He reminded the Punjabis that they owed it to the delegates from southern India, who had come all the way to Amritsar to sympathize with them in their ordeal, to let him speak in English.

Motilal made a detailed and trenchant analysis of the chain of events in the Punjab – the repressive regime of Sir Michael O'Dwyer, the agitation against the Rowlatt Bills, the beginnings of Satyagraha, the Jallianwala tragedy and the martial law regime. From official sources he cited some revealing statistics: 108 persons had been condemned to death and the sentences of imprisonment added up to the staggering total of 7,371 years. 'The figures for whipping, forfeiture, fines and impositions on villages and towns,' he added, 'are not available.' He accused O'Dwyer of trying to convert the Punjab into 'a kind of Ulster

. . . a bulwark of reaction against all reforms' while Lord Chelmsford had failed to serve his King and fulfil his trust by 'persistent refusal to listen or to interfere, by his absence from the scene of these happenings'. He bluntly asked whether the British Democracy would tolerate 'this frightfulness' in India and shield its authors. 'That is the acid test of British policy in India. On the answer to that depends the future goodwill of the Indian people.' To Montagu he paid a tribute: he had 'laboured strenuously for us . . . we must express appreciation of his sincere desire to advance our national aspirations'.

A last-minute addition to Motilal's presidential speech was necessitated by a Royal Proclamation which, besides announcing a political amnesty, had expressed admirable sentiments. 'So far as possible,' King George V had declared, 'any trace of bitterness between my people and those who are responsible for My Government should be obliterated.' The Royal Proclamation came as balm to the assembled leaders at Amritsar. It seemed to confirm their lingering hope that British Democracy would ultimately triumph over the British Bureaucracy; that British justice would triumph over British prestige. Motilal expressed his 'humble appreciation' of the Proclamation. Tilak cabled his 'grateful and loyal thanks' to the King Emperor. 'This is a document,' affirmed Gandhi, 'of which the British people have every reason to be proud and with which every Indian ought to be satisfied. The Proclamation has replaced distrust with trust but it remains to be seen whether it would filter down to the civil service.'

As the new year dawned, it seemed as if the trail of bloodshed and bitterness left by 1919 might after all be obliterated.

CHAPTER SIXTEEN

THE PLUNGE

GANDHI'S moderation at the Amritsar Congress was not an impulsive reaction to the Royal Proclamation; since April, 1919, when he had suspended Satyagraha after violent outbreaks in Bombay and the Punjab, he had been restraining the ardour of his followers and, at the same time, urging moderation and conciliation on the Government. He bombarded the Viceroy, the Governors and even local officials with letters stressing points of agreement rather than of divergence, seeking information, pleading for redress in specific cases of hardship. He did not call upon Lord Chelmsford and Sir George Lloyd (the Governor of Bombay) to sign the Satyagraha pledge, but he did invite them to express their sympathy with the *Swadeshi* movement. To Secretary of State Montagu, he avowed 'our common interest in an Empire to which both you and I belong'. He asked Montagu to believe that Satyagraha was 'a powerful aid on the side of law and order'.[1]

The Viceroy and his colleagues received these protestations with a mixture of bewilderment, incredulity and impatience. It exasperated them to discover that Gandhi, unlike most other politicians in India, could not be fobbed off with studied courtesy, that he adhered to his demands for repeal of the Rowlatt Bills, relief on the Khilafat issue and amends for the Punjab tragedy.

The Khilafat issue was not as simple as the romantic pan-Islamism of Indian Muslims made out: in it were involved the conflicting ambitions of the Turks, the Greeks and the Arabs and the clash of interests – strategic as well as economic – of the Allies at the end of the First World War. The Muslim divines and politicians who had Gandhi's ear were unable to see that the Khilafat was a moribund institution, that the Turks themselves were thoroughly sick of it, that the Ottoman Empire had to go the way of the Hapsburg Empire, that the smaller nations, Arab

[1] Gandhi to Montagu, June 14, 1919. (G.S.N.).

and non-Arab, were struggling to shake off the Turkish yoke. Motilal's healthy agnosticism made him proof against the religious emotion which lay at the heart of the Khilafat agitation. He had consented to be one of the thirty-four signatories to the 'Khilafat memorial', but he did not join the deputation which presented the memorial to the Viceroy in January, 1920.

Motilal's chief interest, both as a lawyer and as a politician, lay in the affairs of the Punjab. When the Privy Council rejected the appeals of Bugga and Rattan Chand, two of the martial law accused, he was shocked. 'Whatever part the other appellants might have taken in the disturbances,' he wrote to Jawaharlal, 'there can be no shadow of doubt that Bugga and Rattan Chand are as innocent as Indu.[2] Everyone in the Punjab – official and non-official – knows it and yet they are to be hanged! However, this is only one instance out of a million in which injustice is daily perpetrated in this country.'[3]

In February, 1920, the Congress sub-committee which had enquired into the Punjab disturbances assembled at Benares to write its report. Motilal had ceased to be a member of the committee after his election as president of Amritsar Congress, but both he and his son were present at the discussions which preceded the preparation of the final draft.

Having been disappointed in Lord Chelmsford and his council, Gandhi and other Congress leaders continued to hope that the British Government and Parliament would override the narrow, insensitive and prestige-ridden policies of their agents in India. Unfortunately the Indian case was not well represented in England. Motilal had remitted £1,000 to Reginald Nevill, his London solicitor, for publicity in England. The money was to be spent in consultation with the British Committee of the Indian National Congress. But the amount was ridiculously small, Nevill was no politician, the British Committee was a derelict body, and the two were soon at loggerheads. Henry S. Polak, a London solicitor, complained that he had the utmost difficulty in obtaining in London a copy of the report of the Congress Inquiry Committee.

The Congress Inquiry Committee published its report in March, 1920. Two months later came out the official report – or rather reports, as the European and Indian members of Lord

[2] Jawaharlal's daughter who was one year old at this time.
[3] Nehru, J. L., *Bunch of Old Letters*, p. 5.

Hunter's committee divided on racial lines. The conclusions of Lord Hunter and his European colleagues, which were described by Gandhi as 'thinly-disguised whitewash', astounded Motilal. 'My blood is boiling,' he wrote to his son, 'since I read the summaries you have sent. We must hold a special Congress now and raise a veritable hell for the rascals.'

Montagu appealed for moderation and sanity, but as Secretary of State he had to defend the men on the spot, from whom incidentally he had to draw all the facts for their own indictment. Suspicious of his pro-Indian bias, the Government of India had taken the precaution of deputing an officer with 'journalistic experience and contacts' to brief the British press well ahead of the publication of the Hunter Committee's report. Unfortunately the nationalist version of the events in the Punjab went largely by default, though Colonel Wedgwood and Ben Spoor put up a valiant fight, and even Churchill came down heavily against Dyer's 'doctrine of frightfulness' and ridiculed the theory of the mutiny in the light of modern developments in communications and techniques of war. The Anglo-Indian lobby had done its work well – indeed, too well for the future of the Raj. There were uproarious scenes in the House of Commons. Montagu was shouted down for encouraging lawlessness in India and asked to resign. The debate in the House of Lords was no less tense. Sarojini Naidu, who was in England at the time, wrote to Gandhi: 'Our friends revealed their ignorance, our enemies their insolence . . . Mr. Montagu has proved a broken reed.' Motilal, whom Nevill had been feeding with press cuttings from the British press, was shocked at the way the guilty officials of the Punjab were being shielded and indeed lionized as saviours of the British Empire. These developments also made a sharp impact on Jawaharlal; many years later in an article on the Quetta Earthquake he recalled that he had been hurt not so much by the jingoism of Dyer as by 'the reaction in England to Dyer's deed . . . the real reaction of the British ruling class was never in doubt. This cold-blooded approval of the deed shocked me greatly. It seemed absolutely immoral, indecent, to use public-school language, it was the height of bad form'.

2

While the political kaleidoscope was shifting fast in the first half of 1920, Motilal was tied down to the small town of Arrah in Bihar by a professional engagement. It was the famous Dumraon case, in which Motilal and a Calcutta barrister, N. N. Sircar, were ranged against C. R. Das, probably the most eminent lawyer in Bengal. The property in dispute was valuable; the stake was high and so were the fees. In eight months Motilal cleared a sum of two lakhs at the rate of Rs. 25,000 a month. But the work was strenuous: the original brief ran to nearly 8,000 pages; the battle of wits continued outside as well as inside the courtroom. The atmosphere in Arrah was heavy with intrigue; most of the witnesses and local underlings had been bribed – sometimes by both sides. It was not quite safe to send letters by post, and a private courier service ran regularly between Arrah and Allahabad where Jawaharlal, in the absence of his father, was looking after domestic, legal and political affairs.

The Dumraon case, involving as it did a continual battle of wits with C. R. Das, was no picnic. In February, 1920, while Motilal and his client were in Calcutta for the examination of certain witnesses on commission, Das abruptly closed the plaintiff's case at Arrah, compelled Sircar to open the case for the defence and himself turned up in Calcutta. 'The whole thing was engineered by Das at Arrah,' Motilal wrote to Jawaharlal, 'you would simply be shocked at the practices to which the big guns of the Calcutta Bar lend themselves.' A few days later Motilal confessed: 'Das is by far the cleverer of the two Calcutta men. I cannot for the life of me understand the tactics he employed today. He has tendered *our* documents as *his* evidence'. Motilal spent the night studying the documents in an attempt to understand and checkmate this move.

The case had its exciting moments. On February 27th Motilal noted:

'The turn the case has taken will not admit of my absence from Arrah for an hour. The fate of a large estate depends upon the reading of an Arabic word, and I am the only person on Hariji's[4] side who has pretensions to some smattering in the language. They have examined a formidable witness today . . . a Persian by birth and the author of many books. He has, however, proved too much and herein lies my chance. I have to work

---

[4] Motilal's client.

tonight as hard as I can and refresh my memory with the aid of
the books you have sent.'

As if these headaches were not enough, Motilal was distracted
by dissensions in his own camp. He had a quarrel with Sircar,
his colleague.

Motilal to Jawaharlal, April 12, 1920: 'There was a difference
of opinion between him [Sircar] and me . . . the other day, and
he exhibited some temper forgetting who he was talking to. This
was in the presence of Hariji. I gave it hot to him on the spot as
you might easily imagine. He had to apologize and did so meekly
enough, but I have reason to think that he has since been trying
to get rid of me . . . He felt a bit cowed down after the apology
incident. He complained to Das that he had never seen a more
insolent *vakil*-junior than I was, and Das replied that having
seen the work of Sircar and myself he would any day deem it an
honour to work as my junior . . .'

Hardly had this storm blown over when both Motilal and
Sircar were engulfed by a minor tragedy. The neat little house
– perhaps the only suitable house in Arrah – in which they were
staying belonged to a retired lawyer who had been hoping to
make a little money by appearing as a witness. When his
evidence was dropped, he took his revenge by abruptly terminat-
ing the tenancy. On returning from Calcutta, Motilal found that
all his belongings had been thrown out of the house. 'There is
considerable amusement in the camp at our expense,' he wrote,
'but the joke was a bit too practical for our nerves.'

But his zest and sense of humour could sustain him under the
most trying conditions. 'Mango session is at its height,' he wrote
from Arrah, 'but we have had no mango for nearly a week. Only
two *safedas*[5] received today for the four of us. What a tragedy!
Are there no *langaras*[6] in Allahabad?'

In June while he was at Benares, he visited the Vishwanath
temple, 'to see what impression it would convey to my mind at
this time of my life'. Unfortunately for him he was immediately
recognized, surrounded by a horde of *pandas* (priests), made to
do *pujas* (worship) and rushed in sweltering heat from one
temple to another through the narrow streets of the holy city.

[5] & [6] Varieties of mangoes.

'I felt a sense of relief,' he confessed to his son, 'on returning to the wide road. Total cost of the experience Rs. 110; net gain: abuses of *pandas* and beggars!'

Whatever his preoccupations, Motilal was never too busy to remember his family. He gave detailed instructions for the treatment of Kamala, his daughter-in-law, whose health had already begun to give cause for concern. During his visit to Calcutta, he asked Messrs Whiteaway Laidlaw to send a perambulator for his two-year-old grand-daughter. 'I am always thinking of Indira,' he wrote on March 8, 1920, 'the very thought of a personification of innocence is soothing. By a very easy slip it justifies idol worship and many other things which modern civilization sets down for senseless superstition. Indira has to be very specially taken care of as she is not at all well'. When Jawaharlal expressed his inability to decipher certain instructions sent by a homoeopathic physician from Calcutta, Motilal wrote to him: 'There is nothing very complicated about Dr Ray's letter if you will only read it carefully after divesting your mind of the Khilafat and Satyagraha.' Such, however, was the spell cast by Satyagraha on young Nehru that it was not easy for him to forget it. The Government were soon to hasten his political education.

3

While Motilal was at Arrah, Swarup Rani and Kamala fell ill at Allahabad. The doctors advised an immediate change to the hills. Early in May, Jawaharlal arrived in Mussoorie with his mother, wife and sisters, and took rooms in the Savoy Hotel. It so happened that the Afghan envoys, who were negotiating the terms of peace after the brief Anglo-Afghan hostilities of the previous year, were staying in the same hotel. The coincidence led to a crisis.

Jawaharlal to Motilal, May 14th, 1920: 'Greatness is being thrust on me. I have just had a visit from the Superintendent of Police. He showed me a letter from the Government addressed to him in which he was asked to take a positive undertaking from me to the effect that I would refrain from seeing or having any communication with the Afghan delegates. In case I refused to give this undertaking, an externment order was to be served

on me. I told him that as a matter of fact I had no intention of
having anything to do with the Afghan delegation. I had not
even seen any of them from a distance so far. He said this was
so. He knew it perhaps from various C.I.D. sources. But I told
him that on principle I was opposed to giving any undertaking.
He was very courteous . . .'

Jawaharlal refused to give the 'undertaking', resisted an impulse to defy the prohibitory order, and left for Allahabad.
Motilal was not at all happy at the turn events had taken. Not
only had the ailing ladies been left unattended at Mussoorie;
there was a real danger that Jawaharlal would defy the ban and
land in gaol – a contingency which his father had been dreading
and staving off for fifteen months. Motilal therefore decided to
address the Governor, Sir Harcourt Butler, whom he knew rather
well. He wrote on May 19, 1920:

'I need hardly say that I wholly approve of Jawaharlal's
action. . . . His politics and mine are well-known. We have never
made any secret of them. We know they are not of the type
which finds favour with the Government, and we are prepared
to suffer any discomfort which may necessarily flow from them.
Young Jawaharlal is known throughout India, and I can con-
fidently say that there is not a man, excepting perhaps in the
C.I.D., who will believe that he is capable of carrying on a secret
intrigue of the nature apprehended from him. You have yourself
had a long talk with him, and knowing as I do the vast and
varied knowledge of human nature you possess, I cannot easily
believe that you could for a moment doubt the material that he
is made of. I am therefore inclined to think that one of two
alternatives has happened: either the order has been issued by
some mistake or inadvertence or under pressure from above.'

The tone of this letter was far removed from the ingratiating
humility to which high British dignitaries were accustomed in
letters from Indian correspondents.
Sir Harcourt's reply was at once courteous and evasive: 'I
am really very sorry that you and your son, and especially the
ladies of your family, should have been inconvenienced by an
official act which your son made it a matter of conscience not
to fall in with . . . I hope, whatever views we may hold on public

matters . . . in private life . . . nothing will interfere with the friendly relations that have existed between us for thirty years.' Motilal appreciated Sir Harcourt's courtesy, but rebutted his arguments. 'I thought,' he wrote on June 14th to his son, 'it was necessary to let Master Butler know, that we are not the people to be overawed by him into servility. I have written to him exactly as I felt and knew how you would feel.' The day after this letter was written, the externment order against Jawaharlal was unconditionally revoked. It lasted exactly one month, but was to have far-reaching consequences.

Early in June, while Jawaharlal was at a loose end at Allahabad, he went to meet a few hundred peasants from the adjoining district of Pratapgarh who had marched to Allahabad to draw public attention to their grievances and were encamping on the bank of the Jumna. They begged young Nehru to visit their district and see things for himself. Their villages were off the beaten track of political leaders; many of them could not boast of a post office, a railway station or even a proper road; their problems, even their existence, were beyond the ken of newspapers and politicians. Jawaharlal found his tour of the countryside an exciting as well as instructive experience. Probably for the first time since his return from England, instead of spending the month of June in Kashmir, Mussoorie or Simla, he was tramping the pot-holed, dusty roads of the Oudh countryside, a wet towel on his head. The peasants were thrilled to have among them the England-trained son of the great Motilal Nehru of Allahabad. As for Jawaharlal, he was 'filled with shame and sorrow, shame at my own easy-going and comfortable life . . . sorrow at the degradation and overwhelming poverty of India'.[7] He ate with the peasants, lived with them in their mud huts; their affection and gratitude had the miraculous effect of dissipating his own diffidence. Since his university days he had had a horror of speaking in public. His first speech at a meeting in Allahabad in 1916 had won him a compliment[8] from his father, and a kiss from Tej Bahadur Sapru, but it had not cured him of his stage-fright. In the presence of these wide-eyed, unsophisticated and pathetically ignorant peasants, whose contact with 'educated' people had so

[7] Nehru, J. L., *Toward Freedom*, pp. 56-57.

[8] Motilal, who was in Kashmir at the time, wrote (June 27, 1916): 'I was glad to read your speech on the Press Act in the *Leader*. Though not very informing it has the rare merit of being free from commonplaces, the besetting sin of all Indian speeches at least in the U.P.'

far been confined to *zamindars*, money-lenders and petty officials, Jawaharlal forgot his nervousness. That his Hindustani diction was not of the purest, that he fumbled for words, did not matter to the peasants. Their faces were strangely transfigured, their eyes glistened and their crushing load of misery seemed momentarily to lift, as they crowded round him and listened.

Motilal was glad to hear of his son's adventures in the villages. 'If one or two more visits like this to other parts of the Pratapgarh district can be arranged,' he wrote from Arrah (June 14th), 'there will be some chance for a pure nationalist getting into the Council in spite of the Raja Bahadur of Pratapgarh.' But the brief incursion into the countryside rewarded Jawaharlal with something more valuable than a ticket for the U.P. Council: it shook off his stage-fright, gave him an insight into the 'naked hungry mass' of India, imparted a socio-economic edge to his politics and laid the foundations of his unique mass-appeal.

4

The Mussoorie episode was no more than an interlude in an exciting drama which was unfolding itself on the wider political stage. The central figure in this drama was Gandhi, whose moves mystified friends as well as opponents. Motilal and C. R. Das, who crossed swords in the courtroom during the day and discussed poetry and politics over a bottle of whisky in the evening, were driven to despair by what they regarded as Gandhi's compromising tactics – his eleventh-hour appeals for peace, his exchanges with high British officials, his repeated and futile overtures to the Moderate leaders. In February Gandhi seemed too much of a reluctant rebel; by June he had swung to the other extreme by irrevocably committing himself to 'non-violent non-co-operation' – the boycott of the whole apparatus of government. Without waiting for the verdict of the Congress, which was to meet in a special session at Calcutta in September, he launched his movement on behalf of the Khilafat party, whose frustration had been completed by the publication of the peace terms with Turkey.

The fact that Gandhi swept the political board by the end of the year must not blind us to the odds against him. Some of the best known public figures among Moderates as well as Extremists questioned the wisdom of his programme. Early in the year

C. P. Ramaswami Iyer, then a brilliant and influential Congressman, had urged Gandhi to avoid, 'what has happened in America, namely the reluctance of gentlemen to enter the political arena'. Annie Besant warned Gandhi against unleashing forces which he would be unable to control, and Srinivasa Sastri begged him to keep out of the Khilafat agitation. 'We have no right to embarrass the Government of India,' wrote Sastri, 'if through causes beyond their control, the Turkish question takes an unfavourable turn.' H. S. L. Polak, a London solicitor, who had been an intimate associate and confidant of Gandhi during the Satyagraha struggle in South Africa, described the non-co-operation programme as 'ill-advised, harmful and inappropriate'.[9] 'I am strongly inclined to think,' wrote Polak, 'that even if you had a national government ruling the country in accordance with the average wishes of your compatriots, you would not feel content, unless you were challenging it upon one point or another. I quite appreciate that this may well be your individual method of self-expression. But does it not occur to you what you may do as an individual you are not necessarily free to do as a member of a group or as a national leader?'

In his presidential speech at Amritsar Motilal had described Gandhi 'as the most revered Indian of the day', and 'the great Satyagraha movement as a new force with tremendous potentialities'.[10] Nevertheless, his conversion to non-co-operation was neither quick nor easy. 'As far as I can see,' he wrote on June 16, 1920, 'it is not likely that the Congress as Congress will bind itself to non-co-operation. It is too big an organization for this.' In the same letter he suggested to his son that it was time they selected for themselves constituencies for the U.P. Council to which elections were due later in the year.

Since 1917 Motilal's politics had been growing progressively more radical. He had broken with his Moderate friends in 1918 over the Montagu-Chelmsford reforms. Yet it was not easy for him to go all the way with Gandhi, to exchange the politics of calculated risks for those of incalculable risks, to make a clean break with the constitutional traditions in which he had been bred, to accept not only new tactics but a new game, the rules of which were being formulated by its author while it was being played. The personal aspect was no less important than the

[9] Polak to Gandhi, August 21, 1920. (G.S.N.).
[10] Natesan (Editor), *Congress Presidential Addresses* (1911 to 1934), p. 431.

political. It required an effort of will to give up legal practice, to slough off the luxury of a lifetime, to deprive the family of comforts to which it was accustomed. During the Mussoorie episode, Motilal had pleaded with his son not to precipitate a crisis. The consequences, he wrote (June 3, 1920), 'are so obvious both from the public and private point of view that it is hardly necessary to discuss them. It will mean the final break-up of the family and the upsetting of all public, private and professional work. One thing will lead to another, and something is sure to turn up which will compel me to follow you to the gaol or something similar'.

Motilal prided himself on his objectivity, but it is a strange paradox that in the greatest decision of his life he was guided as much by his heart as by his head. It was love of his son that enabled him to take the last crucial step over the precipice. The Punjab tragedy had helped to bring Jawaharlal completely under Gandhi's wing. In 1920, young Nehru was frequently seen with the Mahatma, from whom he received from the first extraordinary consideration and affection. In fact Motilal was already looking to his son to interpret Gandhi's moves on the political chequerboard. 'I could not find time to have a quiet talk with Gandhiji as to what he expects us to do,' Motilal wrote to Jawaharlal on June 3rd, 'I hope he has given you some indication before he left this morning.' A few days later, a note in favour of Council-entry, drafted jointly by Motilal and C. R. Das, was carried by Jawaharlal to Gandhi at Bombay.

Jawaharlal seemed determined to go the Gandhi way. In February, 1919, and again in May, 1920, Motilal had seen his son straining at the leash. Was it not better to push himself forward than to try in vain to pull his son back? Was it not better for father and son to march together – even if it was to prison? The image of a doting father trailing after a dashing son is an absurd over-simplification, but there is no doubt that the conversion of the son made that of the father inevitable, and merely a matter of time.

It is only fair to add that the relationship which had been established between Motilal and Gandhi during their stay in Lahore in the last weeks of 1919 facilitated Motilal's conversion. No two men could have been more different. 'Gandhi was the saint, the stoic, the man of religion, one who went through life rejecting what it offers in the way of sensation and physical pleasure,' and Motilal was 'a bit of an epicure, who accepted life and welcomed and enjoyed its many sensations, and cared little for what may come in the hereafter'.[11] Motilal admired Gandhi; he did not, however, pretend to appreciate all the bees in his bonnet; nor did he rate highly the intelligence of the eccentric fringe in the Mahatma's entourage. On his part, Gandhi had good reasons for according high regard to Motilal, who was eight years his senior, a man of outstanding ability, and also young Jawaharlal's father. The links of mutual esteem which were thus forged between Sabarmati and Anand Bhawan were to provide emotional sustenance for the Nehru family. They were also to exercise a profound influence on the course of the Indian freedom movement.

At the Calcutta Congress, Gandhi's plight (as he recalled many years later)[12] was 'pitiable'. He was opposed by an imposing phalanx of veteran leaders including Malaviya, C. R. Das and Lajpat Rai – the President of the session. The discussions in the 'Subjects Committee' were prolonged; the crucial resolution on a boycott of the legislatures was carried with the narrow majority of seven votes. Motilal, as the official historian of the Congress has recorded,[13] was the only front-rank Congress leader who supported Gandhi at the Calcutta Congress. As a result, he found himself in the three-man sub-committee, including Gandhi and V. J. Patel, which worked out the details of the non-co-operation programme – the boycott of titles and honorary offices, of official functions and *durbars*, of Government-owned or aided schools and colleges, of law courts and legislatures and, above all, of foreign goods.

Immediately after the Calcutta Congress Motilal resigned his membership of the U.P. Council, and announced that he would not seek election to the reformed legislatures. He wound up his legal practice, withdrew his daughter Krishna from the local school which she had recently joined, disposed of his horses, carriages, dogs, treasured crystal and china. Life at Anand Bhawan underwent a sudden metamorphosis. The two cuisines were reduced to one; the cellar was abolished altogether. The army of servants was drastically curtailed. Foreign finery was discarded and cartloads of it were consigned to public bonfires.

11 Nehru, J., *Toward Freedom*, p. 66.
12 Gandhi, M. K., *My Experiments with Truth*, p. 610.
13 Sitaramayya, P., *History of the Indian National Congress*, vol. I, p. 207.

From the select club of the *élite* of Allahabad, Anand Bhawan
turned into a caravanserai frequented by humble-looking folk
clad in homespun – party members sojourning in or passing
through Allahabad. With political workers flitting in and out at
odd hours, the household was in chaos – an ordeal for the women
of the family, who found themselves robbed overnight not only
of comfort, but of the quiet and privacy to which they were
accustomed. Thanks to the ascetic streak which lies just beneath
the surface in Hindu womanhood, Swarup Rani, Kamala and the
girls quickly adapted themselves to the changes. The process of
adjustment was helped by the fact that the author of the metamorphosis was a holy man.

For Motilal the final step had not been easy, but once it was
taken, he never looked back. He had spent money with the same
facility with which he had earned it. 'No man in his senses,' he
wrote on October 27, 1920, to his Arrah client, who was making
difficulties about payment of his dues, 'can for a moment doubt
the supreme contempt I have always had for money. My whole
life is an illustration of this. I have so far been sought by it and
have now forcibly closed my doors in its face.'

Before long Motilal was savouring the new simplicity with
the same gusto with which he had relished the luxuries he had
voluntarily renounced. A glimpse into the changed mode of his
life can be had from a letter he wrote to Gandhi in the summer
of 1921 from a health-resort: '. . . The brass cooker . . . has taken
the place of the two kitchens, a solitary servant, not over-in-
telligent that of the old retinue – three small bags containing
rice, *dal* and *masala* that of the mule-loads of provisions . . .
one square meal of rice, *dal*, vegetable, sometimes *khir* [milk and
rice cooked together] in the middle of the day, that of breakfast,
lunch and dinner "a l'Anglaise" . . . The *shikar* has given place
to long walks, and rifles and guns to books, magazines and newspapers (the favourite book being Edwin Arnold's *Song Celestial*
which is undergoing its third reading). "What a fall, my
countrymen!" But, really, I have never enjoyed life better.'

Motilal had laid aside his Savile Row suits, but even the home-
spun *khadi* sat well on him. St Nihal Singh, the journalist, who
had enjoyed Motilal's hospitality in 1910 in the heyday of his
anglicism, noted the contrast twelve years later.

'A tiny *khaddar* cap of Mahatma Gandhi's invention,' St

Nihal Singh recalled, 'sat saucily I thought upon Panditji's head. He wore no coat nor waistcoat. A long *khaddar* shirt – *kurta* we call it in the Punjab – came down to his knees . . . his feet were bare, and he had gold-embroidered shoes . . . The home-spun in which he was clad was coarse. It seemed to add distinction to his handsome face and figure. It certainly did not detract from them. The pure white of the *khaddar* harmonized exceedingly well with his hair and moustaches that had gone grey during the interval between our two meetings. The years had left a few marks upon his face, but he looked robust . . .

' "A great change, Panditji," I remarked as we sat down in a corner.

' "Only in the externals I hope," he replied.

' "Mentally, too, I believe," I said.

' "Hardly, I have been a rebel all my life. I must have been born a rebel." '[14]

[14] *Leader*, February 18, 1931.

CHAPTER SEVENTEEN

HIGH TIDE

'WHAT is a matter of grave concern to me,' Motilal wrote to Gandhi soon after the Calcutta Congress, 'is not the giving up of the [legal] practice, but the fate of the *Independent*.' The *Independent* started its career on February 5, 1919, before the passage of the Rowlatt Bills and the Satyagraha movement brought Gandhi to the forefront of national politics. Motilal had thus defined the aims of his newspaper:

'The *Independent* has come into existence, to lay bare the soul of a nation, of a people ripening into nationhood, of communities merging into a people, of individuals growing into a community. How shall it approach its noble work? or better still, how not? Not along the facile line of opportunism, the fatal line of least resistance. . . But by bringing the fierce light of day to play upon dark spots wherever they exist. By striving to press home the eternal truth that . . . while on the one hand national rights cannot be withheld to be doled out in little bits with a consciousness of high-minded generosity, those rights cannot, on the other hand, thrive in an atmosphere of religious cleavage and racial antagonism. Thus alone can the *Independent* fulfil its mission.'

Not all Motilal's idealism nor all his money could make the venture a success. The high salaries which he offered created a stir in the world of Indian journalism and even succeeded in weaning[1] some journalists from the local rival, the *Leader*, but financial mismanagement ultimately sealed the fate of the *Independent*. B. G. Horniman, the editor of the *Bombay Chronicle*, who was Motilal's chief adviser in starting the new paper, was a fiery journalist, but he had little insight into the business side of a daily paper.[2]

[1] Iyengar, A. S., *All Through the Gandhian Era*, p. 17.
[2] Jayakar, M. R., *The Story of My Life*, vol. I, p. 245.

The first editor of the *Independent* was Syud Hossain, who had served on the *Bombay Chronicle*. Under his editorship the *Independent* made a promising start, but it soon ran into difficulties and became a great drain on Motilal's bank balance just when, owing to his preoccupation with politics, his own income was dwindling. By the beginning of 1920, the *Independent* had become a headache to Motilal. It had not been easy to find a suitable editor after Syud Hossain's departure. Jawaharlal tried to step into the breach, but he had too many other interests. And even Jawaharlal found that it was easier to dash off an article than to unravel the managerial and financial tangles of the paper.

Motilal was the Chairman of the Board of Directors of 'Nationalist Journals' which owned the *Independent*. The other directors were Syed Hyder Mehdi, Syed Nabi Ullah, Janki Nath Chak and Jawaharlal. Early in February there was a crucial meeting of the Board of Directors at Allahabad, but Motilal was unable to leave Arrah even for a few hours.

Motilal to Jawaharlal, February 10, 1920: 'Your note on the "Ind" [*Independent*]. I am sorry I do not follow your figures. It is easy to pass a resolution to continue the paper, but difficult to do so in decent form. What arrangements have been made for the supply of paper, types, etc.? Where is the money to come from? Who is to do the editorial work? I am thoroughly dissatisfied with Ranga Iyer, and cannot give him a free hand to put in any nonsense he likes . . . For the last nine months we have been playing at this stupid game. You say Joseph is out of the question [as editor]. He is a thousand times better than Ranga Iyer, who cannot be trusted to write a single line without pre-censorship either by you or someone else . . . Lajpat Rai is a good idea for the editorship . . . but by the time he is ready to take charge[3] (if at all) the "Ind" will be buried and forgotten. You cannot go on with your present bank balance and income even for a month . . . Had I been present at the meeting I should have voted for complete suspension for a time . . .'

A few days later Motilal tried to sell some shares in 'Nationalist Journals' during his visit to Calcutta, but without success. He could not interest financiers, but was able to enlist

[3] Lajpat Rai was expected to return to India from abroad.

the services of Bipin Chandra Pal for regular editorial assign-
ments. Since the partition of Bengal, Pal had been a popular
hero in Bengal and indeed in the whole of India; in 1920 his
name was still one to conjure with. He was modest in his demands and offered to write four articles a week for sixty rupees.
'He expects payment punctually every Saturday,' Motilal wrote,
'the poor man is really hard up.' In May Pal became editor of the
Independent at a monthly salary of Rs. 500; one of his sons was
appointed a sub-editor at Rs. 100 a month, and another son who
was in England was to work as a foreign correspondent for £6
a week. At the same time Motilal appointed his energetic nephew
Mohan Lal Nehru as the manager of the paper. The hope that
these appointments would bolster up the prestige of the
Independent and bring in fresh capital was not to be realized.
B. C. Pal's politics were out of step with those of the Nehrus; his
flamboyance outran his discretion, and the guns of the *Independent*, to Motilal's consternation, were turned on Gandhi and
the Congress. Within ten days Motilal was asking his son to
'take Bipin Pal in hand. He has run amuck, abusing all
nationalists without any distinction. His last attack on Gandhi
is about "the limit". The *Ind* appears to be doomed. Whoever
comes to it loses his head'.

The *Independent* lingered on for another three years. By
October, 1920, Motilal had sunk Rs. 80,000 in the paper, which
needed a lakh and a half to work off its liabilities. He addressed
a confidential appeal to friends:

'I have given away freely from the earnings of my practice at
the Bar whatever was necessary to keep it afloat, but these earnings have now ceased and I cannot possibly give what I do not
possess. I can therefore no longer give to the *Independent* anything like the help I have so far given single-handed.'

It would be incorrect to regard the story of the *Independent* as
merely one of editorial ineptitude and financial mismanagement.
It provided a useful, perhaps essential, outlet for the political
and literary enthusiasms of Jawaharlal, whose articles gladdened
his father's heart. 'The leading article in the "Ind", which Nagu
brought was excellent,' Motilal wrote from Arrah (February 26,
1920), 'I smelt Jawahar in every word and sentence.' In spite of
all the headaches it gave to the Nehrus, the *Independent* was

decidedly a political asset in the autumn of 1920. 'It is the only English daily in India,' Motilal proudly wrote to Gandhi on September 17, 1920, 'to support the full programme of non-co-operation.'

2

Gandhi's spectacular success in capturing the Congress in 1920 was not the foregone conclusion it might appear in the light of later history. True, he had caught the imagination of the masses, but he had also awakened much doubt and heart-searching in the intelligentsia. The Calcutta Congress, as we have already seen, was no walk-over for him. The Government of India hoped to the last that he would overplay his hand and lose credit with the Congress. 'I think,' Sir William Vincent, the Home Member, wrote on April 26, 1919, 'that a good many people will soon tire of Mr Gandhi and his vagaries.'[4] And as late as September 4, 1920, the Government of India, pinning its hopes on a split in the Congress, told the provincial government that non-interference towards non-co-operation was the 'wisest policy'.[5] These hopes were baffled by Gandhi's consummate skill, patience and humility, which enabled him to win over his critics, to change the creed of the Congress, to amend its constitution and to convert it from a 'three-day picnic of the urban gentry' into a broad-based militant organization in touch with the masses.

Non-co-operation was not a magic wand; it had to contend with the scepticism of the leaders, and the inertia of the rank and file. 'What is troubling me,' Motilal complained to his son, 'is the solid inactivity of our party.' 'There is any amount of work to be done,' he wrote, 'but no workers. You cannot do everything single-handed.'

The Nehrus could not do everything, but they did a lot. Since the spring of 1919, Jawaharlal had virtually given up his practice at the Bar. In the autumn of 1920 Motilal also became a full-time politician. He was elected a member of the Working Committee – the national executive of the Congress – and also one of the three General Secretaries for the year 1921. Since the office

[4] Minute. (N.A.I.).
[5] Nanda, B. R., *Mahatma Gandhi*, p. 220.

of the All India Congress Committee was located in his house at
Allahabad, the brunt of the work was inevitably borne by him.
He brought to his political work the same singleness of purpose,
eye for detail and strong common-sense which had enabled him
to dominate the Allahabad Bar.

As General Secretary of the Congress, Motilal clashed with
the president for the year, C. Vijiaraghavachariar, the veteran
lawyer and Congressman from the South, whose lack of enthusiasm for non-co-operation had been apparent even at the
Nagpur Congress over which he had presided, and who raised
issues which could have seriously distracted the Congress. Motilal
completely by-passed old Vijiraghavachariar who tearfully complained to Gandhi: 'I deeply, very deeply feel the humiliating
position to which the over-enthusiastic Panditji has subjected
me under your auspices.'

The non-co-operation movement confirmed Gandhi as the un-
disputed leader of the Congress and as a great father-figure.
'Gandhism is more than a political movement,' John Clayton, the
correspondent of the *Chicago Tribune* wrote on March 1, 1922,
after an interview with the Mahatma, 'it is a religion among the
followers of this amazing Indian leader . . . He is a master-
philosopher of God to these men and women.' Gandhi's
asceticism, simplicity and saintliness struck deep chords of
Indian humanity. He seemed like a *rishi* [sage] from some
ancient epic come to bring about the liberation of India. His
parables struck home: his analogies were drawn from Hindu
epics. Indian politics became a strange mixture of 'nationalism
and politics and religion and mysticism and fanaticism'. The
mists of Khilafat lent a romantic enchantment to non-co-operation in the eyes of the Muslims. The Hindus needed no
extraneous impulse to yield their willing allegiance to the
Mahatma. Even a hard-headed lawyer like Jayakar could be
so profoundly moved as to write to Gandhi in March, 1922: 'It
is a singular fortune of India that, at this crisis, her greatest
leader is also the humblest *Bhakta* [devotee]. That fact must
secure for his noble mission the blessing and co-operation of
Divine Providence.'[6]

Motilal was not swept off his feet by this emotional tide, but
he was not entirely unaffected by it. The religious impulse behind the non-co-operation movement appealed to Swarup Rani

[6] Jayakar, M. R., *The Story of My Life*, vol. I, p. 586.

and Kamala. The girls turned vegetarian; Motilal himself became an abstainer and could even be seen poring over Sir Edwin Arnold's translation of the *Gita*. As for Jawaharlal, he confessed later that he 'came nearer to a religious frame of mind in 1921 than at any other time since my early boyhood'.[7]

Religious emotion was to prove a two-edged weapon. But while it lasted it produced a sense of exaltation, which may be glimpsed in Jawaharlal's autobiography:

'We were full of excitement and optimism and a buoyant enthusiasm. We sensed the happiness of a person crusading for a cause . . . The old feeling of oppression and frustration was completely gone. There was no more whispering, no roundabout phraseology to avoid getting into trouble with the authorities. We said what we felt and shouted it out from the house-tops . . . We were proud of our leader and of the unique method he had evolved and we indulged in fits of self-righteousness. In the midst of strife and while we ourselves encouraged that strife, we had a sense of inner peace.'[8]

As the morale of non-co-operators went up, that of the authorities went down. A striking example of this new equation was furnished in May, 1921, when Sarup, Motilal's elder daughter, was married to Ranjit Pandit, the handsome barrister-scholar from Rajkot. A number of prominent Congress and Khilafat leaders came to Allahabad to attend the wedding. The concentration of political leaders at Allahabad, coupled with the fact that the date chosen by the priests – May 10th – happened to be the anniversary of the Mutiny, made the imagination of the British officials run riot. Such was the panic into which they worked themselves that there was talk of removing European women and children to the Allahabad fort for greater safety. That anyone could have credited Motilal Nehru and Gandhi with designs of a violent uprising appears fantastic today; but it shows the widening gulf between the rulers and the ruled in those critical years 1920-22.

A few days after the wedding Motilal went to Almora in the Kumaon hills to recover from a particularly malignant attack of asthma. At Kathgodam, the rail terminus, while he was in the

7 Nehru, J. L., *Toward Freedom,* p. 72.
8 *Ibid.,* pp. 69-70.

refreshment room, hundreds of people surrounded his car and decorated it with paper flags and bunting. 'I was so short of breath,' he wrote, 'that I could not say even a few words to them.' At Almora, where he stayed with his nephew Shridhar Nehru of the Indian Civil Service, a crowd collected and insisted that he should speak to them. 'Shridhar looked very uncomfortable,' he wrote, 'each time a lusty *jai* [shout] was sent up by the crowd.'

Henceforth it was to be difficult for Motilal to have any private life: he and his family were to be as much in the public eye as Gandhi himself and as time went on he had his full share of the troubles which are part of public life. He had his first shock in May, 1921, when Gandhi went to Simla for a series of interviews with Lord Reading, who had just succeeded Lord Chelmsford as Viceroy. It was given out that Gandhi had agreed to persuade the Khilafat leader Mohamed Ali to withdraw certain passages in a speech which were considered susceptible of incitement to violence. The official communiqué did less than justice to Gandhi's viewpoint, and the confidential nature of the talks prevented Gandhi from being more explicit. Nevertheless Gandhi did not see any harm in reiterating and emphasizing that non-violence was the sheet-anchor of his movement. This was not how Motilal viewed the episode.

'We have the indisputable fact,' he wrote indignantly to Gandhi (June 3, 1921) 'that the leader of the N.C.O.[9] movement has been in treaty with the Government of India, and has secured the suspension of the prosecution of Ali Brothers by inducing them to give a public apology and an undertaking . . . Very serious questions affecting the whole movement arise for consideration. Indeed it seems to me that the whole principle of non-co-operation has been given away.'

The Viceroy, who believed that he had outwitted and out-manoeuvred Gandhi, gleefully wrote to his son:

'If trouble comes between him [Mohamed Ali] and Gandhi, it means that collapse of the bridge over the gulf between Hindu and Muslim.'

[9] Non-co-operation.

It was not the first time that the real significance of Gandhi's action was lost on his adherents as well as his opponents; they failed to see that Satyagraha did not admit of an irrevocable distinction between friend and foe, peace and war, and that even while the battle was in progress, bridgeheads had to be held for the ultimate meeting of minds and hearts.

In 1921, Gandhi was under increasing pressure from within the Congress to tighten the screws on the Government. There was a clamour for a 'mass movement'. Gandhi described civil disobedience as a 'general upheaval on the political plane'; it was the most drastic remedy in the pharmacopoeia of Satyagraha and it could not be lightly applied. He had been perturbed by outbreaks of violence in Ahmedabad and Amritsar in 1919 and in Malabar and Bombay in 1921. The Mahatma's caution was not appreciated by his adherents who were burning to deliver hammer-blows at the bureaucracy. An eye-witness records that when he argued at a meeting of the Congress Working Committee in November, 1921, that people needed to be trained in hand-spinning before being allowed to offer civil disobedience, 'Pandit Motilal Nehru burst out laughing. Messrs Kelkar and Patel indulged in loud and angry protests'.[10]

If Gandhi had his reasons for restraint, so had the Government. It was anxious not to precipitate a show-down. It did not want to alienate the Moderates, who venerated Gandhi even though they differed from him. It was reluctant to take any measures which might have the effect of strangling the reforms at birth. It hoped for a split in the Congress; but a split did not come. Indeed, by the time Lord Reading became Viceroy Gandhi had acquired a messianic halo which made it difficult for the Government to balance the risks of his arrest against the dangers of inaction.

In September, 1921, the Ali Brothers, the most prominent of the Khilafat leaders, were arrested on a charge of trying to subvert the British Indian army. Soon afterwards forty-five Indian leaders, headed by Gandhi, issued a manifesto affirming that it was 'contrary to the national dignity for any Indian to serve as a civilian and more as a soldier under a system of Government which has brought about India's economic, moral and political degradation'. Both Motilal and Jawaharlal signed the manifesto – the latter in Hindi.

[10] Krishandas, *Seven Months with Mahatma Gandhi*, vol. I, p. 410.

This was an open challenge which the Government would have taken up at once, but for the impending visit of the Prince of Wales in November, 1921.[11] Nevertheless, there were signs of a stiffening of official policy towards non-co-operation. When the Government enforced the Criminal Law Amendment Act and the Seditious Meetings Act to ban volunteer organizations and public meetings, Gandhi made it a *casus belli*. It may seem strange that he challenged the Government on freedom of speech or association rather than on the larger issue of *Khilafat* or *Swaraj*. But he always preferred a concrete to an abstract issue; moreover, he was shrewd enough to see that without these elementary rights, a peaceful popular movement could be quickly snuffed out.

3

'It is essential,' the Viceroy cabled to the Secretary of State on November 24, 1921, 'to take action on more drastic and comprehensive scale . . . Local Governments are being assured by us of our full support should police or military be compelled to fire . . . We are informing them that they should not hesitate to prosecute . . . any person, however prominent, whose arrest and prosecution they consider, is required for maintenance of law and respect of authority . . .'[12]

December opened with the arrests of a number of prominent leaders. Lajpat Rai was arrested in the Punjab. On December 5th, a number of leading non-co-operators were rounded up in Allahabad. On the afternoon of December 6th, while M. S. Godbole, the office secretary of the All India Congress Committee, was in Anand Bhawan showing some papers to Motilal, a servant announced the arrival of a police officer. What followed may best be described in Godbole's words.

Godbole to Gandhi, December 7, 1921: 'Panditji . . . calmly asked him [the police officer] to be introduced . . . He saluted Panditji in his right royal U.P. fashion, shouting courteously: "Adabaraj"[13] and the salute was returned in the same manner by Panditji. After a formal greeting, he presented a search warrant

---

[11] For further details, see the author's *Mahatma Gandhi*, pp. 222-28.
[12] Unpublished. (N.A.I.).
[13] 'I beg to offer my greetings.'

... Panditji told him that his whole house was open for search ... but added ... to search his house they would not take less than six months to do justice to it. This was [Panditji's] inborn humour ...

'I could see the poor fellow [the police officer] wanted to say something more which he could not take the courage to say. But Panditji came to his rescue. Reading the search warrant again ... he asked the [police official] if Government wanted to prosecute him under the Second clause of Section 17 of the Criminal Law Amendment Act. "Yes, sir, and I have a warrant of arrest also in my pocket," was the prompt reply ... "Oh, I am ready for it," said Panditji, "but why did you not produce it all at once?" '[14]

The police officer was visibly nervous, but somehow he made it known that he had a warrant for the arrest of Jawaharlal as well. The grounds of Anand Bhawan were soon filled with friends and admirers. And then, to resume Godbole's account:

'The police ordered a motor, and the Pandits, old and young, father and son, son and father (spiritually Motilalji regards Jawaharlal as his father as you know) gladly entered [the car].'

Motilal dictated a farewell message to his countrymen:

'Having served you to the best of my ability, it is now my high privilege to serve the motherland by going to gaol with my only son.'

Swarup Rani, who was interviewed by a press correspondent, admitted that her heart was not entirely free from 'the wrench of separation', but she 'rejoiced in the great privilege of sending my dear husband and my only son to jail'. The words, 'the only son', were heavily charged with emotion, but Swarup Rani added: 'Mahatma Gandhi told me once that others in the world have also their only sons'.

As the police van drove out of the house the grey-haired, frail Swarup Rani nearly broke down; her 22-year-old daughter-in-law Kamala bravely held back her tears. These last twelve months had demanded much from them; their whole world had

[14] G.S.N. Papers.

been turned upside-down, and now they had taken leave of their menfolk for they did not know how long. Suspense, loneliness and heartache were going to be their portion for the rest of their lives.

The clean sweep of the Congress and Khilafat leaders in Allahabad did not prevent a complete *hartal* on the occasion of the Prince of Wales's visit, which Motilal had organized before his arrest. When Prince Edward arrived at the Senate Hall to receive a welcome address from the Allahabad University, most of the students were absent. Those who were present had to go without food that evening; the servants in the students' hostel refused to serve them.[15]

The following day, on December 7th, Motilal's trial opened in an improvised courtroom in the gaol before K. N. Knox, I.C.S., who had been Jawaharlal's colleague in the local St John Ambulance Brigade. Banerjee, the Government Advocate, was an old friend of Motilal and obviously ill at ease. The charge that Motilal was a Congress volunteer hardly needed any corroboration; his name had headed the list of volunteers published in his own paper, the *Independent*. However, the police did not take any chances; they produced Kirpa Ram Brahmin, a tattered and evidently illiterate fellow, who pretended to verify Motilal's signatures in Hindi by holding the documents upside down. Motilal refused to defend himself; with his four-year-old granddaughter Indira in his arms, he cheerfully sat through the trial, which he described as a 'farce'. He was sentenced to six months' imprisonment and a fine of Rs. 500. A similar sentence was awarded to Jawaharlal who was tried separately for distributing handbills for a *hartal*. The fines were small, but both father and son refused to pay them: as non-co-operators they could not admit the jurisdiction of British courts. This gave the local police a pretext for making raids on Anand Bhawan and carrying away, despite the angry protests of little Indira, furniture and carpets worth thousands in lieu of fines of a few hundreds. For the ladies of the Nehru family, this police vandalism was a valuable training in patience. Soon after the trial, they went to Ahmedabad in response to an invitation from Gandhi to attend the annual Congress session. Swarup Rani, Kamala, Krishna and Indira had their first experience of a train journey in third class. At Ahmedabad they were soothed and uplifted by the presence

[15] *University of Allahabad 70th Anniversary Souvenir*, p. 112.

of the Mahatma, but it was hard to fit in with the *ashram* routine of waking up at 4 a.m., assembling for prayers on the banks of the Sabarmati, partaking of simple but tasteless meals, sleeping on the floor, cleaning plates and washing clothes.

Anand Bhawan

Motilal Nehru launching the *Jalduta*—a ship of the Scindia Steam Navigation Company at Glasgow in 1927. Also seen in the picture are Jawaharlal Nehru, Kamala and Krishna

CHAPTER EIGHTEEN

LOW TIDE

THE Nehrus were lodged in the District Gaol at Lucknow, the headquarters of the Lieutenant-Governor, Sir Harcourt Butler, whom Motilal had known for thirty years. Arthur Moore, a former editor of *The Statesman*, has recently repeated a story which was widely current in the nineteen twenties:

'Motilal was dining with Sir Harcourt and no doubt, feeling his political views changing . . . and possibly shades of the prison house beginning to close around him, said laughingly to Sir Harcourt over their champagne . . . that one day soon he might be in prison. To which Sir Harcourt replied, "Well if that happens, I will see that you get champagne".'

Moore says that the Governor was as good as his word, and throughout Motilal's term in gaol an A.D.C. turned up from the Government House daily with 'a half-bottle of champagne wrapped in a napkin'.[1]

This is a delightful anecdote; only it is not true. For one thing, under the first impact of Gandhian austerity, Motilal had at this time become a teetotaller. For another, it is difficult to believe that even a smart A.D.C. could have smuggled champagne for the elder Nehru without the knowledge of his son and nephews who lived in the same barrack. Arthur Moore has cited for his story Motilal's own testimony. As against this, Dewan Chaman Lall recalls a conversation he heard between Motilal and Aldous Huxley at a dinner party in Western Court during the latter's visit to India. Asked by Huxley if Sir Harcourt Butler had provided him with maple furniture and champagne in gaol, Motilal laughed and said: 'No, it is not true. But in the good old days rivers of champagne must have flowed between us.'

Sir Harcourt's Government did not send champagne, but it did something to make Motilal's lot tolerable in gaol. He had the

[1] Zakaria, Rafiq (Editor), A *Study of Nehru*, p. 173.

company of his son and two nephews, Shamlal and Mohanlal. He was permitted to supplement his food from outside, to write letters, to obtain newspapers and books. Godbole – whose eye-witness account of Motilal's arrest has already been quoted[2] – had noted that the police officer deputed to arrest Motilal was visibly hesitant, almost apologetic. The awe in which prison officials stood of the elder Nehru is illustrated by the story of a visit to Lucknow gaol by Motilal's nephew Brijlal Nehru, who was on a short visit to India from Burma. Accompanied by his wife Rameshwari Nehru, son Braj Kumar, and brother Kishenlal, Brijlal arrived at the gaol gates, but was informed that not more than three visitors could be admitted. Brijlal decided to stay out, and the rest of the party went in. Motilal was furious when he learned that his nephew had been kept out; he sent for the Gaol Superintendent and demanded why the number of visitors had been restricted without his – Motilal's – approval. The Superintendent did not wait to contest the propriety of this remarkable query from his distinguished prisoner, but issued orders that Brijlal should be admitted at once and the new rule should not be applied to the Nehrus.

This was Jawaharlal's first imprisonment, but already he seemed to be in his element. Unlike many Indian nationalists, he did not seek serenity by diving into the Hindu scriptures, but with the zest of a public schoolboy plunged into a feverish routine of physical and mental activity. He swept and dusted the gaol barrack, washed his father's and his own clothes, plied the spinning wheel, read and discussed energetically and con-ducted evening classes for the prisoners. He ministered to his father's wants and nursed him with a devotion which would have been impossible in the servant-ridden Anand Bhawan.

As 1922 dawned, Lucknow gaol resounded with nationalist slogans. Truck-loads of political prisoners arrived daily. The tide of non-co-operation was running high. The climax came on February 1, 1920, when Gandhi wrote to the Viceroy informing him that civil disobedience was about to begin in Bardoli in Bombay Presidency.

2

The Nehrus strained their ears for a clarion call to the final

[2] *Supra*, p. 196.

battle against foreign rule; all they heard was the bugle of retreat. Three days after the Mahatma had sent his ultimatum to Lord Reading, there was a clash between a procession and a party of police at Chauri Chaura, a small village in the United Provinces. The police station was burnt down and twenty-two persons, including the young son of the Sub-Inspector of Police, lost their lives. According to Devadas, Gandhi's youngest son, who visited the scene of the tragedy soon afterwards and sent a confidential report to his father, the procession was unarmed, the initial provocation had come from the police, and the attack on the police station was not premeditated. The High Court came to contrary conclusions, but even Devadas reported that the rioters were heard shouting: 'Gandhi ki Jai'.

Gandhi viewed the Chauri Chaura tragedy as a red signal, a warning that the atmosphere in the country was too explosive for a mass movement. He decided to retrace his steps, to concel the plans for civil disobedience in Bardoli, to suspend the 'aggressive' part of the non-co-operation campaign and to shift the emphasis to the 'constructive' programme of hand-spinning, communal unity, abolition of untouchability, etc.

These decisions were like a clap of thunder to the Mahatma's adherents. Probably no one was closer to him than his faithful secretary Mahadev Desai; but even Desai wrote from Agra gaol (February 15th) that the shock had 'absolutely unhinged' him.[3] Lajpat Rai addressed a circular letter[4] to the Congress Working Committee in which he described Gandhi as 'one of the greatest men of all ages, all times and all countries. Yet that is exactly the reason why we have to swallow the bitter pill of ignominious defeat today . . . Our defeat is in proportion to the greatness of our leader . . . Mahatmaji pitched his standard too high . . . To change the hearts of mobs in such a way as to make it impossible for them to indulge in such brutalities without changing the hearts of Governments, that rule over them is an impossibility . . . Leaders of political campaigns for freedom cannot afford to wear their hearts on their sleeves . . .'

In Lucknow gaol the reactions of the Nehrus were equally violent. Motilal was beside himself with anger, while his son vented his despair in a letter which Gandhi described 'as a freezing dose'. In a long letter the Mahatma sought to justify

[3] Unpublished. Desai to Gandhi (G.S.N.).
[4] G.S.N. Papers.

his *volte face* and to soothe the nerves of both father and son.

Gandhi to Jawaharlal: February 19, 1922: '. . . I see that all of you are terribly cut up over the resolutions of the Working Committee. I sympathize with you, and my heart goes out to Father.[5] I can picture to myself the agony through which he must have passed, but I also feel that this letter is unnecessary because I know that the first shock must have been followed by a true understanding of the situation . . .

'I must tell you that this Chauri Chaura incident was the last straw . . . I received letters both from Hindus and Mohammedans from Calcutta, Allahabad and the Punjab, all these before the Gorakhpur incident, telling me that the wrong was not all on the Government's side, that our people were becoming aggressive, defiant and threatening, that they were getting out of hand . . . I assure you that if the thing had not been suspended we would have been leading not a non-violent struggle but essentially a violent struggle . . . The cause will prosper by this retreat. The movement had unconsciously drifted from the right path. We have come back to our moorings . . .'

Contrary to the belief current at the time, Gandhi's arrest was delayed rather than precipitated by the aftermath of Chauri-Chaura. Reading was being pressed by Montagu, and Montagu was being goaded by Parliament and the press in Britain, to adopt a sterner line towards Gandhi. Uncharitable critics were indeed whispering that India was being lost between two Jews, one in Whitehall, and the other in Delhi, who were not strong enough to grapple with Gandhi.[6] In 1920 Montagu had taken Chelmsford to task for questioning Gandhi's bona fides;[7] in 1922 he was chiding Reading for 'the continued freedom of Gandhi to organize and issue justifications of civil disobedience'.[8] Reading had decided to arrest Gandhi before the Chauri Chaura riot, but considered it politic to give Gandhi just sufficient time to go into reverse. By the end of February, the emasculated programme which Gandhi had already piloted through the Working Committee at Bardoli was finally ratified by the All India Congress

[5] Motilal.
[6] Winterton, Earl, *Orders of the Day*, p. 112.
[7] Nanda, B. R., *Mahatma Gandhi*, p. 197.
[8] Telegram to Viceroy, February 6, 1922 (N.A.I.).

Committee. On March 10th he was arrested, tried for sedition and sentenced to six years' imprisonment.

3

After the Chauri Chaura incident Lord Reading told his son that 'Gandhi had pretty well run himself to the last ditch as a politician.'[9] A few months later, the Viceroy traced the decline 'both of the non-co-operation movement and of the prestige of its leaders . . . from the issue of the Bardoli resolutions which left the organization without any clearly defined and intelligible objectives. From that moment, disintegration and disorganization set in; enthusiasm evaporated, disillusionment and discouragement prevailed in the ranks of the party.'[10]

Motilal would have agreed with this analysis. But he was too shrewd publicly to assail the Mahatma, who was in gaol, whose prestige was in any case independent of the success or failure of particular policies, and whose leadership would be indispensable in years to come. In a speech at Allahabad in June delivered soon after his release, he defended Gandhi's change of front. 'For the war in which we are engaged,' he said, 'we have chalked out an entirely new line. We fight entirely with new weapons unknown to history and only have our own mistakes to profit by.' He deplored the indiscipline that had crept into the non-co-operation movement. Mahatma Gandhi had made himself believe that he was leading a well-equipped army, but had discovered behind him 'a rabble either unarmed or badly armed, and a great number not even in their fighting uniforms'. After Chauri Chaura civil disobedience had not been abandoned but suspended. 'We may have to adjust our sails to the varying winds, we may have to alter our course to avoid the shoals and the breakers ahead, we may even have to drop anchor to allow the gathering mists to clear up. But there can be no question of our changing our destination or our good ship which we have chartered for the voyage.'

Motilal was to be one of the most important influences in setting a new course. In June, 1922, the All India Congress Committee met at Lucknow to consider measures to halt the

[9] Reading, Marquess of, *Rufus Isaacs, First Marquess of Reading*, vol. III, p. 249.
[10] Telegram to Secretary of State, December 5, 1922 (N.A.I.).

growing divisions and demoralization which had been sapping the Congress organization since Gandhi's arrest. Serious differences had arisen on at least one item in the non-co-operation programme – namely the boycott of legislatures.

This was the issue on which Gandhi had waged the hardest battle at the Calcutta Congress in September, 1920, won with the narrowest margin. Among those who had then opposed him was C. R. Das. Das was not at all happy at Gandhi's conduct of the campaign of non-co-operation. He did not like the way Gandhi spurned proposals for a Round Table Conference with the Government in December, 1921;[11] nor did he appreciate the reasons for the *volte face* after Chauri Chaura. Subhas Bose has recorded how Das 'was beside himself with anger and sorrow at the way Mahatma Gandhi was repeatedly bungling'.[12] On his release from gaol Das endorsed Motilal's pleas for council-entry, not in order to co-operate with the Government, but in order to create deadlocks which would compel the Viceroy and the Governors to use their emergency powers and thus expose the true nature of the 'mock parliaments' that had been set up in India.

The All India Congress Committee appointed a Civil Disobedience Enquiry Committee to tour the country and advise whether a reorientation of the Congress programme was necessary. The committee came to the conclusion that the country was not ready for civil disobedience on a large scale, but 'limited mass civil disobedience' on the responsibility of provincial congress committees could be permitted. On the vexed question of council-entry the committee reached a deadlock: three members, Hakim Ajmal Khan, V. J. Patel and Motilal favoured it, while the remaining three, Iyengar, Ansari and Rajagopalachari, were opposed to it. The report of the committee was discussed by the All India Congress Committee in November, 1922, but the final decision was left to the annual Congress session at Gaya.

Those who advocated Congress support for council entry – the 'Pro-Changers' – were led by C. R. Das and Motilal. The two men had been much thrown together during the years 1919-20 as members of the Congress Enquiry Committee in the Punjab, and later as rival counsel in the Dumraon case at Arrah. Temperamentally, they were poles apart. Motilal was severely

[11] Nanda, B. R., *Mahatma Gandhi*, pp. 227-8.
[12] Bose, Subhas Chandra, *The Indian Struggle*, p. 108.

rational, logical, impervious to emotion, particularly religious emotion. Das was alertness itself in the court-room and the legislative chamber, but had a strong vein of mysticism which expressed itself in tender verses and religious trances. Motilal's Olympian manner, stern exterior and caustic wit, while they lent a peculiar distinction to his personality, sometimes engendered in his colleagues a sense of inferiority which not infrequently avenged itself in ingratitude, sullenness and even open rebellion. The more emotional and volatile Das evoked fiercer loyalties.

Despite these temperamental differences Das and Motilal had much in common. Both were able and successful lawyers though success came to Das rather late in life. Both were patriots who gave their all – and they had much to give – to the national movement: Motilal's gift of Anand Bhawan in the last year of his life had an exact parallel in the donation by Das of his Calcutta residence, 148, Russa Road. Both were skilful parliamentarians. Both admired and respected Gandhi but were far from being 'whole-hoggers'. Both favoured flexibility and were irritated by the ethical straitjacket in which Gandhi seemed to wrap his politics. In 1922 both were unable to understand why, after the decline of non-co-operation, a new 'front' could not be opened in the legislatures.

The Das-Nehru combination met with stiff opposition from the 'No-changers' – those who opposed changes in the programme of non-co-operation as framed by Gandhi before his arrest. These included Rajendra Prasad, Vallabhbhai Patel, C. Vijiaraghavachariar; their chief spokesman was C. Rajagopalachari, already a leading Congressman and an exponent of Gandian dialectics. Rajagopalachari's keen wit, subtle logic and stamina in debate, working on the faith of the rank and file in the infallibility of the Mahatma, carried the day for the No-changers at the Gaya Congress. The result, 890 votes for council-entry and 1,740 against, was a crushing defeat for the 'Pro-Changers', particularly for Das, the president of the session.

Das and Motilal did not throw up the sponge. Immediately after the Congress session, on December 31, 1922, they convened a meeting of their supporters at the Gaya residence of the Maharaja of Tikari, a client of Motilal, and formed the 'Congress-Khilafat Swaraj Party'. Das was elected president and Motilal one of the secretaries. In fact the burden of organizing the party fell chiefly on Motilal. The new party, which came to be known as the Swaraj Party, accepted the creed of the Congress and the programme of non-co-operation, but decided to follow an independent line on the issue of council-entry.

The Gaya Congress witnessed only one round in a tug-of-war which was to last for the best part of 1923. While continuing to profess loyalty to Gandhi and the Congress, 'No-Changers' and 'Pro-Changers' engaged in a fierce struggle for the control of the party machine. Attempts at reconciliation invariably ended in fireworks of recrimination. Neither party was willing to change its ground or to accept responsibility for an irrevocable breach. Early in 1923, Abul Kalam Azad arranged a compromise: the Swarajists agreed to suspend propaganda in favour of council-entry while the 'No-Changers' raised funds and volunteers for a revival of mass civil disobedience; but if civil disobedience did not materialize by the end of April, each party was free to go its own way. The call for the revival of civil disobedience – as might well have been anticipated – fell flat. Meanwhile the Swarajists were growing impatient; they had little time to lose if they were to contest the elections at the end of the year. 'The pursuit of a phantasm': this was how Motilal described the attempts at *rapprochement* between the two groups in the Congress. Nevertheless, another attempt at a compromise was made in May, 1923, when the All India Congress Committee met at Bombay. It was proposed that the 'No-Changers' should desist from propaganda against council-entry. Rather than make this limited concession to their opponents, the 'No-Changers' on the Working Committee – Rajagopalachari, Vallabhbhai Patel, Rajendra Prasad and Jamnalal Bajaj – resigned. Das, who had offered his resignation from the presidency of the Congress at Gaya in December, 1922, but had been persuaded to continue, also finally stepped aside. A new Working Committee professing to represent a 'Centre Party' was elected. Dr Ansari became the new president and Jawaharlal one of the secretaries. But the days of the new Working Committee were numbered. 'It represented nobody in particular, and it tried to boss it over those who held the real power in the Congress organization.'[13] Jawaharlal was 'quite shocked at the way some prominent Congressmen could intrigue'. It did not take him long to discover how thankless was the role of a buffer between the warring groups.

[13] Nehru, J. L., *Autobiography*, p. 108.

Within a month of the Bombay compromise, Vallabhbhai Patel, one of the leading 'No-Changers', was provoked by a speech delivered by C. R. Das and fired a broadside at Jawaharlal, the peacemaker.

Vallabhbhai Patel to Jawaharlal, June 24, 1923: '. . . I trust you have been carefully following the adventures of Mr Das in Madras. Do you think that the sinking movement [of non-co-operation] can last long if terrific onslaughts are allowed to be delivered day after day without protest? . . . Is this the kind of propaganda against which the Bombay decision issued an injunction not to open our lips? . . . I have been scratching my brains to find out how, of all people, you could be a party to an arrangement which was expected to create such a complex situation . . . You have an impression that I am obstinate, perhaps incorrigible.'

Das, of whom Patel had complained, was equally critical of Jawaharlal and called him 'cold-blooded' at the next meeting of the All India Congress Committee – which incidentally saw the downfall of the Centre Party.

These wrangles went on until a *modus vivendi* was reached at a special Congress at Delhi in September, 1923, over which Abul Kalam Azad presided. The principles of non-co-operation were reaffirmed, but those who had 'no religious or other conscientious objections against entering the legislatures' were allowed to take part in the elections. This compromise, which was ratified at an annual session at Coconada three months later, was not reached a day too soon. The elections were due in November.

The election manifesto of the Swaraj Party, which Motilal issued on October 14th, described it as 'a party within the Congress, and as such an integral part of the Congress. It is not and was never intended to be a rival organization'. The Swaraj Party did not question the principle of non-co-operation. On the contrary, it proposed 'to carry the good fight into the enemy's camp by entering the councils'.

Though the Swarajists were handicapped by strife within the Congress organization and had only a few weeks to prepare for the elections, they gave a good account of themselves. Motilal's vigorous electioneering at the age of sixty-two was astonishing.

He travelled incessantly by road and rail, addressing an endless chain of meetings- till late at night. The performance of the Swaraj Party at the polls, if not spectacular, was impressive. In the Central Legislative Assembly it won 42 out of 101 elective seats; in the Central Provinces Council it won an absolute majority; in Bengal it was the largest party; in the U.P. and Assam the second largest party; in the Punjab and Madras, it made no headway against sectarian and communal elements.

It was decided that Motilal would lead the party in the Central Legislative Assembly and C. R. Das in the Bengal Council. 'Two of the ablest leaders in the Congress Camp' – this was how the Viceroy described Motilal and Das. In a confidential 'dossier' of the Swarajist legislators prepared for the Government of India soon after the elections Motilal figured as 'an outstanding leader of marked capacity . . . The General Secretary of the Swaraj Party, he engineered the very complete hartal and boycott at the time of the visit to Allahabad of His Royal Highness the Prince of Wales in December, 1921 . . . His family as a whole dabbles in politics . . .'

CHAPTER NINETEEN

LETTERS FROM PRISON

JAWAHARLAL took no part in the controversies which preceded the birth of the Swaraj Party in the latter half of 1922, for the simple reason that he was in prison. His first term had ended prematurely in March, 1922, thanks to a belated qualm of the official conscience: it was discovered that he had been wrongly convicted. It was a wrench parting from his father and almost the first thing he did after his release was to leave for Ahmedabad, where he arrived just in time to meet Gandhi in gaol and to witness his historic trial. The proceedings deeply moved Jawaharlal not only because of the stirring statement of the Mahatma, but of 'the dignity and the feeling' with which the British judge behaved towards the distinguished prisoner. 'It will be impossible to ignore the fact,' Judge Broomfield told Gandhi before sentencing him to six years' imprisonment, 'that you are in a different category from any person I have ever tried, or am likely to have to try. It would be impossible to ignore the fact that, in the eyes of millions of your countrymen, you are a great patriot and a great leader. Even those who differ from you in politics look upon you as a man of high ideals and of noble and even saintly life'.

On return to Allahabad, Jawaharlal threw himself into the non-co-operation movement. His presence – and the threat of picketing – brought the local cloth merchants to heel, and the sales of foreign cloth to a standstill. He was arrested, tried on several counts, including those of 'intimidation and extortion', and sentenced to twenty-one months' imprisonment. He did not defend himself, but gave a statement which *inter alia* recalled:

'Less than ten years ago, I returned from England after a long stay there . . . I had imbibed most of the prejudices of Harrow and Cambridge, and in my likes and dislikes I was perhaps more an Englishman than an Indian. I looked upon the world almost from an Englishman's standpoint . . . as much prejudiced in favour of England and the English as it was possible for an Indian to be."[1]

In giving this flash-back, Jawaharlal was probably emulating his political mentor, who had given Judge Broomfield a dramatic exposition of his transition from a confirmed loyalist to a self-confessed rebel. There was, however, little in common between the political evolution of Gandhi and that of young Nehru. Gandhi's anglicism was an adolescent phase, which he had begun to outgrow even during the student days. But long after his western veneer had peeled off, Gandhi had continued to profess a peculiar attachment to the British Empire – an attachment which survived even his long struggle in South Africa, and the frustrations of the war years after his return to India. The Rowlatt Acts and the Punjab tragedy had almost a traumatic effect upon Gandhi: the depth of his disillusion in 1920 was a measure of the illusion he had been hugging, of a new heaven and earth being established after the war by a grateful Empire for the help rendered to it in its hour of need by a subject people.

Jawaharlal's nationalism ante-dated the Rowlatt Acts, the emergence of Gandhi, even the first world war. It had visibly sprouted when he arrived at Harrow at the age of fifteen; it had not been smothered by the westernized atmosphere of his home and the influence of his European governesses and tutors. It survived the seven impressionable years he spent in the nurseries of the British aristocracy; indeed it was nourished by homesickness at Harrow and invigorated by the bracing climate of Cambridge. His growing familiarity with the literature, the arts and the institutions of England did not reconcile him to her rule over India. On the contrary, it enabled him to judge and criticize the English by their own standards. Jawaharlal did not need the shock of a Jallianwala Bagh to become a rebel; his trauma, if there were one, would have to be traced right back to his infancy: perhaps his nationalism was a congenital disease.

2

On returning to Lucknow gaol in May, 1922, young Nehru found that his father had been transferred to Naini Tal prison

[1] Dwivedi, R. (ed.), *The Life and Speeches of Jawaharlal Nehru*, pp. 4-5.

and the official attitude towards political prisoners had perceptibly hardened. The initial leniency of the authorities may have been due in part to the presence of the elder Nehru – who inspired a strange awe even in his gaolers – and in part to the sudden influx of a new class of prisoners belonging to the *intelligentsia*. The Government had of course no intention (in the words of Lord Reading) of converting imprisonment into 'a comfortable lodging at the expense of the state'.[2]

Jawaharlal's second term in Lucknow gaol began in a barrack housing about fifty prisoners, which was cut off from other barracks and was thus a 'gaol within a gaol'. Jawaharlal found the want of privacy hard to endure. He and his fellow-prisoners bathed in public and washed their clothes in public, and ran round and round the barrack for exercise and talked and argued till they had largely exhausted each others' capacity for intelligent conversation. Yearning for solitude, Jawaharlal would sometimes leave the barrack and braving the sun and the rain, sit in the open part of the gaol enclosures. 'It has been very pleasant,' he wrote to his father (August 17, 1922) 'and I have spent all my time in the open. All day I sit or lie under the *neem* trees spinning or reading or, it may be, writing. And at night, I move out from under the trees so as to have an unrestricted view of the stars and the moon. As I write this letter I am sitting under the starry canopy. An hour ago it was almost a cloudless night – a beautiful sight – and doubly welcome after so many days of mist and cloud. Now the clouds have crept up and try in vain to hide the stars, which peep through them, and twinkle away for all they are worth.'

The new rules for the treatment of political prisoners led to a crisis in Lucknow gaol. Protests from the prisoners were followed by fresh restrictions. The authorities decided to isolate in a remote part of the gaol seven of the ringleaders, including Devadas Gandhi, Mahadev Desai, Purushottam Das Tandon and Jawaharlal Nehru. Whatever other inconveniences this arrangement may have had, it ensured Jawaharlal the modicum of privacy for which he had longed in that crowded barrack. Interviews and newspapers were carefully rationed, but enough information had filtered through to indicate that the non-co-operation movement had passed the magic moment, that the

[2] Reading, Marquess of, *Rufus Isaacs, First Marquess of Reading*, vol. II, p. 236.

people had begun to non-co-operate with each other rather than with the Government. It was only natural that from the melancholy present, young Nehru's mind should have wandered into the recent past or the remote future. 'In the golden days to come,' he wrote to his father, 'when the history of our times and our country comes to be written, shall we not think of the good old days? Shall we not remember the great men who showed us the way, and filled us with the fire of faith? In the words of Meredith (changing but one word Italia for India):

'We who have seen India in the throes
Half-risen but to be hurled to the ground, and now,
like a ripe field of wheat where once drove plough,
All bounteous as she is fair, we think
Of those who blew the breath of life into her frame.'

A regular routine of activity and exercise enabled Jawaharlal to preserve his health and sense of humour. One day he received copies of the *Nation* and the *New Statesman* with marks in blue pencil and a marginal note, by the Gaol Superintendent. 'His interest is touching,' Jawaharlal wrote to his father. 'He is evidently bent on improving our minds, and like the missionary, would save us from the wrath to come in spite of ourselves.' Then, there was a visit from the Inspector-General of Prisons, preceded by 'a good deal of rubbing and scrubbing and soaping and washing and sweeping and cursing . . . and the [staff] put on their newly-washed clothes and tried to look their smartest, and the high officials and the low officials of the gaol put on their uniforms, and tried in vain to look comfortable in them. And so in the evening the grand finale took place. The great one came and walked across and went. So far as I know he did not speak to any prisoner in our barrack.'

3

Jawaharlal took advantage of his enforced leisure to catch up with his reading, which had fallen into arrears since his return from England. It was a tantalizing thought that he might be out of the gaol before he had time to read half the books on his list, that, but for Gandhi and non-co-operation, he would have been leading a pleasant but pointless existence.

Jawaharlal to Motilal: September 1, 1922: '. . . My mind is full of books I ought to read and it is with great difficulty that I refrain from sending you even longer lists than I have done so far . . . I wonder often how I shall be able to compress so much reading, spinning, writing, etc., as I have to do before discharge.

'. . . Ever since my return from England I had done little reading, and I shudder to think, what I was gradually becoming, before politics and N.C.O.[3] snatched me away from the doom that befalls many of us . . . the life I led and that so many of us led, the atmosphere of the lower courts, the uninspiring conversation of the Bar Library, the continuous contact with the sordid side of human nature – all this and the absence of any organized intellectual life – gradually kill . . . the power of free thought. We dare not think or follow up the consequences of our thought. We remain in the ruts and valleys, incapable almost of looking up towards the mountain-tops. And the finer side of life escapes us, we cannot even appreciate art or beauty, for everything that is outside the ruts and the valleys terrifies us. We cling to our physical comfort, and a very second-rate bourgeois comfort at that. We do not even know how to live well or to enjoy ourselves. Few of us have any *joie de vivre* left. And so we live out our lives with little said or little done, that beautifies existence for us or for others, or that will be remembered by anyone after we are dead and gone. That was the fate reserved for us also, till the high gods took us in hand, and removed us from the ruts, and placed us on the mountain side. We may not reach the top yet awhile, but the glory of wide vision is ours, and sometimes the rays of the morning sun reach us sooner than those in the valleys.

'Many years ago Colonel Haksar told me that, after he had finished his academical career, he gave a year or two to reading and thinking and did nothing else during that period. I envied him that year or two. And now the chance has been given to me. Shall I not rejoice? . . .'

In gaol Jawaharlal thought of another of his early loves, the mountains. He sent for two books from the Anand Bhawan library on Western Tibet and the Borderland. 'Khaliq and I,' he wrote, 'came to an agreement long ago to undertake a long pilgrimage as soon as Swaraj is attained. We have chalked out

[3] Non-co-operation.

a beautiful itinerary. We go to Kashmir and Ladakh and Tibet. We pay a visit to the lovely Mansrovar Lake and Mount Kailas. And then we go through the famous cities of Central Asia, may be, Afghanistan and Iran, Arabia, and go to the West . . .'

He hated self-pity and deprecated the sympathy lavished on him by friends and relatives: 'It is those who work and labour outside,' he told his father, 'who deserve sympathy. We have no appointments to keep, no piling up of work with which we cannot cope, no speechifying, no hurry. Time ceases to have significance . . . We might with a stretch of the imagination, think ourselves in Tennyson's island in the Western Sea, where it is always afternoon, and the lotus-eaters dwell. Barrack No. 4 is not such a bad place as outsiders imagine.'

Jawaharlal was protesting too much. That his health was not half so good as he pretended to his family is shown by a diary of his ailments which he used to send to his father so that the latter could prescribe homoeopathic remedies.

Sometimes his thoughts strayed beyond the walls of the prison and the covers of his books. 'I hope mother is not worrying about me,' he wrote. 'I was very pleased to get her note from Bombay . . . Like all mothers, she perhaps exaggerates my ailments and so I am afraid, needlessly alarms herself.' On November 15th he wrote that he had observed his birthday in accordance with his mother's directions: 'I did everything she wished me to do. I have even kept Rs. 5 for the poor. I shall hand these to her when she comes.' The health of his little daughter Indira caused him much concern. 'Tomorrow it will be three months since I saw her,' he wrote on August 18th. When she came to see him, he found her 'very pale and weak'. 'I wish,' he added, 'some arrangements were made for Indu's lessons. I am confident that I could have managed her easily – but I am in Barrack No. 4.' She was probably too small to be able to read the letters her father wrote to her in Hindi.

Jawaharlal to his daughter, October 17, 1922: 'To dear Indu, love from her Papu. You must get well quickly, learn to write letters and come and see me in gaol. I am longing to see you. Have you plied the new spinning wheel which Dadu [grandfather] has brought for you? Send me some of your yarn. Do you join mother in prayers every day?'

November 15, 1922: '. . . Love to dear daughter Indira from her Papu. Did you like Calcutta? Is it better than Bombay? Did you see the Calcutta zoo? What animals did you see? Have you seen a huge tree there? You must get strong and plump before you return to Allahabad.'

From the gaol, Jawaharlal sent 10,570 yards of yarn to Anand Bhawan. 'It took me,' he wrote, 'a considerable time to spin, chiefly because I tried to spin fine yarn. Spinning coarse yarn does not interest me.'

4

On January 31, 1923, before he had completed half his term, Jawaharlal was released. The decline of the non-co-operation movement, and the differences between Hindus and Muslims, Pro-Changers and No-Changers, had encouraged the Government to grant a partial amnesty, for which there was an insistent demand in and outside the provincial and central legislatures.

Just a month before Jawaharlal's release, his father in partnership with Das had founded the Swaraj Party. Jawaharlal, who as a student in England had watched with interest the tactics of Irish nationalists, had argued with Gandhi in favour of council entry in 1920. Three years later, Gandhi was in gaol and his staunch adherents favoured a programme which seemed rather remote from politics as they were commonly understood. Though Jawaharlal did not align himself with either of the parties, he recognized the inevitability of a parliamentary phase following the failure of direct action. We get a glimpse into his mind from Mahadev Desai, who had been his fellow-prisoner in Lucknow gaol in 1922. 'I know you are of the opinion,' wrote Desai, 'that the country is generally in a mood to accept [council entry], if it is allowed to have its own way.'[4]

Curiously enough, Motilal did not press his son to join the Swaraj Party. In 1920, he had looked around for a constituency for Jawaharlal for the U.P. Council; in 1924 he would have been glad to have him by his side in the central legislature. However, the experience of the last four years had shown him how little amenable his son's politics were to merely parental advice,

[4] Mahadev Desai to Jawaharlal, June 6, 1923 (N.P.).

so he left the task of conversion to his friend C. R. Das; but even the able advocacy of Das failed to win over Jawaharlal, who preferred the role of a mediator between the Swarajists and the No-Changers. As one of the chief architects of the ill-fated Bombay compromise, Jawaharlal was elected a member of the short-lived Working Committee representing the 'Centre Party' in the Indian National Congress. His *début* on the stage of national politics in the summer of 1923 revealed his peculiar assets and limitations: while his idealistic and sensitive mind rebelled against pettiness and the scramble for power, he himself was too remote from the personal and factional manoeuvres to be able effectively to control them.

The instinct which kept young Nehru out of political squabbles of 1922-5 was a sound one. If he had been drawn into them, not only would his own intellectual growth have suffered, but he might not have been able to offer in the late 'twenties that romantic and unsullied image which helped to make him the hero of youth, the hope of the national movement and the heir of the Mahatma.

In September, 1923, Jawaharlal attended the Special Congress at Delhi which patched up a truce between the Swarajists and the No-Changers. At the end of the session he decided to take a day off to visit Nabha, which was much in the news because of clashes between Akali demonstrators and the police. Little did he know that a 'strange and unexpected adventure' was in store for him.

CHAPTER TWENTY

TRAPPED IN NABHA

THE Akali movement had originally professed a religious aim: the rescue of the Sikh shrines from the corrupt control of the *Mahants*. But the attack on these vested interests inevitably brought the Akalis into conflict with the Government. In 1923 they started an agitation against the deposition of the Maharaja of Nabha. The tangle of dynastic rivalries between the sister states of Patiala and Nabha, and the squalid intrigues which had preceded the downfall of the ruler of Nabha, could hardly be solved by marching *jathas* – bands of volunteers – from British India. But such reasoning did not enter into the calculations of the Akalis; they could command men, money and emotion for a movement which, so long as it remained non-violent, was designed to enlist nationalist sympathy.

On September 21, 1923, Jawaharlal, accompanied by two of his Congress friends, Dr Gidwani and K. Santhanam, followed an Akali *jatha* from Muktsar in British India to Jaito on the frontier of Nabha state. On arrival at Jaito, all the three were served with orders directing them to leave the state territory immediately. They protested that they were not members of the Akali *jatha* but only spectators, that they had already entered the Nabha state, that the next railway train was not due to leave Jaito for several hours. Their protests were ignored; they were arrested and taken to the police lock-up. In the evening Santhanam's left wrist was handcuffed to Jawaharlal's right wrist; led by a policeman who held a chain attached to the handcuff, the prisoners were marched through the streets of that small town. The experience was deeply humiliating until the humour of the situation dawned upon Jawaharlal: the sight resembled that of 'a dog being led by a chain'. That night he and his two colleagues, handcuffed to each other, remained packed in a third class carriage of a slow-moving passenger train. The following day they arrived in Nabha, the state capital, where they were locked up in the local gaol in a small, damp, insanitary cell with a ceiling so low that their heads touched it.

Immediately after his arrest at Jaito, Jawaharlal had written two letters. 'I have been arrested here, this afternoon,' he briefly informed his wife, 'we do not know exactly where we will be tried and taken to . . . please don't worry.' To his father he wrote: 'We have been fortunate enough to be arrested . . . We have been waiting here for the last few hours in the police station, and do not know what is going to happen. Whatever that may be, we are thoroughly satisfied . . . Do not worry.'

Motilal had seen too much of the world – the world of Indian States – not to worry. Some of the Punjab states were notorious for their sordid atmosphere of intrigue, chicanery and violence. In these states life and honour were cheap and inconvenient persons had a habit of disappearing mysteriously. He sensed the hazards to the health, and indeed the life of his son. He telegraphed (September 23rd) to the Viceroy: 'Starting for Nabha today by Punjab Mail to interview my son Pandit Jawaharlal Nehru, reported to have been arrested under Section 188, and now in state custody. Have so far taken no part in Akali agitation, and the sole object of the present visit is to see my son. Expect there will be no interference or molestation by subordinate officials in exercise of my natural right.'[1] Before leaving Allahabad, he also telegraphed to Harkishenlal – whom he had helped during the martial law days of 1919, and who was now a minister in the Punjab.

Motilal arrived at Nabha on September 24th and lodged himself in the waiting-room at the railway station. What followed may best be described from the contemporary records, which have fortunately survived.[2]

J. Wilson Johnston, I.C.S., C.B.E., Administrator Nabha State, to Pandit Motilal Nehru, September 24, 1923: 'The Honourable Mr Harkishenlal has forwarded to me your telegram of the 22nd despatched from Allahabad . . . I give you a brief outline of your son's case . . . He is being tried under Section 188 and Section 145 . . .'

Motilal Nehru to Administrator Nabha dated September 24, 1923, Waiting Room Nabha Railway Station: 'I beg to acknowledge your letter of this date (unsigned) handed over to me

¹ N.A.I.   ² N.A.I.

at the Nabha railway station by the Chief Police Officer of the State.

'I am obliged to you for the brief outline of my son's case given in your letter . . .

'I have no desire at the present moment to disturb the course of proceedings you have chalked out for the trial . . . but assert the inalienable right of an accused person to have such advice and assistance at the trial as he or his friends may determine. As the father of the accused and the man most interested in him I formally claim the right to have access to him . . .

'I may mention that various reports of ill-treatment of persons arrested by State officials have appeared in the press and I am naturally anxious to find out if my son has been subjected to such ill-treatment . . .'

J. Wilson Johnston Administrator Nabha to Motilal Nehru, September 24, 1923: 'I am in receipt of your letter dated waiting room Nabha station, the 24th September . . .

'As already verbally communicated to you, you have my permission to interview your son upon the following conditions, the acceptance of which I must ask you to give me in writing:

    (i) That you undertake not to engage in any political activity while you are within the state territory.

    (ii) that immediately after the conclusion of your interview with Jawaharlal Nehru, you will leave the state precincts . . .'

Motilal Nehru to J. Wilson Johnston Administrator, Nabha State dated Waiting Room Nabha the 24th September, 1923: 'I beg to acknowledge your letter of date in reply to my letter of this morning. I thought I had in that letter given my clear answer to the conditions verbally imposed upon my interview with Pandit Jawaharlal Nehru which you have repeated in writing . . . I may mention that, besides the right of interviewing Pandit Jawaharlal Nehru, I consider myself fully entitled to watch his trial and to appear for him as counsel if necessary . . .

J. Wilson Johnston, I.C.S., C.B.E., to Motilal Nehru, Dated September 24, 1923: 'As you categorically refuse to accept the two conditions that I have laid down before I could sanction an interview with your son, I have nothing to say. Under the

circumstances, I regret that I must ask you leave the state territory by the first train. I am sending herewith a notice to be
served upon you in this connection under Section 144 of the
Criminal Procedure Code.'

*Endorsement on the Duplicate copy of the Order under
Section 144 of the Criminal Procedure Code by Motilal Nehru:*
'Received notice. My presence in Nabha may be undesirable
from the point of view of the present Nabha Administration,
but it is not true that it will tend to disturb the public tran-
quillity. For the present, however, I am leaving Nabha by the
first available train. Section 144 is wholly inapplicable.'

Motilal returned to Ambala and sent another telegram to the
Viceroy.

*Motilal Nehru to the Viceroy, dated Ambala Cantt. September
25, 1923:* 'Arrived yesterday morning. Despite my assurance
that I had no part in the Akali agitation and the sole object of
my visit was to see my son Jawaharlal Nehru, under-trial
prisoner, Administrator (Nabha) insisted on guarantees. My
request for permission to appear as counsel answered by notice
under Section 144 ordering me to leave Nabha by first train.
Accordingly I left yesterday, while mock trial going on. Besides
absolute denial of justice and fairplay I have strong suspicions
of ill-treatment in gaol . . . Waiting Ambala Cantonment station
for reply.'

Thanks to the intervention of the Government of India,
Motilal was permitted to interview his son and to stay on in
Nabha till the conclusion of the trial; he disavowed, as he had
done from the outset, any intention of taking part in the politics
of Nabha. The interview took place on the evening of September 27th. The police officials who escorted Motilal reported to
the Administrator that he was in high spirits on his way to
the gaol, but visibly dejected after the interview: from this they
inferred that he had recognized how weak and indefensible his
son's case was. This explanation was wide of the mark. To
secure this interview with his son, he had struggled for a whole
week, travelled hundreds of miles by road and rail, kept anxious
vigil in railway trains and waiting rooms, conducted a wordy

duel with the British Administrator of Nabha and even secured the intervention of the Viceroy. Then came the anti-climax. Jawaharlal absolutely refused to be defended. He would not hear of an appeal to the Viceroy; his only advice to his father was to go back to Allahabad and 'not to worry'.

From Ambala, Motilal wrote a letter (September 28th) to the Administrator to say that he had caught 'a chill' on the way, which prevented him from conducting the case personally, and so he was deputing his private secretary Kapil Deo Malaviya to be present at the trial. That the 'chill' was contracted not on the way to Ambala but in Nabha gaol the previous evening is evident from the letter he sent to his son through Kapil Deo.

Motilal to Jawaharlal, September 28, 1923: 'My dear J., I was pained to find that, instead of affording you any relief my visit of yesterday only had the effect of disturbing the even tenor of your happy gaol life. After much anxious thinking, I have come to the conclusion that I can do no good either to you or to my-self by repeating my visits. I can stand with a clear conscience before God and man for what I have done so far after your arrest, but as you think differently it is no use trying to make opposites meet . . . For the present I hardly know what to do with myself and shall wait here for a couple of days or so. Please do not bother about me at all. I am as happy outside the gaol as you are in it.
Your loving,
Father.'

Motilal's irony was merely a cloak for his distress. There was a postscript to this letter:

'Please do not think that I have written this letter either in anger or in sorrow. I have tried my best after an almost all-night consideration to take a calm and practical view of the position. I wish you not to have the impression that you have offended me, as I honestly believe that the position has been forced upon both of us by circumstances over which neither has any control.'

A day's halt at Delhi, where he met his old friend Hakim Ajmal Khan, and Kamala and Indira, revived his spirits. On his way to Allahabad he wrote to Kapil Deo Malaviya:

'I do not know what is going to happen when I get back to Allahabad, but of one thing I can assure you that you will not be ashamed of whatever decision I take.'

Meanwhile in Nabha, the trial – or rather trials – of Jawaharlal and his companions went on. To the original offence of illegally entering Nabha, had been added another, of 'a criminal conspiracy'. The two cases ran their parallel and farcical courses in two separate courts. One of the judges was stupid and illiterate; the other was relatively intelligent and educated, but both of them seemed to be under the thumb of the police. However, the last word was to rest neither with the police nor with the magistrates, not even with the all-powerful Wilson-Johnston.

On September 24th, even before Motilal sent his second telegram, the Government of India had informed the Administrator that the requirements of the case against Jawaharlal and his companions would be 'adequately met' by an order of expulsion from the State. This advice instantly provoked a protest from the Administrator, who had complained to his immediate superior, Lt.-Colonel Minchin, Agent to the Governor-General, Punjab States at Lahore, against the attitude of 'the thinly-veiled impudence which has characterized the whole of Motilal's dealings with me', and against the 'invidious distinction' sought to be made between Jawaharlal and his friends on the one hand and the Akali agitators on the other. The Government of India could afford to look beyond the pride and prejudice of a local despot. Lord Reading and his advisers could not peer into the not far-off future when Jawaharlal was to lead an independent India; but they knew that his father was the General Secretary of the Swaraj Party, which was about to contest the elections and was likely to be the major opposition party in the central and provincial legislatures.

The Nabha episode ended as dramatically as it had begun. Jawaharlal, Gidwani and Santhanam received sentences amounting to two and a half years each; but immediately afterwards 'an executive order' of the Administrator of Nabha, 'suspended' the sentence and expelled them from the State.

On return to Allahabad, Jawaharlal received a letter from his friend Sri Prakasa,[3] congratulating him on his 'lucky escape from Nabha land'. 'Would to God,' wrote Sri Prakasa, 'you did

[3] Now, Governor of Maharashtra.

not put your head into the noose too often.' For Motilal it had been an agonizing fortnight. Jawaharlal went through the ordeal more philosophically, but he had to pay an additional price in the form of a virulent attack of typhoid fever which he and his companions contracted in Nabha prison.

The Nabha episode, which gave Jawaharlal a glimpse of the administration of an Indian State, even under the aegis of a senior British officer, turned him into a stout champion of the rights of the people in 'Princely States'. British officials had unwittingly rounded off young Nehru's political education. The externment from Mussoorie had given him an insight into the problems of the peasantry in 'British India'; the trial in Nabha suddenly illuminated the arbitrary regimes thriving in 'Indian India'.

CHAPTER TWENTY-ONE

LEADER OF THE OPPOSITION

THE Legislative Assembly, the scene of Motilal's triumphs and trials during the next six years, was not a sovereign body like the British House of Commons or the Indian Lok Sabha of today. Its constitution reflected the transitional stage in the unresolved struggle between British imperialism and Indian nationalism. It had a majority of elected members; it enjoyed wider powers of debate and criticism than its predecessor, the Imperial Legislative Council, over which the Viceroy personally presided. But it could not control, much less overthrow, the executive. The Government of India was responsible not to the Indian legislature in Delhi, but to His Majesty's Government in London. In the Legislative Assembly a permanent and irremovable executive confronted a permanent opposition; the disciplined group of forty odd Swarajists was matched by almost an equal number of officials, non-officials and Europeans. Between these two groups, implacably opposed to each other, were fifty-odd members who were wooed by both sides. Early in 1924 Motilal was able to enlist the co-operation of Jinnah and Malaviya and thus obtain the support of about thirty Moderate and Muslim members; the resultant coalition, the 'Nationalist Party', was able to outvote the Government in the opening session.

In this as in other legislatures, there were quite a few members who owed their seats to good fortune, the favour of a patron or the grace of the Government. The names of these mediocrities are buried in the printed record of the Assembly waiting to be momentarily resurrected by a patient scholar. There were, however, eminent figures in that Assembly who would have made a mark in any parliament in any country at any time. Bipin Chandra Pal was the hero of the partition of Bengal, who had thundered from a thousand platforms: in 1924 he was an extinct volcano. Sir Hari Singh Gour was a prolific writer and speaker, who was often on his feet at question-time. Sir Purshotamdas Thakurdas, the Bombay magnate, was noted for his expert knowledge of commercial and industrial matters. Sir P. S. Sivaswamy Iyer specialized in military topics. N. M. Joshi was passionately interested in labour problems. Diwan Chaman Lall and T. C. Goswami were young firebrands of the Swaraj Party, the 'lion-cubs' of Motilal. K. C. Neogy and Shanmukham Chetty were promising young men whose careers were to continue to our own day.

The president of the Assembly, Sir Frederick Whyte, was noted for his dignity, impartiality and the tenacious memory which enabled him to recognize every member by name and face almost on the opening day. The Leader of the Treasury Benches and of the House was Sir Malcolm Hailey, the Home Member, who possessed great experience, astuteness and skill in debate. He was soon to be succeeded by the more genial Sir Alexander Muddiman, whose innate courtesy, good-humour and resilience sometimes helped to· take the edge off the inevitable bitterness.

One of the most distinguished members in the Assembly was M. A. Jinnah, the future founder of Pakistan, who had left the Congress when its reins had fallen into Gandhi's hands. Though during the years 1922-3 there had been a talk of his joining the Swaraj Party, he was the leader of an 'Independent' group. He had a superior, almost supercilious air and his usual attitude to those he encountered was one of withering scorn. Curiously enough, his relations with Motilal were friendly. This may have been because he found it easier to understand a fellow lawyer, treating politics as a practical game, than a saint who professed to spiritualize them. Or perhaps he sensed that calculated insolence would not work with Motilal, but was likely to be returned with interest. In any case, in 1924 Jinnah was still a 'Muslim Mazzini', whose nationalism was not swallowed either by conceit or communalism.

Madan Mohan Malaviya's noble bearing, immaculate dress and silvery eloquence won him respect of all sections of the Assembly. He had attended some of the earliest sessions of the Indian National Congress and had taken an active part in the proceedings. In 1918-19 he was regarded as a firebrand by the Government. However, in the nineteen twenties he seemed a giant laggard from the Moderate era, wavering on the sidelines when Gandhi started his campaigns, at one moment seeking a truce between the Congress and the Government, at another courting imprisonment. His deeply religious outlook and strict orthodoxy, which gave him his unique hold on the Hindu masses, also made his politics, like those of his friend Lajpat Rai, suspect to Muslims. Lajpat Rai himself did not join the Swaraj Party until January, 1926. His powerful intellect and flaming eloquence would have made him a great asset to the party; unfortunately, he could not resist the siren call of Responsive Co-operation which split the Swarajists soon afterwards.

Another colourful personality in the Assembly was Vithalbhai Javerbhai Patel, who became a thorn in the flesh of the executive, first as an unrelenting critic, and then as the president of the Assembly. He was not an easy man to work with, but he had a good deal of the singleness of purpose, subtlety, grit and resilience of his more famous brother Vallabhbhai Patel.

The most striking figure in the Legislative Assembly was perhaps Motilal himself. His entry into the House was always an event: the fascinated eyes of members and visitors fastened on the princely profile, the majestic, immaculately dressed figure of the Leader of the Opposition, moving forward with measured steps and regal dignity to his seat. He seemed to be in his element; it was as if all his life had been a preparation for this supreme moment. He brought to bear on his legislative work the unremitting industry which had been the secret of his success at the Bar. It is significant that while Jinnah stayed in the luxurious Maiden's Hotel. Motilal took up his lodgings in the Western Court where most of the members of his party were staying. He kept a vigilant eye and a firm hand on the Swaraj Party, which came to be recognized in and outside the Assembly as a disciplined assault force.

Jayakar, who knew Motilal both as a colleague and as an opponent, has recorded:

'Whenever he spoke in the Legislative Assembly, it was distilled sense and reason. Even when he let out pyrotechnics, they rose from *terra firma* and came back to *terra firma*'.

Jayakar refers to the superb dignity and self-confidence of Motilal who rose, 'from the daintiest meal with the quiet self-possession of a person accustomed to enjoy the choicest gifts of life, as if they were merely his due'. European members of the Assembly, even members of the Viceroy's Council, found in

Motilal a charming guest and a delightful host. 'My wife and I delighted to entertain him,' writes Sir George Schuster, 'and he always talked freely to her. It was common knowledge that Sir Alexander Muddiman and Motilal hit it off very well. What was it that drew Motilal to the representatives of the Empire which he was openly trying to subvert? Jayakar suggests that 'some secret affinity appeared to exist between them born perhaps of the power to rule and govern men'. It is significant that the finest tribute to Motilal's role as Leader of the Opposition came from Sir George Rainy, a member of the Viceroy's Council, who recalled the 'well-remembered figure . . . that exquisite fitness of attire which symbolized the clean fighter and the great gentleman and that impressive face, deeply lined and careworn, on which character and intellect were so deeply imprinted . . . He had a personality which impressed itself on the most unobservant. Eminent as a lawyer, eminent as a speaker, and in the first rank as a political leader, he could not but take the foremost place wherever he might be, whether within these walls or outside. The quickness of his intellect, his skill in debate, his adroitness as a tactician and his strength of purpose rendered him a formidable adversary in controversy'.

2

On February 8, 1924, within ten days of the opening of the Legislative Assembly, a resolution was moved by Diwan Bahadur Rangachariar, a non-Swarajist member, demanding a Royal Commission for the revision of the Government of India Act so as to secure for India the status of a Dominion within the British Empire. Motilal moved an amendment proposing that the new constitution should be framed by a 'representative Round Table Conference', and approved by a newly-elected Legislative Assembly in India before it was embodied in a statute by the British Parliament.

On behalf of the Government, Sir Malcolm Hailey catalogued the numerous interests which blocked India's progress to freedom : the Indian Princes, European commerce, the Secretary of State's Services, the Minorities. He argued that responsible government promised by the declaration of August, 1917, was not 'necessarily incompatible with a legislature with limited or restricted powers', that India could advance towards its destined goal only gradually, that the British Government was the sole judge of the manner and measure of each step, that the next step, the appointment of a Royal Commission, could be taken only after the ten years stipulated in the preamble to the Government of India Act, 1919, had elapsed.

Motilal blandly questioned Hailey's premises. 'Now, sir,' he said, 'our answer, straight and clear, as unequivocal as the Preamble, is that the Preamble is bad, the whole Act [of 1919] is . . . bad . . . devised to postpone, to stifle, and to suppress the natural desire [for freedom] in the country.' He pointed out that his amendment had been deliberately toned down to secure the co-operation of other parties in the Assembly. 'We have come here,' he added, 'to offer our co-operation, non-co-operators as we are, if you will care to co-operate with us. That is why we are here. If you agree to have it, we are your men; if you do not, we shall, like men, stand upon our rights and continue to be non-co-operators.'[1]

This was Motilal's maiden speech. 'So thoughtfully phrased with such facility,' was the compliment which Hailey paid to it. On the constitutional issue, Hailey did not make any concession: all that he could promise was an inquiry into such defects as might come to light in the working of the constitution.

Seventy-six members voted in favour of Motilal's amendment and forty-eight against it. The latter included the compact bloc of officials, nominated non-officials, Europeans and a few Indian members who were always at the beck and call of the official whip. This was the first and the most spectacular defeat inflicted by the Swaraj Party on the Government; it was made possible by the co-operation of Muslims and Moderates who followed the lead of Jinnah and Malaviya. Thanks to this co-operation, the first four budget grants were rejected in their entirety, the Finance Bill was thrown out on its introduction, and again on the following day, after it had been returned by the Viceroy for reconsideration. Later in the year, the Swaraj Party inflicted a crushing defeat on the Government when the Legislative Assembly rejected the proposals of the Lee Commission on the Imperial Services. In actual practice all this had only a nuisance value for the Government. The Viceroy had the last word under the constitution; with a stroke of the pen he could

[1] Legislative Assembly Debates (Official Report), vol. IV 1924, p. 370.

veto resolutions passed by the legislature, and 'certify' as law measures rejected by it.

Meanwhile, in the provincial field the Swaraj Party had also made a strong impression. In December, 1923, Lord Lytton, the Governor of Bengal, had invited C. R. Das to form a ministry to administer 'transferred' or the 'popular' part of the provincial administration. 'The members of this Party,' replied Das, 'are pledged to do everything in their power by using the legal right granted under the Reforms Act to put an end to the system of Dyarchy.' Das was able to forge a working alliance with other groups in the Bengal Council which gave him a clear majority. In Bengal, and in the Central Provinces (where the Swarajists had an absolute majority) there were votes of no-confidence in the ministers, their salaries were refused, the emergency powers of the Governors had to be invoked and the system of 'dyarchy' became unworkable. These developments thrilled the intelligentsia, the press was full of them, and the Swarajists were glad to see the all-powerful bureaucracy humbled for once.

The emergence of the Swaraj Party on the Indian political stage coincided with a new development in Britain: the advent of a Labour Government in January, 1924. Since the days of Keir Hardie, Indian nationalism had struck sympathetic chords in the Labour Party. The new Premier, Ramsay MacDonald, had visited India in 1909 and published some forthright criticisms of the Indian Administration. A parliamentary committee of the Labour Party for Indian affairs had been formed under the chairmanship of Colonel Wedgwood – a friend of Motilal Nehru and Lajpat Rai.

Lord Olivier, the new Secretary of State for India, soon after coming into office cabled to the Viceroy his astonishment at the fact that even 'Moderate and well-disposed' sections in India seemed to doubt Britain's good faith. A paragraph in the election manifesto of the Swaraj Party (which Motilal had issued in October, 1923) particularly intrigued Lord Olivier. The paragraph ran:

'The guiding motive of the British in governing India is to secure the selfish interest of their own country, and the so-called reforms are a mere blind to further the said interests under the pretence of granting responsible government to India, the real object being to continue the exploitation of the unlimited resources of the country by keeping Indians permanently in a subordinate position to Britain and denying them at home and abroad the most elementary rights of citizens.'

In response to Lord Olivier's request to Lord Reading, a confidential memorandum was prepared in February, 1924, by Mr Crear of the Home Department, listing the causes of Indian discontent: the political and economic forces generated by the war, the emergence of Gandhi, the Punjab tragedy of 1919 and the 'political immaturity of the Asiatic peoples'. 'The East has always oscillated,' wrote Crear, 'between inertia and cataclysm. Political unrest once aroused, there is general impatience with all gradual development, and particularly with the cautious and empirical methods of British constitutional traditions. Circumspection is interpreted as insincerity.'

To this memorandum Sir Alexander Muddiman, who was soon to succeed Hailey as Home Member, added a footnote, the brutal candour of which strangely contrasted with the vague generalities and judicious evasions of Government spokesmen in and outside the legislature. Muddiman wrote:

'My own feeling is that very many people thought that full Dominion Status has to be granted in 1929. Montagu made no secret of his intentions to secure this. Indians realize that they are a very long way off this; the actual powers granted to the Legislature are circumscribed in every direction; whenever they talk about Dominion Self-Government, we tell them that there is still a great deal to be done before they dare think of it; and as a consequence they believe that the whole of the scheme was merely intended to delude them. It is the most dangerous thing in the world to give the semblance of power without its authority – it is bound to cause irritation and charges of bad faith. I think this is the truth of it. Add to this the insistent demand in England that we should keep the European services at full strength; that we should keep and strengthen European hold on the army.'[2]

3

Lord Olivier's first speech in the House of Lords was con-

[2] Unpublished (N.A.I.).

ciliatory. 'The Government has the same ultimate aim,' he declared, 'as the Indian Swaraj Party.' Thanks to Gandhi's emphasis on national 'self-reliance', there was not the same air of expectancy in India in 1924 as had followed the formation of the Liberal Government in 1906 with John Morley as Secretary of State. Nevertheless, there is evidence to suggest that in the first months of the Labour Government hopes of a reconciliation between the Congress and the Government rose high – for a while.

In the spring of 1924, S. R. Bomanji, a Bombay politician, a friend of Motilal, Lajpat Rai and Colonel Wedgwood, was in London and in touch with several ministers including Ramsay MacDonald himself. A glimpse of his activities behind the scenes is furnished by his letters to Motilal.

S. R. Bomanji to Motilal, March 20, 1924: 'I must congratulate you on the brilliant way you have defeated the Government and rejected the whole budget. Your successive rejections, even by the diminishing majority, had a very chastening effect on the die-hards here. If you can exert still greater pressure on your side, I clearly see victory for us . . . Wedgwood told me that he had received your letters and he had found them very useful and asked me to tell you about it.'

Bomanji had a poor opinion of the new Secretary of State. 'Olivier is a bureaucrat by instinct,' wrote Bomanji, 'and claims to know Indians by his experience in Jamaica. He is dominated by the India Office . . . completely . . . I have heard Olivier being called a Tory by the Labour Party.' Bomanji was, however, heartened by the attitude of other influential members of the Labour Party in and outside the Cabinet. 'Lansbury, Spoor, Wedgwood and other Labourites are firm,' he wrote, 'and the Prime Minister himself is firm.' A conference in London between Indian leaders and British statesmen, on the Irish model, seemed on the cards, and Bomanji even speculated on the personnel of the two delegations. MacDonald, Olivier, Wedgwood, Chelmsford and C. P. Trevelyan were mentioned as British representatives; C. R. Das, Motilal, Ansari, Jinnah, Kelkar and a few others were expected to represent the Indian side. Bomanji's optimism was suddenly deflated by an interview with

MacDonald who professed great annoyance at the Swarajist tactics in the Indian Legislative Assembly.

Bomanji to Motilal, March 27, 1924: 'Since writing to you last mail, I saw the Prime Minister. He complained of your holding a pistol at him till he was finally in the saddle. I remonstrated that we gave a fortnight's notice asking for a Round Table Conference, and the Government's reply left us no hope or opening and we were bound to stop the budget grants; otherwise we would be powerless to have our grievances redressed for another twelve months. Your prompt reply was very timely. I showed it to the P.M. . . . I have assured the P.M. as to your sincerity and reasonableness, but he fears that your moderation may not be shared by your colleagues. I have tried to disabuse his mind . . . I have sent you a wire today drafted by Wedgwood.'

Bomanji had an uneasy feeling that senior officials of the India Office in London had got wind of 'what I am doing, and that the Prime Minister has been passing over the regular channels, and I have been made to communicate with . . . Motilal and C. R. Das'. Bomanji suspected that the British bureaucrats in Delhi were conspiring with the British bureaucrats in London to sabotage the negotiations. A few days later, Premier MacDonald, seizing on what he considered a premature leakage of the talks in the Indian press, sent a note to Bomanji expressing his 'profound regret at the way things had gone . . . if you had seen your way to have kept things going for a few days more, something might have come out of it, as we are working very hard indeed at this end to come to some arrangements.'

It is difficult to say how far Bomanji's initial hopes were based on political possibilities and how far on wishful thinking. In his first brief innings as Prime Minister, MacDonald revealed great energy, initiative and drive, particularly in the conduct of foreign affairs. So far as India is concerned, even if we assume (and it is a large assumption) that MacDonald the Prime Minister endorsed the opinions of MacDonald the Leader of the Opposition, it is important to remember that in 1924 the Labour Party was in office on the sufferance of the Liberals and the Conservatives. Srinivasa Sastri, who was in London in the summer of 1924 shrewdly summed up the situation: 'The ministry has

no big plan for India. It only wishes to tide over the difficulty
somehow.'[3] In April, 1924, Beatrice Webb, whose husband was
in the Cabinet, noted in her diary that MacDonald was determined to prolong the precarious life of his Government by
shedding the radical wing of his party, by courting the
Conservatives, and generally playing the role of a 'political
charmer.'[4] This was hardly the posture for a British Prime
Minister who wanted to take a bold initiative in India.

[3] Jagadisan, T. N., *Letters of V. S. Srinivasa Sastri*, p. 260.
[4] Cole, Margaret (Editor), *Beatrice Webb's Diaries 1924-1932*, p. 25.

CHAPTER TWENTY-TWO

TUSSLE WITH GANDHI

JUST when the Swarajists were mounting their assault upon the Government, a new and important development took place. Gandhi, a state prisoner in Yeravda gaol, was operated upon for appendicitis and released on February 5, 1924, on grounds of health before he had served a third of his six years' term.

Gandhi's illness once again revealed the strength of his bond with the Indian people. Leaders of all parties united in expressing their concern; among the numerous resolutions tabled in the Legislative Assembly demanding his release, there was one by Jinnah. Another member, Mahomed Yakub, gave notice of a resolution recommending the award of the Nobel Prize to Gandhi. Colonel Maddock, the surgeon who had operated on the Mahatma in the Sassoon Hospital at Poona, received congratulations and thanks from all over the country. Gandhi himself was inundated with letters and telegrams expressing hopes, which, he confessed, 'staggered' him. There was nothing which he was not expected to solve – from political conundrums to domestic differences. The Nizam of Hyderabad sought his support for the rendition of Berar, the Maharaja of Nabha for the restoration of his throne, Hindu and Muslim leaders for their mutually contradictory claims, the Swarajists for their council programme, the 'No-Changers' for the reaffirmation of the undiluted doctrine of non-co-operation.

The Bombay Government, when recommending the Mahatma's release had mentioned the possibility that he 'would denounce the Swarajists for their defection from the pure principles of non-co-operation, and thus considerably reduce in legislatures their power for harm'. Motilal was naturally anxious to secure Gandhi's support, or at least benevolent neutrality, in the unresolved tug-of-war with the No-Changers. In March the Mahatma moved down for convalescence to Juhu, a seaside suburb near Bombay. As the Legislative Assembly was in session Motilal could not immediately leave Delhi; but he tried to impress Gandhi with the spectacular achievements of his party. On March 18th, when the Legislative Assembly rejected the Finance Bill for a second time, Motilal telegraphed the good news to the Mahatma. 'I have your telegram,' Gandhi replied, 'I rejoice because the victory gives you joy but I cannot enthuse over it . . . I never doubted your very great tactfulness and persuasive eloquence.' What Gandhi questioned was not the immediate success of the Swarajist tactics but the ultimate wisdom of their strategy.

The basic differences between Motilal and Gandhi came into relief during the long negotiations at Juhu in April-May, 1924. 'The two minds so strongly dissimilar,' wrote C. F. Andrews, who was at Juhu at this time, 'would not always work together.' Motilal's arguments were reinforced at a later stage by C. R. Das, but even the combined advocacy of these two brilliant lawyers could not convert Gandhi. Eventually they agreed to differ and issued separate statements.

Gandhi described the Swarajist leaders as 'the ablest, most experienced and honest patriots'; at the same time he acknowledged that his differences with them were not of 'mere detail'. Though he advised the 'No-Changers' not to obstruct the activities of the Swarajists, he argued that council-entry was inconsistent with non-co-operation; that a general policy of 'obstruction' in the councils was undesirable; that the councils should be used, if at all, to implement the constructive programme of the Congress.

Gandhi's arguments were refuted in a closely reasoned statement issued by C. R. Das and Motilal. The rift between the Mahatma and the Swarajists was open. It was much deeper than the studied courtesy of the press statements made it out to be. Motilal's own views were expressed candidly, even pungently, in a memorandum he prepared on an earlier rough draft of Gandhi's press statement.

'I agree,' he wrote, 'that the difference between Mahatmaji and me is in some respects one of principle and not of mere detail. Indeed on a close examination, I have come to the conclusion that it goes deeper and lies more in the theory on which the principle is based than in the principle itself. Let us take Non-violence and Non-co-operation separately . . . Mahatmaji's Non-violence is carried on a very much higher plane than what I have agreed to adopt . . . The doctrine of *Ahimsa* (non-violence) with all its implications and logical deductions has not been and cannot be adopted by the Congress . . . Whilst Mahatmaji is not prepared to resort to violence under any circumstances whatever in thought, word or deed, many true Congressmen would under certain conditions consider it their highest duty to resort to actual physical violence. In fact I hold that it would be doing violence to the highest and noblest feelings implanted in man, if we ruled out violence in any shape or form under all conceivable circumstances. If I see a bully ill-treating or assaulting a person weaker than himself, I would not merely interpose my body between the assailant and the victim, and thus enable him to have two victims instead of one, but to try to knock him down and thus save both his victim and myself. Again, if I were assaulted, I would defend myself, if necessary, by inflicting violence on my assailant, and that violence under certain circumstances may extend even to the causing of the assailant's death . . .

'As for violence in thought it is obvious that one who is prepared to resort to actual violence on certain occasions, cannot be entirely free from the thought of it. By joining the movement of non-violent non-co-operation, all I have undertaken to do is, to refrain from inflicting, or even contemplating, violence of any kind in carrying out the programme of non-co-operation against the Government . . . If a Government official chooses to behave to me like 'the bully of my illustration in matters wholly unconnected with the Congress programme, he shall receive exactly the same treatment as I would give to the bully. The doctrine of non-violence has, so far as I am concerned, a limited application for the very special purpose for which I have adopted it . . .

'Mahatmaji says entry into councils is tantamount to participation in violence. I understand this to refer to the fact that the councils are established by a Government which is based on violence. I maintain that no one living under such a Government can help participating in violence in that sense . . .

'Mahatmaji has been pleased to doubt the accuracy of the statement, "that most Congressmen confine the definition of non-violence to mere abstention from causing physical hurt to his opponent". There may be some who take the extreme view in theory, but I do not know a single follower of Mahatmaji who acts upon it. It is true that non-violence, even in the limited sense that I give to it, must relate to both word and deed and cannot be confined to abstention from causing physical hurt only. But non-violence in thought must be ruled out entirely as impracticable. Otherwise, we shall be weaving a cobweb of casuistry around us from which it would be impossible to extricate ourselves.'

Motilal was dealing with the practical and not the theoretical aspects of non-violence. If he treated its philosophical and spiritual implications somewhat casually, he had at least the courage to cut through the thickets of make-believe behind which many of Gandhi's close associates were often tempted to take shelter. In the last year of his life Gandhi was to realize the truth of some of these criticisms and to discover how few of those who professed to follow him were prepared to pursue non-violence to its logical conclusions.

Motilal applied the same ruthless logic to the rest of Gandhi's thesis. He deprecated the continuing emphasis on the Khilafat and Punjab wrongs (which were 'practically dead') and on the 'triple boycott' proclaimed in 1920. 'The honest thing to do,' he asserted, 'is to admit failure and frankly give up the triple boycott. The Swarajists would have done it, had it not been for their belief that they had no chance of success with the masses against Mahatmaji's teachings.' Council-entry, he argued, was not a negation but an extension of non-co-operation to a new field. The legislatures, with their peculiar composition and limited powers, were an ornamental rather than essential part of the apparatus of British rule in India. By creating deadlocks in these legislatures, the Swarajists hoped to expose to the world the true nature of these 'sham parliaments'.

Gandhi had suggested that the programme of obstruction had a strong smell of violence. 'Our Swarajist nostrils,' Motilal retorted, 'are not trained enough to smell violence in it and fail to see how the Swarajist programme can have a stronger smell of violence than the breaking of the Criminal Law Amendment Act and the various forms of picketing and hartals authorized by the Congress. I take civil disobedience itself as the highest form of obstruction.'

Motilal and Gandhi were picking up the threads of a debate which had begun in 1922 and was not to end until 1925. Non-violent non-co-operation, propounded as a political programme in the special conditions of 1920, had already hardened into a dogma. The Swarajists were – to borrow a phrase from the current coinage of Communist polemics – the 'revisionists', with one important difference: they had to contend with the living Marx of non-violent non-co-operation.

No dish is colder and less appetizing than that of a dead controversy. Nevertheless, the ideological debate on council-entry, which rocked the Indian National Congress for nearly three years, can be viewed in better perspective today than was possible at the time. The founding fathers of Indian nationalism had taken it for granted that self-government would come through legislatures which would progressively become more representative and exercise wider control over the executive until they approximated to the Dominion Parliaments. This was a belief shared by Hume, Dadabhai Naoroji, Gokhale, Tilak and even Gandhi until the beginning of 1920. Gandhi had served his political apprenticeship in South Africa where the Indian minority was unrepresented in the local legislatures; his entire political experience, extending over two decades, was confined to agitation outside the legislatures; Satyagraha itself was an extra-constitutional technique. In *Hind Swaraj*, Gandhi's political manifesto written before the First World War, there are some caustic comments on the British Parliament. It is therefore arguable that the tragic events of 1919 served only to accelerate Gandhi's journey along a path to which he was inclined alike by temperament and past experience. Not all the arguments he advanced against council-entry in 1924 were convincing. It seemed as if he regarded the councils as an 'evil thing' whose touch would contaminate and corrupt the true nationalist. Motilal's logical mind refused to swallow the curious mixture of politics, metaphysics and sheer intuition which Gandhi advanced against the Swarajist case. As we shall see later, the Mahatma's intuition turned out to be less fallible than Motilal's logic.

A footnote to this controversy suggests itself. Gandhi's proposal that councils should be used, if at all, for the 'constructive programme', not for mere obstruction, was rejected out of hand by the Swarajists who were anxious to appear as good non-co-operators as their opponents. Nevertheless important consequences might have ensued, if the Congress had done in 1924 what it did in 1937 and decided to work the constitution for what it was worth. With the elimination of 'obstruction' from the Swarajist programme, a number of Moderate and Muslim leaders, including Jinnah, might have joined the Swaraj party, or at least collaborated with it, on an enduring basis.[1] At the same time a sympathetic administration in Britain might have found it easier to hasten the pace of constitutional advance. This line of reasoning is of course based on the assumption that the British would have relaxed their grip on India within a measurable time without extra-constitutional pressures. This assumption is rather a large one. As we have already seen, the first Labour Government did not make a new departure in its policy towards India. At the end of 1924 the Conservatives came into power. 'I am not able,' Birkenhead, the new Secretary of State, told the House of Lords in July, 1925, 'in any forseeable future, to discern a moment when we may safely, either to ourselves or India, abandon our trust.'[2]

2

In spite of their polite phraseology, the statements issued by Motilal and C. R. Das on the one hand and Gandhi on the other proclaimed to the world that there was a serious division in the Congress leadership. 'I seem to see,' Mohammed Ali, the Khilafat leader, wrote to Jawaharlal, 'an unholy glee on the face of some No-Changers . . . Your father has preserved his good temper more than I was inclined to expect; but that is perhaps more for the public and especially for the Government.' The Government were not deceived.

Viceroy to Secretary of State for India, June 6, 1924. 'The probability of a split between Swarajists and Gandhi is increasing. Interviewed by Associated Press . . . Motilal Nehru says, the Swarajists have determined to stand on their own legs. Moonje, the leader of the Central Provinces Legislative Party says that the effect of Gandhi's dictum would be a clear cleavage in the Congress and practically all the intelligentsia will be excluded from it. He adds that the Swarajists are now driven to concen-

---

[1] Jayakar, M. R., *The Story of My Life*, vol. II, p. 76.
[2] Birkenhead, Earl of, F. E., *The Life of F. E. Smith*, First Earl of Birkenhead, p. 509.

trating all their energy on breaking Gandhi's hold on the Congress.'[3]

The conflict came to a head at the Ahmedabad meeting of the All India Congress Committee in the last week of June. Previously anyone who paid four annas and accepted the creed of the Congress could become a member. Gandhi's proposal to limit membership of the Congress to those who sent in 2,000 yards of self-spun yarn was resisted by Motilal and Das, who carried their protest to the point of staging a walk-out from the meeting. They were persuaded to return, but another, and from Gandhi's point of view a more serious clash took place, when Das did not whole-heartedly support Gandhi's resolution condemning the murder of an English official by a young Bengali, Gopinath Saha. That some of his senior colleagues should have mental reservations about non-violence even in its political applications came as a bitter disillusionment to Gandhi. There were tears in his eyes. 'I felt,' he confessed later, 'that God was speaking to me . . . and seemed to say, "Thou fool, knowest not thou that thou art impossible? Thy time is up".'[4]

A split in the Congress, wider and deeper than that which had paralysed it for a decade after the Surat Congress, loomed large. But Gandhi, who was to preside over the Belgaum Congress in December, 1924, was not spoiling for a fight – least of all with Motilal.

Gandhi to Motilal, August 15, 1924: 'I thank you for your letter. The more I think of it the more my soul rises against a battle for power at Belgaum. But I do not want to be mixed up with the councils' programme. This can only happen by Swarajists manning the Congress or their not acting upon the Congress . . . I would gladly occupy the place I did from 1915 to 1918. My purpose is not to weaken the power of the Swarajists, certainly not to embarrass them. Show me the way and I shall try my best to suit you . . .'

Gandhi was ready to step off the political stage. Motilal was as fair-minded in rejecting the offer as Gandhi had been in making it. He replied to Gandhi on August 25th:

[3] Unpublished telegram (N.A.I.).
[4] Tendulkar, D. G., *Mahatma*, vol. II, p. 189.

'I for one will be no party to an agreement which is based upon your retirement from the Congress as a condition precedent, not because I have the least doubt in my mind of being fully able to run it with my colleagues throughout the country according to our lights, but because of the fact [that] stipulating for your retirement goes against my very soul, quite apart from the public odium involved in it. I have the misfortune to differ from you and am prepared to take the consequences at the hands of the country in the normal way, but not by taking from you an agreement disabling yourself . . . You are of course your own master and can take what step you think proper, but it shall not be at our request, if it imposes the least disability or restraint on you . . .'

There were good reasons on both sides for not pressing differences to a breach. Motilal and Das were aware of the unique influence exercised by Gandhi on the masses. With his position beyond the possibility of damage by any temporal authority, Gandhi had no desire – and no need – to control the party machine. His faith in the ultimate victory of his doctrine and his method was so firm that he could afford to wait for more propitious times. Moreover, he was anxious about the growing communal antagonism in the country which was clearly more dangerous than the Swarajist heresy. He had too wholesome a respect for Das and Motilal – the two giants of the Swaraj Party – to seek a head-on collision with them. With Motilal his relations transcended the political nexus. In the last week of July when the controversy was at its height Motilal learned from press reports that Gandhi was indisposed, and immediately sent him an affectionate rebuke.

Motilal to Gandhi, July 28, 1924: '. . . I am getting very anxious about your health. The most obvious thing to do is to stop all work at once and take complete rest. But the misfortune is that you will not do this . . . I shall be perfectly frank with you even at the risk of offending you. Let me tell you plainly that the kind of work you are doing at present can wait, and the nation will not be poorer if it is not done at all . . .

'I should cut you off from all communication with India for a time and send you out in the open sea for a very long cruise without any land being in sight for six weeks . . . Your dak

[mail] should wait for you at the *ashram* during your absence. But it is useless to go on writing in this strain. I am afraid I can make no impression on you. I have, however, made up my mind about one thing, and that is that I will not be a *particep criminis* in the suicide you are committing by troubling you with any further correspondence or talk about any work, however urgent it may be, till you have considerably improved in health . . .

'Let me ask you a question. Would you put me down as mad, if I were to ask you to spend a few weeks on the bank of Ganges some five miles out of Allahabad, at a garden house belonging to a friend of mine which is at my entire disposal? This is the only alternative to your going out to sea that I can think of for the benefit of your health.'

The sins and sorrows of his countrymen made it impossible for the Mahatma to take a holiday. In September, 1924, he went, not on a cruise, but on a twenty-one-day fast, in a desperate effort to stem the tide of communal bitterness and bloodshed. He had not recovered from the after-effects of the fast when he had to leave for Bengal where the Government had promulgated an ordinance, raided the offices of the Swaraj Party and arrested its prominent members, including Subhas Bose, a lieutenant of C. R. Das. The authorities accused the Swaraj Party of complicity in anarchical crime. Gandhi challenged them to prove the charge in a court of law. 'The Rowlatt Act is dead,' he wrote, 'but the spirit that prompted it is evergreen.' As an answer to what he considered an offensive against the Swaraj Party in Bengal, Gandhi decided to throw his weight in favour of unity in the Congress and in the country. He reached an agreement with Das and Motilal, according to which non-co-operation (except for the boycott of foreign cloth) was to be formally suspended and the Swaraj Party was to become an integral part of the Congress with powers to raise and administer its own funds. In November, 1924, he was present at an All Parties Conference in Bombay at which he invited the leaders of various parties including Jinnah, Mrs Besant, Motilal, Chintamani and others to explore a common political platform and present a united front to the Government.

The Belgaum Congress over which Gandhi presided in December, 1924, ratified his agreement with Das and Motilal. The Mahatma made yet another chivalrous gesture to the

Swarajists by giving them a majority of seats in the Working Committee for the year 1925. To some observers, including his faithful 'No-Changers', it seemed that Gandhi had yielded too much ground to the Swarajists. The Viceroy wrote home: 'Gandhi is now attached to the tail of Das and Nehru although they try their utmost to make him and his supporters think that he is one of the heads, if not the head.'[5]

By the end of 1924 the Swaraj Party under Das and Motilal had scored all along the line. Das was president and Motilal the general secretary. The imaginative insight and emotional appeal of Das formed a perfect foil to the objectivity and down-to-earth empiricism of Motilal; their complementary qualities made them an excellent team. Such was their mutual confidence that each of them could, without prior consultation, use the other's name for any statement or declaration. Their partnership was soon to be cut short.

Das was determined to make the working of the new constitution impossible in Bengal. He succeeded in his object. His health was, however, broken by the terrific pressure at which he was working. Once he insisted on being carried to the Council Chamber in a stretcher. B. C. Roy recalls that when Motilal came to Calcutta, Das recited his exploits and exclaimed: 'Motilal in Bengal, Dyarchy is dead.' 'Yes, Chitta,' Motilal replied, 'Dyarchy is dead, but it has been a costly death.' This premonition proved too true. In June, 1925, Das died. The news reached Motilal at Chamba in the Punjab hills. 'For a long time,' writes Jawaharlal, 'father sat still without a word, bowed down with grief. It was a cruel blow to him.' Henceforth Motilal alone had to shoulder the burden of leading the Swaraj Party. How heavy the burden was to be was mercifully hidden from him in the summer of 1925.

About the same time Lord Birkenhead delivered a speech which aimed at the Congress the usual mixture of bullying and banter. 'The speech,' declared Gandhi, 'is a notice to Indians to set their house in order.' The Mahatma finally closed the rift in the Congress ranks by making further concessions to the Swarajists. The 'yarn franchise' became an alternative to the four-anna membership; the Swaraj Party became not only an integral part of the Congress, but its sole agency for political work.

The triumph of the Swarajists within the Congress was complete. Within three years the rebels of 1922 were in possession of the party machine. They had survived even Gandhi's resistance. But this resistance had been half-hearted. The Mahatma's logic may be inferred from a letter he wrote to Dr Ansari in November, 1925: 'I could not convince the Swarajists of the error of council-entry, and knowing also that my best friends and co-workers had become Swarajists, I took it that I could not do less than throw my weight with them as against other political parties.'[6]

[6] G.S.N. Papers.

CHAPTER TWENTY-THREE

EVOLUTION OF JAWAHARLAL

IN January, 1924, while Gandhi was in hospital, Ramsay Mac-Donald about to form the first Labour Government and Motilal on the threshold of his legislative triumphs, Jawaharlal nearly landed in gaol. An account of the melodramatic incident during the *Ardh Kumbh Mela* was given by him soon afterwards to Gandhi's youngest son, who had been his fellow-prisoner in Lucknow gaol.

Jawaharlal to Devadas Gandhi, January, 1924: '. . . The fact is that I have done my utmost to land myself in jail. I have taken part in a petty riot and richly deserve a spell of jail to quieten my over-excitable nature . . . Malaviyaji [was] greatly put out at a silly order of the Magistrate (against bathing at the confluence of the Ganges and the Jumna) . . . It was difficult for me to restrain myself when there was talk of Satyagraha specially by Malaviyaji, and on I went, like the men of the Light Brigade, with little thought or reasoning. However, it is something to be tried for a disobedience of law with Malaviyaji as one's co-accused . . . But I do not like to go to jail on a false issue. And then I miss seeing Bapu[1] . . .'

In fact, there was no prosecution; the Government were not at all anxious to stir up the dying embers of political agitation in what the Khilafat leader Mohammed Ali picturesquely called the 'Disunited Provinces'. 'Let us all go forth, purged of all narrowness, bigotry and intolerance,' Mohammed Ali wrote in 1923, while his brother Shaukat Ali referred to Gandhi as 'our dear chief.' There were however only grandiloquent phrases. Gandhi found on his release from gaol that the Hindu-Muslim dissensions were no less serious than the group rivalries within the Congress. Gandhi pleaded that religion was meant to unite and not to divide; he talked long and earnestly to the leaders of

[1] Mahatma Gandhi.

both the communities; he devoted a whole issue of his weekly paper *Young India* to an analysis of the communal malaise; but all in vain. Even his three weeks' fast for communal unity in the autumn of 1924 failed to purge the hearts of the fanatics on both sides. If many a Congressman was a 'communalist under his national cloak',[2] many a nationalist Muslim turned out to be more Muslim than nationalist. Gandhi was blamed by bigots on both sides. The Hindus charged him with having roused Muslim fanaticism and ambitions by his support of the Khilafat. The Muslims accused him of leading them up the garden path.

Jawaharlal was completely out of tune with these communal and factional politics, and did not align himself with any particular party. But this did not prevent him from holding high office in the Congress organization. Before his imprisonment in 1921, he was the secretary of the U.P. Congress. His election as general secretary of the All India Congress Committee for the years 1924 and 1925 was a pointer to the new status he was acquiring in national politics. When Motilal wrote to Sir Harcourt Butler in 1920 that 'Young Jawaharlal is known throughout India',[3] the wish was father to the thought; but in 1923-5 the statement would have been perfectly valid. As a young and favourite disciple of the Mahatma, Jawaharlal occupied a special position. In March, 1922, during the brief interval between his two terms in gaol, he had rushed to Ahmedabad to see his beloved leader. In January, 1924, while Gandhi was lying in hospital at Poona, Jawaharlal was longing for 'even a distant glimpse' of '*Bapu*' (father). Intellectually young Nehru was probably nearest to Gandhi during the non-co-operation movement. He began to drift away during the years 1922-5, a process which was accelerated during the next three years. They often disagreed, but the emotional bond between them never gave way. The same could be said of the relations between Jawaharlal and Motilal. Motilal's political views were firmly held and vigorously expressed, but he did not try to ram them down his son's throat. Only rarely were the tensions of national politics reflected in the family: for the most part he was as tolerant of Jawaharlal's political views as he was of Swarup Rani's religious beliefs. Co-existence was practised in the Nehru

---

[2] Nehru, J., *Toward Freedom,* p. 114.
[3] Motilal to Harcourt Butler, May 19, 1920.

family long before it became a political catchword in the world outside.

An imperfect appreciation of the emotional bonds between Gandhi and the Nehrus often led the critics astray. In 1924 it was seriously suggested that Motilal was trying to push Gandhi off the political stage; four years later Jawaharlal was credited with the same ambition. The Trinity of 'the Father, the Son and the Holy Ghost', was something more than a gibe of foreign correspondents; it was one of the realities of the Indian politics in the nineteen-twenties. The ties between Sabarmati and Anand Bhawan were stronger than a political partnership could ever supply. Their nature is illustrated by an incident in 1924 when Gandhi heard of an estrangement between father and son over the admission of little Indira to St Cecilia's School in Allahabad, run by three European sisters, the Misses Cameron. The Mahatma hastened to intercede on behalf of Jawaharlal.

Gandhi to Motilal, September 2, 1924: 'This is again early morning after prayer. I hope you received my long letter . . . This letter like the former is meant to be a plea for Jawaharlal. He is one of the loneliest young men of my acquaintance in India . . . I don't want to be the cause, direct or indirect of the slightest breach.'

Motilal, who was at Simla, telegraphed to Gandhi to say that the story was a 'tissue of lies from beginning to end', that the school to which Indira had been admitted was wholly unconnected with the Government, that Jawaharlal's objections were based not on principles of non-co-operation but on unsuitability from the educational point of view. 'I was solely prompted,' he explained, 'by desire to give Indira companionship of children of her age regardless of instruction and Jawaharlal agreed. Other things reported to you [against me are] absolutely false . . . too mean for the proudest father in the world . . .'

2

On April 3, 1923, Jawaharlal was elected Chairman of the Allahabad Municipal Board. The 'non-co-operating' wing in the Municipal Board had unanimously decided to nominate Purushottamadas Tandon, but when it was suggested that the honour should go to a Muslim, he backed down in favour of a local Khilafatist Kamaluddin Jafri. It was then realized that Jafri was too ill to be able to function as Municipal Chairman, and so almost at the last moment Jawaharlal was nominated as a candidate likely to command the widest measure of support. Just when his father had become the Leader of the Opposition in India's central legislature, Jawaharlal became the civic chief of his home town. Curiously enough, the 'No-Changers', who regarded membership of councils as a sin, did not object to working the local bodies: one of the most prominent 'No-Changers', Vallabhbhai Patel, became the Chairman of the Ahmedabad Municipality.

Jawaharlal took the direction of civic affairs seriously; he tried to rouse the enthusiasm of the citizens, to accelerate the tempo of the municipal organization and to pull the city fathers out of the well-worn ruts in which many of them had moved all their lives.

In Allahabad, as in many other Indian towns, membership of civic bodies was (and is still) regarded as a sinecure, yielding prestige, profit and patronage without definite responsibility. But Jawaharlal made surprise inspections, called for quarterly reports from the standing committees of the Board, set precise targets for performance and prescribed codes of conduct. He frowned upon nepotism. 'Members will remember,' he wrote on April 19, 1924, 'that last year I wrote a note on patronage. I was, and am, very much against chits and testimonials and recommendations. We discussed this matter, and it was felt that where a recommendation had to be made it should be in writing and reasons should be given. On no account should a recommendation be made orally.' He encouraged the idea of a municipal volunteer corps, 'a strong civic guard, open to all classes and communities . . . thus a spirit of *camaraderie*, which has been lacking amongst our citizens of late, might develop.' He discouraged extravagance; when the expenditure on an address of welcome to Maulana Shaukat Ali exceeded the sanctioned amount, the city fathers, led by the Chairman, paid the difference out of their own pockets.

There was hardly a civic issue on which Jawaharlal did not try to educate his colleagues. He wrote a long minute on a proposal for segregation of prostitutes: 'Last year the Board made a brave effort to abolish prostitution by passing a resolution and appointing a committee.' Segregation of prostitutes, even if feasible (he wrote) was as undesirable as segregation of criminals. 'I do not believe in issuing a fiat that prostitutes must not live in any part of Allahabad except a remote corner. If this is done, I would think it equally reasonable to reserve another part of Allahabad for men who exploited women and because of whom prostitutes flourish.' The solution lay not merely in punitive measures but in socio-economic reforms. He suggested a number of constructive measures such as educative propaganda on venereal disease, the building of 'homes' for widows and helpless women and improvement in the legal and economic status of women.

This enthusiasm and industry did not produce the results young Nehru had expected. Many of his colleagues on the Municipal Board were more interested in securing appointments for friends and relatives than in making Allahabad a model city. The powers of the Municipal Board were circumscribed by the Government, and almost every important reform faced administrative or financial hurdles. Between the hopeless apathy of his colleagues and the nagging interference of hide-bound officials Jawaharlal felt frustrated. In April, 1924, he felt he had had enough of the Municipal Board and resigned from the chairmanship. He was persuaded to continue, but finally resigned in February, 1925. Pim, the British Commissioner of Allahabad, asked him to reconsider his decision. 'You have had a very difficult and uphill task,' Pim wrote, 'and everyone recognizes that you have carried it out with much ability and conspicuous fairness to all parties in the board . . .' The U.P. Government formally regretted 'Pandit Jawaharlal's decision to vacate a post he has filled with great ability and fairness'. However, Jawaharlal had no intention of losing himself permanently in the local affairs of Allahabad. 'I feel that it is within the power of a [Municipal] Board,' he wrote to an officer of the Board from Nabha gaol in September, 1923, 'to make life a little more bearable, a little less painful to the inhabitants of Allahabad. This is worthy work. To me . . . it is only secondary work. My real passion, as I have repeatedly informed the Board, lies in a different direction, and, God-willing, I shall go that way till my purpose is achieved'.

Among those who had complimented Jawaharlal was C. Y. Chintamani, the editor of the *Leader*. 'I hope,' he wrote, 'in spite of political differences you will not think it impertinent on my part if I take the liberty of saying with what genuine admiration your administration of the Allahabad Municipality is regarded by friends. Differ from your political opinions as I unfortunately do, allow me to assure you of my great esteem for you for your exemplary sacrifice in the cause of the country.'

3

During the years 1923-5 Indian politics were in the doldrums. The Congress was riddled with personal and factional dissensions. Gandhi, though still the most revered Indian, was ploughing a lonely furrow. The middle class had relapsed into the torpor of the pre-Gandhian era, from which it was occasionally roused by the noisy advocates of communalism. For the landed and titled gentry and the high officials life again was on an even keel; once again they could look forward to such prizes as an invitation to a Government House party.

For Jawaharlal the aridity of politics was partly offset by domestic happiness. In the first flush of Satyagraha in 1919-21 he had lived in public meetings and railway trains. It took him some time to realize how much he had drawn upon the patience of his family, particularly that of his wife.

Both father and son had given up legal practice during the non-co-operation movement. After his release from gaol Motilal resumed it in his spare time, but Jawaharlal could not bring himself to go back to his profession. Jawaharlal and his wife did not spend much, but the thought of being dependent upon his father at the age of thirty-four made him unhappy. He welcomed a proposal which would have made him a salaried General Secretary of the All India Congress; but to his chagrin the prejudice against payment for political work from public funds proved too strong, and the proposal fell through. He could of course have got a well-paid job, but he feared it might distract and even compromise him. Torn between these conflicting considerations he sought Gandhi's advice. The Mahatma was sympathetic.

Gandhi to Jawaharlal, September 15, 1924: '. . . Shall I try to arrange some money for you? Why may you not take up remunerative work? After all you must live by the sweat of

your brow even though you may be under Father's roof. Will
you be correspondent to some newspaper or will you take up a
professorship?'

Jawaharlal knew that even a reference to this subject was
likely to hurt his father. Somehow he screwed himself up to
broach it. Motilal pointed out that it was foolish and unnecessary for Jawaharlal to sacrifice all or most of his political
activities in order to make ends meet. After all, the father could
easily earn in a week what the son would take a year to spend.
The argument was not without force, though it did not resolve
the son's conflict. The consolation young Nehru offered to
Mahadev Desai in August, 1923, applied equally to himself.

'I have also the good fortune of having experienced to the full
the depths of a father's love and many times I have wondered if
I was repaying in any way the love and care that had been
lavished upon me from the day of my birth. I have had to face
that question often and every time I have felt shame at my
own record . . .
'The lesson of service you learnt from your father you have
carried to the outer world. Your father could hardly have
grudged this or preferred a narrow domestic sphere for you to
the wider service of the country.'

4

Jawaharlal's wife, Kamala, had not been well for some time.
In November, 1924, she gave birth to a son who died after a few
days. Her health took a serious turn; in November, 1925, her
illness was diagnosed as tuberculosis. Dr M. A. Ansari, equally
eminent as a nationalist leader and as a doctor, was consulted
and suggested that she should be taken to Geneva for treatment.
Gandhi, to whom the family always turned for solace in
moments of crisis, agreed.
During the winter months Kamala lay in a hospital at Lucknow, and Jawaharlal, who was the General Secretary of the
Congress, was kept busy travelling between Allahabad, Lucknow and Cawnpore, the venue of the 1925 Congress. Difficulties
arose over the issue of a passport. Jawaharlal refused to give an
undertaking that during his stay in Europe he would not take

part in politics. Motilal spoke to Sir Alexander Muddiman and the Government of India advised the U.P. Government that 'having regard to all the circumstances it would be undesirable that such an undertaking should be required.'

In March, 1926, Jawaharlal sailed from Bombay with his wife and daughter; with them in the same boat were his sister Vijayalakshmi and her husband Ranjit who had planned their holiday in Europe long before Kamala's illness.

Jawaharlal had expected to be away from India only for six months; actually he did not return till December, 1927. In the summer of 1926 he was joined by his younger sister, Krishna. Kamala was under treatment at Geneva for the first few months before she was taken to a sanatorium in Montana. Her progress was slow. 'It is a year, almost to a day,' Jawaharlal wrote to Gandhi (March 15, 1927), 'since we landed at Venice, and it must be confessed that the results of the year's treatment have been far from satisfactory.' So long as Kamala was bed-ridden it was not possible for Jawaharlal to leave her for long periods. Still, Geneva as the headquarters of the League of Nations and the venue of international gatherings, was not a bad place from which to study the world scene. With a letter of introduction from Gandhi, Jawaharlal went to see Romain Rolland. He made a few friends, such as the young German poet Ernst Troller and Roger Baldwin. Jawaharlal also came across some of the Indian revolutionaries, Barkatullah, Madame Cama, Raja Mahendra Pratap, Shyamji Varma. He found them a quaint mixture of the picturesque and the pathetic, shadowed by the British secret police, haunted by a past beyond recall, living in their own airy castles out of touch with the political realities of the day.

Jawaharlal went to Europe at a time when the First World War was still a recent memory, and the Second World War not yet in sight; the aftermath of 1919 persisted, the pity and fear of 1939 were still unguessed. A semblance of stability had come to Western Europe with the signing of the Locarno Pacts, but the canker of suspicion continued to poison relations between Germany and France, between the Western Powers and Russia. Asia and Africa were awakening from their long slumber. The United States had left Europe to its own political and economic chaos and retired behind the Atlantic moat. Europe was in the grip of labour unrest, unemployment and muffled echoes of class-war which gave rise to a variety of nostrums, Socialism, Communism and Fascism.

Jawaharlal saw that powerful forces were at work in the world which could not but affect India. In Geneva, and even more in Montana, there was plenty of time for reading and reflection. From his vantage point in Switzerland, he was able to survey Indian politics in a fresh perspective. The petty squabbles which filled the columns of Indian newspapers faded out, and the basic issues of Indian nationalism came into focus. He realized how narrow and parochial the outlook of most Indian parties and politicians had been. A hundred years before, Raja Ram Mohun Roy had given a public dinner in Calcutta to celebrate the grant of a constitution to the people of Spain. But in 1926-7 few Indian politicians knew or cared about what was happening in the world. Until 1920 the Indian National Congress had been running a branch and a journal in England, but with the advent of non-co-operation and emphasis on 'national self-reliance', foreign propaganda had been relegated to the background.

Jawaharlal also began to see the limitations of a purely political approach to his country's problems; a brand-new constitution alone could not carry India far without those social and economic changes which had been arrested by the natural conservatism of a foreign bureaucracy and its anxiety not to antagonize vested interests.

It was perhaps because he was stimulated by his son that Motilal began to show a keener appreciation of the economic factor in Indian politics.

Motilal to Jawaharlal, January 27, 1927: 'You ask me to read books on the world situation. My misfortune has always been that I could never find the time to read anything which was not necessary for the immediate need of the moment . . . You have done a lot of reading . . . But let me again impress on you the great need of the most careful study of economics and finance for a public man in India. The present controversy on the currency question has revealed the fact that many hundreds of crores [of rupees] have been taken out of the country by the simple process of manipulating the exchange and adjusting the tariff to suit the British manufacturer and merchant. And yet the first and the latest protest made by any public man in India

was by Gokhale! Dadabhoy, Dutt and Digby only approached
the fringe of the problem.'

After going through the Currency Commission's Report,
Gandhi had publicly confessed his ignorance of the mysteries of
high finance in an article in *Young India* entitled 'Wanted a
Teacher'. The Indian merchants in Bombay were only too willing to instruct the Mahatma and the Swaraj Party.[4] Motilal had
a shrewd suspicion that the Bombay merchants were not swayed
by undiluted patriotism, that they tended to represent the views
of the manufacturer and the middleman, rather than those of
the primary producer and the consumer. From Europe, Jawaharlal had been impressing on his father the importance of
encouraging aircraft manufacture in India and even named some
German firms from which technical help could be obtained.
Early in 1927 Motilal met Sir Samuel Hoare, the British
Minister for Air, at a luncheon party in Delhi. Sir Samuel
assured Motilal that the British aircraft industry was no less
advanced than the German. Reporting the conversation to Jawaharlal, Motilal wrote (February 3, 1927): 'The difficulty in our
case is that we cannot afford the capital. There is an offer by the
Government [of India] to subsidize the industry (for their own
purposes of course), but even men of the type of Sir Purshotamdas and Sir Victor Sassoon are not ready to take it up. These
men look for fat dividends and they get enough from cotton
[not] to think of anything else.' A few days earlier, Motilal
referred to 'the sudden love of the masses' among the textile
magnates one of whom frankly told Motilal that he could not
contribute to the funds of the Swaraj Party as it was trying to
establish 'Cooly Raj' in India.

The highlight of Jawaharlal's European trip came in
February, 1927, when he attended the 'Congress of Oppressed
Nationalities' at Brussels, along with representatives of a
number of countries in the Middle and Far East, North Africa,
Central and South America, Italy, France and Britain. At Jawaharlal's suggestion the Gauhati Congress (December, 1926) decided to participate in the Brussels Conference and nominated
him as its delegate. Jawaharlal wrote to Srinivas Iyengar, the
Congress President, to ask whether he might define the political
goal of the Congress as independence; the word 'Swaraj' had

---

[4] Moraes, Frank, *Sir Purshotamdas Thakurdas*, pp. 102-3.

been rather vaguely employed in Congress resolutions. 'I have seen your letter to Srinivas Iyengar,' Motilal told Jawaharlal. 'You are quite right in saying that you cannot put the case for India any lower than the people of other countries do. Saklat-wala [Communist] M.P. is here and is making great fun of the Dominion Status theory. It is of course unnecessary for you to mention it. We (the Congress) ask for *Swaraj* and you can in-terpret it to mean independence, as indeed it is.'

Jawaharlal's speech at the plenary session of the Congress was a trenchant attack on Britain. He described the early history of British rule in India as 'an epoch of predatory war – a period in which freebooters prowled about and committed plunders and robberies in an unbridled manner'. He accused British im-perialism of encouraging India's communal divisions, uprooting her educational system and undermining her economy. He was hopeful that the liberation of his homeland would lead to the liberation of Asia and of Africa. The resolution on India drafted and moved by him declared, 'that this Congress accords its warm support to the Indian national movement for the com-plete freedom of India, and is of the opinion that the liberation of India from foreign domination is an essential step in the full emancipation of the peoples of the world. This Congress trusts that peoples and workers of other countries will fully co-operate in this task; this Congress further trusts that the Indian national movement will base its programme on the full emancipation of the peasants and workers of India, without which there can be no real freedom.'

During and after the conference, Jawaharlal took a keen in-terest in mobilizing public opinion against the despatch of British troops to China. In a joint resolution of the British, Indian and Chinese delegates, the Congress of Oppressed Nationalities demanded immediate withdrawal of all foreign troops from Chinese territory and waters and urged 'the need of direct action, including strikes and imposition of embargo to prevent the movement of munitions and troops either in India or China, and from India to China'.

There was something ironic in a conference of 'oppressed nationalities' meeting in the heart of Western Europe, the countries of which had parcelled out most of Asia and Africa among themselves. But it would have been impossible for such a 'subversive' gathering to take place in any of the 'dependencies' or 'colonies'. The Brussels meeting was by no means a product of undiluted idealism. It was financed by the Mexican Government, which resented American intervention in Latin America, and by the *Kuomintang*, the Chinese Nationalist Party, which resented British interference in China. The Soviet Government was quick to see the propagandist value of the conference. But though Marxist phrases were bandied about and there were sincere Communists among the delegates, there were also many socialists and 'pure' nationalists whose only ambition was to end the domination of one country or race by another.

George Lansbury, the British Labour leader, presided over the conference and was also elected president of the League Against Imperialism, the 'permanent' organization to which the conference gave birth. Jawaharlal was elected to the nine-man executive committee of the League, which included such celebrities as Romain Rolland, Mme Sun Yat Sen and Albert Einstein. Jawaharlal sent home detailed and enthusiastic reports of the conference, and recommended that the Indian National Congress should maintain links with Asia and Africa through the League Against Imperialism. 'Your participation in the Brussels Conference,' wrote Motilal, 'has brought home to everybody who has read your reports the importance of our having a full-time representative in Europe and America.' Gandhi was less impressed.

Gandhi to Motilal, May 14, 1927: 'I read the public printed report of the [Brussels Conference] from beginning to end and I have now read the confidential report. Both are worthy of Jawaharlal. I appreciate the view he presents about foreign propaganda. But somehow or other, I still feel that our way lies differently. I feel that we will not get the support of Europe beyond a certain point, because after all most of the European states are partners in our exploitation. And if my proposition is correct, we shall not retain European sympathy during the final heat of the struggle . . .'

Gandhi had written to Jawaharlal in the same vein, and sounded a note of warning against reliance upon external support.

'I fancy,' Jawaharlal wrote back on April 23, 1927, 'you have got a wrong impression about my idea of the utility of the League Against Imperialism. I do not expect much from it and indeed I am quite sure that none of the members of the so-called imperialist or oppressing nations will help us in the least whenever their interests conflict with ours. I have no illusion about their altruism. But I welcome all legitimate methods of getting into touch with other countries and peoples so that we may be able to understand their viewpoint and world politics generally. I do not think it is desirable, nor indeed is it possible, for India to plough a lonely furrow now or in the future. It is solely with a view to self-education and self-improvement that I desire external contacts. I am afraid we are terribly narrow in our outlook and the sooner we get rid of this narrowness, the better. Our salvation can of course come only from the internal strength that we may evolve, but one of the methods of evolving such strength should be study of other peoples and their ideas.'

Gandhi had feared that the League Against Imperialism would not go far enough. But before long, it was the League which branded Gandhi as a 'reactionary'. In November, 1929, when the 'joint manifesto' under the signatures of several Indian leaders, including Gandhi and the Nehrus, was issued to welcome Lord Irwin's declaration on Dominion Status for India, the League Against Imperialism, without understanding the shifting complexities of Indian politics, hurled abuse in stereotyped phrases ('chronic reformism' and 'the betrayal of the cause of workers and peasants') at Gandhi and the Congress. This denunciation came, curiously enough, at a time when the Mahatma was about to launch a campaign of mass civil disobedience. Jawaharlal had no intention of dancing to the League's tune; the final break came in April, 1930, when he told the office of the All India Congress Committee not to correspond with it.

In September, 1927, Motilal was at last able to take his holiday in Europe. He was received in Venice by Jawaharlal. Fortunately, Kamala was feeling better and during the next three months the family travelled together in Italy, Britain, France and Germany. In October they were in Berlin and decided, at Jawaharlal's suggestion, to visit Russia to attend the tenth anniversary celebrations of the Russian Revolution for which they had received invitations from the Soviet Government. It took them twenty-eight hours in a not-too-comfortable train to travel from Berlin to the small town of Niegeroloje on the Polish-Russian frontier. The people of Niegeroloje accorded the Nehrus a welcome as simple and spontaneous as that of their own Indian villages.

'Pandit Motilal Nehru, one of the outstanding leaders of the Indian National movement is expected here, today or to-morrow,' the *Pravda* announced on November 5th. 'He will come to Moscow with his son Jawaharlal Nehru, leader of the left wing of the National Congress.'

On arrival in the Soviet capital they were greeted by officials of the reception committee and S. J. Saklatwala, the young Indian Communist member of the British Parliament whom Jawaharlal had met in Brussels. They arrived a day too late to witness the spectacular parade in Red Square, but spent four busy days in Moscow. Motilal did not record his impressions, but those of his son have survived in a series of articles in the Indian press which were published in book form as *Soviet Russia*. His intellectual curiosity sharpened by months of reading and reflection, Jawaharlal arrived in Russia in a peculiarly receptive mood. He was impressed by what he saw, and felt India could learn much from the Soviet struggle to shake off its feudal past. The constructive side of the new regime made a strong impression upon him. He noted that in Moscow the contrast between luxury and poverty was less glaring than in the big towns of India and Western Europe,[5] that high officials in Moscow did not live in a lavish style; that the State Opera House was patronized not only by the upper class but also by the common people; that literacy was increasing fast; that the legal and economic status of women had risen; that conditions in prisons – at least, those shown to him – had improved.

Jawaharlal of course could not foresee the political and economic changes which the next three decades were to bring to Russia and the world. Communism was at this time linked in his mind with opposition to alien rule and economic injustice. 'Whatever its faults,' he wrote about Communism in his autobiography, 'it is not hypocritical and not imperialistic'. Though he learned to use the Marxist idiom, his affiliation to Communism was never doctrinal, then or later. It was the constructive side of the Soviet experiment which appealed to him – the

[5] Nehru, Jawaharlal, *Soviet Russia*, pp. 13-4.

massive and planned assault on poverty, disease and illiteracy, the tremendous push towards industrialization and away from cramping custom and obscurantism. In 1927-8 he was not alone in not seeing the other side of the Stalinist medal.

'Pandit Jawaharlal Nehru,' wrote J. Coatman in his *Years of Destiny* in 1932, 'has now one secret ambition which is to rival Lenin or Stalin in the history of Communism.'[6] Coatman, like many others then and later, failed to see that Jawaharlal was too firmly tied to Gandhi, to non-violence and to individual liberty to lead a Communist revolution in India, that even his drive for social and economic changes would be pressed only as far as was compatible with Indian freedom and unity.

[6] Coatman, J., *Years of Destiny*, p. 95.

CHAPTER TWENTY-FOUR

RIFT IN THE LUTE

WHILE his son was seeking fresh perspectives in the solitudes of Switzerland, Motilal was in the centre of the parliamentary arena. The opposition to the Swarajists within the Congress had died down. Gandhi let them hold the political stage, while he and his close adherents – the few that remained – engaged themselves in the task of 'nation-building' by propagating hand-spinning, Hindu-Muslim unity and the abolition of untouchability.

The Swarajists had gone to the councils to wreck them 'from within', by throwing out official resolutions, refusing supplies and creating a constitutional impasse. They succeeded in inflicting a series of defeats on the Government during the years 1924-25. But their very success contained the germs of ultimate failure. Except in the Central Provinces they did not command an absolute majority in any legislature and needed the support of other parties to out-vote the Government. That support was sometimes (though not always) forthcoming, but at a price. The price was the whittling down of the original Swarajist programme. In Bengal Legislative Council Das was able to hold the Government at bay, but only after conceding sectarian claims which survived long after Das was dead and his Muslim supporters had dropped off from the Swaraj Party.

In the Central Legislative Assembly Motilal was at first able to reach an understanding with the Moderate and the Muslim groups. The coalition, which came to be known as the Nationalist Party, commanded the allegiance of more than 70 of the 101 elected members; it carried everything before it in the opening session in 1924. But like all coalitions it had to take into account the lowest common measure of agreement among its component elements. The alignment of forces on the floor of the Legislative Assembly thus made the Swarajist strategy of 'uniform, continuous and consistent obstruction' impracticable. In his maiden speech in the Central Assembly on February 8,

1924, on the grant of self-government to India, Motilal admitted[1] that he had 'toned down' his resolution 'to meet the wishes of friends who are not Swarajists in this Assembly'.

Motilal's resolution on self-government secured seventy-six votes; the forty-eight members who voted against it included officials, European non-officials, and a few Indian members who had either been nominated by the Government or were in any case at its beck and call. The utmost that the Government could concede was an 'investigation of defects or difficulties in the existing constitution'. The investigation which was to be within the scope of the Government of India Act of 1919, was entrusted to a committee headed by Sir Alexander Muddiman, the Home Member of the Government of India. Motilal declined to serve on a committee which had such circumscribed terms of reference. Not until September, 1925, did the recommendations of the committee come up for discussion before the Assembly. The minority report signed by Jinnah and Sapru called for major changes in the constitution, which the majority report, representing the official views, ruled out. Motilal assailed the narrow and niggardly spirit in which the Government had approached the issue. He called for the dismantling of the halfway house of dyarchy and for the setting up of full provincial autonomy. He proposed that the Government of India should immediately be made responsible to the central legislature, except for defence and foreign and economic affairs which could be 'reserved' to the Viceroy for a short 'transitional' period.

Official spokesmen, while counselling Indians to be patient, drew attention to the provision in the preamble of the Act of 1919 for a review of the constitutional position after ten years. 'Wise men,' Muddiman said, 'are not the slaves of dates.' 'I say,' Motilal retorted, 'wise men are not the slaves of preambles either. What sanctity is there in a preamble? Is not this Act of Parliament, the Government of India Act of 1919, just like any other Act of Parliament? [Is not] any legislative authority, not to speak of the Mother of Parliaments, perfectly at liberty to set aside its own Act under whatever circumstances it may have been passed.' The struggle for freedom, he declared, would sooner or later have its appointed end. 'It remains to be seen whether England will share the credit of that achievement by willingly giving a hand, or suffer that achievement to be wrested

[1] Legislative Assembly Debates 1924, vol. IV, Part I, p. 370.

from her unwilling hands. It is for England to choose.'

England's choice – or at least the choice of her representatives in India – was to mark time. Eighteen months had passed between the Assembly's resolution demanding responsible government and the presentation of the Muddiman Committee's report. During those eighteen months the edge of the Swarajist opposition had been blunted. 'The Nationalist Party,' the informal coalition of Swarajists, Moderates and Muslims which had made possible the triumphs of 1924, had disintegrated. The Swaraj Party had been sliding gradually but unmistakably from its original creed of 'uniform, continuous and consistent obstruction.' In August, 1925, V. J. Patel, the deputy leader of the party in the Legislative Assembly, became its first elected president. Motilal himself accepted a seat on the Skeen Committee which was to report on the setting up of an 'Indian Sandhurst'. The Committee was headed by Lieutenant-General Sir Andrew Skeen, Chief of the General Staff in India, and included Motilal, Jinnah, Phiroze Sethna, Sahibzada Abdul Qayum Khan, Jogendra Singh, Rama Chandra Rao, Ziauddin, Captain Hira Singh, Capt. J. N. Banerjea, Captain Gul Nawaz Khan, Major Dafle and E. Burden.

Though the committee was nominated by the Government and its composition was not all that Motilal could have desired, he decided to serve on it. One of the strongest arguments in the armoury of the enemies of Indian independence was that Indians could not defend themselves against external danger and internal chaos. In 1917 Motilal had interested himself in the campaign for the grant of the King's commission to Indian nationals and in the organization of the Indian Defence Force; eight years later he was anxious to hasten the Indianization of the officers' cadre of the British Indian army.

In September, 1925, it was decided that a sub-committee of the Skeen Committee consisting of Motilal, Jinnah, Phiroze Sethna, Abdul Qayum and Major Zorawar Singh with Major Lumby as Secretary should tour England, France and Canada in the following spring. Motilal, who was to preside over the sub-committee, hastened to give the news to his son.

Motilal to Jawaharlal, September 14, 1925: '. . . As I have perhaps already told you I was previously consulted about the constitution of the sub-committee, and that [it] was approved by

me as the best we could have out of the bigger committee. I do
hope Dr Ziauddin and Capt Hira Singh will never know that
their exclusion is due to me. Abdul Qayum with all his communal leanings is at least a gentleman, and Major Zorawar
Singh is a fine type of Rajput soldier, very well educated and
thoroughly independent. He was introduced to me at Juhu by
Ranjit . . . He has only recently been taken on the Skeen Committee, and from the first day supported the Indian view, and
took the attitude adopted by Jinnah and myself. He held a
King's commission and threw it up in disgust. From this alone
you can imagine how valuable a colleague he will prove to
Jinnah and me . . .'

The prospect of a trip abroad after seventeen years pleased
Motilal, the more so because his daughter Sarup (Vijaya
Lakshmi) and son-in-law Ranjit Pandit had also planned a
holiday in Europe about the same time. He asked them to cancel
their passages, to travel by the same boat and to stay in the
same hotels as himself and his colleagues.

This pleasant prospect was to be shattered by a political storm
which not only made it impossible for Motilal to continue on
the Skeen Committee, but rocked the Swaraj Party from top to
bottom.

2

The discipline of the Swaraj Party, which had won the admiration of friends and foes, received a rude jolt early in October,
1925, when Tambe, the Swarajist president of the Central
Provinces Legislative Council, accepted a seat on the Governor's
executive council. Motilal lost no time in denouncing Tambe's
action, but was shocked to discover that it had apologists, if not
supporters, among his senior colleagues in the Swaraj Party. One
of them, N. C. Kelkar, telegraphed his congratulations to
Tambe, and another, M. R. Jayakar, openly advocated a change
in the Swarajist strategy by harking back to Tilak's slogan of
'Responsive co-operation'. There was hardly a distinction,
Jayakar argued, between Tambe's appointment as an executive
councillor, Patel's election as Speaker of the Legislative
Assembly and Motilal's acceptance of a seat on the Skeen Com-

mittee: the time had come to seize 'all places of power, influence and constructive responsibility'.

Jayakar's analogy was fallacious. Tambe had agreed to become a limb of the provincial government without the knowledge of his colleagues and party leaders. Patel was elected in the teeth of official opposition and was to be a thorn in the side of the Government throughout his five years tenure of office. Motilal's membership of the Skeen Committee did not in the least compromise his politics. As for the Responsivist talk of capturing places of 'power, influence and responsibility', there was no doubt that one day Indian nationalists would have to fill those places. But had that day come? Could an Indian executive-councillor or minister exercise real authority in the field of provincial administration? Was it not a dangerous pastime for a nationalist opposition to accept responsibility without power? It was one thing to storm and occupy the governmental citadel; it was quite another to seek a premature and partial entry on sufferance.

'The Pandit is on the war-path,' Jayakar wrote[2] when the controversy was at its bitterest. Many years later in the evening of his life, he complained that Motilal forgot 'his usual dignity and restraint', and drove him (Jayakar) into opposition and open rebellion. Motilal's temper, once it was roused, was a terrible thing and could lead him into untenable positions. In 1926 he had a sharp argument with V. J. Patel, when the latter refused to resign his seat in the Legislative Assembly or to contribute part of his salary to the funds of the Swaraj party on the ground that as President of the Legislative Assembly he could not directly associate himself with one party. There is no doubt that on this issue Patel was right and Motilal was wrong.

It is possible that if Jayakar had been handled more gently he might not have led the revolt of 1926. But their differences were not merely those of emphasis or tactics. Motilal rightly sensed that the very foundation of the Swaraj Party, as he and Das had fashioned it, was at stake; his resolve is reflected in a letter he wrote to Gandhi.

Motilal to Gandhi, November 25, 1925: 'I quite agree that the differences which have arisen are quite unfortunate – but as a matter of fact they have always been there, and have only come

[2] Jayakar, M. R., The Story of My Life, vol. II, p. 668.

to the surface. As you know the Marhatta group never took kindly to non-co-operation. They were compelled to join the movement by the pressure of public opinion. The same causes led them to join the Swaraj Party without believing in its principles . . . I am going to put it to them quite plainly that I can under no circumstances agree to make it permissible to take ministerships and executive councillorships by any member of the Swaraj Party – "Responsive Co-operation" is a mere camouflage for taking these offices . . . If [they do not agree], there is nothing for it but an open fight. We have been living on patched-up compromises too long . . . The Cawnpore Congress will settle the question.'

The Cawnpore Congress witnessed a tug-of-war between the rival ideologies within the Swaraj Party. The Responsivists, Jayakar, Kelkar, Moonje and Aney, were supported by Malaviya; they asked for the same freedom of action within the Swaraj Party as Motilal and Das had claimed within the Congress during the years 1922-3. They appealed to Gandhi. The Mahatma preferred to be a 'neutral' and 'peace-maker', but his closest adherents supported Motilal at Cawnpore. 'The more I study the councils' work,' Gandhi wrote, 'the effect of [the Swarajist] entry into the councils upon public life [and] its repercussions upon the Hindu-Muslim question, the more convinced I am not only of the futility but the inadvisability of the council-entry . . . I would welcome the day when at least a few of the comrades of 1920 leave the councils to their fate.'[3]

The day to which Gandhi was looking forward was to be hastened by the fissures within the Swaraj Party. One of the consequences of the Responsivist revolt was to make the official programme of the Swaraj Party more militant. Motilal realized that the only way of preventing the slide downhill was to resume the climb uphill. If the Swaraj Party were to remain the spearhead of the nationalist struggle the drift from non-co-operation to co-operation had to be stopped. At Cawnpore he reiterated his faith in mass civil disobedience, 'the ultimate sanction', and carried a resolution directing the Swarajists to resign their seats in the legislatures if the Government failed to respond to the 'national demand' for responsible self-government.

[3] Gandhi to Srinivas Iyengar, April 27, 1926 (G.S.N. Papers).

In accordance with the mandate of the Cawnpore Congress the Swaraj Party walked out of the Legislative Assembly on March 8, 1926. On this occasion Motilal delivered a memorable speech in which he recalled his resolution of February 8, 1924. That resolution was, he said, a message to the people of the United Kingdom which had gone unheeded. 'We know the great power that this Government wields. We know that in the present state of the country, rent as it is by communal discord and dissension, civil disobedience, our only possible weapon, is not available to us at present. But we know also that it is equally unavailing to remain in this legislature and in the other legislatures of the country any longer. We go out today, not with the object of overthrowing this mighty Empire. We know we cannot do it even if we wished it. We go out in all humility, with the confession of our failure to achieve our objects in this House on our lips.'

The 'walk-out' earned banner headlines in the nationalist press, but it could not stop the rot that Tambe had started within the party. The C.P. Swarajists had been joined by Malaviya and Lajpat Rai. Motilal summoned the dissidents to a conference at Gandhi's *ashram* at Sabarmati in the last week of April. An agreement was reached, but remained a dead letter. Another attempt at a *rapprochement* was made by Sarojini Naidu at Simla, but it shared the same fate. It soon became apparent that the differences between the two wings of the party were not confined to the constitutional issue. 'The angle of vision,' Lajpat Rai wrote to Motilal, 'with which we look upon questions relating to matters on which the Hindus and the Muslims differ is entirely different.' With the elections in the offing, the appeal to religion was a crude but serviceable hook for catching votes. Motilal was accused of bartering away the interests of his own community. In fact, his agnosticism placed him above the storms of religious passion. He had no patience with fanaticism, whether it was of the Hindu or the Muslim vintage. Of the latter he had a bitter taste when he visited Delhi in April, 1926, to confer with Maulana Mohammed Ali and other Muslim leaders.

Motilal to Gandhi, April 28, 1926: '. . . while I was there, the conversation was more or less desultory interspersed with a few acrimonious passages-at-arms between Mohammed Ali and me.

All Hindu Congressmen, with the exception of yourself, Jawahar and me were condemned as open enemies of Muslims . . . On the other hand it was claimed that not a single Khila-fatist of standing had ever deviated from the strict principle of nationalism . . . I am sorry I was unable to agree either in the sweeping condemnation of all Hindu Congressmen or in the general commendation of all Khilafatists, and it was in this connection that some heat was imported in the discussion . . .'

In 1924 Gandhi had made a heroic but vain effort to halt the communal conflict. There were not a few who put down the tension between Hindus and Muslims to the non-co-operation movement and its alliance with the Khilafat cause and blamed Gandhi for having played with the masses and roused them prematurely. 'The awakening of the masses,' Gandhi wrote, 'was a necessary part of the training. I would do nothing to put the people to sleep again.' He tried to divert this awakening into constructive channels and to educate the two communities out of the mental morass into which they had slipped; he even tried the shock-therapy of a three weeks' fast; but all in vain. Gandhi found that the communal leaders were 'fighting not for loaves and fishes, but fighting like the proverbial dog, not for the bone but for the shadow'.

Since the basis of the franchise was communal, communalism reached a peak in 1926, the election year. Faced with fanaticism on both sides, Motilal reaffirmed his own secular faith. Jointly with Abul Kalam Azad, who was to play an important role in Congress politics during the next thirty years, he issued on July 31, 1926, the manifesto of 'The Indian National Union' which was to be open to all Indians 'not under the age of eighteen', who accepted the principles of religious liberty, absolute tolerance of the views and practices of others, and 'adjustment of communal relations on the basis of strict legal rights of communities and individuals'. 'I do hereby solemnly affirm,' ran the pledge of membership, 'that the only way to India's lasting prosperity and freedom lies in realization by all communities of India of a common united nationality and harmonious co-operation between them . . . My sole objective shall be the good of the nation as a whole . . .'[4]

The Indian National Union received the support of a number

[4] Indian Quarterly Register, 1926, vol. II, pp. 90-94.

of eminent Indians of all creeds and shades of opinion, including Sapru, Sastri, Ajmal Khan, Maharaja of Mahmudabad, Ansari, and Sarojini Naidu. But it failed to make an impression on the communal leaders or on the masses. The aims of the Union were wholly unexceptionable; that they needed to be restated at all was a melancholy commentary on the politics of that period, charged as they were 'with artifically produced, deliberately sustained, tensions – communal, internicine, personal and all sorts'.[5] These tensions put the Swaraj Party at a disadvantage in the electoral fight. It did rather well in Madras, Bengal and Assam, not so well in Bombay and the Central Provinces, badly in the Punjab; but in the United Provinces it suffered a rout. Motilal later described the election as a fight 'between the forces of nationalism and a low order of communalism reinforced by wealth, wholesale corruption, terrorism and falsehood'.

'Pandit Motilal is a solitary figure,' a friend wrote to Jawaharlal, who was in Switzerland at that time, 'with the whole of educated India against him, but he is a giant of a man and fights boldly and chivalrously.'[6] Motilal's own nephew Shamlal Nehru was working against him; the communal tide had swept away old colleagues and trusted workers and left him high and dry. He was shocked at the vulgarity and vehemence of his opponents, who accused him of being anti-Hindu, of plotting to legalize cow-slaughter, and even of intriguing with Kabul. It was difficult to believe that colleagues and friends of yesterday could be so factious, so bitter, so unfair.

Motilal to Jawaharlal, January 6, 1926: 'You say that you wished you were here to help me. You do not know how often I have felt this while plying my lonely furrow after being deserted by all the active workers. If you were here, and given me your personal support, the result of the elections in the U.P. and the other provinces, where we have suffered heavy defeats would have been very different to what it was.'

Motilal himself had fought with his back to the wall; he had sought no quarter and given none. Early in 1927 he demanded from Lajpat Rai's paper *Bande Mataram* an unconditional

[5] Sarojini Naidu to Jawaharlal, October 15, 1926 (N.P.).
[6] Sri Prakasa to Jawaharlal, November 26, 1926 (N.P.).

apology, or else one lakh as damages for libel. The case was filed but withdrawn thanks to Gandhi's mediation.

The elections left him disillusioned and disgusted. The Swaraj Party was still the largest party in the country's legislatures, but its strength and moral fibre had perceptibly weakened. The 'Indian National Union' had proved still-born. To Motilal, the political landscape appeared so grim that he seriously thought of announcing his resignation at the annual Congress session to be held in Assam at the end of December.

On the way to Gauhati his spirits revived. He travelled by a small river steamer which cruised slowly down the Ganges and the Brahmaputra. His only companions were Upadhyaya his secretary, and Hari his personal servant. His only regret was that he had no rifle with him with which to do a little shooting as the steamer passed along the Sunderbans. The voyage and the solitude and scenery of the Sunderbans helped to relax the accumulated tension of the election weeks. He was already talking of 'returning vigour'.

He had expected another trial of strength with the dissidents at Gauhati, believing that Lajput Rai and Malaviya, 'aided by Birla's money', were trying to capture the Congress. These fears proved groundless. At Gauhati all was plain sailing for Motilal. This was partly due to the presence and support of Gandhi, whom he had persuaded to attend, and partly to the failure of the Responsivists to muster their forces. Lajput Rai, Jayakar and Kelkar were absent; Aney and Moonje were present but passive. Malaviya's pleas for the acceptance of office had no effect. The original Swarajist programme as advocated by Motilal was confirmed. 'We have stood firm,' he told his son triumphantly, 'against all reactionaries and carried everything we wanted by overwhelming majorities.'

CHAPTER TWENTY-FIVE

END OF THE TETHER

In January, 1927, when the newly-elected Legislative Assembly met at Delhi, Motilal discovered that the ratification of his programme by the Gauhati Congress had not ended his difficulties within the party. Only three years had passed since he had embarked on his legislative career, but he no longer felt the optimism he had felt in January, 1924, when C. R. Das was alive, public interest at a high pitch, the press favourable, the Swaraj Party well-knit, when the support of other parties was forthcoming and the bureaucracy was momentarily bewildered. By 1927 the political kaleidoscope had violently shifted. C. R. Das was dead, the Swaraj Party had suffered a deep schism; the united front of progressive elements in the Legislative Assembly had disintegrated; old colleagues and comrades turned against Motilal and the elections had left a bitter taste in his mouth. He had not yet drained the cup of ingratitude and disloyalty to the full. Tortuous intrigues in the Swaraj Party came to light early in 1927. C. S. Ranga Iyer, the journalist whom Motilal had employed on the staff of the *Independent* and then brought into the Legislative Assembly, was in open revolt, with the surreptitious backing of Srinivas Iyengar, the deputy leader of the Swaraj Party and President of the Congress.

Motilal to Jawaharlal, March 24, 1927: 'We are practically at the end of the Assembly session, but it is difficult to say whether I shall continue to be a member up to the moment it is prorogued. Things have been going from bad to worse in the party. Srinivas Iyengar, being the Congress President, was allowed by me to have a full and free hand in party affairs, while I remained more or less in the background. He took advantage of this to promote disaffection in the party by encouraging Ranga Iyer and others to discredit me in various ways. When I felt compelled to take disciplinary action he interceded on their behalf, and cultivated sympathy for them among the members. After the proceedings were withdrawn, he set them up again for some fresh mischief . . . The only alternatives before me are either to put down the spirit of rebellion with an iron hand or to retire. I think the latter is the better course, but I have not definitely made up my mind . . .'

But the letter continues with characteristic cheerfulness:

'Even with these worries, I have carried on very well – looking younger and younger as I am getting older and older (so say the New Delhi ladies).'

To Kamala, his daughter-in-law, who was slowly convalescing in a sanatorium in Switzerland, he wrote:

'I feel as strong as a horse in spite of all I have gone through. Many European members of the Assembly come and ask me to divulge the secret of health, which, they are sure, I have discovered. I wish I had, as in that case I would first impart it to you.'

Rarely had the political outlook been bleaker in India than at the beginning of 1927. Communal antagonisms, factional rivalries and personal animosities seemed to have submerged basic issues. 'The Muslims do not want to hear anything,' Shaukat Ali, the Khilafat leader, confessed to Gandhi,[1] 'they want us to organize them in the defence of Islam against the Hindus.' This pandering to the worst passions of the mob – by leaders of both communities – had brought about an atmosphere which was deadly to rational politics.

Gandhi had told the Cawnpore Congress in December, 1925: 'Today I would commence civil disobedience if the necessary fire and fervour were there in the people. But alas, they are not.' Later he told a meeting at Comilla in Bengal that the Hindu-Muslim problem had passed out of human hands into God's hands. Nobody knew better than Gandhi that the communal problem was not a simple equation between the Hindu and the Muslim. At the request of a member of the Independent Labour Party, the Mahatma gave a candid analysis of the political triangle in India.

[1] Shaukat Ali to Gandhi, March 4, 1927 (G.S.N. Papers).

'If we were not disposed to quarrel,' he wrote, 'no outside power could make us. But, when an outside power notices our dissensions, it takes advantage of them consciously or unconsciously. Everyone in India knows this and feels the effect of it . . . Some honest British officials have not hesitated to make the admission before me . . . I am well aware that you can do nothing to remedy this evil, even if you (the Labour Party) believed in it. The remedy lies in our own hands. All that you can do is to give us, if you are in power, a good and workable constitution. But you will certainly not be able to control your agents here. The agents themselves know that they are agents only in name, but in reality they are principals. I have before now described the [Indian] Civil Service as a gigantic and most powerful secret corporation that the world has seen. Like the Masonic Brotherhood, it has got its signs and its unwritten language through which it corresponds with its members.'[2]

Even during these lean years when the Mahatma had retired from active politics, nothing important in the Congress was done without his advice. He was the keeper of the consciences of politicians who were at loggerheads with one another. This was a fortunate circumstance for Motilal, who could always bank upon Gandhi's advice and assistance in a crisis. His opponents did not fail to notice his special relationship with Gandhi. During the fierce controversies of 1926, Jayakar bluntly asked Gandhi whether it was not a fact that Motilal counted for more with him than he (Jayakar) did. 'I do not know,' replied Gandhi, 'if it is true in any sense, I can only say that it is a human failing which I have not yet overcome because I am unconscious of it.'[3] Whether he was conscious of it or not, Gandhi never failed to support the elder Nehru in a crisis; and but for this support, Motilal might have thrown in his hand during the years 1925-27 when nationalist politics passed through a particularly disheartening phase. As it was, he felt deeply despondent about the future of his party and country. His mood is mirrored in a letter he wrote to Gandhi on May 6, 1927, his sixty-sixth birthday:

'By the way, I have entered upon my 67th year today and

[2] Gandhi to Dr Norman Leys, M.P., July 23, 1926 (G.S.N. Papers).
[3] Gandhi to Jayakar, August 1, 1926 (G.S.N. Papers).

Sarup [Vijayalakshmi] is celebrating the event by inviting a number of people this afternoon to tea. Looking back through the vista of 66 long years it presents to myself an almost unbroken record of time wasted and opportunities missed. It is depressing to think of little, if any output of all these years, and of the less that can be reasonably expected within the brief span still left to me . . . I have already begun the process of 'slipping out' of the Assembly. During the last session I kept in the background as far as possible. When the next session comes round in September, I shall most probably be in Europe. It will be open to the Governor-General to declare my seat vacant, but I am afraid he will not. In that case . . . I shall occupy myself outside in the best way I can . . .'

Now, when he thought that his innings was drawing to a close, his thoughts turned often to his son, to whom he wrote when the new Assembly had met in Delhi.

Motilal to Jawaharlal, January 27, 1927: '. . . I wish first of all to tell you what has since the opening of the Assembly forced itself upon me many a time. We have among the members two men who were your contemporaries at Cambridge (Mackworth Young and Ruthnaswamy). The former is the Secretary to the Government in the Military Department, and the latter a nominated non-official. What I feel on seeing these men is that you should have been in my place. This would have been more in the fitness of things than my being there. I don't know why this idea recurs to me repeatedly on seeing your contemporaries.'

In the summer of 1927 there were informal discussions among Congress leaders on the choice of the president for the ensuing session which was to be held in Madras in December. A Royal Commission was expected to be appointed, and 1928 promised to be an eventful, perhaps a crucial year. At the instance of Jinnah and the Maharaja of Mahmudabad, Sarojini Naidu suggested that Motilal should preside over the Madras Congress. She sought Gandhi's support for her proposal. 'There are too many forces just now working against Motilalji,' Gandhi told her. Motilal himself declined the offer, but in a letter to Gandhi suggested Jawaharlal for 'the crown' as the Congress presidency was described in Congress circles. 'Jawaharlal presiding has an irresistible appeal for me,' Gandhi wrote back, 'but I wonder whether it would be proper in the present atmosphere to saddle the responsibility on him.'

The Mahatma sounded young Nehru, who was in Switzerland at the time:

'There is some talk of your being chosen as President of the coming Congress,' Gandhi wrote to him. 'I am in correspondence with Father [Motilal] about it. The outlook here is not at all happy . . . We have lost hold upon the masses . . . The question then is how your services can be best utilized. What you yourself think, you should do. I know you are capable of taking a detached view and you will say quite unselfishly like Dadabhai: "Put the crown on my head".'

Jawaharlal did not feel – or at least did not show – much enthusiasm for the proposal. Meanwhile, both his father and the Mahatma had agreed that the time had not yet come for him to take command. Gandhi wrote to Motilal:

'He is too high-souled to stand the anarchy and hooliganism that seem to be growing in the Congress, and it would be cruel to expect him to evolve order all of a sudden out of chaos. I am confident, however, that the anarchy will spend itself before long and the hooligans will themselves want a disciplinarian; Jawaharlal will come in then.'[4]

The choice finally fell on Dr M. A. Ansari, who (Gandhi confided to Motilal) 'won't control the hooligans. He will let them have their way; but he may specialize in the Hindu-Muslim question and do something in the matter'.

If Motilal felt any embarrassment in sponsoring his son's candidature for the Congress presidency, he did not betray it. He could of course write in complete confidence to Gandhi, in whose heart there was a special place for Jawaharlal. But he was careful to keep the issue on a public rather than a private plane:

'You have put it very well to Jawahar to say whether he wishes the "crown" to be put on his head. His own letters,

4 Gandhi to Motilal, June 19, 1927.

which to my mind, breathed an unshakeable faith not only in'
the ultimate victory against the forces of reaction, but also in
our present capacity to put up a strong fight, suggested the
idea to me and I forthwith communicated it to you. His reply
to you will show the extent to which he is confident himself.'
Motilal concluded: 'My only fear is that the habit of playing
the role of the humble soldier in the presence of his great general
may check the necessary assertiveness required for the occasion.'

2

Having reached a dead-end in national politics, Motilal decided to take his long-deferred holiday in Europe. His plans for
going abroad with the sub-committee of the Skeen Committee
in March, 1926, had fallen through. Nor did he feel free, with
the chaos in the party and the country, to leave India in 1926.
Early in 1927 he was eager to re-join his son in Switzerland, but
there were two obstacles. One was the progress of the new house
which he was building in the compound of Anand Bhawan. For
many years Motilal had felt that Anand Bhawan was too large
for his family, particularly after his nephews had set up on their
own. With the cessation of his practice and the change in his
style of living which had followed his plunge into the non-
co-operation movement, Anand Bhawan seemed more and more
of a white elephant. He decided to build a new house, smaller
and more compact. But it was not easy for him to do anything
in a small way; eventually the new house turned out to be more
compact than small. He took a keen interest in the design and
construction, but he was too preoccupied with professional and
political affairs to supervise the work; and the local engineers
had not much experience of modern sanitary and electrical installations. After a good deal of wasteful experiment, an
engineer was sent for from the Tatas, and the work had to be
done over again. The result was that in June, 1927, when the
house should have been receiving the finishing touches, holes
were being knocked in walls and ceilings and the floors and
verandas dug out.

The second hurdle which barred the way to Europe was
financial. Motilal's legal practice since his release from gaol had
been a sporadic affair. What with demands of his family and
party, he had long since run through his savings. The new house

proved a serious drain on his resources. In 1927, when politics began to stink in his nostrils, he was devoting greater attention to his profession. But legal practice at the age of sixty-six was a strenuous affair. A fortnight's pleading in an election case at Farrukhabad in June left him 'more dead than alive', and the offer of Rs. 2,000 a day for the next fortnight in Lucknow failed to tempt him. He came back to Allahabad to rest, but there was no rest for him. He had to drive himself to the limit if he were to meet his immediate liabilities and find the wherewithal for the European trip. When Gandhi, who was slowly recovering in Nandi Hills in Mysore from a serious attack of high blood pressure, asked for a donation for the Spinners' Association, Motilal let him into his financial secrets.

Motilal to Gandhi, May 6, 1927: '. . . I see your eagle eyes have penetrated into my empty till from the heights of Nandi Hills and have discovered something lying at the bottom. Yes, I am making some money, but not much to speak of. April brought me Rs. 15,000 out of which £500 (a little less than Rs. 7,000) went to Switzerland, and the balance to pay outstanding bills mostly on [house] building account. May has opened very well with a single fee of Rs. 13,000, the whole of which has gone to clear overdrafts in the various banks. The bigger creditors have not yet been paid anything. These must be tackled now as they have the first charge, and your "poor spinners" only the second. I must be just before I am generous. Remember my offer [in 1920] to contribute a lakh a year to the Tilak fund if you would let me continue my practice. But you refused to be bribed, as you then put it . . .'

The empty till was to be replenished by the Lakhana case, which also determined the timing of Motilal's trip to Europe.

As we have already seen,[5] the District Judge had decided the case in 1918 in favour of Rani Kishori. The appeal against this decision came up before the Allahabad High Court in 1921. During these three years, the fortunes of the opposing counsel had undergone a remarkable metamorphosis. Tej Bahadur Sapru had become the Law Member of the Viceroy's Executive Council. Motilal had renounced his practice at the Bar, but decided to make an exception of this case; his reappearance at the High

[5] *Supra*, p. 29.

Court was a memorable event. In his homespun *sherwani* he presented a different, though not less formidable, figure than he had done in his Savile Row suit.

Narsingh Rao engaged a distinguished lawyer (B. E. O'Connor), but Dunnaju's refusal to agree to a medical examination sealed his fate. Chief Justice Sir Grimwood Mears and Justice P. C. Banerjea dismissed the appeal without going into the question of law. 'We are driven to the conclusion,' they observed, 'that the only reason for her refusal is the fact that she is well aware that she has never given birth to a child.'

The High Court also turned down Narsingh Rao's request for a review. Nor would it grant him leave to appeal to the Privy Council. Fortunately for Narsingh Rao, the Judicial Committee of the Privy Council took a more sympathetic view and the rather unusual step of granting him leave to appeal direct to the Privy Council. 'The case is a very important one,' Motilal advised the London Solicitor H. S. L. Polak, 'and I shall probably have to look after it personally in the Privy Council, however much I may try to avoid it. It is one of the two cases which I had to conduct after giving up my practice.'

In 1925 Narsingh Rao left for England. 'He has,' Motilal warned Polak, 'a special dread of my appearance in the Privy Council and has declared his intention to arrange the hearing in such a manner and at such a date as would make it impossible for me to be present. I do not know how he hopes to achieve that object ...'

The case took a sudden and unexpected turn in London. Their Lordships of the Privy Council did not see why another chance should not be given to Dunnaju to refute the allegation that she had never borne a child. They selected for her medical examination two lady doctors whose names were not disclosed. One afternoon, at an appointed time, the parties with their counsel reported themselves at a given address. Presently the gynaecologists appeared and examined a woman who claimed to be Dunnaju. The doctors gave a certificate that the woman had given birth to a child. To this certificate, as proof of the woman's identity, were attached her photograph and thumb impressions. On the receipt of this certificate the Privy Council remitted the case back to the Allahabad High Court.

The finding of the London doctors introduced a Sherlock Holmes touch into the case. If they were right, the question naturally arose why Dunnaju had so long and stubbornly held out against a medical examination. There was a spate of rumours. It was alleged that Dunnaju had never gone to London and that another woman, M., had impersonated her; that the thumb impressions of the two women were identical; that the thumb impressions on the certificate were Dunnaju's, but the woman actually examined was M.

Motilal made a thorough investigation. The passenger lists of the ships s.s *Devanha* and s.s. *Rawalpindi* by which Dunnaju was supposed to have travelled to and from England were scrutinized to see whether any other woman had accompanied or followed Narsingh Rao. A professional detective was engaged to look for clues. And incredible as it may seem, even Gandhi was made to take a hand in this detective hunt. From Sabarmati Ashram, where he was spending the 'year of silence', he telegraphed to Motilal (May 6, 1926): 'S – wires, K wires no other woman in party.'

It was a wild goose-chase. Ten months later, as the time came for the hearing before the High Court, Motilal confessed to his son: 'the mystery remains unsolved . . .' The mystery deepened, when some important papers relating to this case were lost and then recovered in Anand Bhawan.

The opinion of the London gynaecologists swung the pendulum in favour of Narsingh Rao. It was no longer possible to contest his legitimacy; but, even on the point of law, the Allahabad High Court took the view that Narsingh Rao was entitled to the disputed estate under the ordinary Hindu Law and not under the 'gift deed' of his grandfather.

The last round of the legal battle was fought before the Judicial Committee of the Privy Council. Rani Kishori had long been dead but her daughter Beti Mahalakshmi Bai insisted that Motilal should personally conduct the case in London. Eminent counsel were engaged on both sides. Sir John Simon, F. H. Maugham and Motilal appeared for Beti Mahalakshmi Bai, while Narsingh Rao enlisted the services of W. H. Upjohn and Sir George Lowndes, a former Law Member of the Government of India. The case was heard by Viscount Sumner, Lords Atkinson and S. P. Sinha, Sir John Wallis and Sir Lancelot Sunderson. Their Lordships disagreed with the Allahabad High Court and decided the case in favour of Motilal's client. They came to the conclusion that Narsingh Rao's claim could only be considered in terms of the 'gift deed', that Raja Jaswant Singh's bequest in favour of a grandson who had not been born at the time of the execution of the deed was invalid.

More than three decades had passed since the Lakhana case had come to Motilal. In its long and tortuous course it had brought him some headaches, but it had also brought him high fees. In the concluding phase of the case he received nearly Rs. 152,000. 'The expenses for my trip to Europe,' he told his son, 'must come out of the fees for the work in Europe.'

Apart from the Lakhana case, he had other reasons for not delaying his departure for Europe. In February Jawaharlal had attended the Congress of Oppressed Nationalities at Brussels and sent home some photographs. 'I have never seen worse photographs,' was Motilal's comment, 'but perhaps they suit the occasion, as you are the very picture of the representative of an oppressed country.' Incomparably superior to these photographs was a likeness of Jawaharlal in a Berlin journal, but it had the wrong caption: 'Barkatullah of *Ghadr* Party'. 'I know, Motilal added, 'that Barkatullah is wanted by the police of various countries and am living in hopes that we shall not hear of a case of mistaken identity in the near future.'

Motilal's banter concealed a real concern for the safety of his son. Sir Alexander Muddiman, the Home Member, with whom Motilal was socially, if not politically, on the best of terms, had recently met him at a dinner, and thrown hints that the Government was keeping track of young Nehru's doings in Europe. Motilal at once took Gandhi into confidence.

Motilal to Gandhi, May 6, 1927: '. . . I am afraid he has attracted too much attention of the India Office and things may not prove to be quite pleasant to him and to us. Muddiman has already hinted at it. He said: "Jawahar was sailing too near the wind". I replied that there was nothing strange in it – and in fact it was the business of both father and son to do so. We laughed it away, but he added significantly: "He has been to Berlin and met some people who are not of the right sort." "How can you help meeting people of all sorts when they come your way?" was my answer.

'He [Jawaharlal] says he has himself noticed that he has of late been the object of attention on the part of the British Secret Service which, he says, is the most perfect on the continent.

One of the reasons for my intended trip to Europe is to escort the young gentleman safely home.'

3

It was not until the end of August that Motilal was able to sail. There was a last-minute hitch. Dr Ansari, the president-designate of the 1927 Congress, insisted on issuing a long statement including comments on the Swaraj Party's work which Motilal considered both ill-advised and ill-timed. Having failed to dissuade Ansari, he urged Gandhi to advise him 'to keep his opinions to himself'. The Mahatma administered a strong, though good-humoured, rebuke to Ansari:

'I have this suggestion, keep these views to yourself. You are in no way called upon to publish them. For, if I am no politician, you are still less. When Swaraj is established you won't belong to the diplomatic service, nor to the military . . . You would be content if you are placed in charge of the medical service, even as I would aspire after nothing more serious or important than the spinning department. The law, diplomacy, military and the rest we shall leave to Motilalji and Company . . .'

Ansari was a good friend of Motilal and a faithful adherent of the Mahatma, but he ignored their advice and published the statement. Gandhi did what he could to soothe the elder Nehru; he undertook to take Ansari in hand, to patch up internal differences in the Swaraj Party, particularly those between Srinivas Iyengar and Shanmukham Chetty, which were weighing on Motilal's mind on the eve of his departure for Europe. 'I want you to leave India with a light heart,' Gandhi wrote to Motilal, 'and to return to India with Jawahar and Kamala within the Congress week.'

Motilal sailed at the end of August for Venice, where he was received by Jawaharlal. Fortunately, Kamala was well enough to move about, and during the next three months the family (except for Indira who was in school in Switzerland) travelled together in Italy, France, Britain, Germany and Russia. The Nehrus took the most expensive suites in the best hotels. Motilal's presence gave the tour the real flavour of an aristocratic holiday. 'Wherever we stayed with Father,' writes

Krishna, 'we were treated right royally. No sooner did we arrive at a hotel than the manager sent flowers with his compliments. He then came himself to see that we were comfortable. Everyone hovered around us all the time.'[6] Motilal himself seemed to have finished with politics. He was in high good humour. Once when the rest of the family was in Paris, he went to a well-known firm of drapers in London to buy a coat for his daughter. Not having the exact measurements with him, he suggested to the manager to have a few shop girls – about 5 feet 2 inches in height – lined up in order to enable him to select the right size. It was a most unusual request, but the manager was either so flabbergasted or awed by the peremptory manner of the customer that he did as he was told.

Early in November the Nehrus were in Berlin and from there paid a brief visit to Moscow. In December Jawaharlal, Kamala, Indira and Krishna sailed for India via Colombo and arrived at Madras just in time for the Congress session during Christmas.

Motilal decided to remain in Europe for a few months more. In January he was in Monte Carlo, which he described as 'the most charming little place that I have seen. You seem moving about in a huge picture laid at your feet'. He visited the Casino thrice, won and lost 'with the net result of some Fr. 2,000 to the good', but found it 'a disgusting affair'. What he enjoyed most was motoring to Nice, Menton and San Remo.

The holiday mood was shattered when a medical check-up revealed traces of albumin, and of glucoma 'implying stone blindness sooner or later'. It was an unduly alarming diagnosis, but Motilal read into it 'the beginning of the end'. 'I feel,' he wrote to his son (January 4, 1928), 'I will be happier in the old familiar surroundings and have accordingly made up my mind to leave Europe as early as I can.' A month later he was back in India.

[6] Hutheesing, Krishna, *With No Regrets*, p. 46.

CHAPTER TWENTY-SIX

RISING TEMPO

'My only hope,' Gandhi wrote in May, 1927, when the political horizon seemed darkest, 'lies in prayer and answer to prayer.' Strange are the ways of Providence: it chose Birkenhead, the Conservative Secretary of State for India, as its instrument for the welcome change in Indian politics. If there were two things in the world on which Birkenhead had no doubt, they were the permanence of Indian discord and the permanence of British rule in India. Of Hindu-Muslim differences he said: 'All the conferences in the world cannot bridge the unbridgeable'. He could not foresee a time when the sun would set on the British Empire. 'There is, my Lords,' he told the House of Lords on July 7, 1925, 'no "Lost Dominion", there will be no "Lost Dominion" until that moment, if ever it comes, when the whole British Empire, with all that it means for civilization, is splintered in doom.'

Birkenhead was in no hurry to prepare the next instalment of constitutional reform. But he had to reckon with the clause in the Indian Reforms Act of 1919 which had prescribed an inquiry into the working of the constitution after ten years. The appointment of a Royal Commission was not due until 1929, but it seemed to Birkenhead 'elementary prudence' not to run the risk of its nomination by a Labour Government. 'You can readily imagine,' he told the Viceroy, 'what kind of a commission in its personnel would have been appointed by Colonel Wedgwood and his friends.'[1] The Act of 1919 was accordingly amended so as to permit the appointment of the Commission two years ahead of the schedule.

In the summer of 1927 V. J. Patel, the President of the Indian Legislative Assembly, was in England ostensibly studying the procedure of the House of Commons. He was in close touch with George Lansbury, Graham Pole, Pethick-Lawrence, Fenner Brockway and other Labour M.Ps. who were regarded as 'friends

[1] Earl of Birkenhead, F. E. *Life of F. E. Smith, the first Earl of Birkenhead*, pp. 511-2.

of India'. Patel had an audience with the King and interviews with Baldwin and Birkenhead. Motilal felt tantalized and embarrassed by the reports of Patel's activities.

Motilal to Jawaharlal, June 15, 1927: 'Patel has, I am afraid, already done enough to compromise Gandhiji and myself. He is a dear but dangerous friend. While extolling us to the skies and telling people in England that nothing can succeed in India without the active support of the two of us, he hit upon the absurd idea of putting me on the Royal Commission on Reforms, which he says will come out in November . . . I am receiving letters from "friends of India" extending warm welcomes . . . My misfortune is that all mention of the Royal Commission and the great things that it will accomplish falls flat on me . . .'

These speculations had in fact no basis. Birkenhead decided to appoint a purely parliamentary commission. For this decision he had the backing of Lord Irwin, who had succeeded Lord Reading as Viceroy of India in April, 1926. A number of plausible reasons could be, and indeed, were, advanced for the exclusion of Indians: that a royal commission answerable to the British Parliament had necessarily to draw its personnel from that Parliament, that the representation of the 'numerous' Indian parties would have made the commission an unwieldy body, that the political and religious differences of Indian members would have endangered its cohesion and impartiality. The fact is that Birkenhead was afraid that Indian members might join hands with the Labour M.Ps. on the commission in producing a scheme, which the Conservatives might not be able to swallow.[2] The Chairman of the commission was Sir John Simon, an eminent lawyer and a Liberal politician; of its other six members, the only one now remembered is Clement Attlee, the future Prime Minister of England who was then a Labour back-bencher in the House of Commons.

The announcement of an all-white Royal Commission in November, 1927, deeply hurt Indian opinion, which came to look upon it as an inquisition by foreigners into India's fitness for self-government. 'Not since the Ilbert Bill,' writes the historian of Irwin's Viceroyalty, 'had racial feelings been stirred

[2] Halifax, The Earl of, *Fulness of Days*, p. 115.

so deeply.'[3] The Indian National Congress decided to boycott the commission, 'at every stage and in every form'. Even Moderate and Muslim elements, whose co-operation Birkenhead had taken for granted, joined in the boycott.

As a sop to Indian feeling, Sir John Simon announced immediately after his arrival in India early in February, 1928, that the central and provincial legislatures would be invited to constitute committees to assist the commission in its labours. But these committees were to have only advisory status; they were to have no say in drafting the report, and could even be excluded from the recording of evidence. This belated and half-hearted concession failed to assuage wounded Indian pride.

Motilal was in England when the announcement was made. 'The only honest course,' he remarked, 'is to declare what Government wants to do and then to appoint a commission to draft a scheme giving effect to that declaration.' He elaborated his views in a speech in the Legislative Assembly on February 18, 1928, soon after his return from Europe. The occasion was Lajpat Rai's famous resolution calling for a boycott of the Simon Commission. 'I have the honour,' Motilal said, 'of knowing Sir John Simon personally, of working with him . . . I have myself described him as a very big man . . . but . . . the biggest thing that he, as an Englishman and as an Imperialist, quite apart from being a lawyer of great eminence, is capable of doing is bound to be the smallest possible thing from our point of view.' He could not (he continued) advise his countrymen to surrender their right of self-determination to the biggest man in the world. He affirmed the principle 'that the British Parliament, the British public and the British Government have no shadow of a right to force a constitution upon us against our own will'. The Madras Congress had defined the goal of the Indian people as 'complete independence', but the Congress was prepared to confer with 'all the other parties concerned, including the Government' as to the kind of constitution which was to be framed, the length of the 'transitional' period and the arrangements suitable for that period. Motilal made a pointed reference to Birkenhead's 'exhibitions of temper'. 'It is easy to reply in the same strain, but I shall resist the temptation, and will only remark that heads that are swollen contain little wisdom and pride always rides for a fall.'

[3] Gopal, S., *The Viceroyalty of Lord Irwin*, 1926-31, p. 21.

He concluded his speech on a minatory note: 'Governments which have not paid attention to the lessons of history have invariably come to grief, to an ignominious end, and I have no doubt that what has not been accomplished by the statesmanship of England will be accomplished by destiny, and destiny and the people of India will add one more to the long list of fallen Empires.'

By providing a common grievance, the Simon Commission brought together parties and politicians who were poles apart. The Congress, the National Liberal Federation, the Jinnah wing of the Muslim League, all spoke with one voice. The bitter feuds of 1926-7 were forgotten; Malaviya, Lajpat Rai, Jayakar and Motilal presented an unbroken front to the Government. The boycott resolution passed through the Legislative Assembly by sixty-eight votes to sixty-two.

Sir John Simon and his colleagues were subjected to social as well as political boycott. A number of Indian legislators, who were staying in the Western Court at New Delhi, where the 'Simon Seven' were also accommodated, cut the Commissioners dead. The boycott movement was intensified when the Commission paid its second visit to India later in the year. The railway track was patrolled and the most rigorous precautions were taken. 'It is a strange comment upon the democratic spirit of friendliness which should inspire the relationship today between Great Britain and India,' wrote the *Pioneer*, 'that the Enquiry Committee of the Mother of Parliaments should be smuggled ashore by zealous policemen and shepherded by unimaginative officialdom.'

On October 30th, when the Simon Commission arrived at Lahore, the police beat up a crowd which was demonstrating in front of the railway station. Lajpat Rai, the most popular leader of the province, received two blows on his chest. His death on November 17th, which sent a wave of humiliation and indignation through the country, had the result on the one hand of intensifying the boycott and on the other of hardening the official attitude towards the demonstrators.

It was during the visit of the Simon Commission to Lucknow that Jawaharlal felt for the first time baton blows on his back – an experience without which his political education would not have been complete. The first assault came on November 29th in the course of a rehearsal for the big demonstration which was to greet the 'Simon Seven' on their arrival. A ban was imposed by the local authorities on processions, but the local Congress committee decided to defy it. A number of small processions were taken out from different parts of the town and were intended to converge on a fixed spot for a public meeting. While Jawaharlal was marching at the head of one of these groups of volunteers, he heard the clatter of horses' hoofs. He looked back and saw a bunch of mounted police, bearing down rapidly upon his little procession; his immediate reactions are graphically described in his autobiography:

'My own instinct had urged me to seek safety when I saw the horses charging down upon us . . . But then, I suppose, some other instinct held me to my place, and I survived the first charge, which had been checked by the volunteers behind me. Suddenly I found myself alone in the middle of the road.'

He might have swerved aside, had not his pride again overcome his instinct of self-preservation. This, he recalled later, was

'a matter of a few seconds only but I have the clearest recollections of that conflict within me . . . the line between cowardice and courage was a thin one and I might well have been on the other side'.

He made up his mind just in time to receive some more resounding blows from a mounted policeman who came trotting up to him, 'brandishing his long new baton'.

Shaking and nearly stunned, he was relieved to find himself still on his feet. Fearing that press reports of the assault next morning might alarm his family, he telephoned his father and told him not to worry. Motilal was not so easily reassured; he could not sleep and, late at night, when the last train had already gone, decided to leave for Lucknow by road. The motor car broke down on the way and he arrived at Lucknow early in the morning of November 30th, just when Jawaharlal, in spite of his injuries, was ready to leave for the railway station for the great demonstration which had been planned to greet the Simon Commission on its arrival. There was another assault by the mounted police; Jawaharlal received more baton blows, but was fortunately carried off to safety by some Congress volunteers.

Motilal was distressed when he saw his son's injuries. A touching letter came from Gandhi.

'My dear Jawahar,' he wrote, 'my love to you. It was all done bravely. You have braver things to do. May God spare you for many a long year to come, and make you His chosen instrument for freeing India from the yoke.'[4]

Jawaharlal was lucky to escape the kind of permanent disability which was sustained during these police assaults by his colleague Govind Ballabh Pant. A curious commentary on the whole episode is provided by the report of the deputy commissioner forwarded by the U.P. Government to the Government of India, in which the clash between the police and the demonstrators at Lucknow was described as 'rather like the clearing of a football ground in England when the crowd have broken loose'.

2

While the Simon Commission continued what Gandhi called its 'blood-red progress',[5] Indian political leaders were busy with the 'constructive side of the boycott'. A challenge from Birkenhead had stung them to frame an agreed constitution:

'I have twice in three years, during which I have been Secretary of State, invited our critics in India to put forward their own suggestions for a constitution to indicate to us the form, in which in their judgment any reform of constitution may take place. That offer is still open.'

The Madras Congress had directed the Congress Working Committee to draft a 'Swaraj' Constitution in consultation with other parties. In February, 1928, an All Parties Conference met in Delhi with Dr Ansari, the Congress president, in the chair, and voted for 'full responsible government'. At its Bombay meeting in May, it appointed a sub-committee to determine the

---

[4] Gandhi to Jawaharlal, December 3, 1928.
[5] Young India, December 6, 1928.

principles of an Indian constitution. The sub-committee was presided over by Motilal and included Sir Ali Imam and Shuaib Qureshi (Muslims), Aney and Jayakar (Hindu Mahasabha), Mangal Singh (The Sikh League), Tej Bahadur Sapru (Liberals), N. M. Joshi (Labour), G. R. Pradhan (Non-Brahmins). Jawaharlal, who was the General Secretary of the All India Congress Committee, also acted as the Secretary of the Constitution-making Committee, which came to be known as the Nehru Committee.

The Nehru Committee had to find an answer to the sinister question which was to shadow Indian politics for the next twenty years: the position of the minorities, and especially of the Muslim minority, in a free and democratic India. If British autocracy was to be replaced by an Indian democracy, would it give a permanent advantage to the Hindus, who heavily outnumbered the Muslims? Was it, as Sir Syed Ahmed had put it, a game of dice in which one man had four dice, and the other only one?

One method of protecting Muslim interests was to incorporate special provisions or 'safeguards' in the constitution. One of the safeguards was the institution of separate electorates, the election of Muslim candidates by Muslim voters, which was first introduced in the Minto-Morley Reforms. In 1909, J. Ramsay MacDonald, then a Labour Member of British Parliament, wrote after a visit to India:

'The Council Act has come, and the Mohammedan has received preferential treatment. The flags are flying over the Mohammedan camp; not a square inch of bunting flies over the Hindu's head.'[6]

Ten years later the 'preferential treatment' was extended by the Reforms Act of 1919 even though its authors acknowledged that 'division by creeds and classes means the creation of political camps organized against each other, and teaches men to think as partisans and not as citizens'.

The Lucknow Pact of 1916 between the Muslim League and the Congress committed the latter to separate electorates. Unfortunately, communal claims had an inconvenient habit of growing. By 1928 Muslim demands embraced 'communal

[6] MacDonald, J. Ramsay, The Awakening of India, p. 60.

provinces' as well as 'communal electorates', guarantees of Muslim majorities in the Punjab and Bengal, 'weightage' for Muslim minorities in other provinces, reservation of one-third of the seats in the central legislature and the posts under the Government. The memorandum of the Ahmediya community to the Hartog Committee went so far as to ask for special schools employing Muslim teachers for Muslim students! The communal climate of the twenties encouraged a fantastic political arithmetic of percentages of seats and jobs, which baffled the Nehru Committee as soon as it set to work. Of the difficulties of the Committee we have a first-hand version in a letter written by Ansari, the Congress president, to Gandhi, dated June 28th, 1928:

'When I reached Allahabad there was a complete deadlock [in the Nehru Committee]. The Sikhs would have no reservation of seats at all anywhere, neither for the majority nor for the minority. The [Hindu] Mahasabha people would allow reservation for the minorities, but none for the majorities. The Congress and Muslim proposal was for a reservation of seats both for the majorities and the minorities. I tried in private discussion with different people to come to a common formula . . .'

The common formula stipulated for a Declaration of Fundamental Rights assuring every citizen the fullest liberty of conscience, belief and culture, and for a reservation of seats in legislatures under joint electorates. The Muslim demand for constituting North West Frontier Province and Sind into separate provinces was conceded on the basis of 'cultural' autonomy, which was also held to justify a Kanarese-speaking province in southern India. The committee expressed the hope that in a free India political parties would follow political and economic rather than religious alignments. The committee framed its constitution on the basis of Dominion Status, 'not as a remote stage of our evolution, but as the next immediate step'.

The constitution was drafted by Motilal with the help of his son, before Tej Bahadur Sapru took a hand. 'Tej Bahadur is very pleased with the draft report,' Motilal wrote to Jawaharlal on July 21, 1928. 'In the sixty pages of typed matter he had only six or seven verbal changes to suggest and said it was "A-I". He is now writing a few paragraphs on Indian States, Dominion Status versus Responsible Government.'

The Nehru Report offered not a constitution, but the outline of a constitution, which could be amplified and put into the form of a bill by a parliamentary draftsman. Among its important recommendations, which were to find their way into the constitution of independent India, were a declaration of rights, a parliamentary system of government, a bicameral legislature, adult franchise, allocation of subjects between the centre and the provinces, redistribution of provincial boundaries on a linguistic basis, and an independent judiciary with a Supreme Court at its apex.

Much hard work and heart-searching went into the report. It was not easy to secure a consensus of opinion in a committee whose members diverged widely in their views and aspirations. The committee tried to reconcile the conflicting communal claims and to find a via media between the radicalism of the National Congress and the conservatism of the Indian Liberals. The significance of an agreed constitution was quickly recognized. 'The day of bondage is ending,' Mrs. Besant declared, 'and the dawn of freedom is on the Eastern horizon.' Dr Ansari recalled the 'years of utter darkness in which the spectre of communal differences oppressed us like a terrible nightmare', and was glad that the work of the Nehru Committee had 'at last heralded the dawn of a brighter day'. 'It is an achievement,' Motilal himself said in December, 1928, 'of which any country in the world might well be proud.'

All this optimism was a little premature. The constitution had been accepted 'in principle' by the All Parties Conference in Lucknow at the end of August, but there were a number of mutually contradictory amendments, which were referred back to the Nehru Committee for consideration. The committee, which was enlarged by the appointment of additional members, including Mrs Besant, Malaviya and Lajpat Rai, issued a supplementary report, which was submitted for approval to an All Parties Convention at Calcutta during the Christmas week. It soon became obvious that communal claims had no fixity. No sooner was an issue closed, than it was sought to be reopened. 'I see,' Gandhi wrote to Motilal in November, 'you are having no end of difficulties, with Mussalman friends regarding your report. But I see you are unravelling the tangle with consummate patience and tact.' But not all Motilal's patience and tact could unravel the communal tangle, particularly as the British Government was an invisible third party in possession of the cake the two communities pretended to divide. The communal politicians had one eye on the Nehru Committee and the other on the Simon Commission which was then touring India. The dilemma was described by Motilal in December, 1928: 'It is difficult to stand against the foreigner without offering him a united front. It is not easy to offer him a united front while the foreigner is in our midst domineering over us.'

At the All India Convention in Calcutta which was one of the most representative gatherings of its kind, efforts were made to reopen the communal issue. 'We admit,' Motilal argued, 'that there are in this report recommendations which perhaps we ourselves might not have made individually [but they] are likely to bring about unanimity and harmony between the parties.' The report, he pleaded, was a 'structure. If you pull out one brick, it is likely to crumble'. These pleas had no effect on a vocal Muslim section led by Jinnah, who soon afterwards lined up with the reactionary part of the Muslim League (led by the Aga Khan) and the Ali Brothers to denounce the Nehru Report. The issues on which the breach occurred at the Calcutta Convention were separate electorates, reservation of one-third of the seats in the central legislature, and the vesting of residuary powers in the Provinces.[7] These were modest demands – compared with those of ten years later. It is, however, difficult to say whether their acceptance in 1928-29 would have halted the crescendo of communal claims which culminated in the demand for Pakistan. The narrowness and rigidity of the Hindu and Sikh politicians in these negotiations was bad enough, but the fluidity of Muslim demands was worse. From 1906 to 1947, each communal 'settlement' became the starting point for a harder bargain, until nothing was left to bargain about.

Motilal himself was prepared to go very far in writing safeguards for the minorities into the constitution, but he felt a line had to be drawn somewhere so that the growth of a common citizenship and national spirit were not permanently stunted. This is why he opposed separate electorates. The rejection of Jinnah's demands by the Calcutta Convention in December, 1928, has been described as a turning point in his

[7] The Proceedings of the All Parties Convention, p. 95.

career,[8] away from nationalism towards Muslim separatism. But it would have been impossible to find, then or later, two Hindu leaders who were freer from communal prejudice or could take a more rational and sympathetic view of the place of the Muslim minority in a democratic India than Motilal Nehru and Sapru, the joint authors of the Nehru Report. At the Calcutta Convention, Motilal and Jinnah had conferred on the disputed issues. Jinnah seems to have had a grievance that Motilal had given him a cold reception. 'If the cold reception of an individual,' Motilal wrote, 'however great in one place, and a rather hot reception of the same individual in another place is to affect the solution of a great national problem we had better say goodbye to it.' 'What Mr Jinnah said on the occasion,' Motilal added, 'left me cold and I could not work up an artificial warmth to please him.'[9]

Motilal's own views on the place of religion in politics were stated bluntly at the Calcutta Congress.

'Whatever the higher conception of religion may be, it has in our day-to-day life come to signify bigotry and fanaticism, intolerance and narrow-mindedness . . . Not content with its reactionary influence on social matters, it has invaded the domain of politics and economics . . . Its association with politics has been to the good of neither. Religion has been degraded and politics has sunk into the mire. Complete divorce of the one from the other is the only remedy.'[10]

As 1928 drew to a close, the Nehru Report was running into difficulties created by the supporters of communal claims. But Motilal was no less worried by the opposition from a radical wing of Congressmen led by Jawaharlal. The clash between father and son is important not only in itself but for the profound influence it was to exercise on the course of the national movement.

[8] Bolitho, Hector, *Jinnah*, p. 95
[9] Motilal to M. A. Ansari, February 17, 1930.
[10] Natesan, *Congress Presidential Addresses 1911-34*, p. 865.

CHAPTER TWENTY-SEVEN

THE CLASH

'HIS Excellency desires,' Home Secretary Haig wrote on October 18, 1928, 'that the utterances of Jawaharlal Nehru should be watched carefully.'[1] It was not only the Viceroy who had reasons to be perturbed by the activities of young Nehru. In Christmas week of 1927, soon after his return from Europe, he had presided over a 'Republican Conference' and carried through the Madras Congress a bunch of resolutions with an aggressively anti-imperialist and pro-socialist slant. One of the resolutions described 'complete national independence' as the goal of the Indian people; another denounced in advance any 'warlike adventure', in which the British might be involved for the furtherance of their imperialist aims. Gandhi was present at the Madras Congress; though he did not attend all its meetings, he kept a vigilant eye on what was happening. He was scandalized by what seemed to him an utter lack of restraint in Jawaharlal's activities and speeches after his long absence from India. 'You are going too fast,' he wrote on January 4, 1928, 'you should have taken time to think and become acclimatized.' Jawaharlal tried to explain, but that made matters worse. 'The differences between us,' wrote Gandhi, 'are so vast and radical that there seems to be no meeting ground between us.'

The European visit had given a sharp edge to Jawaharlal's politics which prevented them from sliding smoothly into the well-worn grooves of the Congress. The passion for intellectual clarity fostered by travel, study and discussion had made him impatient of the empiricism of the Congress elders, who believed in muddling through problems as they arose, and were in perpetual quest of nice formulae to maintain a facade of unity in the party and the country.

Early in 1926, when Jawaharlal sailed from Bombay, India had seemed to him 'still quiescent, passive, perhaps not fully recovered from the effort of 1919-1922'; on his return in

[1] N.A.I.

December, 1927, he found her 'fresh, active and full of suppressed energy'. To this subtle change in the atmosphere, testimony has been left by the Viceroy in his memoirs. Lord Irwin had concurred in Birkenhead's proposal for an all-white Royal Commission, because he had been assured by his trusted advisers that the Muslims would never boycott the commission and therefore the Hindus dared not do so. 'Those who argued thus,' Irwin recalled in the evening of his life, 'were wrong, and the mistake was perhaps evidence that some new force was working, of which even those, whose knowledge of India went back for twenty or thirty years, had not yet learnt the full significance.'[2]

The 'new force' was galvanizing into activity almost every sector of society, the urban intelligentsia, the young people, the industrial workers, the peasantry. The sharp reaction to the appointment of the Simon Commission revealed the increased sensitivity of the intelligentsia. Youth Leagues were springing up all over the country and students' conferences demanded radical solutions for political and economic ills. The Communist Party was active in important industrial centres. A spate of strikes affected steel and tin-plate works at Jamshedpur, jute mills in Calcutta, cotton mills in Sholapur, woollen mills in Kanpur and the railways in southern and eastern India. The strike in Bombay cloth mills embracing 60,000 workers lasted for more than five months. It has been estimated that nearly half a million workers were involved in these strikes and thirty-one million working days were lost.[3]

Even the long-suffering peasantry was astir in 1928. There was an agitation for the revision of tenancy laws in the United Provinces. In Gujarat, Gandhi's home province, a peasants' resistance campaign was organized under the leadership of Vallabhbhai Patel to resist the increase of land revenue in Bardoli *taluk*. A successful struggle after years of inertia was an exhilarating experience for lovers of Indian freedom; the campaign showed the latent energy which was waiting to be harnessed to the national cause.

[2] Halifax, Earl of, *Fulness of Days*, pp. 115-116.
[3] Dutt, R. Palme, *India Today*, p. 337.

2

With this new mood of the country Jawaharlal was in harmony; his tours and speeches helped to crystallize it, even though they alarmed the more sedate sections in and outside the Congress. He was invited to preside over numerous conferences of students, peasants and workers in all parts of the country. In his speeches and writings he made frontal attacks on feudalism, capitalism and imperialism. He advocated a 'revolutionary outlook', questioned age-old assumptions and suggested root-and-branch solutions. His position as General Secretary of the Congress – an office into which he had stepped back in December, 1927 – did not appear to hamper him. On the contrary, he used his position to push the Congress, so far as he could, in the direction in which he wanted it to go.

Jawaharlal's position as General Secretary of the Congress, and the fact that his father was chairman of the committee charged by the All Parties Conference with the task of framing a Swaraj constitution, brought him into intimate touch with the work of the committee. To some extent he shared the easy confidence of that period that if a communal settlement could be devised, it might serve as a bridge to Indian unity and freedom. He helped his father in collecting and sorting data for the report and even in drafting it, but he did not see eye to eye with him on the fundamental postulate of the new constitution, that it should be based on Dominion Status.

Since 1920, when the reins of the Congress had fallen into Gandhi's hands, its avowed goal had been Swaraj (self-rule). Gandhi's definitions of *Swaraj* had been delightfully vague. Once he described it as 'the abandonment of the fear of death'. On other occasions he referred to it as the 'ability to regard every inhabitant of India as our own brother or sister', and as 'the capacity of the people to get rid of their helplessness'. These definitions had the merit of being homely; they did not so much define as give a glimpse of the new order the Mahatma wished to usher in. The nearest Gandhi got to a political definition was when he explained Swaraj as 'a parliamentary Government of India in the modern sense of the word'. In 1921 he frowned upon Hasrat Mohani's motion at the Ahmedabad Congress in favour of 'complete independence'.[4] Six years later he reacted

[4] Natesan, *Speeches and Writings of Mahatma Gandhi*, p. 745.

equally sharply against a similar resolution which was passed by the Madras Congress at Jawaharlal's instance. Gandhi's opposition stemmed partly from his dislike of theoretical discussion of political issues, and partly from a feeling that for a weak and divided people to talk of 'complete independence' was an idle boast. A clean break with Britain also went against his ethical grain; it ran counter to the basic urge in Satyagraha for the 'conversion' of the foe of today into the friend of tomorrow.

'In my opinion,' Gandhi told the Belgaum Congress in December, 1924, 'if the British Government mean what they say and honestly help us to equality, it would be a greater triumph than a complete severance of the British connection. I would, therefore, strive for Swaraj within the Empire, but would not hesitate to sever all connections if severance became a necessity through Britain's own fault. I would thus throw the burden of separation on the British people. The better mind of the world desires today not absolutely independent states, but a federation of friendly interdependent states.'

Motilal's legal, precise mind did not shrink from constitutional definitions; nor were his politics coloured by moral prepossessions. He recognized that in a negotiated settlement there was bound to be a transitional period for which special arrangements by mutual consent would be necessary. He knew that Dominion Status was not to be despised. He had referred to it in the Swaraj Party's manifesto in 1923; he had put it forward as the united demand of non-official groups in the Legislative Assembly in February, 1924, and September, 1925. True, he had not objected to Jawaharlal's advocacy of complete independence at the Brussels Congress in February, 1927, and had declared for complete independence in his speech in the Assembly on the boycott of the Simon Commission a year later. But it was one thing to announce the goal of the Congress, another to reconcile it with the views of the numerous parties, big and small, which were represented on the All Parties Conference.

The popular view that in 1928 Motilal stood for Dominion Status, and Jawaharlal for 'complete independence' is an oversimplification. The differences were not so much on the ultimate goal, as on the immediate tactics. Motilal was prepared to accept a compromise so that he could carry his colleagues on the All Parties Committee and give an effective answer to Birkenhead's challenge.

A compromise on this issue was, however, something which Jawaharlal could not swallow. It contradicted the creed of the Congress, defined, at his instance, by the Madras Congress only a few months earlier. It ran counter to his inmost convictions. It made nonsense of the tirades he had delivered against British imperialism from a hundred platforms since his return from Europe. He did not equate Dominion Status with the substance of freedom. He was doubtful if it could confer genuine equality of status with Britain; and even if it did, he believed it would only translate India from the 'exploited' to the 'exploiting' wing of the empire. The concept of Dominion Status was still in evolution in 1928; the Statute of Westminster was not to be enacted until 1931. British statesmen were chary of using the phrase 'Dominion Status' with reference to India; obviously they were prepared to accord her only, in the words of the Viceroy, 'a second class membership in the graded imperial society.'[5] In April, 1928, Birkenhead had privately admitted[6] to Irwin that 'His Majesty's Government were averse from using the phrase Dominion Status to describe even the ultimate and remote goal of Indian political development, because it has been laid down that "Dominion Status" means "the right to decide their own destinies", and this right we were not prepared to accord to India at present or in any way to prejudge the question whether it should ever be accorded'. When Irwin used the phrase 'Dominion Status' in his declaration of October, 1929, he provoked a first-class political crisis in Britain. In 1930, the Simon Commission Report discreetly avoided a reference to Dominion Status. And in 1931, even a sympathetic critic like Professor A. B. Keith could argue that the authors of the declaration of August, 1917, could scarcely have intended it to cover 'the greatly enlarged conception of Dominion Status'.[7]

The controversy on dominion status versus complete independence created a new obstacle for the Nehru Report. When it came up for approval before the All Parties Conference at Luck-

---

[5] Halifax, Viscount, *Fulness of Days*, p. 121.
[6] Birkenhead, Earl of, *F.E., The Life of F. E. Smith, first Earl of Birkenhead*, p. 518.
[7] Keith, A. B., *Letters On Imperial Relations*, p. 200.
K*

now in August, 1928, the younger radical wing led by Jawaharlal and Subhas Bose suggested that the communal pact should be ratified, but the question of 'Dominion Status' versus complete independence should be kept open. The Nehru Report was thus threatened by communal reactionaries on the one hand, and young radicals on the other. Among the latter were some who were neither so young nor so radical, but were using the controversy to pay off old scores. The loyalty of Srinivas Iyengar, the deputy leader of the Swaraj Party, to his chief had long been in doubt; in 1928 he was vociferously advocating 'complete independence', because Motilal was advocating Dominion Status. Iyengar became the president of the 'Independence for India League' of which Jawaharlal and Subhas Bose were secretaries. Strangely enough, when the Indian National Congress actually unfurled the flag of independence and launched a Satyagraha struggle in 1930, Iyengar discreetly dropped out of politics. The liveliest verdict on this veteran Swarajist from the south was passed by Shankar in a cartoon entitled 'Little Boy Blue' with the tell-tale caption: 'Wanted information of the whereabouts of Sjt Sirinivas Lyengar, Ex-President of the Congress, short, thick-set, very peremptory, last heard of proclaiming Independence for India.'[8] The Independence for India League was no more than a pressure group within the Congress,[9] but it was an unwelcome addition to the numerous and conflicting pressures with which Motilal, as chairman of the constitution-making committee, was already contending.

He had been persuaded to agree to preside over the ensuing session of the Congress which was to meet at Calcutta in December, 1928, but he made it known that if he did not secure a majority for his report, he would resign. He was in an irritable and combative mood; the fact that his son was leading the opposition to Dominion Status seemed to add to his irritation. 'I do not think,' Jawaharlal writes in his autobiography, 'that at any previous or subsequent occasion the tension [between us] had been so great'.

3

The controversy over Dominion Status only high-lighted in-

[8] *Hindustan Times*, December 12, 1934.
[9] Brecher, Michael, *Jawaharlal Nehru*, p. 130.

tellectual and temperamental differences which had always existed between father and son. These differences had crystallized as early as 1907, when Jawaharlal was in his teens. They had brought on a first-class crisis in 1919 which was resolved only after the entire family had plunged into non-co-operation. During the years 1923-6, father and son were content to follow their independent lines of activity. But in 1928, after Jawaharlal's return from Europe, the intellectual gulf between them was wider than ever.

Motilal's political philosophy was derived from his long association with the Indian National Congress; it had been influenced by Gokhale and Gandhi; it enshrined parliamentary democracy, equality before the law, and freedom from the thraldom of caste and creed.

Proud, fearless and stubborn as he was, Motilal's approach to politics was rational, sceptical, almost cynical. Unlike his son he did not romanticize India's past nor idealize her 'naked hungry-mass'. Forty years at the Bar and in national politics had dispelled such illusions as he may have had; he had seen something of the seamy side of life and knew the weaknesses of his countrymen; he was incapable of following a leader or a dogma blindly. He was suspicious of excessive emotion in politics. After hearing Sarojini Naidu's poetic – and impromptu – presidential address at the Cawnpore Congress in 1925, which moved the audience to tears, his only comment was: 'But what did she say?'

Motilal had visited England, but the England he knew and admired was Victorian England. His mentor was Mill, rather than Marx; his chief driving force was political liberty, not social justice. He had an aristocratic disdain for money, which he had earned and spent with an equal facility, but he did not look askance at the institution of property. To him, as to most of his contemporaries in the Congress and on the All Parties Conference, property was a symbol of status and respectability, a reward for initiative and hard work. The guarantee in the Nehru Report of the vested rights in property to the zamindars of Oudh, which so much shocked Jawaharlal,[10] must have seemed the most natural thing to his father, to Sapru and to other members of the constitution-making committee, who had been nurtured on Anglo-Saxon conceptions of individual liberty.

[10] Nehru, J., *Autobiography*, p. 173.

Jawaharlal inherited his father's pride and fearlessness, but not his caution and circumspection. He was one of those who needed a cause to live and die for. The ecstatic politics of 1919-22 satisfied this craving. But when the curve of popular enthusiasm fell, his faith did not sag. The enforced leisure in gaol gave him time to read and think and to re-charge the battery of his mind. Even as he occupied himself in the dull grind of municipal administration, or the routine of the All India Congress Committee's office, his mind was being continually renewed by fresh reading, a process which received a fillip from his stay in Europe during 1926-7.

A Superintendent of Lucknow Gaol, an English Colonel, once told Jawaharlal that 'he had practically finished his general reading at the age of twelve'.[11] For most of Jawaharlal's colleagues in Indian politics, general reading had ended not at twelve but at twenty-five. Were it not for his reading habit, which had been acquired early and preserved by spells in prison, Jawaharlal's mind might also have been 'frozen'; he would then have been spared troublesome thoughts and the agonies of appraisal and re-appraisal from which most practising politicians are so happily immune. His reading was eclectic, but with a preponderance of history and economics. The image of the past that he acquired and was to project in his historical writings, the Glimpses of World History and The Discovery of India, did not reek of the dust of the library shelf. It was the fruit of an exciting voyage into time and space, from which he returned with a sharper awareness of the present and an indomitable faith in the future. He tried to balance himself on 'a point of intersection of the timeless with time', and saw India less as a geographical and economic entity, composed of millions of individuals pursuing their separate ambitions, than as a great nation whose spirit, despite the humiliations of the recent past and the melancholy present, was unconquered and unconquerable. This buoyant optimism seemed almost romantic thirty years ago, but it had a heart-warming quality which sustained not only his own faith but that of millions of his countrymen through the vicissitudes of the national movement. 'There was a time not long ago,' he wrote to his sister in 1931, 'when an Indian had to hang his head in shame in foreign countries . . .

11 Nehru, J., Toward Freedom, p. 90.

Today it is a proud privilege to be an Indian.'[12] It was perhaps this quality which made Rabindranath Tagore describe Jawaharlal as 'the *Rituraj* representing the season of youth and triumphant joy of an invincible spirit of fight and uncompromising loyalty to the cause of freedom'.[13]

If history gave a perspective to Jawaharlal's politics, economics gave a practical edge to them. He saw political liberty not as an end in itself, but as the means of a new social and economic order. He was not alone in conceiving political liberty as a prelude to social justice. Gandhi had never ceased to lay stress on the needs of the downtrodden and the under-privileged. Indeed, he claimed to be a socialist. 'But my socialism,' he wrote, 'was natural to me and not adopted from any books. No man could be actively non-violent and not rise against social injustice wherever it occurred.' The Mahatma's social philosophy was yet to go through its own peculiar evolution during the nineteen-thirties in response to the needs of the time. In 1928 it appeared to Jawaharlal, after his recent exposure to Marxist ideas, too vague, too amorphous and inchoate, to form the basis of a political programme.

4

Father and son, proceeding from different premises, did not find it easy to argue at home. But they did argue in public. The addresses they delivered at the Calcutta and Lahore sessions of the Indian National Congress were in a sense their dialogue, reflecting their differences on the tactics as well as the strategy of the national movement.

Motilal's outlook was that of a trained lawyer and a seasoned politician. 'Pure idealism completely divorced from realities,' he said, 'has no place in politics and is but a happy dream, which must sooner or later end in a rude awakening.' He had, he said, no quarrel with the ideals of the young men: 'I hold with them that all exploitation must cease and all imperialism must go. But the way to it is a long and dreary one . . . The masses want bread. They have no time for theories and dogmas imported from abroad . . . The occasion calls for skilful generalship not academic discussions which take us nowhere.' Dominion status

[12] Hutheesing, Krishna, *With No Regrets*, p. 75.
[13] J. Nehru, *A Bunch of Old Letters*, p. 173.

was 'a very considerable measure of freedom bordering on independence'. And independence did not mean 'walking out of
the world . . . Indeed the more independent you are, the more
necessary it will be to establish relations all round'. Severance
of relations with Britain did not mean a cessation of all relations, but 'such appropriate change in existing relations as is
necessary to transform a dependency into a free state'.

This was the voice of experience, of circumspection, of a man
who claimed to see 'the world as it is, and not as it should be'.
Against this, his son affirmed that 'success often comes to those
who dare and act . . . We play for high stakes and if we seek
to achieve great things it can only be through great dangers'.
The prospect of revolutionary changes did not appear to disturb
young Nehru; on the contrary, it seemed to uplift him. 'We
appear to be in a dissolving period of history,' he said, 'when
the world is in labour and out of her travail will give birth to a
new order.' This was not mere rhetoric. Everyone could see how
impatient he was of half-measures, compromises, vague generalities. He was, he said, a socialist and a republican – 'no believer
in kings or princes, or in the order which produces the modern
kings of industry'. The central problem, he asserted, was the
conquest of power: 'the total withdrawal of the army of occupation and British economic control from India'. He questioned the
right of the British Parliament to decide the measure and
manner of India's progress. India was 'a nation on the march',
which no one could thwart. 'If we fail today,' he said, 'and
tomorrow brings no success, the day after tomorrow will bring
achievement.'

As one reads these words in cold print today, it is difficult to
visualize the impact they made thirty years ago, when they fell
like burning coals on sedate Indian politicians and indignant
British officials. The three-pronged attack on imperialism,
capitalism and feudalism was calculated to antagonize at once
bureaucrats and businessmen, landlords and princes, to whom
young Nehru must have seemed a romantic idealist if not an
enfant terrible of Indian politics. His economics were no less
aggressive than his politics. 'Our economic programme,' he told
the Lahore Congress in December, 1929, 'must be based on a
human outlook, and must not sacrifice men to money. If any
industry could not be run without starving its workers, then
the industry must be closed down. If the workers on the land

have not enough to eat, then the intermediaries who deprive them of their full share must go. The philosophy of socialism has permeated the entire structure of society the world over and almost the only point in dispute is the pace and methods of advance to its realization . . . India will have to end her poverty and inequality, though she may evolve her own methods and may adapt the ideals to the genius of her race.'

This enthusiasm for socialism was not shared by Motilal, whose aristocratic, legal background, saturated with ideas of political liberalism and *laissez faire*, predisposed him against an economic philosophy which aimed at an artificial egalitarianism. There is a significant reference to socialism in Motilal's presidential address to the Calcutta Congress, when he sounded a note of warning against the fate which 'has been pursuing [us] for the last twenty years or more . . . It is close upon our heels already in the garb of socialism and will devour both complete independence and dominion status if you let it approach nearer'.

The conflict between father and son was in a sense a conflict between age and youth. Every generation has its angry young men, though the objects of anger change. Had not Motilal himself defied the superstitions and the taboos of his caste and community as tenaciously as his son, thirty years later, was fighting the political and economic shibboleths of the Congress Old Guard?

During the closing months of 1928, tension in Anand Bhawan was at its peak. Braj Kumar Nehru (now India's Ambassador in Washington) was a student at Allahabad, and stayed at Anand Bhawan during 1928-9. He recalls that Motilal told him one day: 'Father and son are atilt, but Jawahar would not be my son if he did not stick to his guns.' Motilal's irritability was exacerbated by the impetuosity of his son, who appeared to be taking extreme positions, associating with young firebrands, and making himself an easy target for the Government. 'If Jawaharlal lives for ten years,' Motilal told Braj Kumar, 'he will change the face of India,' and then added sadly: 'such men do not usually live long; they are consumed by the fire within them.'

5

As the Calcutta Congress drew near, Motilal wondered whether, like his friend C. R. Das at Gaya in 1922, he would see his policies repudiated by the very session over which he presided. He summoned Gandhi to the rescue. The Mahatma was none too well, but agreed to attend the Congress session.

Motilal was received with royal pageantry at Calcutta. He rode in a carriage drawn by thirty-four white horses ridden by youths. It was an impressive spectacle – men volunteers on horseback; women volunteers in green-and-red bordered *saris* with red bangles and small swords; the medical unit, the long rows of motor cyclists with Subhas Bose in the uniform of a Field Marshal of the Congress Volunteers Corps.

The pageantry without could not conceal the tension within. Behind closed doors, Congress leaders discussed the crucial issue of 'Dominion Status' versus 'Independence', which threatened to split the Congress. In the 'Subjects Committee' which screened resolutions for the plenary session the discussions were long, heated and bitter. On December 27th, Gandhi suggested a *via media*; the Congress should adopt the whole of the Nehru Report, including the Dominion Status formula, but if it were not accepted by the Government within two years, the Congress should opt for complete independence and fight for it, if necessary, by invoking the weapon of civil disobedience.

Jawaharlal described the acceptance of Dominion Status as 'an extremely wrong and foolish act', and advocated civil disobedience if complete independence were not granted within a year. That evening there were further discussions, as a result of which Gandhi moved on the following day (December 28th) an amended resolution giving London only one year to accept the Dominion Status formula. The amended resolution was carried in the Subjects Committee by 118 votes to 45, but Jawaharlal was absent and Subhas Bose did not take part in the debate. Three days later, when Gandhi's resolution came up before the plenary session, Bose opposed it and was supported, rather inconsistently and half-heartedly, by Jawaharlal. Gandhi was furious at this change of front by the young men. 'When we have no sense of honour,' he said, 'when we cannot allow our words to remain unaltered for twenty-four hours, do not talk of independence.' The voting – 1,350 for, and 973 against – gave a clear majority to Gandhi's resolution, but the issue hung in the balance till almost the last moment.

Jawaharlal's vacillation at Calcutta, his conflict between his convictions and his loyalty to his father and Gandhi and the

Congress, was then and later the subject of adverse comment. But vacillation, like silence, is sometimes useful in politics. It was a sound instinct which kept Jawaharlal from breaking with the Congress Old Guard in December, 1928. As events were to show, it was he, not they, who had won at Calcutta. 'Complete Independence', instead of being the catchword of young radicals, bade fair to become the battle-cry of the Indian National Congress. And, most important of all, the way had been opened for Gandhi's return to active politics.

The Nehru Report was an earnest attempt on the part of Indian leaders to come to terms with each other and with Britain. Gandhi aptly described Motilal as 'an eminently worthy ambassador of a nation that is in need of and in the mood to make an honourable compromise'.[14] The Report could not claim the adherence of all the parties; but it was endorsed by a vast majority of them. Yet there is little evidence to show that it received a serious consideration in official circles. 'The British Parliament could never accept a position,' said the Viceroy on January 28, 1929, 'which would reduce it to being a mere registrar of the decisions of other persons.'[15]

Birkenhead's allergy to the 'extremist politician' was such that anything which came from that source was tainted in his eyes. In April, 1928, he chided the Viceroy for the attention which the local authorities in the North West Frontier Province had given to Motilal and Srinivas Iyengar during their visit. 'It does not do to take these people too seriously,' Birkenhead exhorted Irwin. 'Indeed I find it increasingly difficult to take any Indian politicians very seriously.'

On August 29, 1928, Irwin telegraphed to Birkenhead:

'We have received a resolution [for the Legislative Assembly] recommending immediate steps for establishing the Commonwealth of India on lines indicated in the All Parties [Nehru] Report . . . Our attitude could only be that Governor-General in Council can take no such steps when the Indian Statutory Commission is conducting its enquiry . . . we will decline to be drawn into the discussion of [the merits of the Nehru Report].'[16]

[14] Young India, July 26, 1928.
[15] Speeches of Lord Irwin, vol. I, p. 538.
[16] Viceroy to Secretary of State (N.A.I.).

The appointment of the Simon Commission had provoked Indian parties to frame an alternative constitution. But the very existence of the Simon Commission became an argument for ignoring that constitution. Ironically enough, events were soon to move fast and to consign the Simon Commission's own report – even before it was completed and published – to the waste-paper basket of history.

CHAPTER TWENTY-EIGHT

ON THE BRINK

GANDHI had gone to Calcutta reluctantly. He had not intended to take an active, much less a leading, part in the deliberations of the Congress, but the tide of events overtook him and left him, and indeed the entire Congress leadership, a little breathless and bewildered. If the Calcutta session registered a rise in the political barometer, it also revealed a disconcerting lack of discipline and cohesion in the party. On return to Allahabad Motilal sent his thanks to Gandhi.

Motilal to Gandhi, January 12, 1929: 'Now that I have shaken the dust of Calcutta I wish to apologize for all the trouble I gave you. This is not a mere formality which is quite out of the question between you and me. I cannot help feeling that . . . I took you out of your clean surroundings into an atmosphere charged with unreality and untruth. It was quite apparent that a good deal of what you saw and heard was not only not to your liking, but even painful to you . . . I know you are not at all satisfied with what we have been able to achieve in Calcutta, but there can be no doubt as to how I would have fared without your support. You have saved a complete fiasco . . .'

Gandhi's reply was characteristically gracious.

'No apology whatsoever is necessary for taking me to Calcutta,' he wrote back. 'Of course I had never expected to have to take such an active part . . . as circumstances forced me to take. But it was as well. I was quite happy over it and it gave me an insight into the present working of the Congress organization which I certainly did not possess. And after all, we have to battle both within and without . . .'

The battle within was going to be a hard one. It seemed scarcely possible that the British Government would accept the

Nehru Report and grant Dominion Status by the end of 1929. But what chance had the Congress of putting up a fight, if it did not put its own house in order? Immediately after the Congress session, Gandhi wrote urging Jawaharlal, who had been re-elected as the General Secretary of the All India Congress Committee, to tour the country and reorganize the Congress committees. Jawaharlal complained of 'an extraordinary paucity of workers'. 'They are practically non-existent,' he told the Mahatma.

Early in 1929 Gandhi was planning a long trip abroad – leaving in April and returning to India in October after visiting Germany, Austria, Russia and possibly Poland, France, England, the United States, Italy, Turkey and Egypt. A trip abroad had been discussed, planned and abandoned by the Mahatma several times in previous years. In January, 1929, he was wondering whether the time had come for him to deliver the message of non-violence to the world before the experiment in India had succeeded, and whether, after having piloted the ultimatum to the Government through the Calcutta Congress, he could leave the country for such a long spell. He discussed the pros and cons of the trip with his entourage and with friends in India and abroad. Motilal, who was also consulted, advised a postponement.

Motilal to Gandhi, January 14, 1929: 'It is quite certain that the year just begun is going to be an eventful one. What precise trend the events will take, it is impossible to say, but it is highly probable that there will be considerable excitement both at home and abroad . . . Hailey [Governor of the U.P.] will come back in March . . . His first move will be against Jawahar for whom he has expressed the highest admiration to those who were likely to be communicative to me. "It is such men that make history," he said to one of these. To others he spoke in a different strain . . . It is the easiest thing in the world to take a thoroughly straight and earnest patriot like Jawahar. All that need be done (and I am almost sure will be done) is to get some flunkey zamindar, or *talukdar* to oppress his tenantry beyond endurance. The one man they will appeal to is Jawahar, and no power on earth will restrain him from answering the call of duty. The Government knows it and will profit by it, and Jawahar will walk into their parlour. You can understand what this will mean to me, but will it do any good to the country? Perhaps some, but in my opinion out of all proportion to the price ...

'I have pictured this . . . and have looked round to see what support and guidance would be available to me when any such occasion arises. Sabarmati is indicated at once when any such occasion arises. But what, when the *gadi* [throne] of Sabarmati has shifted to Europe? The answer is plain. While there will be a hopeless muddle in India, the occupant of the *gadi* would feel miserable in Europe.'

Jawaharlal, who was reported by his father to have 'put himself in training for gaol by giving up smoking and resorting to a harder life than usual', urged the Mahatma to stick to his schedule. 'I am afraid,' he wrote, 'Father's love for me makes him take too tragic a view of the possibility of my arrest.' Gandhi cancelled his trip, though he told Motilal: 'I do not know that Hailey will lay his hands upon Jawaharlal quite so easily as you think.'

Motilal's apprehensions were not entirely groundless. As we have already seen, in October, 1928, the Viceroy had directed a special watch to be kept on Jawaharlal. Before long there was an opportunity for a prosecution. The Government of India suggested to the Bombay Government that a speech delivered by Jawaharlal on December 12, 1928, at the Bombay Presidency Youth Conference might give grounds for proceeding against him. The speech was pronounced seditious by the Advocate-General, but the Bombay Government did not recommend a prosecution. 'The speech in question,' wrote the Bombay Government, 'does not appear to be a particularly favourable one on which to base a prosecution. With much of what is said in it, everyone must agree, for instance that the present system of society is imperfect, and that much needs to be done to improve the lot of the poor. Of the rest of the speech, a great part is abuse of imperialism and of the British and Indian Governments, which is a commonplace among the opponents of the Government today.'[1]

The Government of India were rather taken aback by what seemed to them the complacent reasoning of the Bombay

[1] Bombay Government to Government of India, January 11, 1929 (N,A,I.).

Government, but they did not press for a prosecution. After a high-level review, it was decided to issue a new directive to all provincial governments to warn them of the dangers ahead. In a secret circular letter dated February 21, 1929, the Government of India described the Calcutta Congress,

'as a clear triumph for extremism. An ultimatum which everybody knows cannot be complied with, has been presented to the British Government . . . Though this resolution may to a large extent have represented a political manoeuvre to avoid a breach in the Congress ranks . . . [it was] a definite declaration from which the Congress would find it difficult to recede. It is no doubt true that the older leaders like Pandit Motilal Nehru and even Mr Gandhi, the author of the resolution, are not anxious to see these developments. But just as they have been forced into the acceptance of a resolution in which they do not really believe, so they may be unable to resist . . . the action that resolution foreshadows. If the experience of the Calcutta Congress is any guide, the decision of future policy appears to lie almost entirely with the young men, notably Pandit Jawaharlal Nehru and Babu Subhas Chandra Bose. There is a tendency for the political and communist revolutionaries to join hands, and Pandit Jawaharlal, an extreme nationalist, who is at the same time genuinely attracted by some of the Communist doctrines, stands almost at the meeting point . . . The situation contains serious potentialities of danger . . . If the extremist leaders press on with their programme, it appears to the Government of India that they should not have a free hand to develop their organization, and increase their following with a view to striking at the moment most favourable to themselves.'

2

Motilal's forecast that 1929 would be a year of excitement proved true. In March Gandhi was arrested in Calcutta on the charge of using a public thoroughfare for a bonfire of foreign cloth. He was fined one rupee, which was paid by someone without his knowledge. The debates in the Legislative Assembly became piquant. The Public Safety Bill and the Trade Disputes Bill brought on a clash between the Government and the Opposition, and an undeclared war between Speaker Patel and the official benches. Verbal explosives were followed by chemical explosives. On April 8th, two young men, Bhagat Singh and B. K. Dutt, threw bombs in the Legislative Assembly with the intention (as they put it later) 'not to kill but to make the deaf hear'. There was a chain of terrorist outrages and a number of conspiracy cases were started. Some of the young revolutionaries caught popular imagination and became heroes overnight; their names resounded in the bazaars and made headlines in the news-papers; their pictures adorned the walls of mud-huts in remote villages; even those who denounced their method, applauded their motive. Public feeling reached a peak when a number of these young revolutionaries went on hunger-strike to protest against the treatment of political prisoners in gaols; one of them, Jatin Das, died after a two-month fast, and was honoured as a martyr.

Meanwhile, the industrial unrest which had characterized the preceding year continued. The Government struck at the trade-union movement, particularly at its Communist fringe. Thirty-one labour leaders were arrested at one swoop in March, 1929, and sent up for trial to Meerut, which was pre-ferred to Bombay and Calcutta to avoid the inconvenience of a jury. 'It seems to me,' Gandhi wrote, 'that the motive behind these prosecutions is not to kill Communism, but to strike terror.' Jawaharlal took a leading part in organizing a Meerut Prisoners' Defence Committee with his father as Chairman. It was not easy to defend the ill-assorted group of prisoners in the Meerut case, which was to drag on for three and a half years. The lawyers who were entrusted with the day-to-day conduct of the case charged heavy fees, and neither Motilal nor Jawa-harlal could afford to give the case sustained attention. At one stage the prosecution tried to rope in Jawaharlal by calling upon him to produce the numerous letters, which he, in his capacity as General Secretary of the Congress, had received from abroad. Secrecy was against the policy of the Congress, but if these letters had been produced they could have been used against the accused and perhaps even against Jawaharlal himself; a refusal to comply with the orders of the court could also lead to trouble. Jawaharlal's arrest seemed on the cards and Motilal had a few anxious days. However, the political climate was changing and, as we shall soon see, Irwin had his own reasons for not baiting the Nehrus.

The Calcutta Congress had given 'a year of grace and a polite ultimatum to the British Government'. A struggle in 1930 seemed not a possibility but a certainty. It was obvious that the next Congress session was going to be a momentous one; the choice of its president had therefore a special significance. Since Gandhi alone could lead a struggle, his choice for the presidency seemed natural, almost inevitable. Ten Provincial Congress Committees voted for him, five for Vallabhbhai Patel and three for Jawaharlal. But as we have already seen, the choice of the Congress president was really made in the informal discussions which preceded the formal election. In 1927 Gandhi and Motilal had discussed Jawaharlal's candidature before Ansari was finally chosen. In 1928, when Motilal's own name was proposed, he suggested that the honour should go to Vallabhbhai Patel, the hero of Bardoli Satyagraha, and failing him, to Jawaharlal. The claims of young Nehru were not so evident to Subhas Chandra Bose and J. M. Sen Gupta, the two young leaders of Bengal, where the Congress was meeting. These two rivals, who seemed to disagree on everything else, were agreed on Motilal being the only possible choice for the Congress presidency for the Calcutta Congress.

In 1929 Motilal again pressed the claims of his son on Gandhi. As in 1927, he put the issue on a public rather than a private plane.

Motilal to Gandhi, July 13, 1929: '. . . Your accepting the chair will give additional weight, dignity and prestige to the office, though as you put it in your letter from the train, there will hardly be any practical difference if you put Jawahar or Vallabhbhai in it. You are the real power, whether on the throne or behind it . . .

'I have been thinking hard on the matter. It appears to me that, leaving one awkward element in the case, all reasons point to your accepting. That element was present in my case. It consists in our apparent stinginess in parting with power and keeping the younger set out of it . . .

'The revolt of youth has become an accomplished fact . . . It would be sheer flattery to say that you have today the same influence as you had on the youth of the country some years ago, and most of them make no secret of the fact. All this would indicate that the need of hour is the head of Gandhi and the voice of Jawahar . . . There are strong reasons for either you or Jawahar to wear the "crown", and if you and Jawahar stand together, as to which there is no doubt in my mind, it does not really matter who it is that stands in front and who behind.'

It is significant that in July, 1929, Motilal should have rated Jawaharlal as indispensable to Gandhi, as Gandhi was to Jawaharlal. The radicalism of his son, which had seemed so inflammable and inopportune only a few months before, struck him now as a vital spark which would light anew the torch of the nationalist struggle. The 'revolt of youth', which had so nettled him at the Calcutta Congress, was now 'an accomplished fact', which he was prepared to recognize and indeed to support. The political radicals, whose irresponsibility had so much troubled him in 1928, now seemed to him as the repositories of the nation's future, to whom power must be transferred by the Old Guard of the Congress.

One may be tempted to argue that paternal affection was clouding Motilal's judgment, that it is easy to talk of parting with power when the recipient is one's own son. Motilal's apparent inconsistency was in fact an indication of the slow and painful process of conversion he had undergone since the Calcutta Congress. In 1929 he was doing exactly what he had done in 1920 and 1917; he was championing the views of his son after initially repudiating and resisting them.

While Motilal was pressing his son's claims for the Congress presidency, Jawaharlal himself was imploring Gandhi to leave him alone. 'I am very nervous about the matter,' he wrote to Gandhi on July 9th, 'and do not like the idea at all.' On August 21st, he telegraphed to the Mahatma: 'Beg of you not to press my name for presidentship.' A few days later he enumerated at length his limitations for the high office of the Congress president: 'I represent nobody but myself. I have not the politician's flair for forming groups and parties. My one attempt in this direction – the formation of the Independence for India League last year – was a hopeless failure so far as I was concerned . . . Most people who put me forward for the presidentship do so because they want to keep someone else out . . . If I have the misfortune to be president, you will see that the very people who put me there . . . will be prepared to cast me to the wolves.'

Gandhi was not moved by these arguments. At the Lucknow meeting of the All India Congress Committee in September, he made it clear that he would not accept his own nomination, and pressed for Jawaharlal's. Vallabhbhai Patel withdrew. Jawaharlal was elected unanimously, but felt hurt and a little humiliated by the mode of his election; as he put it later, he climbed to his high office not by the 'main entrance, or even a side entrance', but 'by a trap door'. He was conscious of the gulf between his ideas and those of most of the Congress leaders. Motilal was delighted at the election of his son, and seemed hardly aware of the conflict that was raging in Jawaharlal's heart. It was left to the poetic diction of Sarojini Naidu to capture their divergent moods.

Sarojini Naidu to Jawaharlal, September 29, 1929: 'I wonder if in the whole of India there was yesterday a prouder heart than your father's, or a heavier heart than yours. Mine was in the peculiar position of sharing in almost equal measure both his pride and your pain . . . You are so sensitive and so fastidious in your spiritual response and reaction, and you will suffer a hundred-fold more poignantly than men and women of less fine fibre, and less vivid perception and apprehension in dealing with the ugliness of weakness, falsehood, backsliding and betrayal . . . You said to me that you felt you had neither the personal strength nor sufficient backing to put your own ideas and ideals into effect . . . I feel you have been given a challenge as well as offered a tribute.'

3

If the Lahore Congress was a challenge to Jawaharlal's capacity for leadership, it was even a greater challenge to Irwin's statesmanship. In March, 1929, Geoffrey Dawson, the Editor of *The Times*, after a three-month tour of India, noted[2] that the situation was 'one of comparative calm on the surface but expectancy beneath', that official circles acknowledged Irwin's sympathy and sincerity, but were not so sure of his being a man 'of active determination'. Of the latter quality Irwin gave (in Dawson's opinion) welcome evidence by launching the Meerut Conspiracy case. Special powers were also assumed by the

[2] Wrench, John Evelyn, *Geoffrey Dawson and Our Times*, pp. 271-2.

executive through the enactment, in the teeth of non-official opposition in the Legislative Assembly, of the Public Safety Bill and the Trade Disputes Bill. There were not a few in the Viceroy's entourage who would have liked him to go further, to put the Congress in its proper place, to nip the challenge of 'complete independence' in the bud, to lock up Jawaharlal and Subhas Bose, to dismiss Speaker Patel and to give India a salutary dose of 'resolute government'. But Irwin was a wiser and sadder man since he had concurred in the proposal for an all-white commission. He sincerely wished to reverse the process of estrangement of Indian opinion which had gone on unchecked since November, 1927. The Simon Commission's report was not to be published for another year, but Irwin already felt that the commission would not be able to placate Indian opinion.

In the summer of 1929, the Viceroy went to England for a mid-term holiday and took the opportunity of discussing Indian affairs with British statesmen. He was in touch with V. J. Patel and Tej Bahadur Sapru, whom he hoped to use as 'honest brokers' with the Congress.

'You may rest assured,' he wrote to Sapru, 'that I shall do everything in my power that may lead to a solution of our present difficulties, and I am sure that I can count upon your help in that direction at this end.'

To Patel he wrote:

'You may rely upon me to do my best to find a way of peace, and I hope that you, on your side, will use whatever influence you have, if anything is done at this end, to get the Congress leaders to meet it half-way.'

Irwin's mission was facilitated by a change of government in England. A Labour ministry headed by Ramsay MacDonald took office in June, 1929. The new Secretary of State was W. Wedgwood Benn (later Lord Stansgate). Though Benn acknowledged to a Labour M.P. that he knew little about India 'on the principle', as he put it, 'that cabinet ministers should be appointed to the posts about which they know least',[3] testimony was borne to his sincerity by friends of the Congress in England.

[3] Brockway, Fenner, Inside the Left, p. 202.

H. S. L. Polak urged Gandhi to seize 'every opportunity of contact that now presents itself owing to the change of Government and circumstances in this country'. Graham Pole assured Sapru that 'Benn is entirely with us and working magnificently . . . [and] regards himself as representing Indians not British'.

Irwin secured the endorsement of the British Cabinet for his proposal for a Round Table Conference in London between the representatives of India and Britain to discuss the framing of a new Indian constitution. He was authorized to herald the announcement of the conference by a declaration affirming that the goal of British policy in India was Dominion Status. Neither Lloyd George nor Lord Reading, the two stalwarts of the Liberal Party, on whose support the Labour ministry's life depended, gave much encouragement to the Viceroy. Nor did the idea of a new declaration evoke much enthusiasm among his own friends of the Conservative Party.

Irwin returned to India on October 25, 1929. Six days later came his long-expected declaration:

'In view of the doubts which have been expressed both in Great Britain and India regarding the intentions of the British Government in enacting the Statute of 1919, I am authorized to state clearly that in their judgment it is implied in the declaration of 1917 that the natural issue of India's constitutional progress, as there contemplated, is the attainment of Dominion Status . . .'

The Viceregal announcement was an 'ingeniously worded document' which could mean much or little. The moderate leaders, to quote Irwin's biographer,[4] saw the conference 'as their supreme opportunity for the full exercise of their intellectual power and from henceforth they were Irwin's faithful allies'. The Congress leaders, scanning the horizon for a gesture which could open the path to self-government and prevent a clash with the Government, discerned the possibility of a change of heart.

The Viceroy had done his public relations job so well that Sapru, V. J. Patel and Malaviya were able to arrange a leaders' conference on November 1st – a day after the declaration – and to issue a 'joint manifesto' welcoming the declaration, under the

[4] Campbell-Johnson, Alan, *Lord Halifax*, p. 225.

signatures of Gandhi, Motilal, Ansari, Sapru, Maharaja of Mahmudabad, Vallabhbhai Patel, and even Jawaharlal.[5]

The Viceroy's announcement was thus well received in India, but in England a storm broke over him and the Labour Government. The British Press and Parliament subjected his words to a protracted post-mortem. Lord Reading, whose opinion as a former Viceroy carried much weight, declared that the announcement was calculated to undermine the prestige and authority of the Simon Commission. Lloyd George, the leader of the Liberal Party, poured scorn on Wedgwood Benn, whom he called 'the pocket-edition of Moses'. Baldwin, the leader of the Conservative Party, whose protégé Irwin was believed to be, did not really rally to the support of the Viceroy's policy. Sir John Simon and his fellow-commissioners, who had not been consulted, felt that they had been shabbily treated by the Labour Government; after the announcement of a Round Table Conference, their report was likely to have only an academic interest.[6] Under such heavy fire, the Labour Government was driven to the defensive. The Secretary of State explained away the declaration as 'a restatement', and an 'interpretation' of Montagu's declaration of August, 1917. The Times compared Irwin's words with a speech delivered by Birkenhead in 1927 and saw no difference between them.[7] Birkenhead himself, in the course of a speech in the House of Lords, exhorted the Simon Commission to treat the Viceroy's declaration as an 'irrelevance'.

Thus circumstances compelled the Labour Government to belittle in Britain what the Viceroy was endeavouring to boost in India. The difficulty, as Morley had bewailed twenty years before, lay in synchronizing clocks in different hemispheres. It was not easy to devise a formula that could pass for self-government in India, and for British Raj at Westminster.

4

The debate in the British Parliament damaged the emotional bridge which the declaration of October 31 had sought to build. During the succeeding six weeks, Irwin set out with the willing co-operation of Sapru, Patel and Jinnah, to repair the damage.

[5] Indian Quarterly Register, 1929, vol. II, pp. 49-50.
[6] Simon, Viscount, Retrospect, p. 151.
[7] The Times, November 4, 1929.

Sir Tej Bahadur Sapru to Lord Irwin, dated Allahabad November 11, 1929. 'I may be permitted to make two suggestions to Your Excellency. The first is that if Pandit Motilal Nehru could personally see Your Excellency, the chances of a favourable atmosphere may in my humble opinion be enhanced . . . The second is . . . some measure of conciliation in the provinces.'

Lord Irwin to Sir Tej Bahadur Sapru, November 12, 1929: 'As regards my seeing Pandit Motilal Nehru, I am unfortunately starting on an extended tour on the evening of November 15th. I had looked forward to seeing Pandit Motilal when next he was in Delhi after my return just before Christmas, and having a frank talk with him. If you think that it would be useful if I were to see him before I go off on tour, I should of course be very glad to do so . . .'

Sir Tej Bahadur Sapru to Lord Irwin, November 15, 1929: 'Last night I received Your Excellency's kind letter of the 12th. I at once put myself into touch with Pandit Motilal over the telephone at Lucknow . . . He has a professional engagement in the Chief Court there . . . he would wait [on you] on your return just before Christmas . . .'

Irwin went off on his tour. Sapru requested Motilal to summon a meeting of the signatories of the Delhi Manifesto at Allahabad where the Congress Working Committee was to meet on November 16th. Sapru succeeded in securing an endorsement of the Delhi Manifesto, and passed on the good news to the Viceroy's camp.

Sapru to Irwin, November 25, 1929: '. . . My task was made difficult . . . by the comments that had appeared in the Press in England and the debate in Parliament . . . On the 18th November the conference met at Pandit Motilal's residence. I received a measure of support which was beyond my expectations . . . Towards the end of the conference the atmosphere was heated, but notwithstanding the fact that Mr Gandhi's point of view was different from mine, I was impressed with the obvious desire on his part to maintain a peaceful atmosphere . . . nevertheless he felt that the situation was such that the country expected that something should be done by the Government which would

enable him to put the advanced section of his following consisting mostly of young men in a reasonable and hopeful frame of
mind . . .

'My mind is not free from doubt and I cannot say what line
the Congress may take at Lahore . . . It is unfortunate that
Pandit Motilal could not wait on Your Excellency on 15th
November . . . My view is if Mr Gandhi could see Your Excellency and have a free talk with you, it might lead to an
easier situation.'

Jinnah, who met the Viceroy at Bombay, also advised him to
see Gandhi. Sarojini Naidu – at Jinnah's instance – readily com-
mended the proposal to the Mahatma. V. J. Patel and Sapru
remained in touch with Motilal.

The interview with the Viceroy, on which such great hopes
had been built, took place in the Viceroy's House at New Delhi
on December 23rd. It proved a complete fiasco. The Viceroy felt
almost personally betrayed; the edifice he had been constructing
laboriously since the summer crumbled to pieces before his eyes.
The intermediaries professed to be bewildered, and blamed the
failure on Gandhi. Sapru's frustration can be seen in a letter
he wrote to two friends in England.

Sapru to Graham Pole and H. S. L. Polak, January 9, 1930: 'At
my suggestion, and also that of Jinnah, the Viceroy agreed to
interview Mr Gandhi, Pandit Motilal Nehru, Jinnah, Patel and
myself. Accordingly we assembled at Delhi on 23rd December.
In the day, we met at Patel's house and the only three things
discussed were (i) political prisoners, (ii) the time for the Round
Table Conference (1930 or 1931) and (iii) personnel of the conference. Mr Gandhi was not present during the conversations
as it was the day of his silence. He came to Patel's house at
4.0 p.m., broke his silence at 4.15 p.m., and quietly went into
the motor car with Pandit Motilal Nehru, and drove to the
Viceregal Lodge. We three, that is to say, Jinnah, Patel and I
followed them in a motor car. When we went in, Mr Gandhi
first expressed his horror at the attempt to wreck the Viceregal
train which had been made that very morning. After that,
throughout the conversation, he was most truculent, which
took us all by surprise. Pandit Motilal was scarcely less stiff.
Jinnah and I argued and reasoned with him but it was all wasted.

His point of view was that the Viceroy should guarantee that
immediate Dominion Status would be granted. Our point was
that the door of the Round Table Conference being open . . . It
was quite clear to Jinnah and myself that we had been badly let
down and that these gentlemen had gone there determined to
break off relations with the Viceroy.'

The attitude of Gandhi and Motilal had struck Sapru as incomprehensible, inconsistent, inexcusable. In fact it was not
the volte face which it appeared to him.

The Delhi 'Joint Manifesto' (which Jawaharlal had been persuaded to sign against his better judgment, and Subhas Bose had
refused to sign) had interpreted the Viceregal declaration to
mean that the Round Table Conference 'would meet not to discuss when Dominion Status would be established, but to frame
a Dominion Constitution for India'. This interpretation, as
Irwin complained to Sapru, was a 'strained' one. The sincerity
of the peace-makers (who had no personal axe to grind) was
patent enough; and so was that of Irwin, who was risking his
political future by venturing on a policy which was anathema
to his own party. But no amount of personal sincerity and goodwill could alter the basic facts of the Indian situation in
December, 1929. The Congress was committed to a civil disobedience campaign, if Dominion Status were not granted by
the end of the year. The Viceregal declaration of October 31,
1929, was an attempt to prevent that contingency. But the
strength of that declaration was its vagueness, which was dissipated by the bluntness of Lloyd George, Reading, Simon,
Churchill and Birkenhead. The debates in the British Parliament
deflated the initial optimism of the Congress leaders. To Jawaharlal, who was repenting his signature to the Delhi Manifesto,
which he described as 'a dangerous trap', Gandhi wrote on
November 7th: 'I believe myself that there is a greater chance
of the Congress coming over to your view than your having to
resign from the presidentship.' A week later, Gandhi gave a
glimpse into the working of his mind[8] to Horace Alexander and
Fenner Brockway, who had cabled for moderation:

'I have done whatever was possible, but you will be patient

[8] Gandhi to Brockway and Horace Alexander, November 14, 1929 (G.S.N.
Papers).

with me if I do not take things quite on trust. I would want some absolute guarantee that things are not what they seem. The Parliamentary debates contain nothing, not even in Benn's speech, that could give me assurance that I may approach the conference with confidence and safety. I would far rather wait and watch and pray than run into what may after all be a dangerous trap . . .'

What Gandhi wanted – and needed – on the eve of the Lahore Congress, was something definite, some proof of the British desire to part with power. Irwin, chastened by recent criticisms in England, was not in a position to make a precise commitment; on the contrary he was deliberately playing for safety. When the news of the forthcoming interview with Gandhi and Motilal appeared in the press early in December, the Viceroy sent frantic messages from his camp to Sapru and Patel urging them to emphasize that the interview had been arranged at their (the intermediaries') suggestion 'otherwise, those who wished to make mischief in England would at once say that the Viceroy was trying to buy off Congress Extremists'.

As for Wedgwood Benn, despite the eulogies he earned from his colleagues in the Labour Party, he was under no illusions as to his limitations. 'We cannot face an election on an Indian issue,' Benn had frankly told Brockway soon after taking office.[9] The Labour Cabinet could not last a day without the support of the Liberals; a radical departure in India was sure to unite Liberals and Conservatives and to sweep the Labour Party out of office. There is no evidence that Benn and Irwin were convinced of the feasibility, or even of the justice of conceding full Dominion Status in 1930, but even if they had been, they could not have carried the British Parliament and public opinion with them. It needed a series of Satyagraha campaigns, the Second World War, and a Labour Government in power (not merely in office) to effect a real transfer of power from Britain to India. It is impossible to resist the conclusion that the chances of a settlement in December, 1929, were overrated by the 'peacemakers', who were victims of their own optimism.

That Gandhi's attitude at the interview of December 23rd was not so perverse as it seemed at the time to the Viceroy and the intermediaries, is evident from the official summary of the

[9] Brockway. Fenner, *Inside the Left*, p. 203.

interview. Though Motilal considered this summary not quite fair to Gandhi, it does not (as one reads it today) reveal the Mahatma in an unfavourable light.

Record of the meeting held at the Viceroy's House on December 23, 1929:[10] Mr Gandhi expressed the horror he and those who accompanied him felt at the attempt on H.E.'s train that morning, and their congratulations on Their Excellencies' escape. He then asked His Excellency if he agreed with the interpretation put by the Delhi Manifesto on his announcement of October 31st, with particular reference to the question of the function of the proposed conference in London. Mr Gandhi said that unless agreement was reached on this point, he felt it fruitless to proceed further.

'His Excellency said that he had thought that the meaning of his announcement was quite plain . . . if any misunderstanding existed, he thought that this might largely be attributed to a confusion of thought about the meaning of the term "Dominion Status". The English view of Dominion Status was of an achieved constitutional state . . . Indians . . . were liable to look on it as a process which might contain a series of degrees. The object, however, of the conference was to thrash out the problems which arose out of His Majesty's Government's definite declaration of policy, and he pointed out the chance there was of doing something big, and the danger of losing a great opportunity.

'Sir T. B. Sapru . . . visualized the conference framing a policy, which when the intermediate safeguards were removed, would mean Dominion Status for India.

'His Excellency said that . . . while it was impossible to lay it down that the conference was to draft any particular constitution, it would have the fullest opportunity to discuss any proposals before it . . . [The Conference] would rather follow the lines of the Imperial Conference, a record being kept of the general sense of the members and the extent of unanimity received.

'Mr Gandhi felt that the Imperial Conference was on a different footing. There all the parties to the discussion were more or less of one mind. At the Indian Conference this would

[10] As made by Cunningham, Private Secretary to the Viceroy, and amended by Sapru (Sapru Papers).

not be so . . . Unless the establishment of Dominion Status would be presumed at once as an immediate result of the Conference, he [Mr Gandhi] would not take part in it . . .

'Pandit Motilal Nehru said, he agreed with Mr Gandhi. The British people exaggerated the difficulties in the way of Dominion Status for India. There was no difficulty about having Dominion Status at once, though he did not mean that the Indian form of it would necessarily be exactly the same, as any particular form of Dominion Status already in existence.

'His Excellency . . . referred to the case of Canada, she did not rise to full Dominion Status in a jump . . .

'Pandit Motilal admitted this, but said that the starting point was there all the same. What India wanted was the starting point.

'Sir T. B. Sapru and Mr Jinnah reasoned at length with Mr Gandhi and Pandit Motilal Nehru . . . They thought that the phrase in the Delhi Manifesto "suitable for Indian needs" was specifically put in with the idea that the Conference would discuss safeguards.

'Pandit Motilal denied this. Mr Gandhi said that his point briefly was, that not Parliament, but India, ought to frame India's future . . .

'His Excellency said that the real test was whether Mr Gandhi and his friends believed in British purpose. If they did believe in it, their present attitude seemed to him inexplicable.

'Mr Gandhi said that he doubted the sincerity of British purpose broadly, though he recognized that of individuals.

'His Excellency said that then there was obviously no common ground between himself and Mr Gandhi . . .

'Mr Gandhi blamed British rule [for lack of unity] . . .

'His Excellency asked Mr Gandhi, as a matter of historical interest, whether India was more united when the British came to India than it was now.

'Mr Gandhi replied that the British had not helped India to bring about unity in the country during the time they had been here. Could the R.T.C. [Round Table Conference] bring about unity in England? . . .

'Pandit Motilal gave it as his opinion that no Indian would be satisfied with less than Dominion Status. He saw no difficulties in the way himself. The whole crux was the transfer of power from Great Britain to India.'

The last words were apparently borrowed by Motilal from the presidential address which his son was to deliver at the Lahore Congress. Throughout the interview, Gandhi and Motilal stuck to one fundamental issue – whether the proposed Round Table Conference would frame a scheme of Dominion Status or get bogged down in subsidiary matters.

Sapru seems to have had a lingering regret that the game was spoilt by the unpredictable Mahatma, that things might have turned out differently if Irwin and Motilal had been able to meet by themselves on November 15th. Motilal, who 'lacked the stout optimism of an Indian Liberal which can read a definite "no" as a clear "yes",'[11] and was a party to the Calcutta Congress compromise of the previous year, could hardly have taken a line in opposition to his own son and Gandhi. A shrewd observer had predicted early in December that 'Motilal Nehru will in the end be overcome by his paternal affection'.[12] It was not only paternal affection, but the aftermath of the parliamentary debates and the imminence of the Lahore Congress, which had led him to fall into line with his son. He had indeed confessed to V. J. Patel, a fortnight before the interview with the Viceroy, that he 'did not expect any results' from it. 'At present,' he added, 'all roads lead to Lahore.'[13]

[11] Motilal to Ansari, February 17, 1930.
[12] Jagadisan, *Letters of Srinivasa Sastri*, pp. 296-7.
[13] Patel, G. I., *Vithalbhai Patel (Life and Times)*, vol. II, p. 1071.

CHAPTER TWENTY-NINE

FREEDOM'S BATTLE

JAWAHARLAL arrived at Lahore on December 25th to preside over the 1929 Congress. He received a welcome which, in the words of the local nationalist daily, 'even the kings might envy'.[1] He was the first president-elect of the Congress to ride a horse – a white charger – followed by a detachment of Congress cavalry. The capital of the Punjab wore a festive look; the streets were canopied with bunting and sparkled with coloured lights. The procession swelled as it surged through the narrow streets of Lahore. Windows, roofs and even trees were crowded with spectators. Motilal and Swarup Rani watched the spectacle from the balcony of the Bhalla Shoe Company in Anarkali, and joined with others in showering flower-petals on their son. Never before in the history of the Indian National Congress had a son succeeded his father as president. As Motilal made over charge to Jawaharlal, he quoted a Persian adage: '*Herche ke pidar natawanad, pesar tamam kunad.*' (What the father is unable to accomplish, the son achieves). This fatherly wish was prophetic.

The Congress was meeting again in the Punjab after exactly ten years. The Amritsar Congress had been held in December, 1919; non-co-operation had followed in 1920. Was history going to repeat itself? The 'ultimate sanction', as Gandhi put it, was civil disobedience, but conditions did not seem ripe for a mass movement. There was no rallying-cry like the Rowlatt Bills, no rankling grievance like the Punjab martial law, no emotional bridge for Hindu-Muslim differences like the Khilafat. Violence was in the air: this was evident not only from the numerous 'conspiracy cases' being tried by the courts, but also from the angry opposition to a resolution moved by Gandhi himself to congratulate Lord and Lady Irwin on their lucky escape from a bomb which had exploded under the Viceregal train a few days before the Congress session.

The Khilafat was dead and most of its exponents had drifted

[1] *Tribune*, December 27, 1929.

into communal politics. The Ali Brothers were no longer the
bellicose nationalists they had been in the early twenties;
Mohammed Ali indeed warned Jawaharlal: 'Your present colleagues will desert you. They will leave you in the lurch in a
crisis. Your own Congressmen will send you to the gallows.'[2]
The Moderates – or as they preferred to call themselves – the
Liberals – Sapru, Chintamani, Sastri and others, had anchored
themselves to Irwin's project of a Round Table Conference; they
made no secret of their fear that Gandhi, Motilal and the Congress were heading for disaster at the heels of Jawaharlal and
the young men. Among the Congress leaders themselves there
were pleas for restraint. Ansari, Sarojini Naidu and Malaviya
were inclined to trust in the sincerity of Irwin and to oppose
any precipitate action. The debates in the 'Subjects Committee',
were long and tense. The inaugural session was in fact held up
for six hours while the committee discussed and voted on the
main resolution. In the end, Gandhi's personal prestige and the
enthusiasm of the rank-and-file carried the day.

The Lahore Congress declared that the agreement to
Dominion Status in the Nehru Report had lapsed; henceforth
Swaraj would mean 'complete independence'. Congress members
in central and provincial legislatures were called upon to resign.
At midnight on December 31st, the flag of independence was
unfurled on the bank of the Ravi. There were scenes of wild enthusiasm in the Congress camp; Jawaharlal danced round the
flagstaff.

The die had been cast. Once again after nine years the Con-
gress had dared to defy the British Empire. Once again it was
going to be blood, sweat and prison for those who followed the
Mahatma. But Motilal's mind was made up. To Ansari, who in
February, 1930, was poised on the razor-edge of indecision,
Motilal wrote:

'I hope you will give me the credit of fully realizing what it
means to me and mine to throw my lot with Gandhiji in the
coming struggle. Nothing but a deep conviction that the time
for the greatest effort and the greatest sacrifice has come would
have induced me to expose myself at my age and with my
physical disabilities, and with my family obligations to the

[2] Nehru, J. L., *Toward Freedom*, p. 106.

tremendous risks I am incurring. I hear the clarion call of the country and I obey.'[3]

2

The Lahore Congress had authorized the All India Congress Committee to launch civil disobedience. But everyone knew that the lead would be given by Gandhi. As the new year dawned, the Government as well as the people waited for the Mahatma's next move. He called for the celebration of 'Independence Day' on January 26th. On that day, hundreds of thousands of people in the towns and villages of India met and took a pledge that 'it was a crime against man and God to submit to British rule'. But soon afterwards Gandhi made an unexpected offer to the Viceroy: if the British Government would accept the 'Eleven Points', he would not press on with civil disobedience. These 'Eleven Points', which included reduction in land revenue, abolition of the salt-tax, scaling down of military and civil expenditure, release of political prisoners and the levy of a duty on foreign cloth, seemed to the Government a conveniently wide net to secure for Gandhi's movement peasants as well as workers, professional classes as well as business interests. To Gandhi's own colleagues, a month after the declaration of independence, the proposal was something of an anti-climax. Gandhi well knew that the 'Eleven Points' did not add up to political independence, but by listing them he was setting a tangible test of the Government's willingness to part with power.

The popular response to the celebration of 'Independence Day' heartened Gandhi. Towards the end of February he announced that he proposed to open his campaign by breaking the salt laws. The salt-tax, though relatively small (in 1930 it amounted to no more than three annas per head) hit the poorest in the land. But somehow, salt did not seem to fit into a struggle for national independence. The first impulse of the Government, as of the Congress intellectual, was to ridicule the 'kindergarten stage of revolution' and to laugh away the idea that the King-Emperor could be unseated by boiling sea-water in a kettle. B. C. Roy, who was at Allahabad when Gandhi's plans for the breach of the salt laws became public, recalls that Motilal was amused, even angered, by the apparent irrelevance of Gandhi's

[3] Motilal to Ansari, February 7, 1930.

move. To Motilal, as indeed to many others, it seemed that salt had become, like fasting and *charkha*, another of the Mahatma's hobby-horses.

Gandhi decided to inaugurate the campaign by leading a band of volunteers from Sabarmati to Dandi on the west coast. The prayer meeing in the *Ashram* on March 11th had a record attendance. 'Our cause is strong,' said Gandhi, 'our means the purest and God is with us. There is no defeat for Satyagrahis till they give up truth. I pray for the battle which begins tomorrow.' Next morning, Gandhi and his seventy-eight companions began the 241-mile trek from Ahmedabad to Dandi. The march did not, as the Government anticipated, prove a fiasco; it electrified not only the districts through which Gandhi's path lay, but the whole country. Salt became the symbol of national defiance. 'At present,' said Gandhi, 'Indian self-respect is symbolized, as it were, in a handful of salt in the Satyagrahi's hand. Let the fist be broken, but let there be no surrender of salt.' 'Today the pilgrim marches onward on his long trek,' Jawaharlal wrote, 'the fire of a great resolve is in him and surpassing love of his miserable countrymen. And love of truth that scorches, and love of freedom that inspires. And none that passes him can escape the spell, and men of common clay feel the spark of life.'

Both Motilal and Jawaharlal were present at the meeting of the All India Congress Committee at Ahmedabad in the third week of March, which empowered Jawaharlal, as Congress president, to act on its behalf, to nominate his successor, and to fill vacancies in the Working Committee. From Ahmedabad, the Nehrus hurried to Jambosar, a small village in Broach district, where Gandhi was scheduled to halt on his way to Dandi. It was at this meeting in the early hours of March 23rd that Motilal decided to make a gift of Anand Bhawan (renamed as *Swaraj Bhawan* – 'The abode of independence') to the Congress. The family had already moved into the smaller house which had been built in the compound and which was to be and is still called Anand Bhawan.

Motilal's decision to give rather than sell the old house, which might have fetched a lakh or two, was prompted by his resolve to throw his all into the battle which Gandhi had begun. The formal ceremony took place on April 6th, the D-day for the Salt Satyagraha, when Jawaharlal as Congress president accepted the gift from his father.

By early April, the Government of India had discovered the dangerous potentialities of Gandhi's strategy.⁴ Immediately after the Lahore Congress, the Viceroy had been assured of support for 'firm executive action' by Secretary of State Benn, and exhorted to handle 'the revolutionary leaders with firm determination' by Premier MacDonald. From April onwards the Congress was subjected to the sternest repression in its long history; the Government sought to strangle Satyagraha with an iron ring of ordinances, ten of which were issued during the next nine months. 'Those who were responsible for executing his orders testify,' writes the Viceroy's biographer, 'that his religious convictions seemed to reinforce the very ruthlessness of his policy of repression.'

As always, the Government were cautious in laying their hands on Gandhi, but other leaders were not spared. Vallabhbhai Patel was arrested on April 7th. Jawaharlal, who had been energetically co-ordinating the movement from Allahabad, was arrested on April 14th. He was sentenced to six months' imprisonment and taken to Naini gaol. He nominated his father as 'acting president' of the Congress

For some months Motilal's health had been causing concern. Dr Ansari, who examined him on his return from Jambosar, was so alarmed that he immediately communicated his findings to Gandhi.

Dr Ansari to Gandhi, March 30, 1930: '. . . I found Panditji's health in a very unsatisfactory condition this time. The continuous anxiety and strain which he has recently gone through, and his visit to you [at Jambosar] and dusty walks had caused a fresh exacerbation of asthmatic attack, and had placed a further strain on his dilated heart. He could hardly walk or even perform ordinary movements without losing his breath. As you know, he has been running an erratic and high blood pressure . . . His age is also such that he has little power of recuperation. But he has not been sparing himself and is determined not to spare himself in future . . .'

⁴ Nanda, B. R., *Mahatma Gandhi*, pp. 293-6.

Motilal turned a deaf ear to Ansari's advice. He refused to step aside and rest so long as the country was in the throes of a struggle, and his son in gaol.

3

These were stirring months for Indian nationalism. Once again, and not for the last time, Gandhi's knack for organizing Indian masses for corporate action delighted the nationalists as much as it discomfited the authorities. On July 10th the Director of the Central Intelligence Bureau specially noted the 'awakening among Indian women, and the fact that the movement has spread to the rural areas'. The following week he expressed his concern at 'the self-sacrificing attitude of many businessmen towards the boycott movement, the unending supply of volunteers for picketing, the participation of large numbers of women, and above all, the abundance of funds for every branch of Congress activity. There are signs that the position may be further complicated by the addition of large numbers of the labouring classes to the forces of disorder'. Army Headquarters expressed anxiety at the possibility of sedition seeping into the army.

These developments served further to stiffen the attitude of the Government. On May 5th, Gandhi was arrested and imprisoned without trial in the Yeravda gaol near Poona. His efforts to keep the movement non-violent had succeeded to a remarkable degree. But there were stray cases of popular violence, which were well-matched by official counter-violence. On April 23rd there was a demonstration in Peshawar, following the arrest of Abdul Ghaffar Khan when the troops opened fire. The number of casualties was officially estimated at 30 killed and 33 wounded, but was placed at 125 by an unofficial inquiry committee appointed by Motilal. In May martial law was imposed in the mill town of Sholapur following acts of arson and violence.

Of the 'awakening of women', which was the most striking feature of 1930, Allahabad and the Nehru family were a fine example. Not only Vijayalakshmi and Krishna, but the aged Swarup Rani and the fragile Kamala were in the front line, organizing processions, addressing meetings, picketing foreign cloth and liquor shops. Motilal did not like the idea of women rushing about the town in the hot weather, but Jawaharlal was delighted when he received the news in gaol. 'By the time I come out,' he wrote, 'I expect to find the womenfolk running everything.'

In Naini gaol, Jawaharlal occupied two of the four cells in a small isolated barrack, where his only companions were the prison guard, the sweeper and the cook. He kept to a rigorous schedule of reading, spinning and weaving. The news of official excesses in Sholapur, Peshawar and other places tormented him; he felt he could identify himself with the unfortunate victims of that repression only by making his own life in prison as hard as possible. He begged his father not to send him fruit or ice; he could not, he wrote, 'hold high festival in gaol, when imprisonment, floggings, firings and martial law are the lot of those outside'.

Meanwhile Motilal was expending the last of his energy in directing the campaign. He took a keen interest in the work of the Peshawar Inquiry Committee, of which he had appointed his son-in-law Ranjit Pandit secretary and V. J. Patel president. V. J. Patel also headed another committee, which made arrangements with the Bombay mill-owners for the boycott of foreign cloth. To Sir Purshotamdas Thakurdas, one of Bombay's 'cotton kings', who had complained of the dislocation of trade and industry, Motilal wrote: 'Those who sow the wind, have to be prepared to reap the whirlwind. This remark applies with equal force to the Congress and the Government.'

In June Motilal went to Bombay – the storm-centre of the movement; with him went Swarup Rani and Kamala. They received a tremendous welcome, but also witnessed some of the fiercest attacks by the police on Congress processions. It was a crowded and memorable fortnight, but its strain finally broke Motilal's physical frame. On return to Allahabad, he planned to leave for Mussoorie for a short holiday on July 1st, but he was arrested on the previous day and taken to Naini gaol, where his son was already serving a six-month term. The barrack in which the Nehrus were lodged was not too comfortable, and the verandah attached to it was too narrow to serve as a protection against sun or rain. But Motilal would not hear of leaving the company of his son for more spacious accommodation in another part of the gaol. The Government were considerate enough to order the construction of a new verandah, but it was completed too late to be of any use to Motilal.

Jawaharlal took charge of his ailing father and nursed him with a devotion which moved him deeply.

'Hari,'[5] Motilal wrote, 'could very well take a leaf out of Jawahar's book in the matter of serving me. From early morning tea to the time I retire for the night, I find everything I need in its proper place. The minutest detail is carefully attended to and it has never become necessary to ask for anything, which had so frequently to be done at Anand Bhawan . . . Jawahar anticipates everything and leaves nothing for me to do. I wish there were many fathers to boast of such sons.'

To circumvent the gaol rule of one letter a fortnight, Motilal had the brilliant idea of writing 'a circular letter' addressed to all members of the family – outside the gaol. The letter dated July 16, 1930, sounds almost like an after-dinner chat. 'You are doing a little too much for your old bones,' he wrote to his wife. 'Use them sparingly if you wish to see Swaraj established in your life-time.' 'Your letter is not as detailed as I expected it to be,' he wrote to his daughter-in-law, 'and there is no news about your health – not a word.' He gave Kamala detailed instructions for planting fast-growing creepers and *doob* grass, and for keeping trespassers off Swaraj Bhawan: 'All sorts of people are about these days, and every wearer of a Gandhi cap is not a follower of Gandhi.' To Vijayalakshmi he wrote: 'It was silly of you to have left Bombay without proper treatment. You seem to be too anxious to receive an invitation [to gaol]. There would be some point in it, if you could be lodged with [your] brother and myself, but that is impossible.'

He chided Krishna for not writing: 'How is it, madness that you have not sent a line this week?' To his twelve-year-old grand-daughter Indira, who had been drilling the children's volunteer 'army' (*vanar sena*), he wrote: 'What is the position in the "monkey army"? I suggest the wearing of a tail by every member of it, the length of which should ·be in proportion to the rank of the wearer.'

4

The comparative calm of Naini gaol was disturbed on July 27,

[5] Motilal's personal servant.

1930, by the arrival of the Liberal leaders Tej Bahadur Sapru and M. R. Jayakar. They came on a peace-mission which, ironically enough, was initiated by an interview given by Motilal to George Slocombe of the London *Daily Herald*. At the instance of V. J. Patel, Motilal had agreed to meet Slocombe. The interview, which took place on June 20th at Bombay, became the first link in that curious and unexpected chain of events which culminated in the Gandhi-Irwin Pact eight months later. At the end of the interview Slocombe drafted a statement indicating Motilal's views on the conditions on which the Congress was prepared to suspend civil disobedience and participate in the Round Table Conference.

'I asked him,' wrote Slocombe,[6] 'what his attitude would be if he were to receive an invitation to the Round Table Conference. "My reply would be," he told me, "to ask you on what basis the conference is convened . . . if it was made clear . . . that the conference would meet to frame a constitution for free India, subject to such adjustments of our mutual relations as are required by the special needs and conditions of India and our past association, I for one, would be disposed to recommend that Congress should accept an invitation to participate in the conference. We must be masters in our own household, but are ready to agree to reasonable terms for the period of transfer of power from the British administration in India to a responsible Indian Government. We must meet the British people in order to discuss these terms as nation to nation on an equal footing." '

In July, 1930, Sapru (this time assisted by Jayakar) was resuming negotiations where they had been left off on December 23, 1929. Motilal's statement to Slocombe was, on the whole, a restatement of the position Gandhi and he had adopted during the interview with the Viceroy. It did not, however, occur to Motilal, until he joined his son in gaol, that talk of 'peace' in the midst of a Satyagraha struggle was likely to demoralize the people.

In Naini prison Sapru and Jayakar argued at length with Motilal and Jawaharlal, but found both equally impervious to the idea of a settlement with the Government, and obviously unwilling to commit themselves without consulting Gandhi.

[6] Sapru Papers.

The Government then arranged for the Nehrus' journey in a special train to Poona. There were protracted discussions in Yeravda Gaol in which Gandhi, the Nehrus, Vallabhbhai Patel, Sarojini Naidu, Jairamdas Daulatram, Syed Mahmud, Sapru and Jayakar joined. The peace-makers reported the results of these abortive negotiations to the Viceroy.

Sapru and Jayakar to Irwin, dated Bombay: August 16, 1930:
'. . . Our conversation on the first day lasted for four hours; talking was done mostly by Gandhi and Motilal – Jawaharlal taking part in the conversations occasionally. We urged it on them that civil disobedience must be called off and they must advise the Congress to participate in the R.T.C. We pointed out to them that, in our opinion, what Your Excellency had written to us in your published letter was in substance identical with the trend of thought in the statement which had been sent to us at Simla by a common friend with the approval of Pandit Motilal . . .

'The salient feature of Mr Gandhi's position throughout has been his insistence upon Eleven Points, and particularly upon the right to manufacture salt privately . . . In other words, Mr Gandhi's test of the [new] constitution would be whether it gave him the power to enforce all or any of his "Eleven Points", if he so desired . . .

'As for the position of the two Pandits, both at Allahabad and in the Yeravda Gaol . . . we may state that Pandit Motilal was of opinion that the terms of Your Excellency's published letter to us were not sufficiently definite, and that he and Pandit Jawaharlal Nehru would not be satisfied unless an agreement on all vital matters are previously arrived at between the Congress and the Government of India.'[7]

These negotiations showed that Gandhi was willing to bargain on details – a tendency which was to make possible, for good or ill, the conclusion of the Gandhi-Irwin Pact. Motilal and Jawaharlal, on the contrary, insisted on a concrete commitment regarding the devolution of power from British to Indian hands. If Motilal had been by Gandhi's side at Delhi in February-March, 1931, the negotiations with Irwin might possibly have shared the fate of the Yeravda talks with Sapru and Jayakar in August, 1930.

[7] Sapru Papers.

On this visit to Yeravda Gaol, Motilal told Lt.-Colonel Martin, the Superintendent, that he took very 'simple and light food', and then gave a list of his requirements which (as Jawaharlal put it) would have been considered simple and ordinary food only at the Ritz and the Savoy in London. Colonel Martin, who had been feeding Gandhi on goat's milk, dates and oranges, could scarcely conceal his amusement at the sophisticated tastes of the elder Nehru. Not the least amusing part of the story is that the Bombay Government wrote to the Government of India to foot the bill for the extra expenses incurred by the dietary requirements of the Nehrus at Poona.

5

Enforced rest in gaol and devoted nursing by his son could not by themselves restore Motilal to health. He rejected an offer of release on medical grounds, and even telegraphed to Irwin not to show him any favours. But his health was failing fast, he was losing weight and becoming a shadow of himself. The Government had no intention of incurring the odium of his death in gaol and released him on September 11th. Three days later, he left for Mussoorie. With him went Swarup Rani, Krishna, Vijayalakshmi and her children.

Kamala did not accompany her father-in-law to Mussoorie. She was too tied up with the local Congress activities to be able to leave Allahabad. Her own health had begun to fail barely a year after her prolonged convalescence in Switzerland. In December, 1928, she and her husband consulted many doctors in Calcutta. With this background, her plunge in the Satyagraha struggle in the summer of 1930 was a feat of courage which filled her husband with pride, not unmixed with a gnawing anxiety. From the gaol he warned her against 'tempting the midday sun'. Gandhi, who had a special affection for her, gave her much paternal advice: 'I understand you are working too hard; your body will not bear excessive strain or neglect.' But her highly-strung, emotional nature made her completely oblivious of herself. Her mind and heart were set on a great cause which had been her husband's for so long, and had at last become hers as well. Her mood is reflected in a letter she sent to Jawaharlal in Naini Gaol.

Kamala to Jawaharlal, September, 1930: 'Jawahar! I have received your letter. The day of your release is approaching, but I am doubtful if you would be set free. And even if you are, you will again be put behind the bars. But I am prepared for everything . . . How I wish I were arrested before you come out!'

The letter is more like one from a soldier to a comrade-in-arms than from a wife to her husband. The ceaseless toil of these months was before long to take heavy toll of Kamala. Her intuition, that her husband would henceforth be more in gaol than out of it, was a sound one. A few days before Jawaharlal's term was to expire, the Government of India threw a broad hint to the United Provinces Government to take the earliest opportunity of 'putting this irreconcilable out of harm's way'. He was released on October 11th, and tried to make the most of his short-lived freedom for the national movement. He convened a meeting of the executive of the Provincial Congress Committee and persuaded it to launch a no-tax campaign in the rural areas. A district peasants' conference was summoned to meet at Allahabad on October 19th. Meanwhile, accompanied by Kamala, Jawaharlal went to Mussoorie, where his father was convalescing. It was a happy family reunion for three precious days, and a wonderful holiday for Jawaharlal – the last he was to spend with his father.

On October 18th Jawaharlal and Kamala returned to Allahabad in time for the peasants' conference. On the following day, the rest of the family also arrived at Allahabad. Jawaharlal received them at the railway station and immediately afterwards, accompanied by his wife, went to a public meeting. As he was returning home in the evening; his car was stopped almost at the gates of Anand Bhawan, he was arrested and taken to Naini Gaol. Kamala went home alone to give the news to the waiting family. Motilal was deeply distressed by the re-arrest of his son within a week. He pulled himself together and announced that he would no longer be an invalid. Strangely enough he suddenly seemed much better; even the blood in his sputum, which had been defying all treatment, ceased.

Motilal took back the reins of the movement. He was once again in high spirits. 'I take my Gandhi cap off to the Naoroji clan,' he wrote on November 10th to Mrs Gosi Captain of

Bombay, 'for the great part they are taking in the national struggle.' 'It has been decided by Pandit Motilal Nehru,' wrote the Secretary of All India Congress Committee to all Provincial Congress Committees, 'that the 16th of November, 1930, should be observed as "Jawahar Day" throughout the length and breadth of India as a protest against the savage sentence of two and a half years passed on the Congress President.' On November 16th at hundreds of meetings all over the country the offending passages from Jawaharlal's speech were read. At Allahabad, Swarup Rani, Vijayalakshmi, Krishna and Indira joined the procession and the meeting in Purushotamdas Park was addressed among others by Kamala, who read the whole of the 'seditious' speech for which her husband had been convicted.

6

The shock of his son's arrest had enabled Motilal to summon the reserves of his dwindling strength for a last desperate effort. But will-power alone could not stem the progress of the fatal disease. Chronic asthma had resulted in advanced fibrosis of the lungs, forming a tumour on the right side of the chest, which pressed upon the blood-vessels.

On November 17th Motilal left for Calcutta where he was examined by two eminent doctors, Nilratan Sarkar and Jivraj Mehta. The Governor of Bengal generously allowed Dr B. C. Roy to leave Alipore Central prison for a few hours to make a further examination. 'The X-rays have revealed,' Motilal wrote to Vijayalakshmi from Calcutta, 'that the heart, the lungs and liver are all affected.' A virulent attack of malaria further lowered his resistance. He moved into a garden-house in the suburbs of Calcutta, where he was joined by the whole family except Kamala, who was busy with Congress work in Allahabad. He toyed with the idea of making a voyage to Singapore. But he did not go to Singapore. He was approaching not a new voyage but the end of an old one.

The news of Kamala's arrest on January 1, 1931, brought Motilal back to Allahabad. On January 12th, when he turned up for the fortnightly interview in Naini prison, Jawaharlal was shocked to see his swollen face and the rapid deterioration in his health. A fortnight later, Gandhi, Jawaharlal and all members of the Congress Working Committee, 'original' and 'substitute',

were released. This brought Jawaharlal and Kamala back home.
The presence of his son and of Gandhi, who had left for Allahabad immediately after his release, seemed to have a soothing
effect on Motilal. A number of Congress leaders came to
Allahabad to review the political situation. Motilal was too ill
to take part in their discussions but he insisted on meeting them.
He sat up in an easy chair to receive them as they came in twos
and threes; the swelling had obliterated all expression on his
face, but there was a glitter in his eye, his head bowed, and his
hands folded in salutation; his lips opened for a word of greeting
and even of humour. When the constriction in his throat
rendered conversation too painful, he wrote on little slips of
paper.

Three of the most eminent doctors in the country, Ansari,
Jivraj Mehta and B. C. Roy, were attending him. On February
4th, they decided to take him to Lucknow for deep X-ray treatment, which was not available at Allahabad. Motilal was reluctant to go; he preferred to die in his beloved Anand Bhawan.
But he yielded to the persuasion of the doctors – and of Gandhi.

His courage and humour remained till the last. He joked with
Swarup Rani about going ahead of her and waiting in heaven
to receive her. He did not, he said, want anyone to pray for him
after his death; he had made his own way in this world, and
hoped to do so in the next as well. Pointing to the swelling on
his face, he said: 'Have I not qualified for a beauty competition?' Turning to the masseur, who was attending on him,
he asked: 'Mr. Austin, how many Baby Austins do you
possess?' 'Mahatmaji,' he said to Gandhi, 'you have perfect control over your sleep. I have perfect control over my digestion;
it never fails me.'

The end came in the early hours of February 6th, while
Swarup Rani and Jawaharlal were at his bedside. For several
hours his strength had been gradually ebbing; he was speechless
but conscious. One wonders what thoughts crossed his mind,
whether in those twilight hours he recalled the strange adventure that life had been to him: the fatherless childhood in
Agra and Khetri; the sheltering care of Nandlal and the
Persian lessons from the old Qazi; the carefree boyhood in Cawnpore and Allahabad and the good old Principal Harrison; the
death of Nandlal and the struggle for survival at the Allahabad
Bar; the palmy days in Anand Bhawan, the drive in state to the

High Court, the poetry and politics and champagne in the evening; the delightful interludes in Europe, and Jawahar at Harrow, and little Nanni's birthday in Bad Ems; the glorious morning of Jawahar's home-coming in Mussoorie and the Nehru Wedding Camp at Delhi; the Home Rule furore and the coming of Gandhi and Satyagraha; the months of agonizing suspense and the exhilaration of the final plunge; Chauri Chaura and the pleasures and pains of Gandhi's leadership; the bouts with Hailey and Muddiman in the Assembly Chamber; Kamala in Switzerland and the last trip to Europe; the Simon Commission and the framing of a Swaraj constitution, the clash and compromise at Calcutta; the hero's welcome for Jawahar in Lahore – and then another struggle. That struggle continued, but it was in safe hands, guided by 'the head of Gandhi and the voice of Jawaharlal'.

EPILOGUE

In June, 1912, two months before the return of his son from England, Motilal had confided to his brother that he was looking forward to an early retirement 'in peace and comfort after a most strenuous life of active work extending over thirty-five years'. Little did he know that his last years were to be the most crowded, the most strenuous and the most memorable of his life. If he had indeed been able to enjoy his well-earned retirement, he might have lived to a ripe old age, holding court in Anand Bhawan, entertaining his friends, holidaying in Kashmir or the South of France. His children and grand-children would then have cherished his memory as that of a fascinating, if somewhat formidable and mercurial patriarch. And in the Bar Libraries of his province, and more particularly of Allahabad, he would have been remembered as a brilliant lawyer, who had lived well and laughed well – one of those fortunate few who had made – and spent – a fortune at the Bar.

Motilal was destined for a larger role than that of a genial patriarch or a local celebrity. He was to become one of the heroes of India's struggle for freedom. He had not the missionary zeal of his son, nor the ascetic streak of the Mahatma, but Satyagraha appealed to that fighting spirit which in youth had gloried in such sports as wrestling and in defying the tyranny of his caste and community. He had always been ready to 'break his lance with a foeman worthy of his steel'. In the armour of this happy warrior there was a chink: the love of his son, but this was his strength as well as his weakness; it turned the last years of his life from a placid pool into a raging torrent, but it also lifted him from the position of a prosperous lawyer to the apex of national leadership.

So long had Motilal been known to admire English ways, English traditions and English institutions that when he turned rebel against the Raj, the feelings of his numerous English friends (in the words of an Anglo-Indian journal) 'resembled those of a fond Edwardian father whose delightful daughter became a suffragette and broke his windows'. The transition was in fact not so sudden as it seemed to his contemporaries; nearly a decade before Gandhi launched non-co-operation, Motilal's politics had been shifting leftward. Nevertheless, it is doubtful if, at the age of sixty, he would have made a clean break with his past and plunged into the unknown, but for the unshakable resolve of his son to follow the Mahatma. Motilal loved the good things of life, but he loved his son even more.

The political partnership between father and son was the more remarkable because of their intellectual and temperamental differences. Motilal was the stern realist, Jawaharlal the irrepressible idealist; Motilal had the clearer head, Jawaharlal had the larger vision. Jawaharlal – like the Mahatma – learned to strike the deep chords in Indian humanity; he took to the crowd, and the crowd took to him. Motilal's gifts were more suited to a legislative chamber than to the street-corner; his public speeches, though spiced with Persian proverbs, were closely reasoned; it was truly said of him that he gave to the mob what was meant for a parliament. Jawaharlal belonged to an uncommon genre: he was an intellectual in politics; his sensitiveness to currents of thought and events in India and abroad kept his politics perpetually in flux and made it difficult for his father to keep pace with him. This led to a clash, which despite its toll of tension and anguish, did much good to both father and son and also to the common cause they sought to serve. It spurred on the ageing father and restrained the youthful impetuosity of the son: it also made them recognize afresh how much they meant to each other.

The process of political education was not one-sided. Young Nehru also owed much to his father. For one thing, he was spared the distraction of working for a living, which might have compromised his politics and kept him away from the centre of events. For another, he could not but be influenced by his father's example: his integrity, pride, courage, tremendous capacity for work, devotion to detail and freedom from pettiness.

During the nineteen twenties when non-co-operation had collapsed and Gandhi had taken to the *ashram* and the *charkha* and nationalist politics were at a low ebb, the Swarajists led by C. R. Das and Motilal kept up the spirit of resistance to foreign rule. The Swarajists rendered another more important, if unintended service. By bringing the Congress into the legislatures, even for the avowed purpose of wrecking them, the Swarajists helped to acquaint the country with the mechanism, the procedures and the traditions of parliamentary government. The Swarajist experience was thus not so barren as it seemed in 1930; it created precedents which helped the Congress to contest the elections and to accept office in 1937; it facilitated the installation of a fully-fledged representative government at the centre in 1946.

Motilal was one of those outstanding men who were drawn into the national movement under Gandhi's inspiration in 1920, and who gave much to the national movement because they had much to give. He seemed cut out for the role of a great parliamentarian with his splendid presence, his gift of persuasive advocacy, his freedom from doctrinaire rigidity and his capacity for personal friendliness towards political opponents. These are qualities which India will need in her leaders if she is to maintain her democratic institutions in full vigour, and build a better future for her people in freedom and unity.

He also represented another great tradition, that of a liberal secularism. There was hardly any Indian leader of his time who was more fully emancipated from the bonds of orthodoxy and sectarianism. He fought the narrowness of his co-religionists and the mounting ambitions of Muslim communalism with equal tenacity. His secularism did not stem from political expediency, but from that broad-based culture which had nourished several generations of Nehrus in Delhi and Kashmir. He was a product of the mingling of three cultures – the Aryan, the Mughal and the European.

His sacrifices and fighting statesmanship cast a spell on his generation and it is but natural that he should be remembered today chiefly as a legendary figure. He was, however, no copy-book hero. He was refreshingly human in his school-boy exuberance, insatiable curiosity and the bubbling enthusiasm which enabled him to make of his life an unending adventure and to laugh right to the very gate of death. He had his failings too – pride, arrogance and a quick temper – but the sum of all these faults and virtues was a fascinating human being. The heroic and the human were happily blended in him, and in nothing was he more human than in his love for his son. Motilal's ambitions had been all for his son: his son's were all for India. For India Jawaharlal took risks and endured hardship which filled Motilal's heart with a perpetual conflict between paternal pride and paternal anxiety.

Asked to describe Motilal's greatest quality, Gandhi said: 'Love of his son.' 'Was it not love of India?' the Mahatma was asked. 'No,' he replied, 'Motilal's love for India was derived from his love for Jawaharlal.'

BIBLIOGRAPHY

Unpublished Sources: This book is primarily based on original sources, the Nehru family papers, official records of the Government of India, and the unpublished correspondence of Mahatma Gandhi and Sir Tej Bahadur Sapru.

The abbreviations used are: 'N.P.' for Nehru Papers; 'N.A.I.' for National Archives of India; 'G.S.N.' for *Gandhi Samarak Nidhi*.

Published Sources: A large number of books, journals and newspapers have been consulted; the following list is not exhaustive but includes only such publications as have been cited in the footnotes. The year against each book is not necessarily the date of first publication, but of the edition actually consulted.

All Parties Conference (Nehru) Report: Allahabad, 1928.

All Parties National Convention, Proceedings of: December, 1928.

BALL, W. MACMAHON: *Nationalism and Communism in East Asia*; Melbourne, 1956.

BANERJEA, S. N.: *A Nation in the Making*; London, 1925.

BESANT, ANNIE: *India Bond or Free*; London, 1926.

BEVERIDGE, LORD: *India Called Them*; London, 1947.

BIRKENHEAD, EARL OF: *The Life of F. E. Smith, First Earl of Birkenhead*; London, 1960.

BOLITHO, HECTOR: *Jinnah; Creator of Pakistan*; London, 1954.

BOSE, SUBHAS CHANDRA: *The Indian Struggle*; Calcutta, 1948.

BRECHER, MICHAEL: *Jawaharlal Nehru*; London, 1959.

BROCKWAY, FENNER: *Inside The Left*; London, 1942.

BROGAN, D. W.: *The Price of Revolution*; London, 1951.

CAMPBELL-JOHNSON, ALAN: *Lord Halifax*; London, 1941.

CHATURVEDI, BANARSIDAS AND MARJORIE SYKES: *Charles Freer Andrews*; London, 1949.

COATMAN, J.: *Years of Destiny*; London, 1932.

COLE, MARGARET: *Beatrice Webb's Diaries 1924-32*; London, 1956.

COTTON, SIR HENRY: *New India or India in Transition*; 1907. *Indian and Home Memories*; London, 1911.

DUTT, R. PALME: *India Today*; Bombay, 1947.

DWIVEDI, E. (Ed.): *The Life and Speeches of Pandit Jawaharlal Nehru*; Allahabad, 1930.

GANDHI, M. K.: *My Experiments with Truth or an Autobiography*; Ahmedabad, 1945.

GOPAL, S.: *The Viceroyalty of Lord Irwin*; London, 1957. *The Viceroyalty of Lord Ripon*; London, 1953.

GUPTA, J. N.: *Life and Work of Romesh Chunder Dutt*; London, 1911.

HALIFAX, EARL OF: *Fulness of Days*; London, 1957.

HARDINGE OF PENSHURST: *My Indian Years*; London, 1948.

Hindustan Times: New Delhi.

History of the Times: The 150th Anniversary and Beyond; Volume IV, London, 1952.

HUGHES, E.: *Keir Hardie*; London, 1956.

HUTHEESING, KRISHNA: *With No Regrets*; Bombay, 1952.

Independent, Allahabad.

INDIAN NATIONAL CONGRESS: *Reports of the Annual Sessions*.

INDIAN STATUTORY COMMISSION REPORT: Calcutta, 1930.

IRWIN, LORD: *Speeches of Lord Irwin*; Volume I, Simla, 1930.

IYENGAR, A. S.: *All Through the Gandhian Era*; Bombay, 1950.

JAGADISAN, T. N. (Ed.): *Letters of Rt. Honourable V.. S. Srinivasa Sastri*; Madras (n.d.).

JAYAKAR, M. R.: *The Story of My Life*; Vol. I, Bombay, 1958, Vol. II, 1959.

KEITH, A. B.: *Letters on Imperial Relations; Indian Reform and International Law, 1916-1930*; London, 1935.

KRISHANDAS: *Seven Months with Mahatma Gandhi*, Vol. I; Madras, 1928.

Leader, Allahabad.

LEGISLATIVE ASSEMBLY DEBATES: 1924 to 1930.

MACDONALD, J. RAMSAY: *The Awakening of India*; London, 1910.

MALAVIYA, K. D.: *Pandit Motilal Nehru; His Life and Speeches*; Allahabad, 1919.

MASANI, R. P.: *Dadabhai Naoroji*; London, 1939.

MITRA, N. N.: *Annual Register*; Calcutta.

MONTAGU, E. S.: *An Indian Diary*; London, 1930.

MORAES, FRANK: *Sir Purshotamdas Thakurdas*; Bombay, 1957.

MORLEY, VISCOUNT: *Recollections*; Vol. II, London, 1918. *Indian Speeches*; London, 1909.

NANDA, B. R.: *Mahatma Gandhi*; London, 1958.

NATESAN, G. A.: *Congress Presidential Addresses*; 1911 to 1934; Madras, 1934. *Speeches and Writings of Mahatma Gandhi*; Madras, 1933.

NATARAJAN, J.: *History of Indian Journalism, Part II of Report of Press Commission*; Delhi, 1955.

NATARAJAN, S.: *A Century of Social Reforms in India*; Bombay, 1959.

NEHRU, J. L.: *A Bunch of Old Letters;* Bombay, 1958. Soviet *Russia;* Bombay, 1929. *Toward Freedom;* New York, 1941. (British edition entitled *An Autobiography;* London, 1958.)

NEVINSON, H. W.: *The New Spirit in India*; London, 1908.

PARVATE, T. V.: *Gopal Krishna Gokhale*; Ahmedabad, 1959.

PATEL, G. I.: *Vithalbhai Patel, Life and Times*, Vol. II; Bombay, 1950.

Pioneer: Allahabad.

PUNJAB SUB-COMMITTEE: *Indian National Congress*: Reports I and II; Lahore, 1920.

RADHAKRISHNAN, S. (Ed.): *Mahatma Gandhi: Essays and Reflections*; London, 1939.

RATCLIFFE, S. K.: *Sir William Wedderburn*, London, 1923.

READING, MARQUESS OF: *Rufus Isaacs: First Marquess of Reading*; Vol. II, London, 1945.

RONALDSHAY, EARL OF: *The Life of Lord Curzon*, Vol. III; London, 1928.

SAHGAL, NAYANTARA: *Prison and Chocolate Cake*; London, 1954.

SEN, S. N.: *Eighteen Fifty-Seven*; Delhi, 1957.

SHARMA, JHABARMAL: *Khetri ka Ithas* (History of Khetri in Hindi); Calcutta, 1927.

Adarsh Naresh (Biography of Raja Ajit Singh of Khetri in Hindi); Calcutta, 1940.

SHUKLA, CHANDRA SHANKER (Ed.): *Incidents of Gandhiji's Life*; Bombay, 1949.

SIMON, VISCOUNT: *Retrospect*; London, 1952.

SITARAMAYYA, P.: *History of the Indian National Congress*; Vol. I, Bombay, 1946.

SPEAR, PERCIVAL: *Twilight of the Mughals*; London, 1951.

TAYLOR, A. J. P.: *From Napoleon to Stalin*; London, 1950.

TENDULKAR, D. G.: *Mahatma*, Vol. I to III; Bombay, 1951-52.

THOMPSON, EDWARD: *Radindranth Tagore*; London, 1948.

The Times, London.

Tribune, Lahore.

UNIVERSITY OF ALLAHABAD 70TH ANNIVERSARY SOUVENIR; Allahabad, 1958.

U.P. COUNCIL DEBATES.

WEDDERBURN, SIR WILLIAM: *Allan Octavian Hume*; London, 1913.

WILLIAMS, RUSHBROOK (Ed.): *Great Men of India* (n.d.).

WINTERTON, EARL: *Orders of the Day*; London, 1953.

WOODRUFF, PHILIP: *The Guardians;* London, 1955.

WRENCH, JOHN EVELYN: *Geoffrey Dawson and Our Times;* London, 1955.

Young India; Ahmedabad.

ZAKARIA, RAFIQ (Ed.); *A Study of Nehru;* Bombay, 1960.

INDEX

Abdul Ghaffar Khan, 330
Advocate, the, 111
Afghanistan, 214
Aga Khan, 98, 114, 291
Agra, 21-2, 43, 106, 201, 338
Ahmedabad, 194, 197, 209, 240, 246, 248, 328
Ahmedabad Congress, 197, 295
Ahmediya Community, 289
Ahsanullah Khan, Hakim, 20
Aikman, Sir Robert, 99, 123
Ajit Singh, 22, 38, 88
Ajmal Khan, Hakim, 171
Ajudhyanath, Pandit, 50
Akalis, 217-18, 220, 222
Akbar, 19
Alexander, Horace, 320
Ali Brothers, 125, 156, 159, 193-4, 291, 326
Alice in Wonderland, 64
All Parties Conference, 287, 290, 296
All Parties Convention, 290-2, 295
Almora, 192
Ambala, 220
Amethi, Raja of, 118
America, 31, 41, 61, 256
Amherst, Lord, 35
Amritsar Congress, 171-3, 182, 325
Anand Bhawan, 17, 31-2, 40, 42, 51, 63-4, 68, 85, 105, 112, 116, 122-3, 129-30, 140, 151, 184-5, 195-7, 200, 205, 213-14, 247, 275, 278, 328, 332, 338-9
Anderson, Principal, 21
Andrews, C. F., 168, 234
Aney, 265, 269, 288
Angell, Norman, 124
Anglo-Afghan parleys, 178
Ansari, Dr, M.A., 204, 206, 231, 244, 251, 268, 274, 280, 287-8, 290, 316, 326, 329-30, 338
Arabia, 214
Arnold, Sir Edwin, 185, 192
Arrah, 176-8, 180, 185, 188-9, 204
Arundale, G. S., 134
Arya Samaj, 36
Assam, 208, 269
Asthana, N. P., 135

Atkinson, Lord, 278
Attlee, Clement, 145, 283
Austria, 308
Avery, Sir Horace, 112
Azad, Abul Kalam, 125, 206-7, 267

Bad Ems, 16-17, 339
Bad Homburg, 66
Bahadur Shah, 19-20
Bajaj, Jamnalal, 206
Balfour, Arthur, 98
Balwant Singh, 28-9
Baldwin, Roger, 252
Baldwin, Stanley, 283, 317
Bande Mataram, 268
Banerjea, Justice P.C., 277
Banerjea, Surendra Nath, 48, 51, 53-4, 103-5, 114, 125, 150
Banker, 164
Bankipore Congress, 124
Bardoli, 200-3, 312
Barkatullah, 252, 279
Barrow, Rogers and Nevill, 168
Basu, Bhupendra Nath, 114, 144
Belgaum Congress, 240, 242, 296
Benares, 41, 57, 64, 177
Bengal, partition of, 52-3, 57, 124
Benn, W. Wedgwood, 315-17, 321, 329
Berar, 234
Berlin, 257-8, 279, 281
Bernard Shaw, George, 96
Besant, Annie, 36, 64-5, 130-5, 137, 139-40, 142, 145, 147, 149, 156, 159, 165, 171, 182, 242, 290
Beti Mahalakshmibai, 28, 278
Beveridge, Henry, 47
Bhardwaj Ashram, 31
Bhagat Singh, 311
Bhownaggree, Sir Mancherjee, 38
Bihar, 176
Bikaner, Maharaja of, 98
Birkenhead, Lord, 239, 243, 281-2, 287, 294, 305, 317, 320
Bishamber Nath, Pandit, 50
Bishan Sabha, 37
Blavatsky, Madame, 64-5
Boer War, 39, 153
Bomanji, S. R., 231-2

Bombay Chronicle, 187-8
Bombay Congress, 158
Bonnerji, W. C., 51, 150
Bose, Subhas Chandra, 105, 204, 242, 304, 310, 312, 315, 320
Bradford, Captain, 22
Bradlaugh, Charles, 64, 130
Brahmaputra, 269
Brahmo Samaj, 36
Bright, John, 45
Britain, 254-5, 257
British Committee of Indian National Congress, 174
Broach, 328
Brockway, Fenner, 282, 320-1, 329
Broomfield, Judge, 209-10
Brooks, Ferdinand, T., 64, 78, 95, 101, 130
Brown, Dr Lennox, 38-9
Brussels Congress of Oppressed Nationalities, 254-6, 258, 279, 296
Buddha, 41
Bugga, 174
Burden, E., 262
Burke, Edmund, 35
Butler, Sir Harcourt, 40, 179-80, 199, 246

Calcutta Congress, 292, 301-4, 307-8, 310, 312-13, 324
Cama, Madame, 252
Cambridge, 64, 76, 123, 136, 210
Cameron, Misses, 247
Campbell-Bannerman, Sir Henry, 83, 102
Captain, Mrs. Gosi, 336
Canada, 262, 323
Carson, Sir Edward, 112
Cawnpore Congress, 251, 265, 271
Chak, Janki Nath, 188
Chaman Lall, Dewan, 199, 225
Chamba, 243
Chamberlain, Austen, 133, 142, 144
Chamberlain, Joseph, 52
Champaran, 159
Chandavarkar, N. G., 76
Chaudhrani, Mrs. Sarla, 113
Chauri Chaura, 200-4, 339
Chicago Tribune, 191
China, 255-6
Chetty, Shanmukham, 225, 280
Chelmsford, Lord, 95, 133-4, 143-4, 156, 158, 164-5, 167-8, 172-4, 193, 202, 231

Chintamani, C. Y., 111-12, 135, 140, 148-9, 242, 249, 326
Chirol, Valentine, 125
Choudhuri, Jogendranath, 27, 93
Churchill, Winston, S., 175, 320
Civil Disobedience Enquiry Committee, 204
Clark, Sir Edward, 38
Clayton, John, 191
Cleveland, Sir C. R., 166
Coatman, J., 259
Coleridge, S. T., 66
Colombo, 281
Colvin, Sir Auckland, 49-50
Commonweal, 131
Congress of Oppressed Nationalities, 254-7
Cotton, Sir Henry, 51, 54
Craddock, Sir Reginald, 133, 143
Crear, James, 230
Cripps, Sir Stafford, 145
Curtis, Lionel, 147
Curzon, Lord, 52-3, 57, 87, 124, 146

Daffe, Major, 262
Daily Herald, 333
Dalhousie, Lord, 45
Dandi, 328
Darwin, Charles, 101
Das, C. R., 26, 170, 171, 176-7, 181, 183-4, 204-5, 207, 215-16, 229, 231-2, 235, 239-43, 260, 264-5, 270, 303, 340
Das, Jatin, 311
Daulatram, Jairamdas, 334
Dawson, Geoffrey, 133, 165, 314
Dayanand, Swami, 36
de Lambert, Comte, 100
'Delhi Manifesto', 316, 318, 320, 322
Desai, Mahadev, 168, 201, 211, 215, 251
Dhammapada, 65
Dharam Sabha, 37
Dhar, Pandit Bishan Narayan, 37, 112
Dickens, Charles, 64
Digby, 254
Discovery of India, 65, 300
Donnell, C. J. O., 52
Drinkwater, John, 124
Dufferin, Lord, 45-6, 49
Dumraon case, 176, 204
Dunnaju, 29, 277-8
Dutt, B. K., 311

Dutt, Michael Madhusudan, 36
Dutt, R. C., 52, 103-4, 150, 254
Dwarkadas, Jamnadas, 164
Dyarchy, 229
Dyer, General, 165-6, 168, 175

East India Company, 18
Edge, Sir John, 27, 40
Egypt, 308
Einstein, Albert, 256
Ellenborough, Lord, 47
Englishman, the, 82
Essays of Elia, 71
Eton, 73, 95

Fateh Singh, Raja, 21-2
Farrukhabad, 275
Farukhsiyar, 18
Fitzgerald, Sir G. Seymour, 38
Forster, E. M., 31
Fuller, Sir Bampfylde, 87

Gandhi, Mahatma, 9, 10, 26-7, 41,
    54, 124, 135, 145, 151-60, 162, 164,
    168-74, 181-5, 187, 189-97, 200-5,
    209, 212, 215, 230, 234-45, 250-2,
    254, 256-7, 264-9, 271-3, 275,
    278-9, 282-283, 287, 289-90, 293-6,
    301, 304-5, 307-10, 312-14, 316-28,
    330, 332, 334-5, 337-9, 342-3
Gandhi, Devadas, 201, 211, 225, 245
Gandhi-Irwin Pact, 333
Ganga Dhar, 18-19, 21
Ganges, 17, 245, 269
Garibaldi 95, 140
Gauhati, 254, 269-70
Gaya Congress, 204-5, 303
Geneva, 251-3
George V, King, 114-15, 172
George, David Lloyd, 136, 143, 316-
    17, 320
Germany, 252, 257
Ghadr Party, 279
Ghalib, 19
Ghose, Aurobindo, 26, 36, 56, 105
Ghose, Motilal, 146
Ghose, Dr Rash Behari, 91
Gidwani, Dr, 217, 222
Gladstone, William E., 57
Glimpses of World History, 300
Godbole, M. S., 195, 200
Gokhale, Gopal Krishna, 49, 51-2,
    54-5, 57-60, 85, 91, 97, 106, 113-4,
    124, 150, 238, 254, 131

Goswami, T. C., 225
Gorakhpur, 202
Gour, Sir Hari Singh, 224
Gujarat, 156, 294
Gupta, B. L., 103-4
Gupta, J. M., Sen, 312
Gupta, Nagendranath, 111
Guzdar and Company, R.R.M., 31

Hailey, Sir Malcolm, 225, 227-8, 230,
    308-9, 339
Haksar, Colonel, 213
Haldane, Lord, 98
Hapsburg Empire, 173
Hardie, Keir, 82, 229
Hardinge, Lord, 158
Hardwar, 41
Hari, 62, 232, 269
Hariji, 176
Harkishenlal, 167, 169, 218
Harrison, Principal, 23-4, 338
Harrow, 64, 66-7, 70-80, 123, 159,
    210, 339
Hartog Committee, 288
Hewett, Sir J. P., 108
Hindu Mahasabha, the, 114, 289
Hind Swaraj, 238
Hindu College, 35
Hira Singh, Captain, 262-3
Hoare, Sir Samuel, 254
Hodson, Captain, 20
Home Rule League, 132, 135-6
Hooper, Miss, 75
Horniman, B. G., 164, 187
Hossain, Syud, 188
Hume, Allan Octavian, 45, 49,
    50-1, 113, 150, 238
Hume, Joseph, 45
Hunter Committee, 170, 174
Huq, Mazhar-ul-, 145
Huxley, Aldous, 199

Ibbetson, Sir Denzil, 87-8
Ilbert Bill, 283
Imam, Sir Ali, 288
Imam, Hasan, 145
'Independence Day', 327
Independent, 149, 187-9
Indian Civil Service, 272
Indian Defence Force, 136-7, 262
Indian Mirror, 108
Indian National Union, 267, 269
Indian Opinion, 111
Indian People, 84

Indian Social Reformer, 108
India, the, 52
Iqbal, 125
Iran, 214
Irwin, Lord, 257, 283, 305, 314-19, 321, 324-5, 334
Ishwar Saran, 112
Italy, 254, 308
Iyengar, Srinivas, 254-5, 270, 280, 305
Iyer, Ranga, 188, 270
Iyer, Sivaswamy, Sir P. S., 225

Jafri, Kamaluddin, 248
Jagat, Narayan, 148
Jagmohanlal, 38
Jaipur, 22
Jaito, 217-18
Jallianwala Bagh, 166, 168, 171
Jamaica, 231
Jambosar, 328-9
Jameson, Sir L. S., 52
Jamshedpur, 294
Japan, 41, 61
Jaswant Singh Raja, 28-9, 279
Jawaharmul, Pandit, 128
Jawan Bakht, Prince, 20
Jayakar, M. R., 170, 191, 226-7, 263-5, 269, 272, 285, 332
Jeorani, 21
Jinnah, M. A., 126, 145, 164, 171, 225, 228, 231, 234, 239, 242, 261-3, 273, 285, 288, 291, 317, 319, 323, 334
Jogendra Singh, 262
Joseph, George, 188
Joshi, N. M., 225, 288
Juhu, 234
Jumna, 17, 245

Kashmir, 18, 24, 180, 214
Kathgodam, 192
Katju, K. N., 27
Kaul, Lakshmi Narayan, 18
Kaul, Mausa Ram, 18
Kaul, Raj, 18
Kaul, Saheb Ram, 18
Keith, A. B., 297
Kelkar, N. C., 194, 231, 263, 265, 269
Khan, Abdul Qayum Khan, 262
Khan, Captain Gul Nawaz, 262
Khetri, 21-2, 25, 38, 338

Khilafat, 173-4, 178, 181, 191, 193-4, 197, 237, 239, 245-6, 267, 271, 325
Kilian, Professor, 117
Kishori, Rani, 28-9, 276, 278
Knox, K. N., 124, 197
Krishnamurti, 130
Kuomintang, 256

Labour Government, 239, 245, 315, 317
Labour Party, 229, 231, 272
Ladakh, 214
Lahore, 183
Lahore Congress, 301-2, 314, 324-9
Lajpat Rai, 56-9, 88, 96, 184, 188, 195, 201, 226, 231, 266, 268-9, 284-5, 290
Lakhana Case, 28-30, 276-9
Landsdowne, Lord, 57
Lansbury, George, 231, 256, 282
Latin America, 256
La Touche, Sir J. J. D., 99
Lawrence, John, 20, 22
Lawrence, Lord Pethick, 145, 282
Leader, the, 111-12, 127, 136-8, 148, 249
League Against Imperialism, 256-7
League of Nations, 252
Leys, Dr Norman, 272
Lloyd, Sir George, 163, 173
Locarno, 252
Lowndes, Sir George, 163, 278
Lucknow Congress (1916), 125-6, 143, 158
Lucknow Pact, 146, 288
Lytton, Lord, 229

Macaulay, Lord, 35, 46, 61
MacDonald, J. Ramsey, 162, 229, 231-3, 245, 288, 315, 329
Mackenzie, Sir Morel, 38-9
Maclagan, Sir Edward, 169-70
Maddock, Colonel, 234
Madras Congress, 273, 281, 284, 287, 293, 296-7
Maffey, J. L., 135, 164
Maharani, 21
Mahmudabad, Maharaja of, 268, 273, 317
Mahmud, Syed, 334
Malabar, 194
Malaviya, Kapil Deo, 221, 228, 265-6, 269, 285

Malaviya, Madan Mohan, 50-1, 86, 90, 111, 113, 145, 169, 171, 184, 225, 245, 290, 316
Mangal Singh, 288
Maharaj Singh, Rao, 123
Mansrovar Lake, 213
Marris, Sir W. D., 147
Marseilles, 67
Martin, Lt.-Colonel, 335
Marx, Karl, 238
Mary, Queen, 114
Matthai, Dr John, 26
Maugham, F. H., 278
Mazumdar, Ambika Charan, 150
McKinley, President, 38
McRobert, Sir A., 116
Mears, Sir Grimwood, Chief Justice, 29-30, 277
Meerut case, 311, 314
Mehdi, Syed Hyder, 188
Mehrauli, 19
Mehta, Dr Jivraj, 337-8
Mehra, Sir Pherozeshah, 54, 57-8, 131, 150
Menton, 281
Meredith, George, 212
Meston, Sir James, 134, 137-9, 143, 148, 163
Mill, J. S., 57
Minchin, Lt.-Colonel, 222
Minto-Morley Reforms, 288
Mirza Mughal, 20
Misra, Gokran Nath, 142, 145
Moderates, 194
Mohamed Ali, 193, 239, 245, 266, 326
Montagu, E. S., 140, 142, 144-9, 157-8, 165, 167-9, 173, 175, 202, 317
Montagu-Chelmsford Reforms, 147-8, 150, 182
Montana, 252-3
Monte Carlo, 281
Moonje, Dr, 239, 265, 269
Moore, Arthur, 199
Morley, John, 57-8, 87, 97, 99, 108-9, 124, 231, 317
Moscow, 258, 281
Moti Sabha, 39
Mountbatten, Lord, 95, 145
Mount Kailas, 213
Mubarak Ali, Munshi, 63
Muddiman, Sir Alexander, 225, 230, 252, 279, 339

Muddiman Committee, 262
Mukandlal, 19
Muir Central College, 23, 34, 63, 75
Muller, Max, 35
Mushran, Shamji, 112
Muslim League, 125-6, 143, 145, 171, 288, 291
Mutiny, 18-20, 36

Nabha, 216-23, 234, 249
Nadir Shah, 20
Naidu, Sarojini, 140
Naini Gaol, 17-18, 329, 331-2, 335-6, 338
Naini Tal, 210
Nair, Sir Sankaran, 55
Nandi Hills, 276
Nandrani, 25, 42
Naoroji, Dadabhai, 52, 55, 58, 131, 150, 238, 254, 274
Narsingh Rao, 29, 277-8
Nation, the, 212
Nationalist Journals Ltd., 188
Nationalist Party, 260
Nehru, Bansi Dhar, 21, 23, 37, 40, 63, 104, 122
Nehru, Biharilal, 25
Nehru, Braj Kumar, 200, 303
Nehru, Brijlal, 25, 34, 65, 84, 200
Nehru Committee, 288-91
Nehru, Indira (also Indu), 174, 178, 197, 214, 221, 247, 280, 332, 337
Nehru, Jawaharlal, birth, 25; celebration of his birthdays; his childhood, 62-3; early schooling, 63; influence of his tutor, Ferdinand T. Brooks, 64; is initiated into Theosophy, 65; leaves for England with his father, 65; admitted to Harrow, 68; makes a mark in the school, 70; receives prizes and takes part in school sports and the Cadet Corps, 71-4; his correspondence with his father, 75-8; visits India and France, 78; unable to mix with English boys at Harrow, 79-80; signs of his precocity, 81, 84; is happy at his father's entry into active politics, 86; his views on Sinn Fein movement, 90; breeze with his father over the Moderates' attitude at Surat Congress,

Nehru, Jawaharlal (*Cont.*)
91-3; is admitted to Trinity College, Cambridge, 94; effects of public school training upon him, 95; his life at Cambridge, 96-9; resents exclusion of Indians from the Officers' Training Corps, 98; tours the Continent with his father, 100; has a narrow escape, 101; formative influence of Cambridge, 101-3; decides not to compete for entry into the Indian Civil Service, 104-5; is delighted at his father's attack on orthodoxy at the Agra Social Conference, 108; his comments on the titles conferred by the British Government, 117; his intellectual curiosity and love of literature, 119-20; incurs his father's wrath, 121; returns to India, 123; practises at the Bar, 123; his marriage, 127-8; goes on a perilous mountain expedition, 128; attracted by Home Rule movement, organizes the Allahabad Home Rule League, 136; resigns from the Committee on Indian Defence Force, 137; receives Mrs Besant on arrival at Allahabad, 140; attends Bombay Congress, 149; criticizes the Viceroy on the South African question, 158; meets Gandhi, 158-9; decides to join Gandhi's campaign against the Rowlatt Bills, 159-60; attends the meeting of the Congress Inquiry Committee, 174; his comments on General Dyer, 175; is asked to quit Mussoorie, 179; tours the rural areas of Pratapgarh, 180-1; and the *Independent*, 188-90; is imprisoned, 196-7; receives a letter from Gandhi explaining the withdrawal of mass civil disobedience, 202; is released, and rearrested, 209; his political evolution, 210; his routine in Lucknow gaol, 210-12; is released, 215; declines to join the Swaraj Party and acts as a mediator between Pro-changers and No-changers, 215-6; attends the Delhi Special Congress and

Nehru, Jawaharlal (*Cont.*)
is arrested at Nabha, 216-17; refuses to defend himself, 220; is convicted, but expelled from Nabha, 222; takes part in Satyagraha during the Ardh-Kumbh Mela, 245; his emotional bonds with his father and Gandhi, 246-7; his work as chairman of the Allahabad Municipal Board, 248-50; desires financial independence, 250; leaves for Switzerland for the treatment of his wife, 252; attends the Brussels Congress of Oppressed Nationalities, 254-7; visits Russia, 258-9; question of his election as president of the Congress, 274-5; shadowed by the secret police, 279; returns to India, 281; is injured during demonstrations against the Simon Commission, 286-7; official concern at his activities, 293; his role at and after the Madras Congress, 293-5; differs with his father on Dominion Status as political goal for India, 296-8; a conflict of ideologies, 299-303; clash and compromise at Calcutta, 304-5; asked by Gandhi to reorganize the Congress committees, 308; possibility of his prosecution, 309-11; organizes defence of accused in Meerut Conspiracy case, 311; his election to presidency of the Lahore Congress, 312-14; signs Delhi Manifesto, 317; presides over the Lahore Congress, 325-6; his tribute to, and meeting with Gandhi, 328; is arrested and gaoled, 329; delighted at the part taken by the ladies of the Nehru family in the Satyagraha movement, 331; nurses his ailing father in prison, 332; takes part in negotiations with Sapru and Jayakar, 333-4; his wife's heroic role in the national struggle, 335-6; is rearrested, 336; is released, 337; is at his father's bedside in his last hours, 338; emotional and political bonds between him and his father, 340-3.

Nehru, Kamala, 128, 178, 185, 192, 196-7, 221, 251-2, 257, 271, 280-1, 330-2, 335-9

Nehru, Krishna (also Betty), 32, 42, 115, 122, 184, 197, 281, 330, 332, 335, 337

Nehru, Kishenlal, 25, 200

Nehru, Mohanlal, 25, 189, 200

Nehru, Motilal, ancestry in Kashmir and Delhi, 18; family uprooted by the Mutiny, 19-20; brought up by his brother after the death of his father, 21-2; career at school and college, 22-3; qualifies as a lawyer, 24; is married, 24; death of his brother, 25; his success in his profession, 26-8; the Lakhana case, 28-9; builds 'Anand Bhawan', 30-1; his hospitality, 32-3; visits Europe, 38-40; extent of westernization, 40-4; attends the annual sessions of the Indian National Congress, 50-1; delivers presidential address at the Allahabad provincial conference, 59-61; his fits of temper, 62-3; makes arrangements for the education of his son, 63, 65-6; admits his son to Harrow, 66-7; writes farewell letter to his son, 68; his enormous practice at the Bar, 69; receives reports from Harrow, 70; birth and death of a son, 76; his advice to Jawaharlal, 77; on the anti-partition agitation, 84; is drawn into active politics, 84-5; attends Surat Congress, 91; expresses disapproval of his son's political views, 92-3; his friendly feelings for England and Englishmen, 99; visits Europe, 100; presides over the Social Conference at Agra, 106-8; his views on Morley's reforms, 109; his freedom from sectarian politics, 111-12; is elected to U.P. Council, 110-1; and the *Leader*, 111-12; St Nihal Singh's pen-portrait of, 112-13; attends the Allahabad Congress, 113-14; his experiences at Delhi Durbar, 115-17; and homoeopathy, 118; on the profession of law, 120; attends Bankipore Congress, 124; and the

Nehru, Motilal (Cont.) Lucknow Pact, 126; and Home Rule Movement, 132, 135-41; meets Mr Montagu and Lord Chelmsford, 145-6; his attitude to the reforms and differences with the Moderates, 157-9; on Gandhi's Satyagrapha struggle in South Africa, 158; ridicules Passive Resistance, 159; tries to wean Jawaharlal from Satyagraha, 160-1; and the Punjab tragedy, 167-8; experiences as a member of the Congress Inquiry Committee, 170; presides over the Armitsar Congress, 171-2; his reaction to Privy Council judgments and Hunter Committee's Report, 174-5; conducts Dumraon case, 176; his zest and humour, 177-8; addresses Governor of the United Press, 179; takes the final plunge and supports non-co-operation at the Calcutta Congress, 182-5; metamorphosis in his life, 184-6; founds and runs the *Independent*, 187-90; is elected General Secretary of the Congress, 191; celebrates marriage of his elder daughter, 192; differs with Gandhi on the 'apology' incident, 193; is arrested, 195-7; his life in Lucknow gaol, 199-200; is unhappy at Gandhi's withdrawal of civil disobedience, 201; on release favours Congress entry into legislative councils, 204-5; issues the Swaraj Party election manifesto, 207; addressed the Administrator of Nabha State and visits Jawaharlal in Nabha gaol, 218-21; as Leader of the Opposition in Central Legislative Assembly, 224-8; his correspondence with Bomanji, 231-2; his differences with Gandhi on Council work, 234-44; impresses upon his son the importance of the study of economics, 253; declines to serve on the Muddiman Committee, 262; nominated to the Skeen Committee, 262; is confronted with a split in Swaraj Party, 236-7; leads the walk-out of the

Nehru, Motilal (*Cont.*)
Swaraj Party, 266-7; condemns communalism, 266-7; is distressed by dissensions in his party, 270; his relations with Gandhi, 272; addresses Gandhi on Jawaharlal's election as president of the Congress, 217-5; constructs a new house, 275; appears in the Lakhana case, 276-9; visits Europe, 280-1; denounces the Simon Commission, 283-5; frames the Nehru Report, 287-92; differs with his son on Dominion status versus complete independence, 296-8; his political philosophy, 299, 301-3; presides over the Calcutta Congress, 304; advises Gandhi to postpone his visit to Europe, 307-9; corresponds with Gandhi on the election of the Congress president, 312-13; interviews the Viceroy, 319-24; attends Lahore Congress, 325; his decision to join Gandhi's campaign, 326; visits Gandhi at Jambosar, 328; donates Anand Bhawan to the Congress, 328; his ill-health, 329; conducts the campaign after the arrest of his son, 331; is arrested, 331; life in Naini gaol, 333; interview with Slocombe, 333; negotiations with Sapru and Jayakar, 334-5; resumes charge of the movement after the re-arrest of Jawaharlal, 335-337; an estimate of his character and career, 340-3
Nehru, Nandlal, 21-2, 24-5, 30, 40-2, 338
Nehru, Rameshwari, 84, 200
'Nehru Report', 290-2, 297, 304-5, 308
Nehru, Sarup Kumari (see also Pandit, Vijayalakshmi), 32, 41, 65-8, 75, 113, 115-16, 122, 192, 263, 273
Nehru, Shamlal, 25, 136, 200, 268
Nehru, Shri Shridhar, 63, 104, 123, 193
Nehru, Swarup Rani, 24-5, 41-2, 65, 68, 76-7, 115-17, 122, 126, 178, 185, 191, 196-7, 246, 325, 330-1, 335, 337-8
Nehru, Uma, 158

Neogy, K. C., 225
Nevill, Reginald, 174
Nevinson, H. W., 82
New India, 131
New Statesman, 212
Niegeroloje, 258
Nightingale, Florence, 46
Nihal Singh, St, 112-13
Nizam, the, of Hyderabad, 234
Nizamuddin, 20

O'Connor, B. E., 277
O'Dwyer, Sir Michael, 134, 163, 165-71
Olcott, Colonel, 64-5
Olivier, Lord, 229-31
Ottoman Empire, 173

Pakistan, 225, 291
Pal, B. C., 56, 96, 171, 189, 224
Pandit, Ranjit, 192, 263, 331
Pandit, Vijayalakshmi, 252, 330, 332, 335, 337
Pant, Govind Ballabh, 287
Paris, 41, 78
Parmanand, Kanwar, 31
Patel, Vallabhbhai, 205-7, 226, 248, 294, 312, 314, 317, 319, 334
Patel, V. J., 184, 194, 204, 226, 262-4, 282-3, 310, 315-17, 319, 321, 324, 329, 331
Patrani, 21
Paul, Sir Charles, 29
Pentland, Lord, 134-5, 165
Peshawar, 330-1
Pillai, 145
Pim, A. W., 249
Pioneer, the, 81, 90, 104, 111, 137, 166, 285
Polak, Henry S., 174, 182, 277, 316, 319
Poland, 308
Pole, Graham, 282, 316, 319
Poona, 45-6, 234, 245, 330, 334-5
Porter, Leslie, 115-17
Powell, H., 23
Pradhan, G. R., 288
Pratapgarh, 180-1
Pratap, Raja Mahendra, 252
Prithinath Pandit, 24, 39, 117-8
Punjabi, the, 87

Quetta earthquake, 175
Qureshi, Shuaib, 288

Qutab, 20

Rainy, Sir George, 227
Raipur, 58
Rajagopalachari, C. R., 204-6
Rajkot, 27, 152, 192
Rajputana, 21-2
Rajvati, 42
Ramachandra, 19
Ramakrishna, Shri, 36
Rampal Singh, Raja, 48
Ramayana, 31
Ram Prasad, Munshi, 27
Ranade, 36, 54, 106
Rangachariar, Diwan Bahadur, 227
Rao, Rama Chandra, 262
Rattan Chand, 174
Ratan Lal, 76
Rauf, Judge, 170
Ray, Dr, 178
Reading, Lord, 193-4, 201-3, 211, 222, 230, 283, 316-17, 320
Reay, Lord, 45
Responsive Co-operation, 263, 265
Responsivists, 269
Rhodes, Cecil, 52
Ripon, Lord, 45, 81-2
Roberts, Charles, 124
Robertson, M. L., 166
Robertson, Sir Benjamin, 134
Rolland, Romain, 252, 256
Round Table Conference, 204, 227, 231, 316-17, 320, 322-4, 326, 333-4
Rowlatt Bills, 156-9, 164, 166, 173, 187, 210, 242, 325
Roy, Dr B. C., 243, 327, 337-8
Roy, Raja Ram Mohun, 35, 253
Russia, 252, 257, 308
Ruthnaswamy, 273

Sabarmati Ashram, 184, 198, 246, 266, 278, 309, 328
Sadruddin Qazi, 22
Saha, Gopinath, 240
Saklatwala, 255, 258
Salisbury, Lord, 48
Salt Satyagraha, 328
Santhanam, K., 217, 222
Sapru, Sir Tej Bahadur, 10, 29, 85, 112, 135-7, 140, 142, 148, 157, 180, 268, 276, 288-9, 292, 315-24, 326, 332, 334
Sarkar, Nilratan, 337
Sassoon, Sir Victor, 254

Sastri, Srinivas, 157, 171, 182, 232, 268, 326
Saturday Review, the, 97
Satyagraha, 173, 178, 182, 187, 194, 245, 250, 275, 329, 335, 338-40
Savile Row, 17
Scott, Sir Walter, 64
Schuster, Sir George, 227
Sen, Keshub Chander, 103
Sen, Madame Sun Yat, 256
Servants of India Society, 124
Sethe, 164
Sethna, Phiroze, 262
Shakespeare, William, 35
Shaukat Ali, 245, 248, 271
Shaw, George Bernard, 64, 130
Shelley, P. B., 35
Shibli, 125
Shiva Prasad, Raja, 50
Sholapur, 294, 330-1
Simla, 180, 247, 266, 334
Simon Commission, 283-87, 291, 294, 296-7, 306, 315, 317, 339
Simon, Sir John, 278, 317, 320
Singapore, 337
Sind, 289
Sinha, Sir S. P., 108, 157-8, 167, 278
Sircar, N. N., 176-7
Skeen Committee, 262-4
Skeen, Lt.-General Sir Andrew, 262
Slocombe, George, 333
Smuts, General, 154
Sobhani, 164
Song Celestial, 185
South Africa, 27, 99, 152-4, 156, 182, 219, 238, 254
Soviet Russia, 258
Spain, 253
Spoor, Ben, 175, 231
Sri Prakasa, 222
Statesman, the, 99
Stansgate, Lord, 314
Stephen, Sir Fitzjames, 47
St John Ambulance Brigade, 197
Strachey, Sir John, 47
Sumner, Viscount, 278
Sunderbans, 269
Sunderlal, Pandit Sir, 27, 30, 76, 86, 90, 93, 99
Sunderson, Sir Lancelot, 278
Surat Congress, 90-1, 124, 240
Swaraj Bhawan, 31, 328, 332

Swaraj Party, Swarajists, 205-9, 215-16, 222, 224-6, 228-9, 231, 234-44, 254, 260, 263-5, 268-70, 280, 296, 342
Switzerland, 253, 260, 268, 271, 275-6, 335, 339
Syed Brothers, 18
Symond, Addington, 124

Tagore, Satyendranath, 103
Tagore, Rabindranath, 168, 301
Tambe, 263, 266
Tandon, Purushottam Das, 211, 247
Tatas, 275
Taylor, A. J. P., 48
Telang, 36
Tennyson, Lord, 214
Thackeray, W. M., 64
Thakur, S. B., 103
Thakurdas, Sir Purshotamdas, 224, 254, 331
Three Men In A Boat, 64
Tibet, 213-14
Tikari, Maharaja of, 205
Tilak, B. G., 56-9, 85, 91, 124, 126, 133, 136, 140, 142, 147, 150, 156, 159, 171-2, 238, 263, 276
Times of India, the, 166
Times, The, 47, 81, 84, 133, 314
Tolstoy, L., 153
Trevelyan, C. P., 231
Trevelyan, G. M., 95
Troller, Ernst, 252
Turkey, 125-6, 308
Twain, Mark, 64
Tweedy, Mr, 116
Tyabji, Abbas, 170
Tyabji, Badruddin, 150

Ullah, Syed Nabi, 188
United States, 38, 52, 252, 308
Upadhyaya, 269
Upanishads, the, 65

Upjohn, W. H., 278
U.P. Council, 180, 184, 215

Varma, Shyamji, 252
Varma, Gang Prasad, 111
Venice, 257
Victoria, Queen, 36-7
Vijiaraghavachariar, C., 191, 205
Vincent, Sir William, 156, 163, 190
Vishwanath Temple, 177
Vivekananda, Swami, 44, 129

Wacha, Sir Dinshaw, 131, 150
Wadia, B. P., 134
Wales, Prince of, 93, 195, 197, 208
Wallis, Sir John, 278
Warner, Sir W. Lee, 38
Wavell, Lord, 95
Webb, Beatrice, 233
Wedderburn, Sir William, 51, 113, 144, 150
Wedgwood, Colonel, 175, 229, 231, 282
Wednesday Review, 108
Wells, H. G., 64
Western Court, 199, 226
Whiteaway Laidlaw, Messrs., 178
Whyte, Sir Frederick, 225
Wilbee & Co., J. C., 74
Willingdon, Lord, 134
Wilson Johnston, J., 218-19, 222
Wood, Dr Joseph, 66, 70-1, 79-80, 84, 94

Yakub, Mahomed, 234
Years of Destiny, 259
Yeravda, 234, 330, 334-5
Young India, 246, 254
Young, Mackworth, 273
Yule, George, 50, 52

Zauk, 90
Zeppelin, Count, 100